EXPLORING
THE
GOSPELS

JOHN

EXPLORING
THE
GOSPELS

JOHN

JOHN PHILLIPS

LOIZEAUX BROTHERS
Neptune, New Jersey

A Publication of Loizeaux Brothers, Inc.
A Nonprofit Organization Devoted to the Lord's Work
and to the Spread of His Truth

Library of Congress Cataloging-in-Publication Data

Phillips, John, 1927 –
Exploring the Gospels: John / John Phillips.
ISBN 0-87213-658-2:
1. Bible. N.T. John—Commentaries. I. Title.
BS2615.3.P52 1988
226'.507—dc19   88 - 13345

Printed in the United States of America

10   9   8   7   6   5   4

CONTENTS

PREFACE

His brother James was dead. Peter, the leading apostle to the Jews, was dead. Paul, the intrepid apostle to the gentile world, was dead. Thomas, Andrew, Philip, Nathanael, all the apostles, were dead—all except one. There in Ephesus lived a lonely old man, the first and the last of the apostles, the great apostle to the church. His name was John.

He had lived through a marvelous time. In his days the Son of God had become the Son of man. He had been incarnated at Bethlehem, baptized in the Jordan, tempted and proved sinless in the wilderness. He had healed the sick, cleansed the leper, raised the dead. He had made the blind see, the deaf hear, the dumb speak, the lame walk. He had turned water into wine, walked on the waves, fed hungry multitudes with a handful of bread. He had taught God's truth in a pungent, memorable way. He had been love incarnate, God manifest in flesh. He had been betrayed, falsely accused, manhandled, mauled, crucified. He had been buried, but had risen in triumph from the tomb. He had ascended into heaven, and John had his sure word for it that he was coming back.

All these memories lingered in John's heart, in the innermost thoughts of this very old man. John was Jesus' human cousin and for some three-and-a-half years his best friend. John knew the truth about the Lord Jesus Christ as did no other person on earth.

Enormous changes had taken place. The terrible Jewish war with Rome had brought the end of Jerusalem as the Jewish capital. The burning of the temple and the beginning of another long exile for the Jews all heralded a new dispensation. Undaunted, and bitterly hostile still to their rejected messiah, the Jews had taken all this in their stride. So there was to be no temple, no sacrifices, no capital city, no homeland, no king but Caesar. Exiles and strangers in alien lands, the Jews nonetheless would survive, nursing their rejection of Jesus century after century in the hope of a later return to their ancestral home and a rebuilt temple in Jerusalem.

On earth a new entity had arisen, the Christian church. It

had been born on the Jewish annual festival of Pentecost in a crowded upper room in Jerusalem just ten days after the bodily ascension of Jesus into heaven. John had been there. The Holy Spirit had come like a mighty, rushing wind, like cloven tongues of fire. The disciples had been baptized into one body, a mystical body, the body of Christ the church.

John had known all the apostles, all the disciples, all the early members of the church. He was a charter member, now the last one left. He had seen the church grow from 120 to over 3,000 in a single day. He had seen it take root and spread, until now, near the end of the first century, its branches were reaching into all the world. No living man knew that story better than he.

All the books of the New Testament were written except his own gospel, three short epistles, and a remarkable apocalypse. Three gospels, the book of Acts, Paul's epistles, and the general Hebrew epistles were all in circulation. Doubtless John was at home in them all.

So why write another gospel? His friend and colleague Matthew had written such a masterpiece. John Mark—he knew him well—had given a precise account of Peter's preaching. Luke had written a Christian classic. So why was the Holy Spirit urging him to write? Because so much was still unsaid. The other gospels dealt primarily with Galilee. But what about the work of Christ in Judea? The other gospels prepared their hearers for the kingdom of heaven, but what about the deeper mysteries Christ had taught? Many of those mysteries, indeed, had subsequently been revealed to Paul. But what about their origins in Christ's teaching?

Matthew had written primarily for Jews, Mark for Romans, and Luke for Greeks. There was a desperate need for one more gospel record. Someone needed to write for the church.

It was now the third generation. The ominous warnings of Paul, Peter, and Jude about a coming apostasy in the church, about "grievous wolves, not sparing the flock," were no mere alarmist fancies. By the time of the third generation all kinds of heresies were being spread about.

The third generation always brings particular problems for a movement. In the first generation a perceived truth is a conviction; in the second generation it settles down to a belief; in the third generation it becomes merely an opinion. John could clearly see this declension. It was evident on every hand.

All kinds of false teachings were either flourishing already or soon would flourish. Soon they would have names attached to them and they would be written into church history books:

—Apollinarianism: the word became "flesh," not a body or its like;

—Gnosticism: the Lord only assumed the appearance for a time of something that was really quite alien to himself; at his baptism the divine *Logos* was united with the man Jesus;

—Eutychianism: if the humanity of the Lord had any real existence at all, it was because the result of the incarnation was a third nature;

—Nestorianism: the Lord had both a divine personality and a human one, and all aspects of his life must be referred to one or the other of them;

—Ebionism: the Holy Spirit was first imparted to Christ at his baptism.

Yes, there was need for a fourth gospel, three more epistles, and an apocalypse. Only John remained with the knowledge, experience, and apostleship to write them. And so he did, rising magnificently to the occasion. He wrote his gospel out of personal experience, out of a memory quickened and clothed in inerrancy by the Holy Spirit. As a result we have in our hands "the gospel according to John," a priceless document, "written, that ye might believe that Jesus is the Christ, the Son of God, and that believing ye might have life through his name" (20:31).

INTRODUCTION

The moment we pick up John's gospel we are aware that it is different from the others. There is no genealogy, no manger scene, no boyhood, no baptism, no temptation, no mount of transfiguration, no Gethsemane. There are only a few special miracles chosen by John as "signs." We have the famous I AM sayings of Jesus and many discourses found nowhere else. There are no scribes, no lepers, no publicans, and no demoniacs. There are no parables. It would almost seem, as others have pointed out, that John sits with a copy of Luke's gospel open before him, deliberately leaving out things Luke puts in and putting in things Luke leaves out (W. Graham Scroggie, *A Guide to the Gospels*, London: Pickering and Inglis, 1962). Luke had written to show that Jesus was the Son of man; John is writing to show that Jesus is the Son of God.

John's language is Greek but his thoughts are Hebrew. His language is simple, his vocabulary small. There are about six hundred words in John's vocabulary. It is the vocabulary of a seven-year-old child (a child adds about a hundred words to his or her vocabulary every year). But if John's "coins" are few, their denomination is large; they are golden coins, royal sovereigns, the kind one would find in a rich man's purse. The word John uses most is *Father* (121 times) with the companion expression *my Father* (35 times). He is fond of the word *believe* (99 times). Other common words are *world* (79 times), *Jews* (71 times), *know* (*oida* 61 times and *ginosko* 56 times), *abide* (41 times), *life* (36 times), *light* (23 times), *love* (in its various forms and cognates, 57 times), *truth* (and its cognates, 66 times).

John's gospel begins with a prologue (1:1-18), runs through a threefold view of the Lord Jesus—*the signs* (1:19–12:50), *the secrets* (13:1–17:26), and *the sorrows* (18:1–20:31) of God's Son—and ends with an epilogue (21:1-25). The basic structure is simple, but John surprises us. He says the simplest things, uses the simplest words, puts together the simplest phrases and sentences—and at once plunges us into mysterious, mystical, mind-staggering concepts.

The prologue can be divided into three parts, revolving

around three of John's favorite words. We have *the divine life in essence* (1:1-5), *the divine light in evidence* (1:6-13), and *the divine love in experience* (1:14-18). We begin with the first of these introductory passages. Immediately John whirls us away into the eternal ages to confront one who was from everlasting to everlasting, eternal, immortal, invisible, the only wise God, our Lord and Savior, Jesus Christ.

PART ONE

The Prologue
John 1:1-18

I n the beginning was the Word, and the Word was with God, and the Word was God. The same was in the beginning with God. All things were made by him; and without him was not any thing made that was made. In him was life; and the life was the light of men. And the light shineth in darkness; and the darkness comprehended it not" (1:1-5).

I. The Divine Life in Essence (1:1-5)

John does not waste his time arguing with the Gnostic and other heretics. Rather, he states certain facts that he knows beyond all shadow of doubt to be true. Let them speculate; he *knows*.

He begins with:

A. The Lord's Ineffable Person (1:1-2)

John makes three sweeping statements that affirm once and for all the deity of the one he had known so well. Although he did not become his disciple until he revealed himself for who he was, John had almost certainly known "Jesus of Nazareth" since he was a small boy. He was the Lord's cousin. His mother, Salome, was sister of the virgin Mary. The mysterious circumstances surrounding the birth of Jesus, chronicled by Matthew and Luke, were no secret in the family circle. We can reasonably assume that the Lord Jesus, in his boyhood and early manhood days, along with his brothers and sisters, had normal contact with the relatives who lived by the lake. Nazareth was not that far from the sea of Galilee. Annual pilgrimages to Jerusalem for the feasts were always social occasions when families and friends joined together in bands to make the trip.

After becoming one of the Lord's disciples, John knew that Jesus of Nazareth was God. He simply tells what he knows. No turn-of-the-first-century liberal or cultist was in a position to deny the sublime statements John makes in his opening sentences. All John has to do is bear witness to the truth. He was not concerned to confront all the vagaries and varieties of error. He knew what the truth was and he contented himself with that.

1. Jesus Is Eternally God (1:1a)

To equate Jesus with God was a proposition not lightly made. John was a Palestinian Jew, with all the horror such a person would have for blasphemy. He was not a philosopher, not even a theologian. He was a man who had spent three-and-a-half extraordinary years in the company of Jesus. For well over half a century he had thought things over. It was his conviction now, as it had been his conviction then, that Jesus of Nazareth was no ordinary man. He was—and is—God.

John begins with an affirmation, "In the beginning was the Word," that does not refer to a start, but to an infinite state.

The Greek used by John is the word *logos*. It was a word familiar to Greek philosophers and a word adopted for his own purposes by the Jewish philosopher Philo. To the Greeks, the word had reference to the abstract conception that lies behind everything concrete—to the ideal, to what we could perhaps call *wisdom*.

But John did not get his views of Jesus from Greek philosophy or from the speculations of Philo. John borrowed the Greek word but he used it in a new sense, in a more Hebrew sense. The Hebrews left the Greeks far behind when it came to the eternal· verities lying behind the world of time and sense. The Hebrew would argue from the thought to the thinker, from "wisdom" to God. The Greeks did not go that far. Thus, when John calls Jesus "the Word," the *logos*, he is referring to him as the thinker, the omniscient genius behind the created universe.

That, however, does not exhaust the statement, "In the beginning was the Word." We must look also at the verb. The imperfect tense used in the Greek expresses a continuous state, not a completed past. It suggests the idea of "absolute, supratemporal existence." The Lord Jesus, in other words, was pre-existent before the creation of the universe (not mentioned until we get to verse 3). "In the beginning *was* the Word, and the Word *was* with God, and the Word *was* God" (italics added); the imperfect tense is used each time. This is not nearly so arresting in English as it is in the original. In each case it sets before the reader not something past, or present, or future, but something ongoing. It refers to a mode of existence that transcends time.

Time is a device to help finite beings relate to their mode of existence. The verb John uses takes us into the sphere of the timeless. In other words, the one John calls "the Word" belongs to a realm where time does not matter. The word did not have a beginning. The word will never have an ending. The word belongs to eternity.

That in itself is a disturbing statement for some. We can go back in our minds quite easily a century or two, even a millennium or two. Astronomers have accustomed themselves to think in terms of billions of years. But to go back beyond the beginning, to no beginning at all—that is disquieting.

But, says John, when we think of Jesus, that is where we must begin. We must go back to the dateless past, to a time before time. We must think of Jesus as never having begun at all. He is eternally God.

2. Jesus Is Equally God (1:1b)

"In the beginning was the Word, and the Word was with God." In other words, there is more than one person within the godhead, and Jesus was one of those persons.

The Old Testament writers caught glimpses of this. In the great Jewish credal statement found in Deuteronomy 6:4, the Hebrews expressed the unity of God: "Hear, O Israel: The Lord our God is one Lord." But the very first sentence in the Bible expressed the idea of plurality in the godhead: "In the beginning God [*Elohim*, a plural noun] created [a singular verb] the heaven and the earth." This usage is consistent throughout the Old Testament; God is referred to in a plural form accompanied by a singular verb. Thus, embedded in the Old Testament is the idea of the trinity: one God, three persons. Expressed mathematically this would not be $1+1+1$ (which equals three), but $1\times1\times1$ (which equals one). From both Old and New Testaments we arrive at the concept of God existing as three persons (Father, Son, Holy Spirit). Three persons, one God.

Difficult as this concept is to grasp, we are not left without illustrations in the world of time and sense. Ours is a triune universe: space, matter, time. Space is triune: length, breadth, height. Matter is triune: energy, motion, phenomena; time is triune: past, present, future. Nathan Wood has shown that all these relationships reflect the relationships within the godhead, some more than others. When it comes to the relationship of past, present, and future in the realm of time, he produces a startling array of facts. He writes paragraph after paragraph and then substitutes the word *God* for the word *time*, the word *Father* for the word *future*, *Son* for the word *present*, and *Holy Spirit* for the word *past*. Then he rewrites the paragraphs, inserting the exchanged words. The result is a perfect description of the relationships of the three persons of the godhead to one another. It is an awesome proof of the trinity (N. Wood, *The Secret of the Universe*, Grand Rapids, Michigan: Eerdmans).

So, when John says of Jesus, "the Word was with God," he is stating a sublime truth. Jesus is equally God with the Father and the Holy Spirit. He is God the Son, the second person of the godhead.

3. Jesus Is Essentially God (1:1c-2)

"And the Word was God." That is, in his essence, in what he actually is, in his nature, person, and personality, in his attributes and character, Jesus is all that God is. All the essential characteristics of deity are his. He exists in his own right, independent of all creation. Does God have the wisdom and power to create a hundred million galaxies and hold them whirling through space at enormous velocities on inconceivable paths, according to fixed laws, expending prodigious amounts of energy? So does Jesus. Such is the Lord's ineffable person.

B. The Lord's Infinite Power (1:3-5)

Jesus is unique in:

1. His Power of Creation (1:3)

"All things were made by him; and without him was not any thing made that was made." All things. The Greek word *panta* refers to all things individually, all things separately. It is a reference to the infinite detail of creation. The scientist takes his or her telescope and focuses it on the reaches of space. Out there are distances so vast that a special unit of measure is needed with which to express those concepts. The astronomer's yardstick is a light year: the distance light travels in one year (at 186,273 miles per second—the equivalent of encircling the earth at the equator seven and a half times). In round numbers, that is about six trillion miles. Our sun, by that yardstick, is eight light minutes away. But out there in space are suns and stars believed to be billions of light years away. Nor can we count the stars or guess how many billions there are.

Some stars are large beyond all thought. The star Antares,

for instance, could hold sixty-four million suns the size of ours. In the constellation Hercules is a star that could contain one hundred million stars the size of Antares. Our galaxy, the Milky Way, is 100,000 light years in diameter. It is revolving at a speed of two hundred miles an hour. It takes two million years to complete one revolution on its axis.

Not only are we awed by the size of space and the prodigality with which the creator has strewn it with stars, but we are overwhelmed by the precision with which all these vast orbs pursue their appointed paths. Our planet, for instance, does not travel in a true circle. It travels in three directions at the same time. It revolves on its axis, it travels around the sun, and its path is deflected by other planets. Yet it does not lose more than one one-hundredth of a second every one hundred years.

Let us turn from the world of the infinitely large to the world of the infinitely small. The building block of the universe is the atom, an entity so small that each one is less than one hundred fifty millionth of an inch in diameter. If the molecules of a single drop of water could be converted into grains of sand, there would be enough sand to build a concrete highway half a mile wide and one foot thick all the way from New York to San Francisco.

That is the world of inanimate things. When we turn to living things the complexities that confront us on every hand are incredible. Each cell in a living creature contains two hundred billion molecules of atoms. The nucleus of a cell (a complex life factory) is less than four ten-thousandths of an inch in diameter. The membrane that encloses the cell's component parts is only one half of that, or one-millionth of an inch thick.

Jesus made it all. "Without him," says the Holy Spirit through the inspired apostle, "was not anything made that was made." The form of the text in Greek is even more emphatic: "not even one thing."

2. His Power of Communication (1:4-5)

The Lord is said by John to have power in *communicating life* (1:4) and in *communicating light* (1:5). "In him was life; and the life was the light of men. And the light shineth in darkness; and the darkness comprehended it not."

Even before he came into the world in the incarnation, to be the light of the world (8:12; 9:5), he made God known through creation, of which life itself is the most marvelous mystery and the loudest voice. The more we know about life, the more complex and elusive it proves to be. Life, rising from the dust in myriad forms, beckons to us and says, "This is the finger of God" (compare Exodus 8:19). Every cell, every membrane, every complex molecule, every strand of DNA, picks up the chorus: "The hand that made us is divine."

But darkness now enfolds the children of fallen Adam's race. There is the darkness of the religious mind, which leads otherwise intelligent people to harbor superstition or embrace all kinds of high-sounding nonsense. There is the darkness of the philosophical mind, which speculates vainly about the ultimate nature of things. There is the darkness of the carnal mind, which is entrenched in enmity against God and is quite prepared to entertain a thousand hurtful and destructive lusts. There is the darkness of the scientific mind, which says in one breath that life is bewildering in its complexity and in the next breath declares that "life is only chemistry" and that therefore there is no reason to believe in God.

The existence of darkness is evident. Its goal is to envelop the earth completely and prevent the light from penetrating into human souls. That, however, is beyond the power of darkness. "The darkness overpowers it not." A small candle can dispel darkness. When the light shines in all its strength, darkness flees. In the heart of every person is the recognition of God and of right and wrong. That light has never been extinguished. Nor can the most virile propagation of atheism and humanism blot it out. At Calvary the power of darkness had its moment of precarious victory when the light went out. But on the resurrection morning it blazed forth again, triumphant forever. Soon will dawn "the perfect day" (Proverbs 4:18).

II. THE DIVINE LIGHT IN EVIDENCE (1:6-13)

John moves smoothly into his next introductory theme: the light. Looking back at those early days when the Lord Jesus first showed himself, the apostle John now recalls the ministry of John the baptist and marvels at the speed with which Israel's rejection of the announced messiah developed. It will be one of his major concerns in this gospel to show belief and unbelief developing side by side. His prologue gives us an initial glimpse of this.

A. The Witness and the Light (1:6-8)

1. The Messenger (1:6)

The witness in verse 7, of course, is John the baptist, the messenger, the "man sent from God" (1:6). John the baptist was both a priest and a Nazarite. There are only three lifelong Nazarites mentioned in the Bible: Samuel, Samson, and John the baptist. A Nazarite had to keep from touching a dead body and from any contact with the fruit of the vine. He also had to let his hair grow long. Forbidden to touch the dead body of even his nearest and dearest relative, he proclaimed to the world that his affections were on the altar. His love for God eclipsed all lesser loves. Abstaining from wine, he proclaimed to the world that his appetites were on the altar. He kept his body in subjection. Allowing his hair to grow long, he proclaimed to the world that even in his appearance, all was on the alter.

This was a high standard of consecration, much more demanding than normal devotion to the things of God. It is no wonder that in fifteen hundred years of continuous Hebrew history we read only of three who were thus set apart for God. One of them, Samson, failed dismally. The other two, Samuel and John the baptist, were Hebrew prophets—Samuel was the first of them and John the last.

John was a prophet "and more than a prophet" (Luke 7:26). He was also a priest. A prophet represents God to man; a priest represents man to God. John was a priest and more than a priest—he was a Nazarite priest. A priest suggests professional consecration; a Nazarite suggests personal consecration.

John the baptist is injected suddenly into the gospel narrative. John the apostle had been speaking of "life" and "light," two common denominators of a person's belief and behavior. ("Light" has to do with knowing; "life" has to do with showing.) There flashed into the apostle's mind a vision of "a man sent from God," one who on the human level epitomized both light and life. John the baptist lived a life so wholly true to his calling and conviction that he earned the Lord's commendation: "Among them that are born of women there hath not risen a greater than John the Baptist." He was sent from God to bring to the nation of Israel fresh light on the coming of Christ after the darkness of some four hundred silent years. He cast a floodlight of truth and expectation on the times, backed by the authority of a life beyond reproach.

He was "sent from God." No one can be sent from God who has not first been with God. John the baptist, muses John the apostle, came straight from the presence of God. That was what gave him his authority and power.

2. The Motive (1:7)

John had a motive, a reason for his actions. He "came for a witness, to bear witness of the Light, that all men through him might believe" (1:7). A witness is not the same as an attorney. A lawyer argues his or her case, tries to prove a point, tries to influence people to make the desired decision. A witness is called solely to tell the truth, the whole truth, and nothing but the truth. Witnesses are called to testify to what they know. John the baptist knew that Jesus was the light and he testified to that fact.

3. The Method (1:8)

"He was not that Light, but was sent to bear witness of that Light" (1:8). A good illustration in nature is in the relation of the moon to the sun, in the light each sheds on the earth. The moon is a dead world in space, a massive chunk of lifeless rock. It has not a spark of fire, not a glimmer of light of its own. The work of the moon is to be a giant reflector in the sky, to pick up the light of the sun and relay that light to the earth. The moon is not the light. It is poised in space to bear witness to the light. Out there beyond the darkness of the world and of the night is the sun. The sun is a vast orb of burning gas, a kind of nuclear furnace, blazing away, pouring out a continual stream of light. The moon's function is only temporary, for the day is coming. The sun sheds its light directly on the earth, dispelling its darkness in a way the moon could not do.

Such was John the baptist. He was not that light, but was sent to bear witness of that light.

B. The World and the Light (1:9-13)

1. The Light Revealed (1:9)

The apostle John's thoughts go back to Jesus. "That was the true Light, which lighteth every man that cometh into the world." Every man. Every person. All without distinction. All have some light. Those who have received no written revelation have the light of creation and conscience. God gave the Jews the added light of covenant and commandment. Now God has given the world the light of Christ. No one escapes one or another of the sources of light God has made available. The Holy Spirit sees to that. God holds people responsible for the light they have. In lands that have known the full blaze of the light of Christ, people are without excuse.

2. The Light Resisted (1:10-11)

Nothing seemed to astonish John more than the resistance to Jesus. Looking back to the beginning of things, John was still amazed at how quickly and how completely people, both Jews and gentiles, turned away from the light.

The Lord saw the light resisted *by his own creatures* (1:10). "He was in the world, and the world was made by him, and the world knew him not." He walked a hedgerow and plucked a blade of grass. He had created it; he knew about its structure, about photosynthesis, about the mystery of a plant's pollination and germination, and all its complex chemistry. He walked beside the sea of Galilee; he knew the topography of that lake, every deep and shallow place, every pebble on the bottom, each and every fish darting through its waves. The world was made by him; he knew all about astronomy and chemistry, physics and biology, mathematics and medicine. He knew every law now known to science and every law not known to science, not because he had studied them but because he was the author of them all. He looked at the world through the eyes of a man but somehow, in the mystery of his being, he had infinite understanding of all things.

The creator trod those Galilean fields and walked Jerusalem's streets. Wisdom, love, and power looked out of his eyes, and were felt in the touch of his hands. He was in the world, the world was made by him, and the world knew him not. To John, that was a supreme tragedy and irony. People rubbed shoulders with God, yet were too blind to see.

The Lord was resisted not only by his creatures; worse still, he was resisted *by his own countrymen* (1:11). "He came unto his own, and his own received him not." That is, he came to the Jewish people, and they had no use for him. He had been preparing them for that coming for centuries. The prophets had foretold it. Their regathering to the promised land from the Babylonian exile had heralded it. The cold, deadness, and formality of their religion echoed the need for one who could breathe life into dead bones. John the baptist had arisen to announce the imminence of his coming. But Jesus was not the kind of messiah they wanted.

The classic biblical illustration is that of Joseph, the father's well-beloved son, the "firstborn" of old Jacob's heart. Joseph was set apart from his kinsmen, the children of Israel, by the unique position afforded him in the family, as was evident from his coat of many colors. He was set in deliberate contrast to his kinsmen, his goodness and obedience standing in stark relief to the evil and wickedness of the others. As a result he was hated, the more so because of his dreams, which spoke so clearly of his pre-eminence and coming exaltation. The Old Testament historian tells that they envied him and could not speak peaceably to him. At last they conspired against him, sold him for the price

of a slave, and delivered him into the hands of the gentiles—
and that, after he had come to them from the immediate presence of the father.

Thus, too, the Lord Jesus came unto his own, and his own
received him not.

3. The Light Received (1:12-13)

The light, however, was not only revealed and resisted. It was
received. John then gives one of those marvelous gospel texts
that are such a marked feature of his writing, texts that distill
into pure concentrate the essence of God's plan of salvation for
humankind. They are natural stopping places in the onward
march of redemption as recorded by John.

"But . . . " Oh, those revealing *buts* of the Bible. They are
small hinges on which great truths and destinies swing. "He
came unto his own, and his own received Him not. But . . ."
Thank God, that was not all the story. By John's old age the
ranks of the redeemed were already reaching around the
world. Millions had been born again. Here John gives us what
we can call the formula for the new birth. He describes *the
spiritual birth of the child of God* (1:12).

"But as many as received him, to them gave he the power [the
right, the authority] to become the sons [children] of God, even
to them that believe on his name." We must note the three
verbs: *believe, receive, become*—putting them in their chronological order. In the case of a human birth, two factors interact in
the equation of life: the human and the divine. Human beings
do their part, and then God performs a miracle and life is
created in the womb. A child is born. As it is with a natural
birth, so it is with the new birth. We do our part, God performs
the miracle, and life begins—spiritual life, divine life, eternal
life. A new child is born into the family of God. The process
revolves around those three verbs.

First we must believe, believe on his name. The name is not
mentioned here but there is no doubt as to what that name is:
Jesus, the name John more than anyone else uses. Matthew uses
that name 151 times, Mark 13 times, Luke 88 times, but John,
no less than 247 times. John, more than the other evangelists,
confronts us with the Lord's deity, yet keeps his humanity before us from beginning to end. But, while reminding us over
and over again of Jesus' humanity, John never lets us forget that
he was more than human.

So, we are to "believe on his name." Why his name? Well, his
name is the key to our salvation. When he was about to be born,
the Lord sent a messenger to Joseph with the command, "Thou

shalt call his name JESUS: for he shall save his people from their sins" (Matthew 1:21). To believe on his name is to believe in what his name signifies; it is to believe that Jesus can save me from my sins. And that presupposes that I know myself as a sinner in need of a Savior.

It is a great step to arrive at the point where I believe in his name. But that in itself does not put me in the family of God. The second part of the equation (stated first because of its primary importance) is to "receive him." It is to "as many as received him" that he imparts new life. It is not enough to believe that Jesus is *a* Savior, not enough to believe that he is *the* Savior. He must become *my* Savior. The only way that can happen is for me to receive him. That step simply involves inviting Jesus, the one who saves people from their sins, to come into my heart and life as Savior and Lord, to live and to reign in my innermost being.

How does believing and receiving make one a child of God? Well, that is our part. When we do our part, God performs the miracle. He says, "Become!" And we become a child of God. He imparts new life. The Holy Spirit comes in and indwells the human spirit, bringing with him the life of God. The life-giving power of God flows in and regenerates our human spirits. We have life from above. We share the divine nature. We become children of God.

By way of comparison and contrast, John next describes *the supernatural birth of the Christ of God*. The Authorized Version reads: "Which [who] were born, not of blood, nor of the will of the flesh, nor of the will of man, but of God." If that reading is correct, the verse amplifies the statement of the previous verse. It shows that a person's new birth is *not of human descent* (1:13a). It is "not of blood." Just because my parents are God's children does not make me one of God's children.

It is *not of human desire* (1:13b). It is not "of the will of the flesh." No amount of wishful thinking makes me a child of God. I might wish I were the child of a millionaire but that does not make me one. I may even live in a fantasy world where I convince myself that I am the son of a millionaire, but to do so is folly.

It is *not of human design* (1:13c). It is not "of the will of man." No amount of parental or personal resolve can make me a child of God. My parents may have me baptized as a baby, but that does not make me a child of God; that is only "the will of man." I may use all my strength of character to live a good life, perform religious duties, achieve spiritual goals, but those things will not impart new life. It is a birth. We are "born of God," according to the three spiritual laws given in verse 12.

But there is another view of this verse. There are those who argue that the phrase "who were born" should read "who was born" which changes the sense entirely. In this case it refers to the Lord Jesus, the one in whose saving name we are to believe, the one who himself was born "not of blood, nor of the will of the flesh, nor of the will of man, but of God." If so, this is John's definition of the virgin birth of Christ and it prepares us for the statement in the next verse.

III. THE DIVINE LOVE IN EXPERIENCE (1:14-18)

"And the Word was made flesh, and dwelt among us, (and we beheld his glory, the glory as of the only begotten of the Father,) full of grace and truth"(1:14).

There are three turning points in John's prologue, which, in fact, is really a summary of his gospel. The first key statement is found in verse 1, where John categorically states the eternal and essential deity of Christ. The second key statement is this one here, in verse 14, where John emphasizes the mystery of the incarnation—the fact that the word now assumed a new form of existence. There was a unity of the Lord's person before and after the incarnation. He did not cease to be God, the second person of the godhead at his incarnation, God the Son; but at the same time his humanity was both real and complete. He remained the same person as before, but "he became flesh." The humanity of the Lord Jesus was not something to be temporarily assumed and then later discarded. It expressed a new form of existence, not a new existence. The third key statement in this summary is found in verse 18, which closes the prologue.

A. Incarnation (1:14)

John ignores all the wonderful stories of the Lord's birth recounted by Matthew and Luke. He tells us, instead, of the mysterious significance of Christ's birth. He says, "The Word was made flesh, and dwelt among us."

The birth of the Lord Jesus was unique. When any other child is born into this world, it is the creation of a new personality. A new life is created, one that never existed before. But when Jesus was born, it was not the creation of a new personality at all. It was the coming into this world of a person who had existed from all eternity. This was something new in the history of the universe. No wonder the angels awoke the slumbering echoes of the Judean hills that night with their anthems of praise.

"The Word," John says, "was made flesh." Thus he describes the incarnation, using four words in contrast with the 2,500 words used by Luke. He "dwelt among us," John says. The word is *eskenosen*, which carries the idea of pitching a tent. "He tabernacled among us" is another way to put it. Some have attached great significance to John's use of this word to describe the incarnation. They have seen it as a date mark. The thought has been expressed that the Lord Jesus was actually born on the first day of that joyous annual Jewish feast of tabernacles (15th of Tisri; that is, September 29 in the year 4 B.C. by modern reckoning). If that was the case, then his circumcision, which took place on the eighth day, would have fallen on "the great day of the feast" mentioned later by John (7:37). It is an attractive idea.

But John's use of the word *tabernacled* gives rise to many other thoughts related to the rich typology of the Old Testament tabernacle.

That tabernacle was "all glorious within," but its glory was a hidden glory. There was no great beauty about the tabernacle's outward appearance. All the furniture of the outer court was made of ordinary brass (copper). The curtains of the outer court were of unadorned linen bleached white by the sun. The only flash of color was at the gate, which gave access to the brazen altar and hinted at the hidden beauties within. From without, there was nothing particularly glorious about the tabernacle. To the eye of the casual beholder it was just another tent, spaced off from the tents of the common people and more imposing in its dimensions, but just a tent. Even when the tabernacle was moved from place to place, every piece of golden furniture used within the tabernacle itself was carefully covered from the eyes of the curious.

Thus, too, the glory of the Lord Jesus was a hidden glory. When he came to "pitch his tent" among us he did not lay aside his deity, but he veiled his glory.

The inside of the tabernacle, seen only by the priests, was glorious. The inner hangings were of blue, purple, and scarlet, and were fine linen. All the inner furniture was of gold or overlaid with gold. That mysterious shekinah cloud, which overshadowed the camp of Israel, came to rest on the mercy seat in the holy of holies where it bathed all with the light and glory of another world.

"We beheld his glory," says John, "the glory as of the only begotten of the Father, full of grace and truth." Our thoughts go instinctively to the shekinah glory that filled the tabernacle.

The reigning monarch of Great Britain has a number of homes: Buckingham Palace, Windsor Castle, Sandringham, Bal-

moral Castle. The one in which the monarch is currently resid-
ing is always indicated by the raising to the flag pole of the royal
standard. Just so the shekinah glory which filled the holy of
holies indicated that God was in residence. The Lord Jesus had
this inner glory. God was permanently in residence, so to speak,
in him. It was this inner glory that John, who knew him so
intimately, saw in the Lord Jesus Christ. He saw God in Christ,
"the glory as of the only begotten of the Father, full of grace
and truth."

Scholars draw attention to the omission of the definite article
in the original and to the fact that the absence is significant—
intended to emphasize what is specified in the nouns. John was
looking back to those days he had spent in the company of this
glorious person. "We beheld his glory," he says. The word is
etheasametha, which carries with it the idea of being a spectator
but with emphasis on the beholder; the word is used of gazing
with a purpose, of regarding with admiration. "We beheld his
glory," the kind of glory an only begotten Son receives from a
Father. John adds that, gazing on the incarnate Son of God,
they saw one "full of grace and truth"—a Hebraism for the sum
total of divine revelation. Grace corresponds with the revelation
of God as love; truth corresponds with the revelation of God as
light.

B. Identification (1:15)

John comes back now to John the baptist as the one who first
identified the Lord Jesus for who he was.

1. His Person (1:15a)

John the baptist bore witness to the Lord's person: "John bare
witness of him, and cried [cried aloud], saying, This was he of
whom I spake."

2. His Pre-eminence (1:15b)

John bore witness to the Lord's pre-eminence: "He that cometh after me is preferred before me."

3. His Pre-existence (1:15c)

John bore witness to the Lord's pre-existence: "for he was
before me."

John the baptist spoke as the last prophet of the old order. He

knew two things about the coming Christ. First, the Lord had
absolute priority in dignity and pre-eminence. As John put it
himself, he was not worthy to untie his shoe. Second, the Lord
had absolute priority because of his eternal pre-existence. The
significance of that second "before" (*protos*) has been pointed
out. It has reference to time—not just to priority of birth, but
rather to uniqueness in the matter of time. The Lord Jesus
related himself in time in quite a different way from any other
human being. He was related to time as one coming out of
eternity. As to his mother, he was born as a baby in Bethlehem;
as to his Father, he was "the ancient of days."

C. Imputation (1:16)

John the apostle now adds his own comment, rounding off
the prologue. Thus John the baptist speaks (1:15), the herald,
the last messenger of the Hebrew line, and John the apostle
speaks (1:16-18), the last of the apostles, the messenger of the
new line.

"And of his fullness (*pleroma*) have all we received, and grace
for grace." That word *pleromatos* was a favorite of agnostics, but
one that had been wrested from them by the apostle Paul and
endowed with new and higher meaning (Colossians 1:19; 2:9;
Ephesians 1:23; 3:19; 4:13). The word as used in the New
Testament speaks of the sum total of the attributes and powers
of God. Out of that inexhaustible supply every believer is given
all he or she needs. "And grace for grace," John adds: new
grace, continuous grace, uninterrupted grace. All the exceeding riches described by Paul in his Ephesian epistle, all are ours
in Christ. Each spiritual blessing we appropriate becomes the
foundation of greater blessing. God's grace is like a mighty
Niagara, thundering unendingly out of eternity into our hearts.
That is something no Old Testament prophet ever imagined.

D. Implementation (1:17)

"For the law was given by Moses," says John, "but grace and
truth came by Jesus Christ." The law was *given*; grace and truth
came. The law was impersonal, pealed out from Mount Sinai
amid scenes of terrifying grandeur, engraved on cold tablets of
·stone, mediated by angels, given to Moses. Grace and truth
were wrapped up in warm, vibrant human flesh and brought
into this world by Jesus (the man) Christ (the messiah). "He
went about doing good" was Peter's summary—as grand a
statement as any to emphasize our Lord's grace. "Never man

spake like this man" said those sent once to arrest him—as great a statement as any to emphasize our Lord's truth. Not grace at the expense of truth, not truth at the expense of grace, but grace and truth in perfect proportion—demonstrated in the character, conduct, and conversation of the most balanced person who ever lived on earth. Out of hundreds of possible illustrations John selects a few and weaves his gospel around them: the night with Nicodemus, for example; the conversation with the woman at the well; his dealings with the woman taken in adultery and with her accusers. Thus, the law of Moses contained truth—sharp, demanding, penetrating—embodied in the Decalogue, expanded into some 613 edicts of the law. The law of Moses embodied grace. Human failure to keep the moral law necessitated the giving of the ceremonial law so that guilt could be covered until it could be cancelled at Calvary. But it was not until Jesus came that the truth and grace inherent in the law could be fully implemented in a peerless human life and thus be translated into a language all can understand.

E. Illumination (1:18)

In Old Testament times God granted people visions, theophanies, angelic visits. But all fell short of a direct view of God as God. Men like Abraham and Jacob, Moses and Manoah, David and Daniel, Isaiah and Ezekiel, had manifestations of God given to them. The "glory of the Lord," the "angel of the Lord," "the Word of the Lord" came to patriarchs and prophets of old, but none of them saw God as God.

John repeatedly emphasizes the fact of the deity of Christ, the fact that Jesus was God. Yet here he says equally emphatically that "no man hath seen God at any time." We believe in the unquestionable equality of Jesus with the Father in the godhead. We believe that Jesus was God. How then could John say here that "no man hath seen God at any time" (or, more literally, "no one hath yet seen God")? The fact is that John recognized that although Jesus was God, when he came to earth, he deliberately laid aside, not his deity, but those attributes of deity which would be incongruous with true humanity. For instance, God dwells in light unapproachable (1 Timothy 6:16). If Jesus had come into the world not only to be God but also to behave as God, nobody would have been able to approach him. The fact is that although he never ceased to be God he walked this earth as though he were not more than human, a fact that explains many of John's later statements about the Lord Jesus Christ. He was seen as a man even though he was God.

In a message given at a Moody Bible Institute Keswick Conference some years ago, Major Ian Thomas put it like this: "He had to come as he came in order to be what he was; he had to be what he was in order to do what he did. He had to do what he did so that we might have what he has; we have to have what he has in order to be what he was." Major Ian Thomas is very good at this clever kind of definition. This one he expanded. "He had to come as he came (born of a virgin) in order to be what he was (a perfect man inhabited by God). He had to be what he was in order to do what he did (die to redeem us). He had to do what he did so that we might have what he has (his life, all that we lost in Adam). We have to have what he has in order to be what he was (perfect: man inhabited by God)." That is what the gospel of John is all about.

So the Lord Jesus was seen as a man even though he was God. However, "The only begotten Son, which is in the bosom of the Father, he hath declared him." It has often been pointed out that the word *declared* (*exegeomai*) is the one from which we get our English word *exegesis*. It means "to make known by expounding." The person who expounds or exegetes the Scriptures brings out things that were there all the time for people to see, but things that had been overlooked until they were thus brought forth. Jesus is the incarnate exegesis of God. He has brought God forth, set him before us, fully, accurately. He has authoritatively "expounded" him in what he is, in what he has said, in what he has done. For although Jesus was man, in every sense of the word, he was also God in all the dimensions of deity.

The one who thus exegetes God is the one, John says, who "is in the bosom of the Father." That phrase suggests "has his being in." It describes a timeless state, an eternal condition. It refers to a condition of fullest intimacy, of boundless love, of fathomless affection. It describes the mutual love of Father and Son in the eternal godhead, and it affirms that this relationship continued unbroken by the incarnation. It tells us that the revelation of God that Jesus came to exegete was a revelation of the heart of God.

Such is John's introductory statement. If he had written no more, he would have said all we need to know. His prologue thus puts to rest all those philosophical speculations and heresies that, in his day and ours, find expression in attacking the person of Christ with reference either to his deity or humanity.

PART TWO

The Signs of the Son of God

John 1:19–10:42

From out of the wilderness had come striding a spiritual giant of a man. His dress, diet, deportment, and demands made his hearers think of Elijah. His voice thundered until the windows of conscience rattled in everyone's soul. His eyes flashed like lightning, seeming to read the secrets of everyone's heart. Multitudes heard about this new prophet and flocked to hear him. The religious establishment investigated him, disliked him, feared him, rejected him, and was denounced by him. Herod on his throne was afraid of him. John the baptist was his name—the son of a priest, married to the daughter of a priest. His birth had been foretold. He had been raised strictly, with a view to his becoming a priest. He had also been raised as a Nazarite, with a view to his becoming a prophet. There already were priests after the order of Aaron—enough and to spare. Few and far between were prophets after the order of Elijah. What Israel needed was not another priest. What Israel needed was a prophet. John, by birth, training, disposition, conviction, and choice was raised up by God to be that prophet, the last of a long, illustrious line.

Section 1. His Deity Is Declared (1:19–4:54)

His message galvanized the nation: "Christ is coming! Repent! The kingdom of heaven is at hand!" Thousands came to hear him, accepting baptism by him as token of their repentance.

The apostle John tells us very little of all this. He takes it for granted that these facts from the other gospels are general knowledge.

John the apostle begins the first major section of his gospel with a reference to the testimony of John the baptist and to the faithfulness of that testimony.

I. THE TESTIMONY OF JOHN (1:19-51)

A. The Faithfulness of His Testimony (1:19-34)

It would seem that verse 19 begins after the baptism and subsequent temptation of Jesus. The testimony of John the baptist was a logical place for John the apostle to begin his gospel, since one of his overall objectives was to trace the parallel rise of belief and unbelief among the Jewish people living in Palestine at the time of Christ.

1. Questions Asked (1:19-28)

John begins with questions asked of John by the Jews. There were two main questions. One question asked is *about John's identity* (1:19-23).

We begin with *the delegation* (1:19). "The Jews," we read, "sent priests and Levites from Jerusalem to ask him, Who art thou?" John was writing from the standpoint of the close of the first century. Jewish rejection of Christ had hardened into a settled attitude. Just before the fall of Jerusalem the rabbi Zakkai obtained permission from Vespasian to establish a special academy for Jewish studies in Palestine. The astute rabbi could see the writing on the wall for Jerusalem, the temple, and the homeland. He was concerned that Judaism and the Jewish people might survive the impending destruction and dispersal of the Jews. When Jerusalem fell, with Vespasian's warrant he successfully established his center at Jabneh, just north of Jerusalem. He rejected Jesus as the answer to the Jewish dilemma. He set about making the oral traditions and commentaries (which later became the Talmud) the pattern for Jewish survival in the coming centuries. There would be no more Jewish homeland, no more capital city, no more temple, no more altar, sacrifices or priests. So let the Jews find their home, their fulfillment, their means of national survival in hostile gentile lands, in the accumulated wisdom of their rabbis. So those laws and traditions, a seemingly odd assortment of wisdom and folly, became the focus of Jewish life. (See John Phillips, *Exploring the World of the Jew*, Chicago: Moody Press, 1981, pp. 65-66.) The Rabbi Zakkai poured the cement of Jewish traditionalism and exclusivism over the wandering Hebrew people, and it hardened into centuries of rejection of Jesus as the messiah and Savior of Israel.

All this was already in process by the time John wrote. So he calls God's ancient people "the Jews." It is his characteristic word for them in this gospel. He uses the expression seventy times. The word emphasizes the *Lo-ammi* status of the Hebrew people consequent upon their rejection of Christ both in the gospels and in the period covered by the book of Acts (Hosea 1:9; the name *Lo-ammi* means "not my people"). In this age of grace the Hebrew people are not regarded from the biblical standpoint as "Israel" but as "Jews." John adopts the name given to them by the gentiles.

The Jews, John says, sent a delegation to John the baptist. Later he defines the word *Jews* as referring particularly to the Pharisees (1:24), who took the lead in the gospels as the enemies of Christ. The delegation was probably dispatched by the Sanhedrin. The "priests" and "Levites" represented, particularly, the ecclesiastical side of things in the nation. In sending this delegation they recognized in John a priest and a Levite as well as a Judean. Later, they saw Jesus as a Galilean and a carpenter.

"Who are you?" That was the burning question. John's preaching had touched a chord. Not even the Sanhedrin could ignore the vibrating strings of renewed messianic expectation that thrilled the nation as a result of John's testimony. "Who are you?" That was what they wanted to know.

John had been ministering for a considerable time. Even Herod had made it his business to have conversations with this dynamic preacher. It would seem that some in the Sanhedrin had been speculating about whether or not John himself was the messiah. (Remember, John the apostle at this time was a disciple of John the baptist.)

Next, we have *the denials* (1:20-21). "He confessed, and denied not; but confessed." The repetition reflects John's resolution not to accept honors that were not his. The questions were posed by men who knew the Scriptures. His answer was clear: "I am not the Christ." "Then are you Elijah?" They went back to Malachi. The last of the writing prophets of the Old Testament had foretold that, prior to the coming of Christ, Elijah would come. "Are you Elijah?" John's answer was unequivocal. "I am not." The Jewish rejection of Jesus would necessitate a second coming of Christ. Before that coming, Elijah will come (see Revelation 11). The questioners went back even further, back now to Moses (Deuteronomy 18:15). They remembered that Moses had prophesied that one day God would raise up a prophet just like him. "Are you that prophet?" John's answer was a blunt "No." His replies grew shorter with each succeeding guess: "I (the *I* is emphatic) am not the Christ. I am not. No."

Then came *the demand* (1:22-23). Their specific question— very well, who are you then? We need to give an answer to those who sent us—was followed by a scriptural quotation. John took them back to Isaiah 40:3. "I am only a voice," he said. "I am the voice of one crying in the wilderness, Make straight the way of the Lord." He was the Lord's herald. It is likely (from 1:26) that John knew that Jesus was standing in the throng listening to this exchange—standing there, smiling at his faithful ambassador, nodding his head in approval of his words. No wonder John's answers to these questioners grew briefer and blunter.

John continues with questions *about John's ideology* (1:24-28). There now followed a brief clash of swords. We note *the Pharisees' attack on his baptism* (1:24-25). The question about John's ideology was put by his questioners who are now identified. They were the religious party among the Jews particularly concerned with religious rites and ceremonies. "Well," they said, "you are not the messiah, you have no mandate from Malachi or from Moses. On what ground do you take it upon yourself to introduce a new religious rite, baptism, not ordered by the law? (Proselyte baptism might have been practiced by the Jews, though this is not certain. But proselytes baptized themselves and were gentiles seeking admission to Israel. John's baptism was administered by him, to Jews.) The Pharisees strongly objected to John's baptism. If proselyte baptism was practiced at this time then of course they would resent a rite that seemed to treat Jews as if they were aliens. Further, John's baptism was a baptism of repentance. The Pharisees were indignant at any suggestion that they needed repentance and ritual cleansing in the Jordan.

John did not waste much time in answering their questions. He was not accountable to the Pharisees or to the Sanhedrin. He derived his authority from a higher source. So he carried the attack into their territory. We note *John's attack on their blindness* (1:26-28). Who gave him his right to baptize? We know the answer. His authority came from one standing in their midst, one whom in their blindness they could not see. The messiah of Israel, the Christ of God, the hope of every faithful Hebrew heart, was right there, and they did not know it.

"I am not worthy to unloose the latchet of his shoe," said John. This menial task was considered by the religious Jewish authorities as being a servile act, fitting only for a slave to perform. Thus John, the greatest of all the prophets, abased himself in the presence of his Lord.

At this point the apostle John adds a footnote out of his personal knowledge of the event. He says that these things took place at "Bethabara beyond Jordan, where John was baptizing." The name means "house of the ferry." The traditional site is the

Jericho ford some miles north of the Dead Sea. Another view is
that the place referred to is another fifty miles north of the
Jericho ford, a place in the land of Bashan, ten miles south of
the sea of Galilee and about twenty-two miles from Cana.

2. Questions Answered (1:29-34)

About six weeks before, Jesus had been baptized by John in
the Jordan. Right afterward, he had gone into the wilderness
where his temptations took place. John makes no mention of
that. The period of temptation was forty days, a little under six
weeks. Having routed the devil and recuperated from his prolonged fast, Jesus now returned to the Jordan. On the day the
deputation arrived, John had seen and recognized him in the
crowd. It was now the next day, and *the arrival of Jesus* (1:29a)
took place.

John saw Jesus coming toward him. This is the Lord's first
appearance in this gospel. He had come to be publicly announced by his herald to the nation. The day before, the delegation from the Sanhedrin had questioned John about whether
or not he himself was the messiah. The time had come to
remove all doubt. John's repeated denials and refusal to identify
himself as any more than a "voice" must have provoked heated
discussions both among the authorities and the common people.
John the apostle, an eyewitness of these things, no doubt could
remember it all as though it were yesterday.

The arrival of Jesus was a moment freighted with possibilities. The Passover feast was approaching, a feast that commemorated the exodus of Israel from Egypt, the birth of the
Hebrew nation, and the demonstration of redemption by the
blood of the lamb. We can be sure that Jesus chose this moment
unerringly for his formal presentation to the nation by his now
famous herald. From John's first words we can see that he had
the approaching Passover in mind. We have seen the arrival of
Jesus and now we hear the *announcement of John* (1:29b-34).

John the baptist's announcement revolved around a proclamation and a problem. First, we have *a proclamation* (1:29b-30).
"Behold," he cried, "the Lamb of God, which taketh away the
sin of the world. This is he of whom I said, After me cometh a
man which is preferred before me: for he was before me."

John did not introduce Jesus to the nation as the Son of God,
nor as the holy one of God, nor as the Christ of God, nor as the
word of God. He went right to the heart of Israel's need, of the
whole world's need. He proclaimed him to be the lamb of God.
Although John's baptism had confronted people with the need

for repentance, they needed much more than repentance. They needed redemption. No amount of water could remove the stain of sin; that required blood. And not the blood of bulls and goats, which could never take away sin (Hebrews 10:1-4), not the blood of an ordinary lamb. It called for the shedding of "precious blood," for redemption made possible by the lamb of God.

It is a special title for the Lord. He is called the lamb explicitly only twice in the Old Testament, only twice in the gospels, only once in the book of Acts, and only once in the epistles. He is called the lamb, however, twenty-eight times in the book of Revelation; it is particularly his apocalyptical title.

The great question in the Old Testament was voiced by Isaac on his way to Mount Moriah: "Where is the lamb?" (Genesis 22:7). Abraham's answer was equally great: "God will provide himself a lamb for a burnt offering." Now that great Old Testament question is matched by an even greater New Testament answer: "Behold the Lamb of God, which taketh away the sin of the world." As John spoke, it is likely that the bleating of sheep could be heard and that people could see flocks being driven toward Jerusalem in preparation for the Passover feast. John drew attention away from them to Jesus, the true Passover lamb whose sacrifice would procure eternal redemption for all humankind and make obsolete the annual Passover of the Jews.

To complete the identification, John added the words: "This is he of whom I said, After me cometh a man which is preferred before me." John was six months older than Jesus. While still in the womb, John had acknowledged the pre-eminence of the coming Christ (Luke 1:41). Now he acknowledged his pre-existence.

But John had *a problem* (1:31-34). Even though he had been called to announce the coming messiah to Israel, he did not know who he was. First we see *the problem stated* (1:31): "I knew him not," he says. The day before, he had said to the delegation from the Sanhedrin and to those standing around that the messiah was right there, in their midst, one "whom ye know not" (1:26). In both cases he used the same root word to describe their ignorance and his. It is the word *oida*, which means "to know intuitively, without effort." Before he was enlightened he was as much without the knowledge of Christ as they were. He must have known who Jesus was, since Jesus was his cousin (Luke 1:36), or at least a relative. The circumstances surrounding his own birth and that of Jesus must surely have been known to John. The likelihood is, however, that they had never met or that they had not met for many years. John's self-exile to the wilderness to prepare himself for his ministry might account for that. In any case, we have his word for it that he had a problem. He would not recognize the messiah when he saw him. He was going to need special revelation from God to show who it was, who was the true messiah. He had this assurance, however, that "he should be made manifest to Israel" (1:31). On the strength of this assurance he had proceeded with his mission: calling the nation to repentance and baptizing his converts in the Jordan.

We see *the problem solved* (1:32-34) when the time came. When Jesus showed up to be baptized some six weeks before, God had given John the long-awaited sign (1:32-33). It had been made known to John that he would recognize the messiah by seeing the Holy Spirit descend on him and remain on him. What form the Holy Spirit would take remained to be seen. But as soon as Jesus came up out of the water at his baptism, John's doubts dissolved: "I saw the Spirit descending from heaven like a dove, and it abode upon him" (1:32).

Our thoughts go back to the story of Noah and the flood. The storms had passed, the billows subsided, and the ark rocked on the waters. Noah opened the ark's window and sent out a dove. That dove, like the Spirit of God who on creation's morning had brooded over the face of the deep, found no place where it could alight to rest. At last it returned to the ark.

Since Adam's fall the Spirit of God has moved on the face of the waters, brooding over a ruined race, looking for one on whom he could come to rest. The ages rolled on; kingdoms waxed and waned; generation after generation came and went, and not one child of Adam's kin could the Spirit find to give him rest. Then Jesus came. For thirty years the Holy Spirit was with him. Then, at his baptism, came the Father's benediction: "This is my beloved Son, in whom I am well pleased." With that the holy dove of God came down and abode upon him. At last he had found one on whom he could rest.

The word *abode* carries with it the idea of "remaining." The Holy Spirit came on individuals in Old Testament times to enlighten or empower. He came and went. His work was intermittent. He came to remain on the Lord Jesus.

At once John the baptist knew beyond all doubt that Jesus of Nazareth was the one whose coming he had been called to announce. "He that sent me to baptize with water, the same said unto me, Upon whom thou shalt see the Spirit descending, and remaining on him, the same is he which baptizeth with the Holy Ghost" (1:34). This linking of the water baptism, administered by John to repentant sinners, to the Spirit baptism, administered by Jesus to regenerated saints, should be noted in preparation for the Lord's impending midnight talk with Nicodemus (1:35).

The baptism of the Spirit is mentioned by all the evangelists. It took place on the day of Pentecost. It is that operation of the Holy Spirit which takes an individual believer in Christ and makes him or her a member of the mystical body of Christ, the church (1 Corinthians 12:13). It should not be confused with some mythical "second work of grace" or with some ecstatic experience that enables people to speak in tongues. People who adopt those views do violence to the text of Scripture; they play havoc with biblical terminology and misinterpret the baptism of the Spirit as defined by the Holy Spirit himself. The only direct doctrinal reference to this baptism is in 1 Corinthians 12:13, where its all-inclusiveness is clearly taught and its sole purpose explained. No mention of "tongues" is in any way found in this Holy Spirit-inspired definition of the baptism. (For further study of this subject and all relevant mentions of the Holy Spirit and "tongues" in Acts, see John Phillips, *Exploring Acts,* Chicago: Moody Press, 1986.)

Having told people about the sign, John the baptist boldly introduces his listeners to the Son (1:34). "And I saw, and bare record that this is the Son of God."

The Jews were looking for a messiah, but they thought that a human person might be that messiah. The *messiah* was, literally, "the anointed one." In the Old Testament, prophets, priests, and kings were anointed with oil. Jesus was anointed with the Holy Spirit.

The Jews were looking for a messenger, another Moses or Elijah, one who would come in the tradition of David or Daniel, one who would come after these men, the prophet to end all prophets. Jesus was not just one who came after these men; he was before them.

The Jews were looking for a monarch. They wanted a militant leader, one who would break the power of Rome and build an empire ruled from Jerusalem. Jesus was not just a ruler; he was a redeemer. He had come not just to set people free from servitude but from sin.

John proclaimed Jesus as the lamb of God and as the Son of God. He lifted the thoughts of thinking people to much higher ground than they had envisioned. Jesus is the Son of God in an absolute sense that is true of no other human being. His sonship, as set forth particularly in this gospel, is rooted in his eternal sonship. In other words, he whom John the baptist proclaimed to be the Son of God is the one we proclaim to be God, the Son, the second person of the godhead.

B. The Fruitfulness of His Testimony (1:35-51)

The apostle John turns now from the faithfulness of John the baptist's testimony to a consideration of the fruitfulness of that testimony. Some of the Lord's earliest disciples had previously been disciples of John the baptist. John the apostle was one of these. The greatness of John's fruitfulness is seen in two phrases, "They heard him [John]" and "they followed Jesus" (1:37). That should be the primary objective of every evangelist, soul-winner, pastor, teacher, deacon, and elder. When people hear us, they should follow Jesus.

1. Disciples of John in View (1:35-39)

We consider, first, these disciples of John and *how they found the Lord* (1:35-37). John the apostle, now living far from his native land, thinks back to that memorable period in his younger years.

It was "the next day," the third day in a series of days shortly before the Passover. On the first day in the series we have a delegation, the representatives of the Sanhedrin, questioning and challenging John the baptist. On the second day we have a declaration, John the baptist formally presenting Jesus as lamb of God and Son of God. Now on this third day we have a decision. Two of John the baptist's followers leave him in order to become followers of Jesus. It was John the baptist who promoted this move. He saw Jesus walking nearby. The word for "looking upon" Jesus is *emblepo*, which means "to fix one's gaze upon" or "to give a penetrating look." The only other time the word occurs in the gospel is in verse 42, where the Lord Jesus is said to have given the same kind of searching look at Simon. As far as we know, this was the last time John the baptist ever saw Jesus. John's gaze was accompanied by an exclamation: "Behold the Lamb of God!" That was all. The public declaration of the preceding day now became a personal direction to his disciples. Two of them instantly transferred their allegiance to Jesus (1:37), won to him, significantly, not by a declaration of his deity but by a declaration of his death and atoning sacrifice.

We note, next, *how they followed the Lord* (1:38-39). One of the two is identified as Andrew. The other remains unnamed, though there can be little doubt it was John himself, the author of this gospel. He never names himself except in the book of Revelation. The narrative bears the marks of one who was there and for whom every small detail still lived in his memory. From this time on in the gospel, John speaks as an eyewitness, though he withholds his name (1:40; 13:23,25; 19:26,35; 20:2,4,8; 21:7,20,24).

The Lord, knowing that he was being trailed, turned around and confronted these two. "What seek ye?" he asked. Those are his first words in this gospel. Probably the two men were so awed by the thought of who this one really was that they did not dare to speak to him directly. If so, he opened the door for them. John, of course, knew who Jesus was on the purely human level. But the words of John the baptist had set Jesus worlds apart from him. Andrew, too, probably knew him or at least knew of him. He and his brother Simon were business partners of John and his brother James. Now the words of John the baptist, identifying Jesus as lamb of God and Son of God, put awe in the hearts of both these men.

Andrew spoke for both of them; he addressed Jesus as "Rabbi" (Master). "Where dwellest thou?" Evidently Andrew felt that the issues now being confronted were too momentous to be discussed out there in public. He wanted a more personal and private setting. Where could he find this wondrous messiah again? Already he had someone in mind he wanted to bring to Jesus.

The Lord responded with an invitation: "Come and see" (1:39) or "Come and ye shall see." The two men responded at once. This was John's spiritual birthday and to the end of his days he could remember the exact time, "the tenth hour." We cannot be sure whether John was using Hebrew time or Roman time. If it was Hebrew time it was four p.m.; if Roman time it was ten a.m. The likelihood is that it was Roman time. In any case they spent the rest of the day with Jesus and left determined to waste no time in bringing others to Christ.

2. Disciples of Jesus in View (1:40-51)

We look first at *how Peter was drawn to Jesus* (1:40-42). One can picture Andrew and John hurrying away from this momentous meeting. Andrew is saying, "I must tell Simon." John is saying, "I'm going to get James." This is implied by the next verse: "He [Andrew] first findeth his own brother Simon, and saith unto him, We have found the Messiah" (1:41). Now that phrase, "Andrew first findeth his own brother," can legitimately be rephrased, "Andrew findeth first his own brother." The implication is not that he found his own brother before he did anything else or went after somebody else. The implication is that Andrew found his brother first, that is, before John found his brother. It is well within the meaning of the text that both

Andrew and John brought a brother to Jesus but that Andrew was first to do so.

"And he brought him to Jesus," John says, characteristically telling us about Andrew's convert rather than his own. Andrew's convert became the first messenger of the church; John's convert became the first martyr among the apostles.

There can be no doubt that the day of Peter's conversion was a notable day in heaven—almost as notable as the day of Paul's conversion. For Simon Peter preached that famous pentecostal sermon which won three thousand people to Christ in a single day and gave the infant church its first major influx of members.

The Lord looked searchingly at Andrew's big blustering brother. He identified him at once and then gave him a new name which completely eclipsed the old one: "Thou art Simon, the son of Jona [an Aramaic form of the name *John*]; thou shalt be called Cephas [the Aramaic form of the name *Peter*]." The word for "Peter" is *petros* meaning a movable stone, not a rock *(petra)*. It was an indication of what Christ intended to do for impulsive, easily swayed Simon. He was going to give him a rocklike character.

On this important day three (or more likely four) men were attached to Jesus. Three of them (Peter, James, and John) became his most intimate disciples. This was the first day of the Lord's public ministry. The Lord established a personal relationship with these men at this time. Later, as the synoptist writers record, he would call them to fulltime service (Matthew 4:18-22; Mark 1:16-20; Luke 5:1-11).

Next we see *how Philip was discovered by Jesus* (1:43-51). We see *Philip's call* (1:43-44). The next day (the fourth day in the sequence and the second day of the Lord's ministry) the Lord went out soul-winning himself. The Lord had made up his mind to leave Judea and go to Galilee. Connected with this decision was the Lord's approach to Philip, though we are not told just where this meeting took place. We are simply told: "The day following Jesus would go forth into Galilee, and findeth Philip, and saith unto him, Follow me" (1:43). John adds the information that Philip "was of Bethsaida, the city of Andrew and Peter" (1:44). Perhaps they had already prepared the soil. Bethsaida was a city not far from the place where the river Jordan runs into the lake. It was evidently a wicked place and was denounced by Jesus for rejecting him and the "mighty works" he had done in its streets. He said that, given such proofs of a divine visitation, the wicked Phoenician cities of Tyre and Sidon would have repented in sackcloth and ashes (Matthew 11:21).

Actually Bethsaida was a fishing suburb of Capernaum. Bethsaida is said here to be "the city of Andrew and Peter." It is implied in Mark 1:29 that by the time the Lord began his Galilean ministry, Peter and Andrew had taken up residence in Capernaum itself.

We see *Philip's concern* (1:45-51). The Lord's invitation to Philip was trimmed of all verbiage: "Follow me" or "Come, travel with me" as some have suggested it be phrased. We can picture the warmth in the tone of the Lord's voice, the smile that accompanied it, and perhaps the friendly hand on the shoulder. From that moment on Philip was his man, and his first concern was for his friend Nathanael.

The story of Nathanael's conversion is in three parts. We begin with the way in which *Nathanael was introduced to Jesus* (1:45-46). "Philip findeth Nathanael." There is some doubt as to who Nathanael was since he is not mentioned by that name by any other New Testament writers. Generally, however, it is taken for granted that he is the disciple of the Lord called Bartholomew elsewhere in the New Testament.

"We have found him, of whom Moses in the law, and the prophets, did write," Philip said, adding for further indentification: "Jesus of Nazareth, the Son of Joseph." We note that he began by describing Jesus as the one who fulfilled all the scriptural requirements for the messiah. Nathanael was evidently a man who knew the Hebrew Scriptures. It is possible that Philip and Nathanael had often pored over the prophetic pages together. They knew that the messiah was to be a scion of David's royal line, that he was to be born in Bethlehem, that he was to be born of a virgin, that he was to be a sojourner in Egypt for at least a time, and that he was to be identified with the northern part of the promised land. All these details were fulfilled in Jesus of Nazareth.

Still, it came as a shock to Nathanael to hear his friend describe this new-found messiah as "Jesus of Nazareth" and further add the identifying description, "the Son of Joseph" (as was commonly believed). Nathanael came from Cana of Galilee (21:2), less than five miles from Nazareth. We can be sure that Jesus already had a reputation for goodness in that part of the country even though he was generally looked on as a local peasant and known as the carpenter. Probably very few people were aware of the secret of Christ's virgin birth. Everyone, however, must have known of his remarkable reputation for honesty and integrity, for sympathy and kindness, for knowledge and wisdom, for helpfulness and generosity, for scholarship and for godliness. But the messiah? From Nazareth? Impossible. "Can there any good thing come out of Nazareth?" was Nathanael's response.

Because of its proximity to gentile cities and its mixture of gentile population, its backwoods manners, general biblical illiteracy and lack of sophistication, and the coarseness of its dialect, the people of Judea held Galilee in low esteem. Nathanael, a Galilean, exhibited this local prejudice against Nazareth, which seems to have had a poor reputation. Was Nathanael perhaps hedging for time? Jesus, the messiah? The Son of Joseph? Surely not. From Nazareth? Impossible. Nazareth, in the gospels, lived up to its reputation. It was the first city to greet Jesus' claims with violence, and was ready to put him to death on the strength of just one day's exposure to his teaching. He was actively hindered in ministry there because of the town's scornful rejection of his claims.

Philip wasted no time discussing the reputation of Nazareth. He used an unanswerable argument. "Come and see," he said.

We look next at the way in which *Nathanael was interested in Jesus* (1:47-48). The Lord could read Nathanael's soul. Speaking not to Nathanael but to the others he said, "Behold an Israelite indeed, in whom is no guile." It has often been pointed out that the words can be paraphrased, "Behold an Israelite indeed, in whom is no Jacob." Jacob was a man of guile and deceit in his early years, until God broke him at the Jabbok and changed him into Israel. Jesus saw in Nathanael a guileless disposition, a man in whom the spirit of Jacob had been supplanted by the spirit of Israel.

Nathanael's reaction was one of surprise. "How do you know me?" he asked. A less sophisticated reaction would be hard to imagine. Most people, when confronted with such a compliment, would hedge and deny the statement: "Me? guileless? You don't know me!" Nathanael was not like that. He accepted the Lord's evaluation of his character as being true. His problem was not with his own disposition but with the Lord's discernment. How could this man know him?

Jesus went still further. He showed Nathanael that even before Philip had found him he had found him. He knew not only what Nathanael was like, but also he knew where he had been earlier that day: "Before that Philip called thee, when thou wast under the fig tree, I saw thee." It would seem, from the form of the sentence, that Nathanael had actually been right underneath the fig tree, in leaf about this time, possibly looking for privacy in which to ponder and pray. The Lord's subsequent words imply that Nathanael had actually been thinking about Jacob and the Genesis story of "Jacob's ladder" (Genesis 28:12), thinking about the night of Jacob's conversion. The Lord revealed to this thoughtful man Nathanael his own infallible ability to read an individual's soul and thoughts as well as his ability to see him at a distance and in a place where he had secluded himself in order to be alone.

Finally, we see the way in which *Nathanael was inspired by Jesus* (1:49-51). Nathanael's astonishment broke out in words. "Rabbi, thou art the Son of God; thou art the King of Israel." Son of God, on the throne of the universe. King of Israel, on the throne of the world. Son of God—that acknowledged his deity. King of Israel—that acknowledged his destiny. Nathanael acknowledged him as his maker, the king of Israel. Nathanael acknowledged him as his messiah, the Son of David. Nathanael capitulated before omniscience; such was *his confession of Christ* (1:49).

The Lord at once acknowledged Nathanael's tribute. He spoke to him of *his comprehension of Christ* (1:50-51). Nathanael had made what modern physicists would call a quantum leap. In one burst of revelation he had seen this man from Nazareth as God manifest in flesh. When Peter much later would make a similar confession on the mount of transfiguration, the Lord would tell him that such insight was not of flesh and blood but a direct revelation from his Father in heaven.

But Nathanael had touched only the fringe of Christ's garment. His grasp of truth was limited at this moment. "Jesus answered and said unto him, Because I said unto thee, I saw thee under the fig tree, believest thou? thou shalt see greater things than these" (1:50). The picture of Nathanael under the fig tree was in itself symbolic. The fig tree was one of the three trees used in Scripture to symbolize the nation of Israel; invariably it is used to depict the nation in its unbelief, fruitless under the old covenant, subject to God's displeasure and discipline. Nathanael represented the godly remnant in the nation who would come into the blessing of the new covenant by faith in Christ.

Nathanael's grasp of truth would be nearly limitless in a coming day: "Verily, verily, I say unto you, Hereafter ye shall see heaven open, and the angels of God ascending and descending upon the Son of man" (1:51). "Son of man" is the Lord's human and millennial title. "Verily, verily," said Jesus, "Amen, Amen," or "Truly, truly." The word *amen* is a Hebrew word with roots in the ordinary Hebrew for belief, faithfulness, and truth. It is found closing the first book of Psalms: "Amen, and Amen" (Psalm 41:13), the double *amen* being used for solemn emphasis, to express the assurance that the prayer embodied in this doxology psalm would be answered. The same "Amen, and Amen" closes the second book of Psalms (72:19) and also the third book (Psalm 89:52). The fourth book ends with a single "Amen" and then, "Praise ye the LORD" (106:48). The final book of Psalms ends with five psalms each beginning and ending with another great Hebrew word, *hallelujah.* "Praise ye the LORD."

The Lord frequently used the word *verily.* In Matthew we have a single "verily" thirty times, in Mark fourteen times, and in Luke seven times. John alone records a double "verily" and it occurs in his gospel twenty-five times. The double "verily" is used to emphasize the Lord's divine authority, to mark the importance of what he was about to say, and to affirm the certainty of the truth he declared.

It is interesting that John records the word *amen* in the apocalypse as a name of Christ (Revelation 1:18; 3:14). It is the name by which he addressed himself to the lukewarm, endtime, Laodicean church. The word *amen* is also the last word in the Bible. The last thing God has to say to us is to leave us pondering a word that is a name for his beloved Son: "The grace of our Lord Jesus Christ be with you all. Amen." (Revelation 22:21). Thus grace and truth did indeed come by Jesus Christ and, after affirming that, God has no more to say.

Now let us come back to Nathanael. The Lord arrested his attention with the first of his double *amens.* He carried him back in thought to the night of Jacob's conversion and reminded him of Jacob's ladder and how Jacob had seen the angels of God ascending and descending that celestial stairway which linked earth and heaven. "I am that ladder," Jesus said in effect to Nathanael. You have hailed me as "Son of God" and so I am. I put my hand on deity, so to speak, because of my deity. You have hailed me as "King of Israel," great David's greater Son, and so I am. I put my hand on humanity, so to speak, because of my humanity. I am that ladder. I link God and man, heaven and earth. I am the one and only mediator between God and man, the only link between heaven and earth. The angels ascend and descend because of me.

There is so much truth here. Note, for instance, the statement about the angels "ascending and descending." It is not the other way 'round, as we would think. The angels are not coming down to this world from that world and then going back up there again. Exactly the opposite. They are already here. They are down here and are seen as going up to heaven from earth and then coming back down to earth again.

That is important. God has already established beachheads on this rebel planet. God has his angels already here, permanently based in enemy territory, so to speak. Nor can Satan expel them. They are here for a variety of reasons and they have constant communication with heaven.

There are the angels who watch over children, "ever beholding" the face of the Father of these little ones in heaven. How often those angels must ascend that shining stairway heavily burdened by cases of child abuse, of child neglect, with reports of those who hurt the faith of these little ones, who deceive them with lies and withhold from them the truth of God. Up they go, up that long ladder, to present each case at God's throne. Then down they came with fresh instructions for their unseen watch over their charges.

There are the angels who watch over God's own people in this hostile world, those angels "sent forth to minister for them who shall be heirs of salvation" (Hebrews 1:14). What appalling tales they have to tell of Christian inconsistencies, outright worldliness, carnality (even gross sin), weird beliefs, broken homes, damaged lives, ruined testimonies. Of course some have better and brighter reports to make, of victories won, holiness demonstrated, lives transformed, homes reclaimed.

There are the angels who are assigned to churches. What sad reports so many of them have to make. What thoughts must be theirs as they trudge the upward-leading stairs. Churches split over the color of a carpet, pastors run off by vindictive deacons, preachers embroiled in sin, strange heresies entertained and then given honorable status in the family of God. Yet others have glad reports of revival, souls being saved, new missions launched, the Holy Spirit being allowed full sway.

There are the angels of the nations, once glimpsed by Daniel, those "thrones and dominions," who counter Satan's "principalities and powers, his rulers of this world's darkness, his wicked spirits in high places." What reports must those angels have to bring of communist Russia, atheistic China, pagan India, apostate Britain and America. What tales of war and rumors of war, of earthquake and pestilence, famine and want, persecution and pillage, of hellish philosophies, greed and intrigue, treaties broken, and men's hearts failing them for fear. Heavy indeed must be their tread on that stair.

Up they go. God is still on the throne. Time's short day is ebbing fast away. The dawn of a new day is just over the horizon. All the factors of space and time, beyond the ken and scope of human minds, beyond the grasp of angel intellects, all are weighed in the balance of omniscient genius and ordered by omnipotent power and incarnate love to work together, to the eternal glory of him who sits on the throne. So back they come, down that stairway, enlightened, encouraged, energized, to pick up again their secret mission on planet earth.

"Ye shall see," Jesus said to Nathanael. Doubtless the Lord was not only proclaiming himself as mediator but was also pointing to the millennium. When as Son of man the Son of God sits as king of Israel, there will be open communication between the earthly Jerusalem and the heavenly Jerusalem. Doubtless, when the Lord manifests his glory, the full traffic between earth and heaven will be seen as a matter of course. The Lord was thus seeking to lift Nathanael's thoughts to higher ground and to a higher sphere than was then common among the narrow and circumscribed concepts of the kingdom.

Thus ended the first two days of the Lord's public ministry. In this brief time he enlisted six of his twelve disciples, including those who would be numbered as chief apostles.

II. The Triumphs of Jesus (2:1–4:54)

It is of considerable interest and significance that, as far as the Lord's public ministry was concerned, as recorded by John, the first sign was at a wedding, and the last (chapter 11) at a funeral. The first was connected with life's gladdest hour; the last was connected with life's saddest hour. It is of interest, too, that the first miracle of Moses ("the law was given by Moses") turned water into blood; the first miracle of Jesus ("grace and truth came by Jesus Christ") turned water into wine.

A. The Wine at the Wedding (2:1-12)
Triumph over Life's Sudden Disappointments

Now we come to the first of John's "signs." Three words are used in the New Testament to describe what we call miracles, evidence of the supernatural. Peter used all three on the day of Pentecost when he reminded the Jews of the marvelous ministry of Jesus (Acts 2:22). He was "a man approved of God among you by miracles [*dunamis*] and wonders [*teras*] and signs [*semeion*]." *Dunamis* means "powers" or "mighty works"; this word is not used in John's gospel at all. *Teras* means a "wonder" and is used by John only once, in 4:48. *Semeion* means a "sign" and is used by John seventeen times, but in the King James Version is wrongly translated "miracle" thirteen of those times. The word *dunamis* is also used to described the gift of miracles (1 Corinthians 12:10,28). All three Greek words are used to describe the satanic power and signs and lying wonders of the antichrist (2 Thessalonians 2:9). The word *powers* denotes the manifestations of evident power; the word *wonder* underlines the effect produced on those who witness the mighty work; *signs* emphasizes the value or significance of the mighty work. Of all the miracles wrought by the Lord Jesus, John records only eight and all of them are signs.

An astonishing linguistic structure can be seen between the various pairs of signs as recorded by John. This is brought out clearly in *The Companion Bible* (Appendix 176, p. 194). The first sign was at the marriage in Cana (2:1-11) and the background was that of Nathanael's faith; the eighth sign was the draught of fishes (21:1-14) and the background was the unbelief of Thomas. The second sign (4:46-50) was the healing of the nobleman's son who was at the point of death; the seventh sign (second from last) was the raising of Lazarus (11:1-44), the sisters' brother, who was dead already. The third sign was the healing of the impotent man (5:1-47) and the sixth sign (third from the last) was the healing of the man born blind (9:1-41); both these signs were given in Jerusalem on the sabbath and both infuriated the authorities. The fourth sign (6:1-14) was the feeding of the five thousand and the fifth sign (fourth from the last) was the walking on the water (6:15-21); both these signs are the only ones recorded in all four gospels. There are many other points of comparison and contrast connected with each pair.

1. Jesus and the Marriage (2:1-2)

We begin, then, with the first of the signs recorded by John. This sign was given "on the third day" though there is no agreement as to whether this was the third day from the calling of Philip (1:43) or the third day from the Lord's arrival in Galilee. If it was the first of these, then we have a record of the first week of the Lord's ministry. The first day was recorded in 1:19-28, the second day in 1:29-34, the third day in 1:35-42, the fourth day in 1:43-51. "The third day" (2:1) brings us to the end of the week and a marriage. This corresponds with what we have in Genesis where after the six days of creation comes a marriage. It is possible that John wants us to compare and contrast this first week with the last week of the Lord's ministry (12:1).

The Lord and his disciples were invited to a wedding at Cana, the hometown of Nathanael. The site of Cana is disputed. The traditional site is less than five miles from Nazareth. There is something beautiful about this unknown couple inviting the Lord and his followers to be present to share in this occasion.

The Lord should be invited to every wedding. Marriage was God's idea in the first place. There would be few broken marriages if every couple recognized the divine significance of a wedding and actively sought the Lord's presence and experienced his power and endorsement of their union.

2. Jesus and His Mother (2:3-5)

We are told, "The mother of Jesus was there." John never mentions the mother of Jesus by name, although he does name Joseph (6:42). John's omission of the name of Mary may have been part of his divine inspiration. Various Gnostic and cultic errors were already taking deep root in the church. The day would come when the Roman Catholic Church would proclaim Mary as having been immaculately conceived, free from original sin. In the fertile imaginations of men and by false church dogma she would be exalted bodily to heaven, and the devout would be asked to believe in her corporeal presence there. She would be given the old Babylonian title of "queen of heaven." She would be called the "Mother of God." She would be proclaimed as co-redemptrix. The devout would be urged to pray to her (on the assumption that she was possessed of the divine attribute of omniscience—since only one with such an attribute could hear and separate and comprehend and evaluate the millions of prayers addressed to her in a thousand languages from all parts of the world every single day). Miracles were attributed to her. The devout were taught to pray to her because she was the Lord's mother and had influence over him and could get him to do what she wanted. Pope, priest, and people would light candles to her, pray to her, bow down before images of her, and in some sense worship her. Anyone who has been in Catholic churches, seen current news reports of papal activities, studied a Catholic catechism, or read church history knows to what heights Mary has been elevated. Many Catholics still count their beads and say their Hail Marys. Many still subscribe to the dictum of Saint Bernard: "It is God's will," he said, "that we should receive all things through Mary." In many lands, on feast days, the image of Mary is paraded through the streets amid scenes of both revelry and near-hysteria.

John did not know this. Jesus did. Hence his dealings with his mother on this occasion and others.

It was not long before we note *mankind's problem* (2:3a): "The mother of Jesus saith unto him, They have no wine." The wine ran out. Nothing could be more devastating at an eastern wedding. It is always embarrassing to run out of food and drink at a public occasion. Here, at a wedding, it was catastrophic.

Wine was wine. The word used is *oinos,* the only word for wine in the New Testament. In the Septuagint it is used to translate the Hebrew words *yayin* and *tirosh.* The word *yayin* is derived from a root word *yayan* meaning "to ferment." The word *yayin* occurs 142 times in the Old Testament and includes all kinds of fermented wine. The first use of the word is in connection with Noah's drunkenness (Genesis 9:21). It is used of the wine brought forth by Melchizedek for Abraham (Genesis 14:18). The same word is used in connection with Nabal and his extreme intoxication (1 Samuel 25:36-37). It was used at the feasts of the Lord (Deuteronomy 14:23-26) and was the wine poured out in the drink offering (Exodus 29:40; Leviticus 23:13; Numbers 15:5).

The word *tirosh* comes from the root *yarash,* ("to possess"), evidently because of wine's power to take possession of a person's brain. The word occurs thirty-four times in the Old Testament.

There can be little doubt that wine is what was served at the wedding, not grape juice. And they ran out of wine. In the symbolism of Scripture, wine speaks of joy. It suggests the exuberant side of life. It is in this area that life first breaks down. Something adverse happens and the joy goes out of life. Often, in this sad world, joy goes out of a marriage very soon. "The honeymoon is over." It happens so frequently it has become a well-known saying.

Then came *Mary's proposal* (2:3b): "The mother of Jesus saith unto him, They have no wine." It has been suggested that Mary was a close friend of the family, that she perhaps had some responsibility for the supplies. It would certainly seem that Mary had taken note of the fact that Jesus had begun to attract disciples. News of his recent activities in Jerusalem was doubtless already in circulation in Galilee. All her life this woman could have endured suspicion because of the circumstances connected with the birth of Jesus. The story of his virgin birth would be scoffed at by many. The fact, however, that he was commonly known as "the son of Joseph" (1:45) doubtless expressed the general belief.

Gently she tried to prod him into action. But that he would not and could not allow. He knew the idolatrous position that would be given her in centuries to come. Never must there be given the slightest ground for such distortions of truth. She was his mother, but in no way must she be allowed any say in his redemptive work. She must be tenderly but firmly put in her place. A great gulf must be fixed between the mother and the messiah, the master, the one mediator.

So we have the *messiah's prerogative* (2:4-5): "Jesus saith unto her, Woman, what have I to do with thee? mine hour is not yet come" (2:4). Here the Lord put her in a new relationship to him. All the authorities remind us that there is no discourtesy, no harshness, in the term *woman*.

"What have I to do with thee?" he continued. This has been variously rephrased: "What hast thou to do with me?" or, with awkward literalism, "What is there to me and thee?" Or, as it has been paraphrased, "Leave me to myself."

This is emphasized by the words, "Mine hour is not yet come." The Lord, thereafter, spoke frequently of this mysterious and momentous hour. In chapter 7 he said, "My time is not yet come," when his unbelieving brothers likewise sought to prod him into making a move (7:6). When he was teaching in the temple, although there was mounting opposition, "no man laid hands on him; for his hour was not yet come" (8:20). When the Greeks came, harbingers of coming harvest in the gentile world, he again spoke of his hour: "The hour is come, that the Son of man should be glorified" (12:23). In the upper room we have it again: "Jesus knew that his hour was come that he should depart out of this world" (13:1). Still later, in the upper room, in his high priestly prayer, and for the last time in John's record, we have it one more time. Beginning his prayer he said, "Father, the hour is come" (17:1). We observe that his first reference to his "hour" was to his mother; the last was to his Father.

Everything he did had to do with this hour. Mary could not know the timings of God in his life. She knew nothing yet about that hour when he would have his glory displayed, of all things, through his cross.

Mary accepted his words; her understanding was enlightened, her trust unshaken. She turned to the servants who were standing around in consternation and gave them the best advice anyone can give to another human being, "Whatsoever he saith unto you, do it."

3. Jesus and the Miracle (2:6-11)

Jesus' first "sign" and *its preliminary purpose* (2:6-10) was to meet this emergency and bring joy into that wedding where doom and gloom were on the periphery. The Lord used what was available, as he always does. (He said to Moses, "What is that in thine hand?" [Exodus 4:2]. It was only a stick, but it became a symbol of divine power to pharaoh and his people before all was over.)

What they had were half a dozen waterpots, each capable of holding about nine gallons of water (some authorities go as high as twenty gallons apiece). The water in these stone jars was for the ceremonial cleansing of the wedding guests. The Jewish religion demanded close attention to personal hygiene. The "purifying" included the washing of hands and of utensils used in serving the guests (Mark 7:3-4). No amount of ritual religion could make up for the social disaster now about to overtake the newlyweds. The Lord commanded that these jars be filled with water. Evidently their contents had been depleted. The servants obeyed, filling the jars "up to the brim." It was obvious that there was nothing but water in those vessels. So far, so good.

But now came a challenge to the faith of the servants: "Draw out now, and bear unto the governor of the feast" (1:8), the man we would call the master of ceremonies. There was no hesitation. They did as they were told.

It upsets many Christians to think that Jesus actually turned water into wine. Some have claimed it was not really wine but grape juice—a position hard to defend both in consideration of the word used for wine and of the reaction of the emcee who certainly believed it to be wine, and extraordinarily good wine at that. He said to the bridegroom, "Every man at the beginning doth set forth good wine [*oinos*]; and when men have drunk, then that which is worse [inferior]: but thou hast kept the good wine until now" (2:10).

"The good wine"! Some would maintain that there is no good wine. Yet year by year the Creator turns water into wine by a natural process. Who can explain all the mystery of a plant that is able to take water and minerals from the soil, energy from the sun, all that it needs from its environment and transform them into wine-filled grapes? What Jesus did as Creator was short-cut the whole process— with a difference. This was *good* wine. Not just better than inferior wine, but *good* wine. A man could have drunk gallons of it and never have had a bad reaction. Nobody could have made himself drunk on wine that Jesus made. (It is difficult to make a case for total abstinence from the Bible except on the grounds advocated by Paul in Romans 14.)

There was a symbolic meaning to this. The filling of the jars to the brim, those jars used for holding water for purifying "after the manner of the Jews," symbolized Judaism with its rituals, which had now fulfilled its purpose. The new wine symbolized a new creation, Christianity, "full of joy unspeakable," rich and full of glory.

As to *its primary purpose* (2:11), the miracle was a sign, "this beginning of signs" designed to display the Lord's glory and convince his disciples that he was all he claimed to be. "His disciples believed on him," John says, recalling the incident now as an old man. The phrase, "believe on," is characteristic of John and is found only once in the synoptic gospels (Matthew 18:6 and its parallel, Mark 9:42) and only occasionally in Paul's writings (Romans 10:14; Galatians 2:16; Philippians 1:29). The essential thought behind the phrase is that of unreserved transfer of trust from oneself to someone else.

4. Jesus and His Move (2:12)

The final item draws our attention to a move that Jesus made. "After this he went down to Capernaum, he and his mother, and his brethren, and his disciples, and they continued there not many days." The figure of speech (known as polysyndeton), revealed by the deliberate and repeated use of the word *and,* is intended to draw our attention to each member of the party. The Roman Catholic Church, in its exaggeration of Mary's role in redemption, has claimed her perpetual virginity. It argues that the Lord's "brethren" mentioned here were either the sons of Joseph by a previous marriage or else they were cousins. The Lord's brethren are mentioned nine times in the New Testament. Three of them shed no light on their true relationship to him (John 7:3-5; 1 Corinthians 9:5; Galatians 1:19) but the remaining six are more definite. They all speak of his brethren in connection with his mother (Matthew 12:46; 13:55; Mark 3:32; 6:3; Luke 8:19-20; John 2:12). This last reference, the one we are considering here, emphasizes the connection with Mary. The use of the polysyndeton draws attention to it: "He, and his mother, and his brethren, and his disciples." Because these "brethren" are often seen accompanying Mary, the obvious conclusion is that they were her children.

It would seem that the whole family, Joseph being presumed dead, went to Capernaum. At this time or shortly afterward the Lord took up residence there, and that lakeside town became his headquarters for his Galilean ministry. On this occasion, however, he remained in the town only a short while. Jerusalem and the annual Passover feast were beckoning him.

The Lord was now about to give the whole nation a sign of a different kind, not a miracle this time, but an act worthy of a sovereign messiah.

From John's gospel we are able to reconstruct the chronology of the Lord's public ministry, especially from John's references to the various feasts of the Jews, and particularly from references to three Passovers. The feasts in John are as follows:

1. The first Passover (2:12-13)
2. Another feast (5:1)
3. The second Passover (6:4) (Jesus did not attend)
4. The feast of tabernacles (7:2)
5. The feast of the dedication (10:22)
6. The third Passover (12:1)

Now we can assemble the facts as they relate to the Lord's public ministry. (Some of the dating is approximate. See Graham Scroggie, *A Guide to the Gospels,* London: Pickering and Inglis, 1948, 409-411.)

1. From the Lord's baptism (Jan A.D. 27) to the first Passover (Apr 11-18, A.D. 27)
   a. Feb A.D. 27 (1:19-51)
   b. Mar A.D. 27 (2:1-12), a period of about three months
2. From the first Passover to the departure for Galilee (Dec A.D. 27)
   a. Apr A.D. 27 (2:13–3:21)
   b. May A.D. 27 (3:22-24)
   c. Aug A.D. 27 (3:25-36)
   d. Nov A.D. 27 (4:1-3)
   e. Dec A.D. 27 (4:4-42), a period of about eight months
3. From the departure from Galilee to May A.D. 28
   a. Dec A.D. 27 (4:43-45)
   b. Jan A.D. 28 (4:46-54)
   c. May A.D. 28 (5:1-47), a period of about five months
4. From May A.D. 28 to the ministry in northern Galilee (Nov A.D. 29)
   a. Mar A.D. 29 (6:1-15)
   b. Apr A.D. 29 (6:16-71), a period of about twelve months
5. From May A.D. 29 to the final departure from Galilee (Nov A.D. 29)
   a. Sept A.D. 29 (7:1–8:11)
   b. Oct A.D. 29 (8:12-59), a period of about six months
6. From Nov A.D. 29 to the triumphant entry (Sunday, Apr 2, A.D. 30)
   a. Oct A.D. 29 (9:1-41)
   b. Nov A.D. 29 (10:1-42)
   c. Jan A.D. 30 (11:1-54)
   d. Apr A.D. 30 (11:55–12:11), a period of about five months
7. From Sunday, Apr 2, A.D. 30 to the resurrection (Sunday, Apr 9 A.D. 30)
   a. Apr 2 (Sun) A.D. (12:12-19)
   b. Apr 4 (Tues) A.D. 30 (12:20-50)
   c. Apr 6 (Thur) A.D. 30 (13:1–18:12)
   d. Apr 7 (Fri) A.D. 30 (18:13–19:42), period of eight days
8. From Sunday, Apr 9, A.D. 30 to May 18, A.D. 30
   a. Apr 9, A.D. 30 (20:1-25)

b. Apr 9–May 18, A.D. 30 (20:26–21:25), a period of forty days

It is significant that John devotes more than half his gospel to events relating to the Lord's last week on earth, that is, to events leading up to his death and resurrection. Important and essential as was the Lord's life, it is his death that makes our salvation possible.

B. The Traffic in the Temple (2:13-25)
Triumph over Life's Secular Debasements

We begin with one of those chronological notes so characteristic of John: "And the Jews' passover was at hand, and Jesus went up to Jerusalem" (2:13).

The annual Passover feast commemorated Israel's exodus from Egypt. It was celebrated on the anniversary of that event, on the fourteenth day of Nisan (at the time of the March-April full moon). It was immediately followed by the feast of unleavened bread, which lasted a week (15-22 Nisan). Pilgrims from all parts of the Diaspora (that is, the Jews dispersed outside Palestine) assembled in vast numbers for this great national feast.

On the Passover eve the head of each house had carefully gathered up all leaven in the house and removed it, giving the house a good spring-cleaning, as we would say today. Yet no one gave a thought to cleansing God's house. So deplorable was the spiritual condition of priest and people that John habitually refers to this feast as "the Jews' Passover" (see also 6:4; 11:55; and compare 5:1; 7:2) instead of what it was intended to be, "a feast of Jehovah."

1. Jesus and the Building (2:13-17)

It is fitting that the Lord's public ministry should commence in Judea, in Jerusalem, and in the temple. The Lord went straight for the heart. He now offered himself as messiah in the nation's capital and, being rejected, left and offered himself as prophet in Galilee. He would not offer himself openly as messiah in Jerusalem again until his final entry.

Coming suddenly into the temple (as predicted, Malachi 3:1-3) the Lord's eye took in at a glance the desecration of that sacred place. Two words are translated "temple." There is *hieron*, which (as here) takes in the whole area, the sacred enclosure, the courts, the porticoes, and *naos*, a word reserved for the sacred structure itself, which contained the holy place and the holy of holies. This latter word is used symbolically for the Lord's body and of believers who form his mystical body. Here John is describing the entire area (comprising some nineteen acres). The area was divided into four courts. Coming in from the east and moving toward the sanctuary itself, a visitor would successively pass through the court of the gentiles, the court of the women, the court of Israel, and the court of the priests. With their usual contempt for all things gentile, the Jews had designated their court as a suitable place to transact business.

Oxen, sheep, and doves were the creatures generally used in offering sacrifices. The authorities had decided it would be convenient to have a cattle market adjacent to the altar, and the court of the gentiles could be used for the sale of approved animals. Doubtless the authorities received a percentage of the profits.

Then, too, many Jews took advantage of this pilgrimage to Jerusalem to pay the annual half-shekel levied against all Jewish men, worldwide, of twenty years of age and over, for the maintenance of the temple. Obviously no coins bearing the image of the emperor or any other heathen symbol could be paid into the temple treasury. All offerings of money would have to be paid in Jewish coins. There would be a brisk and lucrative business in all this for the moneychangers. Again, the court of the gentiles was designated as a suitable place to allow this business to be carried on. One does not need to be a student of human nature to picture the avarice and cheating (Matthew 21:13). The Lord's heart was moved at the sight of all this business traffic in the temple. The place of prayer for all nations smelled of the barnyard, sounded like a cattle market, was filled with noise and din, was the scene of many a swindle. "There shall be no more the Canaanite [a trafficker] in the house of the LORD of Hosts," the prophet Zechariah had foretold (Zechariah 14:21). The Lord decided to make a clean sweep of this desecration of his Father's house.

He made a scourge of small cords for driving out the oxen. He seized the tables of the moneychangers and with a vigorous heave turned them upside down. We can imagine the resulting scramble after the rolling coins! And, with the dignity and restraint that marked his every move, he ordered those that sold doves to remove their property—thus gently safeguarding the innocent birds. Within a few minutes the place was cleared. All that remained to be done was cleansing of the pavements and picking up of the litter.

This bold attack on the "syndicate" proclaimed Jesus, in the most authentic manner possible, to be the Christ. Alone and single-handed he had taken on the establishment, including the Sanhedrin and the powerful Sadducean party, which both sponsored and doubtless profited from this traffic. He had overthrown an entrenched system of evil that posed as a public benefit. In doing so, he had proclaimed himself the Son of his Father, whose house these profane intruders were defiling. In view of the Passover he had rid that house of the leaven of unrighteousness that had long corrupted it. (When the Lord left that temple for the last time he called it "your house," but by then he had already prophetically handed it over to judgment; see Matthew 23:38.)

The incident made an impression on his disciples, who remembered Psalm 69:9. "The zeal of thine house hath eaten me up." A verse from that impressive messianic psalm was a fitting comment on the Lord's fearless action.

2. Jesus and His Body (2:18-22)

The Jewish authorities were not long in reacting. Instantly they demanded an explanation. How dare he interfere with their rights and prerogatives as custodians of the temple and guardians of Jewish faith? The answer draws our attention to Jesus and his body. The Jews demanded a sign. Wasn't the way he had cleansed the temple sign enough, if they had been able to see it? But they wanted more. Later, Paul would underline this demand of the Jews for signs as being characteristic of an unbelieving people (1 Corinthians 1:22).

The Lord promptly gave them a sign but it was one they neither wanted nor understood. "Destroy this temple," he said, "and in three days I will raise it up"(2:19). That cryptic statement on two subsequent occasions (Matthew 26:61 and Acts 7:14) was used as a basis for accusation and in both cases it was misquoted. The Lord was referring to the fact that his body (the temple, *naos*) would be handed over to them to "destroy" and, when that happened, he would "raise it up." The word he used was *egeiro*, which literally means "to rouse from sleep." It occurs 141 times, of which 70 refer to resurrection.

The Jews failed to discern the Lord's metaphor and took his words at face value. "Forty and six years was this temple in building," they exclaimed in astonishment, "and wilt thou rear it up in three days?" (2:20). Herod the Great, an avid builder, had begun renovations of the Jewish temple in 20 B.C. Josephus says that some eighteen thousand workmen were employed in that task. It was not finally finished until A.D. 64. Three years later, A.D. 67, the Jewish war with Rome broke out and the temple's doom was sealed. It went up in flames at the end of that war in A.D. 70. The Jews by their rejection of Christ and their intransigence did indeed "destroy this temple," the literal temple. The Lord did not raise that one.

John adds the comment, "he spake of the temple of his body" (2:21). It was three years before the Lord's disciples understood this saying. His word was hidden away in their memories, however, and after his resurrection they not only remembered it but understood its significance—that the Lord here, on his first public confrontation with Jewish officialdom, actually foretold his death at their hands.

3. Jesus and the Believers (2:23-25)

All this provoked considerable speculation in the city, a city jammed with Jewish pilgrims from all over the known world. John concludes this part of his record with a reference to Jesus and the believers. He refers first to *the foundation of the faith* (2:23) of those who are said to have "believed in his name" (2:23). They believed because of "the signs" he did. We must remember that John by no means records all the "signs," or miracles, which Jesus performed. Indeed, the gospels are sparing in recording miracles. Only thirty-six are recorded altogether (less than one a month on average when seen in the light of a three and a half year ministry) along with several summary statements.

A faith that rests on miracles is not a very satisfactory or substantial faith. Such a faith always demands more. If it gets more, it becomes surfeited and its appetite jaded. We need to beware of those in Christendom today who profess to have the power to perform miracles and also of those who believe them.

John records *the flaw in the faith* (2:24-25) of those who he says believed. The Lord did not "commit" himself to them, however. The word *commit* is the same as *believed* in verse 23, but the tense is changed. The "belief" of those responding to the signs marks a completed act; the "belief" of Jesus indicates a habitual, continued action. They believed in him; he had no continuing faith in them. John gives the reason: "Because he knew all men, and needed not that any should testify of man: for he knew what was in man" (2:24b-25). This attribute of knowing a person's innermost heart, state, and character is an attribute of God (Jeremiah 17:10; 20:12). Here the Lord's omniscience is clearly stated. It was universal ("he knew all men") and individual ("he knew what was in man"). He had no need for people to express their thoughts and feelings. He could read them infallibly without that.

The whole incident illustrates the Lord's knowledge of what people are like—the greed and cheating of those who profaned the temple, the opposition and resentment of the Jewish leaders, the untrustworthiness of those who professed a faith based on "signs." The Lord read the hearts of them all.

C. The Night with Nicodemus (3:1-21)
Triumph over Life's Spiritual Deceptions

The cleansing of the temple had its impact on a member of the ruling Sanhedrin. Nicodemus came to Christ as a representative of the thoughtful few among the intelligentsia and aristocracy of the nation. His hope for the restoration of Israel and for the speedy inauguration of the kingdom had been stirred by Christ's authoritative action. That, he thought, was how a messiah should act. The miracles now being performed by this remarkable prophet from Nazareth were added confirmation in Nicodemus's mind that perhaps Jesus was indeed the messiah.

Nicodemus was rich, respected, religious. He was a ruler. But somehow none of these things brought the peace and joy for which he longed. Maybe this new prophet had some insights along these lines.

So it was that Nicodemus, as fine a specimen of the natural man as we could wish to find, put his pride in his pocket and sought a private interview with the young preacher.

1. The World's Greatest Tragedy (3:1-10)

The story of Nicodemus, in its larger context, sets before us the world's greatest tragedy (3:1-10), the world's greatest truths (3:11-15), the world's greatest text (3:16), and the world's greatest test (3:17-21).

We begin with *Nicodemus and his belief* (3:1-2), noting two things about him. He was "a man of the Pharisees" and "a ruler of the Jews." The name *Pharisee* identifies them as religious exclusives, separatists by belief and practice. They were strict about all matters pertaining to the keeping of the law: the sabbath, tithing, circumcision, ceremonial cleanliness, eating only certain foods, fasting, observing holy days. They maintained that the oral law was as necessary and as binding as the written law and they were thus the champions of those "traditions of the elders" denounced by Christ. As has been said, Nicodemus was a Pharisee, a righteous man with a well-developed religious conscience. He was a ruler of the Jews, that is, a member of the Sanhedrin. The title *ruler* is used in rabbinic literature for "a great man" or "prince." Rabbinical tradition makes Niodemus one of the three richest men in Jerusalem.

He came to Jesus with his belief: "We know that thou art a teacher come from God: for no man can do these miracles that thou doest except God be with him" (2:2). Therein lay Nicodemus's error. He saw Jesus as a teacher. The word he used was *didaskalos*. The word carries with it the idea of "doctor." Nicodemus (perhaps using the word *we* to avoid committing himself too much; caution seems to have been one of his characteristics) knew that Jesus was not the product of any of the rabbinical schools but he courteously called him "doctor" and cautiously acknowledged his power with God. He thus acknowledged Jesus as a teacher, like any other teacher, though marked by an extraordinary power. The Lord, however, could not accept that compliment, which fell far short of the facts.

The Lord's answer shows us *Nicodemus and his blindness* (3:3-8). In his reply the Lord revealed to this very good man, this very religious man, just how far he was from the kingdom of God. We note how *the need for a new birth was expressed to him* (3:3-5). In his natural state Nicodemus could neither envision nor enter the kingdom of God. Jesus said, "Verily, verily, I say unto thee, Except a man be born again, he cannot see the kingdom of God" (3:3).

Nicodemus was the best kind of person that religion, education, and culture could produce. And his case was hopeless. Thus the ground is cut, once and for all, from beneath those who think that birth and breeding, moral rectitude and religious training, knowledge of biblical truths and punctilious attendance to religious duties, can gain a person entrance into heaven. What is needed is a new birth.

There is an old story about two courtiers of a certain king who wearied their monarch with their incessant arguments as to whether or not a person had to be born a gentleman, or whether he could become a gentleman by training, discipline, and ingrained habit. The king finally dismissed them from court and ordered them to go out into the world and seek conclusive proof for their claims. A year to the date they would each present their proofs and he would settle the argument once and for all.

The year passed. The courtier who said that one could become a gentleman had traveled far. He was in a distant land and still had not found his proof. But one day, sitting gloomily in a wayside inn, he sat up with astonishment. He had ordered a cup of chocolate, and to his amazement he saw that it was being brought to him by the innkeeper's cat. But this was no ordinary cat. This cat had been trained to stand up on its hind legs. It had been dressed in a tiny uniform and it had learned to balance a tray in its forepaws. The courtier watched spellbound as the creature, contrary to nature, walked slowly toward him balancing the tray with his cup of chocolate.

He saw the implications at once. If a cat could be trained to do a thing like that, why couldn't a man be drilled into becoming a gentleman? It proved his point. He paid a vast sum and secured the astonishing feline and headed for home.

News of the cat leaked out and the courtier's rival was plunged in despair. He, too, had traveled far but was returning home empty-handed. He was sure he had lost. But then, just a day or two before the scheduled appearance in court, he saw something in a shop window that brought a smile to his lips. He made a purchase but kept it well hidden from view.

On the day of the trial the first courtier presented the cat to the king as proof that a person could be so trained that he could overcome all natural handicaps and become that most accomplished of civilized persons, a gentleman. As the king sat on his throne, the remarkable cat, attired in miniature court dress, walked carefully on its hind legs, made its way slowly down a red carpet, carrying a tray of chocolate to the king. The court broke into applause. Everyone looked with admiration at the cat and with pity at the other courtier, the one who said one must be born a gentleman.

But the man was ready. With a bow to the king he opened the box in which he had his proof. The courtier released half a dozen white mice and instantly the cat forgot its training and education, its discipline and ingrained habit. Its natural instinct surfaced and, in a flash, off it went after the scampering mice. The discussion was settled once and for all. The cat returned purring loudly several hours later, its courtly attire rather disheveled.

In Nicodemus we see what culture, religious education, and moral training can do. But man in sin is still man in sin, a prey to the fallen instincts of sin which, given the appropriate time, place, circumstance, and opportunity, will override the veneer with which religion, culture, education, and moral conscience overlay the old, fallen adamic nature.

No wonder Jesus said to Nicodemus, "Except a man be born again, he cannot see the kingdom of God." We were born the first time with a sinful nature, born alienated from God, born in sin and shapen in iniquity, born lost and on our way to a lost eternity, aliens and enemies of God, a prey to evil desires, evil deeds, and an evil disposition. We need to be born again.

Someone once approached George Whitefield and asked, "Why do you always preach that we must be born again?" "Because," he replied, "we must be born again."

If anyone among the Jews thought that he was a candidate for the kingdom of heaven, that man must have been Nicodemus. Born into the chosen nation, a member of the commonwealth of Israel, circumcised the eighth day, a Hebrew of the Hebrews; as touching the law, a Pharisee; concerning zeal, one who paid tithes of mint and anise and cumin; touching the righteousness which is in the law, blameless; and willing, indeed, to give a Galilean prophet a fair hearing. The only man who could boast a record like that was Saul of Tarsus (Philippians 3:4-6). But after he came to Christ Paul evaluated all those things as "confidence in the flesh" (Philippians 3:4).

Nicodemus did not understand the Lord's reply. "How can a man be born when he is old?" he asked. "Can he enter the second time into his mother's womb and be born?" (3:4).

There is this to be said for Nicodemus: When the Lord confronted him with the need for the new birth he did not ask *why*. He asked *how*. Somewhere in the depths of his soul the Lord had struck a chord that awoke echoes of deep longings that no religion or moral code could satisfy. Nicodemus did not present the Lord with an argumentative *why* but with an astonished *how*.

The Lord's answer was both simple and profound: "Verily, verily, I say unto thee, Except a man be born of water and of the Spirit, he cannot enter into the kingdom of God" (3:5). His statement has been abused by those who believe in infant baptism and by those who think that Christian baptism is essential to regeneration.

Water and the Spirit. The words take us back to the original creation (Genesis 1:2), to the original shaping of things, to the time when the eternal Spirit brooded over the darkness of primeval chaos.

Water and the Spirit. Whatever else the words mean, they had a meaning that Nicodemus could appreciate, apprehend, and appropriate. The Lord was not trying to be mystical and obtuse. He was trying to lead Nicodemus into the experience of the new birth. The Lord was answering the question *how*. He was not concealing truth but revealing truth.

In seeking to ascertain the Lord's meaning we must observe the law of historical propriety. We must ask ourselves, "What would Nicodemus understand by these words?" Obviously he would not read Christian baptism into them because the Lord had not yet instituted that ordinance nor would he do so for several years. Water and the Spirit. Who had been hammering at the conscience of Israel, seeking to prepare the people for the coming of king and kingdom, using those very two words? John the baptist, of course. Nicodemus would think at once of John's words, "I indeed baptize with water, but there comes one who will baptize you with the Spirit." That is the key to this otherwise cryptic statement.

The key phenomenon of John's ministry was his baptism, essentially a baptism of repentance. "The king is coming," he proclaimed. "Repent!" Thousands had responded. The religious leaders, however, of which Nicodemus was a representative, had rejected the ministry and the baptism of John. They saw no need for repentance. The Lord brought Nicodemus back to the message of John the baptist, back to the need for "water," for all that John's baptism stood for.

In effect he was saying this to Nicodemus: Except you respond to what John's baptism stood for—repentance; except you are, so to speak, "born of water"; except you come by way of repentance; except you respond to what I stand for, regeneration; except you are in fact "born of the Spirit," you cannot enter the kingdom of God. The challenge was this—no John, no Jesus. No repentance and no regeneration mean no rebirth, and apart from rebirth the kingdom of heaven is closed to you.

The Lord had expressed the need for a new birth to Nicodemus. Now, *the need for a new birth was explained to him* (3:6-8). He did this by giving him two illustrations. The first illustration concerned *different worlds* (3:6-7): "That which is born of the flesh is flesh; and that which is born of the Spirit is spirit. Marvel not that I said unto thee, Ye must be born again" (3:6-7). Nicodemus had experienced a physical birth which put him into this world. He needed to have a spiritual birth to make him an heir of that world. It is a fundamental law of nature and of grace. A great dictum of Genesis 1 is "after its kind." No one kind can evolve into some other kind. Cats do not become dogs, monkeys do not become men. Each creature reproduces according to its kind. Thus Adam in his fallen state could reproduce only his own kind. Fallen men can reproduce only fallen men. What we inherit from our parents is a sin nature. What we pass on to our children is a sin nature. We reproduce our own kind. What is born of the flesh is flesh; it can never evolve into some higher kind of life. Fleshly life can never generate spiritual life. That is life of a different kind.

If we are to have spiritual life we must be "born of the Spirit." The Holy Spirit must impart this life to our souls. The life he imparts is the life of God. God made human beings to be inhabited by God. The human spirit was to be inhabited by the Holy Spirit. When sin came in, the Spirit went out. Through the miracle of the new birth, sin is cleansed, the Holy Spirit returns to inhabit the human spirit, and spiritual life begins.

It is a miracle. It opens up a new world. A minister was seeking to reach the heart of a dying doctor. The minister had spoken to him about conversion, forgiveness, redemption—all the themes at the heart of the Christian gospel. Nothing seemed to reach the dying man. Then he spoke to him of regeneration, of the need for being reborn, and that brought enlightenment. Over many years the doctor had attended countless births. "A new birth!" he exclaimed, "Why, that's what I need. A baby has no past—only a future. That's what I need." And so do we all. "That which is born of the flesh is flesh" and can be nothing else but flesh. "That which is born of the Spirit is spirit," born of God, bright with an eternal future as a child of God in God's own wonderful world.

The Lord's second illustration concerned *different winds* (3:8). "The wind bloweth where it listeth, and thou hearest the sound thereof, but canst not tell whence it cometh, and whither it goeth: so is every one that is born of the Spirit." The wind has its own laws. It is not answerable to human demands and dictates. Its paths are mysterious, its direction apt to change without notice.

It is no accident that in Greek and Hebrew the words for *wind* and *spirit* are identical. The Lord's comparison of the ways of the Spirit and the way of the wind was apt. The laws of both are known only to a very small degree. Both are invisible. Both can be sensed, and the presence of both is revealed in their effects. The action of the Spirit on the soul of sinner and saint is analogous to the action of the wind in the natural world. As the branches of a tree betray the passing of the wind, so do a person's thoughts, words, and deeds reveal that an invisible force has influenced him or her. The wind can blow gently or with gale force. It can bring rain, tempest, and storm, or it can drive the clouds away.

The wind of the Spirit was blowing into the soul of Nicodemus that night, but it was not at his beck and call. He had better bow before its gentle influence before it departed, perhaps forever. It is imperative that when the Holy Spirit is visiting a soul, in convicting, converting, regenerating, and renewing power, the soul respond while yet it can.

Nicodemus was not belligerent, but only bewildered. With such a person the Lord can be very patient. We note next

Nicodemus and his bewilderment (3:9-10). "How can these things be?" he exclaimed. Nicodemus confessed he was out of his depth. The man was a teacher of the law. In fact, the Lord spoke back to him the word he had used early in their discussion (*didaskalos*), now with a bit of irony: "Art thou a [famous] master of Israel, and knowest not these things?" (3:10). No doubt Nicodemus, who evidently had a reputation as a teacher, had taught many the minute details of Pharisaic legalism. Now, alas for his religious education which had left him impoverished of basic truth! The Lord had begun by telling him that, apart from the new birth, he could not see the kingdom of God. The twice repeated *how* of this reputed doctor of the law revealed how true that was. But the Lord was not through with him yet. Face to face with this spiritual tragedy, the Lord was patient.

2. The World's Greatest Truths (3:11-15)

The Lord continued his discussion with Nicodemus. He set before him *the secret of salvation* (3:11-12). For the third time in this brief conversation the Lord brought out that emphatic "Verily, verily." *Great facts are revealed* (3:11): "Verily, verily, I say unto thee, We speak that we do know, and testify that we have seen; and ye receive not our witness." The Lord drew a line, as it were, in the sand. On the one side of that line he wrote the word *we*. On the other side he wrote the word *ye*. Nicodemus was still siding with the wrong crowd. The *we* seems to include the Lord and his disciples, those who had received his instruction. The *ye* seems to include Nicodemus and the "blind leaders of the blind" of which he was the present representative, the rabbis with all their weight of tradition and ignorance of spiritual truth.

"We know," Jesus said. "We have seen." Nicodemus had begun this conversation with the words "we know." He had said, "We know that thou art a teacher from God" (3:1). The Lord had just pointed out to this learned doctor that he lacked understanding of things that really mattered. Nicodemus was face to face with omniscient genius, incarnate wisdom—truth that was pure, simple, and divine. Jesus placed before Nicodemus eternal verities, unwavering certainty, uncompromising assurance. "We know." "We have seen." The word for "seen" is *horao*, usually meaning "to perceive with the eyes." The Lord was not setting before Nicodemus some fine philosophy, the fruit of reasoning and high-sounding speculation. He was setting before him hard facts, the kind of facts an eyewitness could present in a court of law.

Great faith is required (3:12). "If I have told you earthly things, and ye believe not, how shall ye believe, if I tell you of heavenly things?" The things of God embrace two spheres. There are "earthly things," things with their sphere on earth. In this sense, regeneration is an earthly thing. It is something we experience on earth. Its origin is heavenly but its manifestation is earthly. There are also "heavenly things." The revelation of Jesus as the Son of God is a heavenly thing. The hope of the millennial kingdom is an earthly thing; the mystery of the kingdom of God is a heavenly thing.

To grasp that spiritual side of things called for faith. If Nicodemus was having trouble with earthly truths, how could his faith rise to grasp heavenly truths?

Next comes *the source of salvation* (3:13). "And no man hath ascended up to heaven, but he that came down from heaven, even the Son of man which is in heaven" (3:13). Probably the best way to view this much disputed statement is to regard it as an explanatory comment by John. We would put it in parenthesis or as a footnote if we were writing this today. The coming of the Holy Spirit at Pentecost made plain much that was baffling and perplexing to the disciples, as well as to Nicodemus. In the light of later events, John could shed this light on the Lord's words to Nicodemus. The Lord Jesus, the source of salvation, had come down from heaven and so knew about "heavenly things." Now, in his resurrected body, he had ascended back into heaven from whence he had come. In other words, the Lord Jesus could speak with such authority on heavenly things because heaven was his home. He knew all about it.

What a comfort to have access to certain knowledge. How much better this is than the speculations and unfounded philosophies of religious dreamers, the deceptions of psychics and spiritists, the delusions of those whose hopes originate from satanic sources.

This interview with Nicodemus concludes with a statement about *the simplicity of salvation* (3:14-15). The Lord had one more illustration for this man to whom his soul went out. "And Moses lifted up the serpent in the wilderness, even so must the Son of man be lifted up" (3:14). The full truth of that probably did not dawn on Nicodemus until Christ was nailed to the cross—perhaps it was then he cast his doubts and difficulties aside and threw in his lot with the Lord.

As was so often his way, the Lord directed Nicodemus back to the Scriptures. Not to the vain speculations and traditions of the rabbinic schools, but back to Numbers 21:4-9. He taught this

Hebrew scholar the value of Old Testament typology. "As . . .
even so . . ." These words in the Scriptures often indicate a
parallel.

The Lord was referring Nicodemus to the last miracle of
Moses, on the borders of the promised land. The sinning people
had been bitten by fiery serpents. They were dying without
hope. Moses was commanded to make a brazen serpent and
hang it high on a pole. It had thus been "lifted up" where all
could see. All a bitten Israelite had to do to procure salvation
was look and live (Numbers 21: 8-9). The solution to the poison
of the serpent, coursing through the victim's veins, was folly to
reason but was life to faith.

The parallel is obvious. Christ was "lifted up" on the cross of
Calvary. So, for all perishing sinners, aware of their need, willing to abandon useless human remedies, daring to venture all
on faith, "there is life for a look at the crucified one."

In speaking to Nicodemus of these things and setting before
him a graphic illustration, the Lord used one of his emphatic
"musts." "Ye must be born again," he had said, pressing home to
Nicodemus his desperate need. "So must the Son of man be
lifted up," he said, pointing him to the remedy.

He added one more explanatory word. "So must the Son of
man be lifted up: That whosoever believeth in him should not
perish, but have eternal life" (3:15).

3. The World's Greatest Text (3:16)

The Lord's conversation with Nicodemus seems to end with
the statement in verse 15, so from here on we seem to have
John's inspired commentary, beginning where Jesus left off and
with similar words.

We have now arrived at the great metropolis of gospel truth.
No other single statement in the Bible so aptly sums up God's
redemptive purpose in Christ for the human race. Volumes
have been written on it. Its each and every word has been
weighed and examined and marveled at and preached on. Who
will ever know until the judgment seat of Christ how many
millions of Adam's ruined race have found their way to heaven
by the discovery of John 3:16?

The text itself revolves around ten words: *God, loved, world,
gave, Son, whosoever, believeth, perish, have, life.* Those ten words
make up the "constellation of the redeemer" in the firmament
of divine revelation. The creative work of God is summed up in
ten commandments in Genesis 1 ("And God said"). The legisla-

tive work of God is summed up in ten commandments in Exodus 20. The redemptive work of God is summed up in ten words here in John 3:16.

These words can be arranged in five pairs. We have (1) "God" and the "Son," the giver and the gift; the author and finisher of salvation; two eternal, self-existing, uncreated members of the godhead. We have (2) "loved" and "gave," a twofold revelation of the benevolence of God; love, the prerequisite of such a gift, and the gift, the proof of such a love. We have the (3) "world" and "whosoever," all people universally, without distinction or exception; and each person individually, as though that person were the only one in the world. We have (4) "believeth" and "have," the hand of faith stretched out in confidence to the giver, and the hand of faith drawn back in contentment with the gift, the trust and the transfer complete. We have (5) "perish" and "life," the unutterable lostness of those who die in their sins and the unending life of those who die in the Savior; two eternal destinies, hell and heaven, with a great gulf forever fixed between banishment and bliss, the extremes of horror and happiness, the terminus of two roads: the broad road that leads to destruction and the narrow road that leads to everlasting life.

The text should be read through, ten times, meditatively, each time putting the emphasis on a different word. "For *God* so loved the world, that he gave his only begotten Son, that whosoever believeth in him should not perish, but have everlasting life." Then: "For God so *loved* the world, that he gave his only begotten Son, that whosoever believeth in him should not perish, but have everlasting life." Next: "For God so loved the *world*, that he gave . . ." And so on. The result will be ten meaningful meditations; for the preacher, ten great sermons. The text is inexhaustible. All the highways of divine truth meet in this metropolis. It is the hub of all revealed truth.

We think, for instance, who it is who loves this poor lost world. It is *God*, eternal, self-existing, uncreated, having need of nothing. It is God, omniscient, omnipotent, omnipresent. It is God, Elohim, Jehovah, Adonai, the God who has revealed himself by so many names, who now reveals himself as incarnate love. It is God, the one who sits, high and lifted up, worshiped by adoring angels, by cherubim and seraphim, and in whose presence they hide behind their wings and cry, "Holy, holy, holy is the Lord." It is God, creator and sustainer of the universe, who gazes out on stellar empires, on galaxy after galaxy, on mighty burning orbs that rush through space that obey laws he has ordained. It is God who takes the initiative, God who loves and gives. John 3:16, like Genesis 1:1 and Exodus 20:1, begins with *God*. We recoil in horror at the zeal for the virgin Mary that led Alfonso Maria dei Liguori to write in his book, *The Glories of Mary* (1750): "Mary so loved the world that she gave her only begotten Son." (Quoted by T. C. Hammond, *The One Hundred Texts*, London: The Society for Irish Church Missions, 1939, p. 18.) No, indeed. It is *God* who thus loved the world.

This text sets before us a glimpse of the heart of God. "For God so loved the world, that he gave his only begotten Son . . ." This is love that is stronger than death, the love that will not let me go, the love that many waters cannot quench, the love that suffers long and is kind, the love that never fails, the love that passes knowledge.

When D. L. Moody was in England on one of his crusades he met a young man named Henry Morehouse. The Englishman was greatly drawn to the American. The story goes that Henry Morehouse asked Mr. Moody if he would let him preach in his church if he were to come to Chicago. The evangelist agreed to the suggestion, lightly enough, never thinking he would have to make good on his promise.

But in due time Henry Morehouse arrived on Moody's door-step to redeem the pledge. A reluctant Moody surrendered his pulpit, assuring his colleagues that the young man could not do much harm in one night and that he himself would follow him into the pulpit and rescue the situation.

That night Henry Morehouse took John 3:16 as his text and preached on the love of God with such passion and power that an awed Moody invited him to speak again the next night. This continued for a week, each night the young Englishman speaking from the same text. Moody was overwhelmed. In fact Henry Morehouse became known as the man who moved the man who moved millions.

On the last night of his series, Henry Morehouse said to the people: "I have been trying to tell you how much God loves you. Suppose I could borrow Jacob's ladder. Suppose I could ascend that shining stairway until my feet stood on the sapphire pavements of the city of God. Suppose I could find Gabriel, the herald angel who stands in the presence of God. Suppose I could say, 'Tell me, Gabriel, how much does God love the world?' I know what he would say. He would say, 'Henry Morehouse, God so loved the world, that he gave his only begotten Son, that whosoever believeth in him should not perish, but have everlasting life. That's how much God loves the world.' "

This text also gives us a revelation of the mind of God, especially along two lines. We have here the thought of God concerning his Son. It is, of course, in some ways an accident of translation, but it is a delightful one. It so happens that in our beloved King James Version there are twenty-five words in this text and the central one is *Son*. That, of course, is exactly the way it should be.

In the thinking of God, all centers on his Son. God has no plan, no program for this world or any other, no purpose in the universe or in time or eternity, that does not center in his Son. Any measure in which our thinking centers in Christ is the measure in which our thinking is in harmony with the mind of God. Any thinking that is not Christ-centered is in that measure out of harmony with the mind of God. Our plans and purposes can succeed in the long run only in proportion to whether or not they are centered in God's Son.

We have here, too, the thought of God concerning our salvation: "whosoever believeth in him . . . " Again we are brought back to Jesus. He is the one who saves people from their sins, writes their names in life's eternal book, secures for them a place in the family of God and a home in heaven.

The word that activates it all is the word *believeth*. Simply and solely, God calls on us to trust his Son. And, since he is able "to save them to the uttermost that come unto God by him," that is no vain thing to do. The damning sin, the ultimate sin God will not forgive, is the sin of refusing to trust his Son. That is the greatest insult one can offer the Lord, to say to him verbally or otherwise, "I can't trust you." When someone came to D. L. Moody on one occasion with the excuse, "I can't believe," Mr. Moody asked, *"Whom* can't you believe?"

This text also gives us a revelation of the will of God. God is "not willing that any should perish" (2 Peter 3:9); it is a great revealed truth. Our text says that whosoever believeth in him "should not perish, but have everlasting life." That is God's earnest desire for all the children of Adam. The idea of a limited atonement, that God chose certain ones of the human race, an elect company, and that Christ died for the elect alone is a slander on the love of God. He died "for the sins of the whole world" (1 John 2:2). The gospel invitation is extended to all. It's when a person sees the personal aspect that the stage is set for the salvation miracle to take place. In dealing with people it is sometimes a good idea to get them to put their own names in the text where the more general words appear: "For God so loved the world (including John Brown), that he gave his only begotten Son, that whosoever (including John Brown) believeth in him should not perish, but have everlasting life."

Perish. That is a word to make the sinner tremble. It is a revelation of the other side of God's character. He is not only a

God of immeasurable love, he is also a God of infinite holiness.
But what does it mean? Someone once approached C. H. Spur-
geon with a problem text and asked him if he knew what it
meant. "Why, of course I do," he said. "It means just what it
says." The word *perish (apoletai)* means just what it says. We find
it used by the disciples in the extremity of their terror on the
storm-tossed sea when they awoke the Lord crying, "Lord, save
us, we perish" (Matthew 8:25). The word is translated "destroy"
in the urgent command to Joseph to take Jesus and Mary to
Egypt out of harm's way, "for Herod will seek the young child to
destroy him" (Matthew 2:13). We have all seen people destroy
their bodies with drink and drugs, with promiscuous sex and its
dread harvest of disease. But God threatens to allow sin to
complete its work beyond the grave by destroying the soul. The
soul does not perish like the body; the soul is immortal. Sinners
take with them into eternity unquenchable thirsts, terrible passions and appetites, mad cravings and inflamed desires, fierce
longings and furious hates, lusts and loathings, white-hot temper and spine-chilling fear. Those destructive character traits
will continue to ravage the soul and will never be either satisfied
or stilled. The word *perish* denotes the final condition of the
soul, the awful state of those who are "filthy still" (Revelation
22:11) under the eye of God.

But that is not what God wills for us. God would have all
come to repentance. That is why the invitation of John 3:16 is
universal, hinging on believing in him. Those who do, become
heirs of "everlasting [eternal] life." The word *aionios* is found
seventeen times in John's gospel, six times in his first epistle,
and eight times in the synoptic gospels. We are engineered out
of the stuff of eternity. Eternal life. The life of God himself.
Thus this great sentence, which summarizes the whole gospel
story, begins with God and ends with everlasting life. It begins
with one who had no beginning. It ends with that which has no
ending.

4. The World's Greatest Test (3:17-21)

The fact that Jesus Christ has come into the world provides
all people with the ultimate test of believing or disbelieving, of
choosing whether to continue in their sins and surely perish or
whether to believe in him and pass from death to life. The
coming of Christ into this world is the watershed of eternal
destiny for all.

We think, first, *why Jesus came* (3:17). "For God sent not his
Son into the world to condemn the world; but that the world

through him might be saved." Looking at John 3:16-17 as a whole we note that one phrase keeps cropping up, "the world . . . the world . . . the world." Something about this world draws out the love and compassion of God. This earth is a rebel planet, one that has gone astray. It is a challenge to the character of God, to his holiness, to his love.

When God's Son stepped off the throne of the universe the first time, to come down to earth, it was God's love he came to reveal. He did not come to condemn; he came to save. Grace, "sovereign grace o'er sin abounding," was the theme. But let no one do despite to the Spirit of grace. When he steps off the throne of the universe the next time, to come down to earth, it will be God's wrath he will come to reveal.

The word translated "sent" here is *apostello*, the word from which we derive our word *apostle*. It carries with it the idea of sending someone forth as a messenger on a mission. It suggests the thought of a definite mission and also of a representative character in the envoy. Jesus, the ambassador from heaven sent into this world, was no ordinary representative of God's throne. It takes all four gospels, not to mention all twenty-one epistles, to reveal what a perfect representative he was.

We think next *whom Jesus condemns* (3:18-19). Although it is true that Christ's mission the first time was not one of condemnation, the manifestation of Christ was both a process of judgment and a sentence of judgment on those who rejected him. The purpose of his coming was to offer peace, love, joy, and the goodness and glory of God's grace. But to those who spurned all that, the product of his coming was inevitably judgment.

"He that believeth on him is not condemned [judged]"; that is the one class of people. "He that believeth not is condemned already [hath been judged already]"; that is the other class of people. This is not the judgment of an arbitrary sentence but the inevitable working out, in the life of a Christ-rejecting individual, of an absolute law. A man who has a disease that a few injections can cure, but who refuses to take the injections and consequently dies of his disease, has no one but himself to blame. He spurned the remedy. What followed in his life was the inevitable outworking of law, of cause and effect. The same is true of sinners. The judgment they reap, by rejecting Christ, they bring on themselves. Christ came to offer eternal life. They chose death.

"And this is the condemnation, that light is come into the world, and men loved darkness rather than light because their deeds were evil" (3:19). They still do, and they still are. Taken by itself, this is a very great text. Some people rarely have their

greatness recognized because they are overshadowed by someone close to them. Thus the greatness of Isaac is overshadowed
by the greatness of his father Abraham and by that of his son
Jacob. The greatness of Barnabas is overshadowed by the stat-
ure of Paul. The same is true of texts. This verse in John's
gospel can afford to stand alone, straight and tall, on its own
two feet. That it rarely does is because it is overshadowed by
the giant three doors down on the same street—John 3:16.
Everyone preaches on John 3:16, but who preaches on John
3:19?

This is a fine Christmas text. "Light is come into the world,
and men loved darkness rather than light, because their deeds
were evil." At Bethlehem, light invaded this darkened world. A
classic illustration of men loving darkness rather than light is
seen in King Herod, whose deeds were evil indeed. Herod—
who murdered his wife's brother, his favorite wife, and both his
sons. Herod—who murdered the rank and file of the Hasmon-
eans, whose favorite sport was to watch while several hundred
of his subjects were crucified before him as he was getting
drunk, who had every leading citizen in his realm arrested just
days before his death and gave instructions that, immediately
upon news of his own death, every one of them was to be
murdered. If ever a man's deeds were evil, it was Herod's. If
ever a man loved darkness rather than light, it was Herod. And
when the light came into the world and he heard about it, he
sent and murdered the babes of Bethlehem in an effort to
overcome light with the "power of darkness."

The reason why people hate the light is because of what it
reveals. It shows us where we are and what we are. It shows us
what a dark place the world is. It shows human beings how dark
and evil they are. And so we note *what Jesus contrasts* (3:20-21):
those who loathe the light (3:20—"For every one that doeth evil
hateth the light, neither cometh to the light, lest his deeds
should be reproved") and *those who love the light* (3:21—"But he
that doeth truth cometh to the light, that his deeds may be
made manifest, that they are wrought in God").

D. The Jews and John (3:22-36)
   Triumph over Life's Saddening Discouragements

The closing verses of this chapter are a sequel to the Lord's
visit to Jerusalem. He had come to the holy city and had offered
himself as messiah by spectacularly cleansing the temple. That
dramatic sign was either ignored or misinterpreted. He there-

upon left the city and retired to the more rural parts of Judea. He evidently made disciples in this area including Lazarus and his sisters, Simeon, and Judas Iscariot.

1. John the Baptist's Witness (3:22-30)

These final verses can be grouped around the two men in the life of the Lord who were named John. We begin with the witness of John the baptist (3:22-30). Our attention is first drawn to *John and his baptism* (3:22-27). Here we have one of those significant notes common to John's gospel about the place involved. It will be helpful to get these locales in order.

A.D. 27 THE CALM YEAR
  Judea (1:1-42)
  Galilee (1:43–2:12)
  Judea (2:13–3:36)
  Samaria (4:1-42)
  Galilee (4:43-54)

A.D. 28-29 THE CROWDED YEAR
  Judea (5:1-47)
  Galilee (6:1–7:9)
  Judea (7:10–10:21)
  Galilee (between 10:21-22)
  Judea (10:22-39)
  Perea (10:40–11:16)

A.D. 30 THE CLOSING YEAR
  Judea (11:17–20:31)
  Galilee (21:1–25)

A general survey of these periods shows that the first period was comparatively quiet and lasted a year, the Lord alternating his ministry between Judea and Galilee. When Herod Antipas put John the baptist in prison (Matthew 4:12; Mark 1:14; Luke 3:19-20; John 4:1-4), the Lord departed to Galilee where he presented himself not as a king but as a prophet. His ministry was designed to draw public attention to himself. The first five chapters of the gospel of John all have to do with this year of comparative calm and tranquility. Apart from these chapters we would know little about the year between the Lord's baptism and the imprisonment of John the baptist.

The silencing of John the baptist was the Lord's signal to begin preaching, "Repent: for the kingdom of heaven is at hand," reiterating the message of the baptist (Matthew 4:12-17). Although the next two years were crowded years, John's gospel practically ignores them. Chapter 6 is the only place where John mentions this period.

The next watershed came when at Caesarea Philippi Simon Peter made his messianic confession (6:68-69) and the Lord began to disclose to his disciples that he was going to be crucified (Matthew 16:13-20). The last six months of the Lord's life were darkened by the shadow of the cross. Much of this busy time was spent in Perea. In John's gospel, chapters 7–21 have to do with events after Caesarea Philippi.

These general movements in the Lord's life are sketched only in a general way but they help us get the feel of what was going on.

As we return to the verses before us, two different baptisms are mentioned by John. There was *the baptism of Jesus* (3:22), though 4:2 states that the baptisms were actually being done by the Lord's disciples. It would seem that this baptism was similar to that of John the baptist, a preparation for the kingdom. We must not confuse either baptism with Christian baptism, which is a baptism into the death of Christ (Romans 6:3) and which was not instituted until after the Lord's death (Matthew 28:19).

There was also *the baptism of John* (3:23-24) at a place called Aenon ("abounding in springs"), said to have been "near to Salim." The spot is disputed by some but was evidently well known to the apostle. Taking the Damascus road northward for about seven miles from Sychar at the foot of Mount Ebal to the lovely valley of Wadi Farah and then following the stream that flows through the valley eastward for another seven miles, the traveler discovers another valley in every way suitable for John the baptist's ministry. The valley is big enough to hold the crowds who still flocked to John's meetings: rabbis and rulers from Jerusalem, publicans and peasants, ordinary folk, even Roman soldiers. A perennial stream and abundant springs provide plenty of water. It was an ideal place for John's preaching and baptism. "For John was not yet cast into prison," says the apostle, reminiscing about those early days.

The aged apostle is now concerned with the burden that weighed on the Lord's ambassador (3:25-27). It began with an argument between some of John's disciples and "the Jews" (some renderings read "a Jew") about "purifying" or, as we may suppose, about the value of baptism, such as John's, which had no foundation in the Old Testament Scriptures. In any case, notice was taken that Jesus was also baptizing people and that his success was now exceeding that of John. "All men come to him," they said. Evidently, John's disciples viewed Jesus as one who owed his success to the baptist's testimony. They viewed Jesus' activities as an invasion of their own master's prerogatives and they nurtured hostility toward him as a result.

John the baptist was above such pettiness and denominational spirit. "A man can receive nothing, except it be given him from heaven," he said (3:27). John's responsibility was to discharge the divine commission entrusted to him by God to be the fore-runner of the messiah; as for Jesus, thank God for his success! As the messiah, he too was entering on the path marked out for him in heaven. How foolish, then, to resent his success; it was a cause for rejoicing, not resentment. John the baptist was free from that dark spirit of professional jealousy which seizes the souls of some preachers when they contemplate someone in the ministry who seems to be having more success than they.

Our attention is drawn next to *John and the bridegroom* (3:28-30). First comes John's *positive denial* (3:28). "Ye yourselves bear me witness, that I said, I am not the Christ, but that I am sent before him" (3:28). John was surprised and disappointed at the dullness of his disciples. Then comes John's *personal delight* (3:29). As the "friend of the bridegroom" his job was to ask for the hand of the bride, to arrange the preliminaries of the wedding, and to oversee the reception of the bride and bridegroom. He had done that. His cup of joy overflowed because now everyone could hear the voice of the bridegroom instead of his own. Then comes John's *primary desire* (3:30), that which marked him out as a truly great man. He knew his work was almost over. "He must increase, but I must decrease," he said. He must now fade increasingly into the background. These are the last recorded words of this noble and valiant man before his arrest and imprisonment. Later he speaks once from prison. There is suspense, martyrdom, and his day is done.

2. John the Beloved's Witness (3:31-36)

We now have reflections by the aged apostle on these events associated with the earliest beginnings of the new movement of which he is the last surviving eyewitness.

He speaks first of *the testimony of God* (3:31-33). This testimony has been *adequately declared* (3:31): "He that cometh from above is above all: he that is of the earth is earthly [of the earth], and speaketh of the earth: he that cometh from heaven is above all." The phrase "of the earth" is repeated three times. It expresses the limitations of all earthly messengers, even though entrusted with a divine message. Even his words are "of the earth." He has the treasure in an earthen vessel. This was true even of John the baptist, whom Jesus called the greatest man born of women (Matthew 11:11; Luke 7:28). The prophets of the Old Testament—men like Moses and Malachi, David and Daniel, Jonah and Jeremiah—were "of the earth." They had human limitations. But in contrast, "He that cometh from above is above all . . . he that cometh from heaven is above all." The thrice repeated word *above* is set in contrast with the thrice repeated phrase "of the earth."

The Lord Jesus was free from the limitations felt by ordinary human messengers. He was from heaven. He had full knowledge of heavenly things, of the eternal counsels of God. Thus we read in that grand opening statement of Hebrews: "God, who at sundry times and in divers manners spake in time past unto the fathers by the prophets, Hath in these last days spoken to us by his Son" (Hebrews 1:1-2). It is like the difference between speaking to an audience through an interpreter and speaking to them in their own language.

His testimony has been *actually disbelieved* (3:32): "And what he hath seen and heard, that he testifieth; and no man receiveth his testimony." What an astonishing fact. It was not just a spirit-inspired prophet, not even an angel from the presence of God, but God himself who came. And people actually disbelieved him—and still do.

"What he hath seen and heard." These are the hallmarks of an impeccable witness. Way back before time began, before the rustle of an angel's wing disturbed the silence of eternity, God the Father, God the Son, and God the Holy Spirit decided to act in creation. They accepted the possibility that if they acted in creation and made a creature—man—and endowed him with intellect, emotions, and will, they would also have to act in redemption. Jesus was there. So when in John's gospel we repeatedly read of him talking about intimate and other-dimensional, extraterrestrial prechronological conversations with his Father we can take his word for it. He is speaking of things he has seen and heard.

When we hear him talking about marriage in terms of Adam and Eve and the garden of Eden, he was there. It was something he had seen and heard. When he spoke of Noah, the ark, and the flood, it is the same. It was something he had seen and heard. When he talked about Abraham or Noah or Isaiah or David or Daniel, these were people he had seen and heard. When he talked about the overthrow of Sodom and Gomorrah, he was there. He had seen and heard. Far more than Lot, whom he knew, his righteous soul was "vexed with the filthy conversation of the wicked" (2 Peter 2:7-8).

When he talked about "that great gulf fixed" and described the torment of a soul in hell, he had seen and heard. When he spoke of his Father's house of many mansions he was talking about things he had seen and heard. When he unveiled the future, talked about building a church, talked about the end-time rebirth of the state of Israel, talked about the desecration of a future temple and about a coming great tribulation, he was talking as one who had stood outside our space-time dimensional limitations in an unwavering present tense and had seen and heard. He was speaking as one "from above." "And no man receiveth his testimony," says John. Truth incarnate had spoken and his word was actually disbelieved.

But his testimony is *absolutely dependable* (3:33): "He that hath received his testimony hath set to his seal that God is true." The idea behind this statement is that of confirming a legal document by affixing an official seal to it. Jesus is God's perfect witness. His words are truth, not in a relative sense, but in an absolute sense. When he speaks, it is God who speaks. Those, therefore, who receive the witness of Jesus are attesting to the truthfulness of God.

Having thus confirmed the testimony of God, John concludes this section with a further statement about *the truth of God* (3:34-36). Each word is meaningful. There is a reference here to *the Spirit of God* (3:34): "For he whom God hath sent speaketh the words of God: for God giveth not the Spirit by measure unto him." In no way did our Lord's humanity impair him from speaking the words of God. The means by which he, the Son of God, imparted as man the words of God, was the Spirit of God. The Old Testament prophets, of course, had their measure of the Spirit of God enabling them so to speak the words of God that we can affirm with confidence the plenary, verbal inspiration of the Scriptures. But with these men the gift of the Spirit was partial and intermittent (1 Peter 1:11; Hebrews 1:1). But the Holy Spirit was not so given to Jesus. He was conceived of the Holy Spirit, indwelt by the Holy Spirit, filled with the Holy Spirit from his very first breath and, from the time of his baptism, fully anointed by the Spirit. "God giveth not the Spirit by measure unto him." In him "dwelleth all the fulness of the Godhead bodily" (Colossians 2:9). The word *giveth* is in the present tense, indicating a continuous and uninterrupted flow of the Spirit in his life.

There is a reference to *the Son of God* (3:35): "The Father loveth (*agapao*) the Son, and hath given all things into his hand." The measure of the love is indicated by the nature of the gift.

Finally, there is a reference to *the salvation of God* (3:36): "He that believeth on the Son hath everlasting life: and he that believeth not the Son shall not see life; but the wrath of God abideth on him." One thing God will not forgive is to have his Son treated with contempt, disbelief, or indifference. The state of soul of those who do such outrageous things is so fearful that they not merely kindle the wrath of God: it actually abides on them. The phrase "the wrath of God" is used to denote a distinct expression of the righteous judgment of God (Romans 1:18). It is used especially of the coming wrath of God soon to be poured out, as described in the apocalypse, on a Christ-rejecting, God-hating, sin-loving world (1 Thessalonians 2:16; Revelation 11:18; 16:19; 19:15).

E. The Woman at the Well (4:1-42)
   Triumph over Life's Sordid Defilements

The contrast could hardly be greater between Nicodemus and the woman at the well. One was a man, the other a woman; one was a Jew, the other a Samaritan; the one was a respected ruler, the other a social outcast; the one was seen as a moral man, the other an immoral woman; the one came to Jesus by night, the other came at mid-day; the one had no arguments, only a wondering *how*, the other was full of questions and debate; the one was cautious, the other was bold; the one did not seem to know what he wanted, the other knew only too well; the one fades out of the story unnoticed, the other went back to her crowd and brought them all to Jesus; the one we hear of again (7:50; 19:39), the other fades into women's usual invisibility in patriarchal society.

We shall look at the story of the woman at the well in three parts. We begin here with the detour (4:1-8), we shall look at the discussion (4:9-30), by far the longest section, and we shall conclude with the disciples (4:31-42).

1. The Detour (4:1-8)

The detour begins with reference to *a necessary way* (4:1-6). The Lord "must needs go through Samaria." It was all part of a plan. The Lord seems to have left the area where his disciples were baptizing to avoid a premature collision with the Pharisees. Perhaps his disciples were only too eager to jump into the developing controversy among John's followers over the news that Jesus was baptizing more people than their master—as though counting the number of baptisms and having a competitive spirit over the resulting numbers had anything to do with truth. The Lord wanted no part of it. Neither, as we have seen, did John. John rebuked his disciples; Jesus moved away.

It is perhaps significant that the Pharisees were eager to stir up controversy between the disciples of John and Jesus. It was the Pharisees who throughout most of the Lord's ministry represented most vocally the unbelieving nation. Not until after the raising of Lazarus did the Sadducees seize the reigns of opposition and thereafter drove the nation headlong to the crime of Calvary. But John never mentions this aristocratic and theologically liberal party by name.

"He left Judaea," John says, "and departed again into Galilee" (3:3). The word for "left" is *atheken*, and there is no exact parallel to the use of this word in the New Testament. The idea the word conveys is that of leaving something to itself, to its own fate, of leaving someone to their own devices, of withdrawing whatever controlling power was exercised before. It is a significant word. From now on the bulk of Jesus' ministry will be in Galilee and elsewhere. He will leave Jerusalem and Judea to their own devices. Indeed, in a decision full of symbolic meaning, he seems deliberately to have made up his mind to make the journey to Galilee via the despised district of Samaria. Scrupulous Jews would always avoid Samaria. They would cross the Jordan and make a long detour to avoid contaminating themselves with any contact with Samaritans.

Pursuing this plan, then, the Lord at length arrived at "a city of Samaria, which is called Sychar, near to the parcel of ground that Jacob gave to his son Joseph." Jacob's well was there and Jesus "being wearied with his journey, sat thus on the well" (3:6). What a picture of our Lord, overwhelmed with fatigue, sinking down, perhaps with an audible sigh to rest.

Some have identified the town referred to here by John with Nablus (the ancient Shechem), about a mile and a half west of Jacob's well. The real Sychar seems to have been Askar, which is scarcely half a mile north of the well. It was one of those little walled villages that crowned every small hill in Palestine.

Some have thought that the name *Sychar* means "town of the sepulcher," a reference to the fact that Joseph's tomb was there.

Jacob's well is one of the few places in the Holy Land about which there is no dispute. The well was originally very deep

(105 feet was one measurement taken in the year 1697). It was
seven and a half feet in diameter and was walled with masonry
to a depth of ten feet, below which it was actually cut through
solid rock. Joseph's tomb is only four hundred yards north of
the well.

So, as Jesus wearily seated himself there on the well at "the
sixth hour" (high noon according to the Jewish reckoning of
time), the sun beat down. The weary traveler longed for a drink
of water. The stage was now set for a momentous meeting. We
are about to learn the reason for that "must needs go" (4:4).
Everywhere around him the Lord could see the marks of the
sacred history of the Hebrew people: Jacob's well, Joseph's
tomb, nearby Mount Gerizim where half of the tribes had assembled to pronounce the blessing contained in the mosaic law.
So with a body weary and thirsty, a mind full of Bible memories,
a spirit in moment by moment communion with his Father,
alone (the disciples had departed in search of food), the Lord sat
in the heat of the day and waited for a woman he knew would
soon arrive at the well.

So *a needy woman* (4:7-8) comes. What was she like, this woman? Her marital and extramarital relationships would seem to
indicate that she was not overburdened by moral scruples. It
doesn't take us long to discover that she had a quick mind and a
sharp tongue. She had a stock of local religious sentiment, a
strange mixture of error and truth. The Lord must have enjoyed talking to her almost as much as he enjoyed the result of
their conversation.

He opened the conversation as soon as she arrived. It was an
unusual hour of the day to draw water, right when the sun was
at its height. But then, this woman probably had no wish to face
the sneers and contemptuous glances of the other woman who
gathered there at cooler times of day. Her lifestyle no doubt
had provided plenty of material for the town gossips.

"Jesus saith unto her, Give me to drink." He, the creator of
the Nile and the Mississippi, the one who filled the Great Lakes
and designed Niagara Falls—he was thirsty. There was the well;
she had the bucket; he asked for a drink. As if, had he so
desired, he could not have commanded the deep, unseen, allu-
vial spring that fed the well and it would instantly have filled the
well to the top and overflowed at his feet! Centuries before, he
had brought water from the flinty rock for Moses. A short while
before, he had changed the water into wine. The devil had
challenged him to command stones to become bread. But never
once did Jesus perform a miracle for himself. He was here, after
all, to taste of life to the full. And part of life on ordinary

human terms is to be hungry and thirsty and to go on being hungry and thirsty if the ordinary means of obtaining bread and water are not around.

The needy woman! It looked, on the surface, more like the needy man. But then, with Jesus, things are not always what they seem to be. He had "seen and heard." He knew this needy woman better than she knew herself.

2. The Discussion (4:9-30)

A remarkable conversation takes place with Jesus responding to the woman's statements at every step. Seven times we read "the woman saith," or its equivalent (9,11,15,17,19,25,28).

We begin with *a word of indignation* (4:9-10): "How is it that thou, being a Jew, askest drink of me, which am a woman of Samaria?" She begins with the question of racial prejudice; later she brings in the issue of religious prejudice (4:20). "The Jews have no dealings with the Samaritans," she added.

The racial issue went back a very long time. When the northern ten tribes were led into captivity by the Assyrians, the conquerors (following their usual policy of population redistribution) brought foreign settlers into the territory. Before long these newcomers adopted a bastard form of Judaism. The Jews of Judea rejected the colonists and their clumsy attempts to imitate the Hebrew religion, refusing to have anything to do with them. Later, after the Jews themselves had suffered through the Babylonian captivity and returned to repossess their ancestral homeland, they found the Samaritans still entrenched in the land.

When the Jews began to rebuild their temple in Jerusalem, although the Samaritans wanted to help, their overtures were rejected out of hand. The resulting enmity was fostered on both sides and grew increasingly bitter as years went by (2 Kings 17:24-29; Ezra 4:1-5; Nehemiah 2:10,19; 4:1-3).

The Samaritan answer to the Jewish temple was to build a rival temple on Mount Gerizim for themselves. The destruction of this temple by the Hasmonean ruler John Hyrcanus (about 108 B.C.) only increased Samaritan hostility. Most Jews would not think of asking a favor from a Samaritan for fear of becoming ceremonially defiled; indeed, many Jews assumed that all Samaritan women were in a perpetual state of ceremonial uncleanness. By asking the woman of Samaria for a drink, Jesus swept aside such racial and gender-based prejudices.

The Lord did not answer the woman's question directly. Rather, he directed her attention to God: "If thou knewest the

gift of God, and who it is that saith to thee, Give me to drink;
thou wouldest have asked of him, and he would have given thee
living water" (4:10). He had said, "Give me." Now he says, "If
you had asked him, he would have given you . . . "

Here were two marvels. The first was that he, a Jew, had
asked her for a drink. The second was that he claimed to have
"living water," which he was quite willing to give her. In this
statement Jesus told her all she needed to obtain salvation: what
it was ("the water of life"); who controlled it (he did); how to get
it ("ask of him" and receive it as "the gift of God") (compare
Romans 6:23).

Next comes *a word of indecision* (4:11-14). We note at once *the
woman's innate thoughtfulness* (4:11-12). Already this Jew has
gone up in her estimation. She now calls him "Sir." But she was
confused. She was still thinking of the water in the well. It was
very deep; her daily trips there over many years had taught her
that. Her thoughts went back to the Hebrew patriarch Jacob
who had dug that well through solid rock—no small achieve-
ment. She claims Jacob as "our father Jacob," a spurious claim
since Jacob was not the father of the alien Samaritans. But the
Lord did not quibble about that. He was soon to introduce her
to his Father, one who could indeed become her Father.

The Lord simply held before her again the attractive offer of
never thirsting, appealing to *the woman's inner thirstiness* (4:13-
14). "If you drink of this water, you will thirst again. If you
drink of the water I give, you will never thirst again. On the
contrary, you will receive an inner 'well of water springing up
into everlasting life' " (4:14). She was thinking in literal terms;
he was talking to her in figures of speech. The physical was used
as an illustration of the spiritual. The woman had not yet
caught on. She was still thinking of some magical well of water,
as her next words show.

Now comes *a word of intimation* (4:15). The woman asks for
this mysterious water that would relieve her of the necessity of
making daily trips to the well. She could not follow the symbolism but she could intimate her own deep need; she could ask for
the water of life this stranger was talking about. And she did.
Now she was asking him for a drink, just as he had previously
asked her. It was a great step forward in her spiritual odyssey.

But the Lord does not give the gift of eternal life without first
dealing with the question of sin. As soon as the woman revealed
her receptiveness to the gift of living water, the Lord put a
finger on what was causing her quenchless thirst: sin.

At once comes *a word of insulation* (4:16-18), as the woman
instinctively backed off from the sensitive issue, trying to insu-

late herself from exposure. First came *a disturbing reservation* (4:16). Jesus said, in effect—"You want this water of life? Then I, like a physician, must first put my hand on that malignant growth of sin in your life which makes eternal life impossible; it is the sentence of death in your life. I must deal with that first." At the first hint of this unwelcome but unerring knowledge of her condition she shrank back. That was a sore spot and she knew it. She may have been telling herself for years that there was nothing wrong, that it was all right—when all the time she knew it was all very wrong.

The disturbing reservation, that this water of life could only be obtained subject to some definite, personal, and awkward preconditions, led to *a defensive reaction* (4:17a). "The woman answered and said, I have no husband." She shied away from this topic, probably disturbed by the sudden change of subject. Still, she may have thought to herself, this wandering Jew could not possibly know the story of her life; he could be put off with an evasion. So she simply stated her present marital status, concealing the true situation.

This led to *a damaging revelation* (4:17b-18). "Thou hast well said, I have no husband: For thou hast had five husbands; and he whom thou now hast is not thy husband; in that saidst thou truly." Five husbands in a row during her life so far had at least some semblance of respectability. We are not told how or why these marriages were dissolved, whether by death or divorce. But whatever the reasons, it was no part of the Lord's purpose to rake over the ashes of dead fires. There was enough flame in her present dishonorable situation. The Lord was always a perfect gentleman, possessed of impeccable manners. He wanted only to expose the sore, not poke and pry into all the details of her life. "Love covers a multitude of sins" (1 Peter 4:8).

All this led to *a word of inspiration* (4:19-24). First came *a notable tribute* (4:19-20). She had begun by calling him "Jew," and she had progressed to calling him "Sir." Now, astonished by his insights, she called him a "prophet." And, like so many others, when the soul-winner approaches the sin question in their lives, this woman resorted to a tactical diversion. She raised a religious question, one that would steer the discussion away from that area. It happens all the time, as any experienced soul-winner knows. When the issues began to become plain and personal, at once the question is raised: "Where did Cain get his wife?" or "Are the heathen lost?" or some such irrelevant religious issue.

She said, "Our fathers worshiped in this mountain; and ye say, that in Jerusalem is the place where men ought to worship" (4:20).

The destruction of Solomon's gorgeous temple in Jerusalem sadly tarnished its superiority as "the exclusive place for worship"; the rebuilt temple had none of the former grandeur of the original. Not long after it was rebuilt, Manasseh, son of the high priest Joiada and brother of the high priest Jonathan, married the daughter of Sanballat, the Persian governor of Samaria (Nehemiah 12:10-11; 13:28). The governor of Jerusalem ordered him to dissolve this marriage which had all the marks of an unequal yoke, but Manasseh refused to do so. He was thereupon thrown out of Jerusalem by that redoubtable reformer Nehemiah. But that was not the end of the story. His father-in-law, Sanballat, made Manasseh high priest of the Samaritans and arranged to build a temple for him on Mount Gerizim. Manasseh left Jerusalem during or about the year 332 B.C. The temple on Mount Gerizim remained there for about two centuries.

There was no doubt about the religious interest of the location. Mount Gerizim and its chief neighboring city, Shechem, figured often in Old Testament history. It was associated with Abraham (Genesis 12:6-7), Jacob, (Genesis 33:18), and Joseph (Genesis 37:12-13). It was the site of one of the cities of refuge (Joshua 20:7-9). Here the children of Israel rehearsed the law's blessing and curses, soon after entering the promised land (Joshua 8:33). Here Joshua gave his last address to the tribes (Joshua 24:1-31). Moreover, the place was important at the time Israel set up its rival kingdom (1 Kings 12:1,25). To all this, the Samaritans added all kinds of other special (highly speculative) claims for the place: that the garden of Eden crowned Mount Gerizim, that it was of the dust of Gerizim that Adam was made, that the ark came to rest on Mount Gerizim, and that here Noah offered the first postdiluvian sacrifice. Here, too, they said, Abraham offered up Isaac and here he met with Melchizedek. And this was the true place where Jacob saw his vision of the ladder reaching from earth to heaven. Great claims!

But if the woman at the well thought she could divert the Lord into a discussion of such details, she was mistaken. The Lord ignored her tactic and confronted her instead with *a notable truth* (4:21-24).

He began with *a word about the future* (4:21). "The hour cometh, when ye shall neither in this mountain, nor yet at Jerusalem, worship the Father." Over against this woman's boast, "our fathers," the Lord places "the Father." He lifted her thoughts above any earthly shrine. He knew that within a generation the temple at Jerusalem would be as extinct as the temple that once stood on Gerizim. Temples made with hands had no relevance in the new age about to dawn.

He continued with *a word about the faith* (4:22) and dismissed out of hand the woman's question about the sanctity of Mount Gerizim. He did it not because he was a Jew but because he was Jesus, incarnate truth. He said, "Ye worship ye know not what: we know what we worship: for salvation is of the Jews." In both cases the pronoun is emphatic in the original. At best, the Samaritan form of worship was incomplete, tainted by its origins, devoid of all the later prophetic revelations given to the Jews. True, the Samaritans had their Pentateuch, but their worship was a crude mixture of truth and error and, in any case, they were outside the mainstream of God's revealing process and redemptive purpose. "Salvation was of the Jews." It was of the seed of Abraham, of the tribe of Judah, of the family of David, of the city of Bethlehem—of the Jews—that the Savior of the world was to come. God had chosen this people for this purpose, nor could all the faults and failings of the Jewish people alter or annul the divine purpose.

He concluded with *a word about the Father* (4:23-24), and a marvelous word it is. How remarkable that this lofty concept of worship should have been revealed not to the scholarly Nicodemus, but to this wayward woman, not to that aristocratic scion of the Jewish faith, but to this eager Samaritan seeker. God is no respecter of persons; God looks on the heart. The Lord had looked into the heart of Nicodemus and had found himself obliged to go back to the word pictures of the Old Testament, back to the kindergarten stage of divine revelation, and to talk to him about the serpent on the pole—so dull was his spiritual apprehension, so hedged about with tradition, caution, and mental reservation. He looked into the thirsty, empty soul of this bright and thoughtful woman and saw her longing for truth and holiness. So it was to her he gave one of his greatest revelations about God.

He talked to her about the Father, about *his passion* (4:23): "The hour cometh, and now is, when the true worshipers shall worship the Father in spirit and in truth: for the Father seeketh such to worship him." He drew her mind away from a place to a person. Very rarely in the Old Testament is God spoken of as a Father. But it was the Lord's characteristic name for him. (No wonder, he was his Son.)

True worship has to be "in the spirit." Judaism was largely a worship of the letter rather than of the spirit. It was concerned with rites and rituals, forms and ceremonies, sacrifices and offerings, feast days and fast days, circumcisions and sabbaths. All of that was to be set aside in favor of a spiritual form of worship.

Real worship had to be "in truth." Samaritanism was largely a worship of the false, rather than worship in truth. It was concerned with a hodgepodge of religious ideas. At best it was a sterile hybrid thing, lifeless, dead, and false.

The Lord lifted her thoughts to a living, loving Father, one who yearned for the worship of any—Jew or Samaritan—who would worship him in spirit and in truth. What was needed for that, of course, was the regeneration of the Spirit of God, so that she could worship in spirit, and a full revelation of the Son of God, so that she could worship in truth.

The Lord proceeded to explain, as he went on to talk to her further about the Father, about *his person* (4:24): "God is a Spirit: and they that worship him must worship him in spirit and in truth"—in spirit because of what he is; in truth because of what we are.

The woman was overwhelmed. Now comes *a word of indoctrination* (4:25-27). Evidently the woman had picked up echoes of the truth concerning the messiah. No doubt the preaching of John the baptist and the recent stirrings of messianic hopes in Israel had been talked about in Samaria. She had at least some understanding along these lines. She voiced what little she knew and believed: "I know," she said (and this stands in contrast with Nicodemus's pompous "we know" in 3:2), "that Messias cometh, which is called Christ: when he is come, he will tell us all things" (4:25). The pronoun *he* is emphatic.

Now comes the final revelation: "Jesus saith unto her, I that speak unto thee am he" (4:26). This was the last of the Lord's seven utterances to this woman: "Give me" (4:7), "If thou knewest" (4:10), "I shall give" (4:4), "Go, call" (4:16), "Well said" (4:17), "Believe me" (4:21), and "I . . . am he" (4:26).

It was the critical moment. And as so often happens, it was disturbed. Again, everyone who has sought to lead a soul to Christ is familiar with this interruption at the critical moment. You get a person right to the point where a decision is about to be made—and the telephone rings. But, no matter. The Holy Spirit is not to be hindered from doing his work by a disturbance. In this case it was the return of the disciples which caused the interruption (4:27).

They were speechless that the Lord should be talking to a woman, and a Samaritan woman at that. It was contrary to Jewish taboos. Look again at these men. On their way into the village to buy provisions they must have met this woman with her waterpot on her way to the well. Perhaps they passed her by on the other side without any sort of friendly greeting.

But now comes *a word of invitation* (4:28-30). "The woman

then left her waterpot, and went her way into the city." Why did she leave it? Was it an act of thanks and appreciation, leaving it for Jesus to use? Was her heart so overflowing with living water that it was a subconscious, symbolic testimony to the new life within? Was she already sure that she'd be back in a very short time?

She hurried home. She rounded up the men. What men? The men she had once been married to? The chief men of the village? The word used is *anthropos*, the general New Testament word for a human being. Some have translated it, "she saith to the people." In any case her testimony was clear, a call to action: "Come, see a man, which told me all things that ever I did: is not this the Christ?" Her testimony was simple; it was also successful. "Then they went out of the city, and came unto him" (4:30). Thus ends the evangelist's description of this remarkable encounter.

3. The Disciples (4:31-42)

Any woman who has slaved over the kitchen stove, prepared a delicious meal, called her husband to come and eat—only to be told that he's not hungry—can empathize with the disciples at this point. But the Lord was never discourteous, never thoughtless of others. His behavior at this point in the story is all of a piece with his divine purpose in this world. He had forgotten his physical thirst in his greater thirst for the Samaritan woman's soul. Now he forgot his physical hunger in his hunger to reach a lost world.

The section begins, then, with the disciples and *their meat* (4:31-34). They had gone into the Samaritan village to purchase provisions. That in itself was not a task any of them would have relished. They wanted as little as possible to do with Samaritans. We can read between the lines. Why did they all have to go on such a minor mission? We can imagine what went on. "Well, you'd better go, Judas. After all, you have the money bag." Judas would indignantly refuse—he a Judean, no less! Certainly he wasn't going. They would look at Peter. "You like to take the lead, Peter. You go. Take the lead in this." And Peter would be as unwilling as Judas. Philip might say to Nathanael, tongue in cheek, perhaps: "Here's your opportunity, Nathanael. You thought no good thing could come out of Nazareth. Go and see what good thing can come out of Sychar." So in the end they all went.

And a hot, tiresome business it was. But now they were back. They had drawn water from the well. They had spread out their provisions on the wall of the well. They were hungry. They looked inquiringly at the Lord for the blessing. But his mind and heart were far away. He was with that woman even now bursting into the city with her good news. "Master, eat!" they said (4:31).

"I have meat to eat that ye know not of," he responded. The disciples looked at each other in bewilderment. "Has someone brought him something to eat?" They were as unable to grasp the metaphors he used as were the Jerusalem Pharisees, Nicodemus, or the woman from Sychar.

The Lord translated for them; "My meat is to do the will of him that sent me, and to finish his work" (4:34). When Satan, a short time before, had tempted him to turn stones into bread and to satisfy his hunger, Jesus had simply pointed to the word of God: "Man shall not live by bread alone, but by every word that proceedeth out of the mouth of God." He was quoting from Deuteronomy 8:3. That was the principle he lived by. He was hungry above all to do his Father's will in this world and to finish (teleioo, "accomplish," "bring to a perfect end") his work (4:34). He had just brought to such a perfect end a part of that work in the conversion of the Samaritan woman. The satisfaction that gave him was more real than any ordinary meal could give.

This naturally paved the way for a discussion of the disciples and their mission (4:35-42). The Lord turned their attention to the harvest field of which he had just reaped a token of the firstfruits.

He spoke first of the time of the harvest (4:35-38). "Say not ye, There are yet four months, and then cometh harvest? behold, I say unto you, Lift up your eyes, and look on the fields; for they are white already to harvest" (4:35). There has been considerable discussion as to what the Lord meant by the expression, "Say not ye, There are yet four months, and then cometh harvest?" Some take it to mean that the grain fields of Moreh were green with growing grain and that they figured it would be four months to harvest time (about the middle of April) since it was then (calculating backward) about the middle of December. There is, however, no general agreement as to this time.

The other view is that the saying was proverbial because, in the Greek, the words have a rhythm to them. In this case the meaning would be that patience, but not undue patience, must be exercised from seed time to harvest.

The Lord, in any case, directed the disciples' thoughts away from the grain fields to the other harvest of which he was speaking. His eye may have already caught sight of the approaching figure of the woman from Sychar and the crowd coming with her. "Look!" he seems to be saying. "Just moments ago I sowed the seed and here comes the harvest already!"

And, while waiting for this throng of Samaritans to arrive, he spoke further to his disciples about the joys and rewards of sowing and reaping in the field of the world. He spoke first of *the need for reapers* (4:35). "Look on the fields; for they are white already to harvest." If they were ripe then, what must they be now as we stand at the other end of the long dispensation of grace? The sunset burns across the sky. Millions, still untold, lift up their anguished voices to the heavens. The church has dillied and dallied with the great commission, careless, for the most part, of the tragedy of a soul dying in nature's darkness. The terrible indictment, "No man cared for my soul" (Psalm 142:4), will be raised by a million million voices at the last assize. How will we ever explain our lethargy and neglect when the charge is referred to us by the billions of our own generation who will say to God, "I never knew you had a Son"? Are we any less culpable than those first disciples who saw in the woman of Samaria not a mission field but one whom they could afford to despise?

Jesus spoke to them, so patiently, of *the nature of rewards* (4:36-38). In "the crowning day that's coming by and by" the reaper and the sower will rejoice together. So often the reaper, the evangelist, gets the glory down here—the one who gets the souls into the kingdom. There will be no such distinction at the judgment seat of Christ. Paul plants, Apollos waters; but God gives the increase (1 Corinthians 3:6). So often some unknown Christian plants the seed, waters it with prayers and tears, and never sees the harvest. "I sent you to reap that whereon ye bestowed no labor: other men labored, and ye are entered into their labors" (4:38). All such distinctions will be swept aside at the judgment seat by the all-seeing eye of him who knows the spiritual history of each soul.

The point is, the time is now for sowing and reaping. We are to seize our opportunities while we may.

The Lord sees *the token of the harvest* (4:39-42). The crowd of Samaritans arrived on the scene, an eager, welcoming throng. They wanted to know more. They asked this strange Jew, who had already showed himself to be so singularly free from racial bias, to come and visit in their town. He gladly obliged and remained there two days, breaking who knows how many Jewish shibboleths, visiting in their homes, eating their food, sleeping in their beds, teaching them the word of God. Revival broke out. "And many more believed because of his own word" (4:41). Unlike the Jews, the Samaritans asked for no signs. The Lord performed no miracles in their midst. Like those of Berea, who were "more noble than those in Thessalonica" (Acts 17:11), these despised Samaritans received the word with readiness of mind. Their faith came to rest on something more solid than someone else's testimony. They said to the woman: "Now we believe, not because of thy saying: for we have heard him ourselves, and know that this is indeed the Christ, the Savior of the world" (4:42). It is significant that this lovely title for the Lord Jesus, found also in 1 John 4:14, this great concept, was first expressed by Samaritans. Jesus had said to the woman at the well, "Salvation is of the Jews." These Samaritans said, "And so it is! We have found not just salvation, but the Savior, and not just the Savior of the Jews, but the Savior of the world."

F. The Faith of a Father (4:43-54)
Triumph over Life's Sorrowful Disasters

The two eventful days in Samaria were over and Jesus continued on his way to Galilee. He quoted a proverb. "A prophet hath no honor in his own country." We learn from all three of the synoptic gospels that he quoted the proverb again on another occasion in connection with his home town of Nazareth (Matthew 13:57). Here the quotation seems to have been directed toward Judea. Judea was "his own country" too; he had been born there. The reception the Lord had just received in Samaria contrasted significantly with that given him in Judea. Jerusalem had given him no honor, and his messianic claim had not been welcomed. He did not trust himself to the Jews there. True, many followed him, but theirs was a faith that rested on miracles. So a homespun proverb fell from his lips.

If his reception in Judea had been cool this first time, it would be far worse the next time. Soon he would be saying, "I have come in my Father's name, and ye receive me not" (5:43). Soon, too, John would be writing into the record that although the Lord "had done so many miracles before them, yet they believed not on him" (12:37).

1. The Return to Cana (4:43-46a)

The Lord found a warm reception awaiting him in Galilee. His works at Jerusalem, although they produced no lasting effect in the area, seemed to have impressed the Galileans who had been there. It is likely that returning Galilean pilgrims must be counted among the many who had believed in Christ at the

Passover (2:23). The Lord found a welcome awaiting him in Galilee.

When he arrived back in Galilee, the Lord headed for Cana where he had performed his first miracle.

2. The Request from Capernaum (4:46b-54)

But the Lord had no sooner arrived in Cana than he received the request from Capernaum. We note first *his plight* (4:46b). The request came from "a certain nobleman."The word for nobleman is *basilikos* and literally means "king's man." The probability is that this nobleman was an officer of Herod Antipas, the tetrarch of Galilee who was popularly known as "king" (Matthew 14:9). The man's son was sick in the nearby city of Capernaum.

Next comes *his plea* (4:47-49). The nobleman wasted no time. As soon as he heard that Jesus was in the vicinity he seized his opportunity. He hurried to Cana to plead with Jesus "that he would come down, and heal his son: for he was at the point of death" (4:47). His plea received an instant check. Jesus looked at the man, ignored his request, and challenged the ground of his faith. "Except ye see signs and wonders, ye will not believe," he said. The words were also meant for the bystanders. The word *ye* is in the plural. The words *signs* and *wonders* underline the two chief aspects of miracles. They were "signs." That suggested the spiritual aspect of the miracles, the fact that the miracles were intended to convey some deeper truth, that they proved that he who performed them was acting under the direct authority of God. They were "wonders." That drew attention to the external aspect of the miracles. They were designed to attract attention, to startle people by their uniqueness. The nobleman was seen by Jesus as a representative of the kind of people whose faith has to be constantly bolstered by miracles; this, in contrast with the Samaritans who believed without having their faith thus propped up.

The nobleman was obviously irritated by what seemed to him an unnecessary discussion of the niceties of faith. His boy was dying, indeed was already at the point of death when he rushed out of the house in a desperate race with time to find the only one he felt could help. To have that one launch instead into a challenge to him and the bystanders as to whether or not they would believe in him without miracles was a frustration. One can almost hear the exasperation as well as the desperation in his voice as he said, "Sir, come down ere my child die" (4:49).

On his first plea he had used the word *son*; now he uses the diminutive. The word is *paidion*, "my little child," my dear one. Perhaps the picture of a little child would touch the heart of this teacher.

"Go thy way," Jesus said to him, pointing out *his path* (4:50) of true faith. "Thy son liveth." In effect Jesus said to him: "All right, let us find out whether or not you will believe without seeing. You want me to come down to Capernaum. Well, I'm not coming. It's not at all necessary for me to come. I don't have to be physically present to heal a sick child at the point of death. I'll stay here and heal him. You go on home. Your son lives. I have commanded death to leave him." There is a word of assurance in that for us too. The Lord does not have to be physically present to act on our behalf; distance is no obstacle to him.

It was not long before the ruler had *his proof* (4:51-54) that the Lord was worthy of his trust. He was on his way home when he saw some of his servants hurrying toward him. Evidently they had news. Did his heart skip a beat as a flash of doubt surfaced in his soul? Did his heart leap within him as faith triumphant soared? What news could it be but good news! And sure enough, it was. The servants met him with the identical words of Jesus: "Thy son liveth."

Now, as a matter of interest, the nobleman compared notes with his servants. "When did he start to get better?" he said, remembering that he had left him at death's door. "It was yesterday at the seventh hour they said—at one o'clock in the afternoon, the precise hour in which Jesus had said to him, "Thy son liveth."

It was about twenty-two miles from Cana to Capernaum. The father could have arrived home the same day. His confidence in the Lord, however, seems to have been so secure that he did not hurry. Perhaps he was tired and hungry. Perhaps he stopped for rest and refreshment. There was no need for breakneck speed. All was well.

Now he had complete confirmation that Jesus was indeed the Son of God, the messiah of Israel. John notes that the nobleman himself believed, "and his whole house." Previously he had believed the Lord's promise (4:50); now he believed in the Lord's person.

In closing the account of this miracle, John calls it "the second miracle [sign] that Jesus did, when he was come out of Judaea into Galilee." It was not, of course, the second miracle Jesus performed. It was the second of John's selected signs and, like the first one, was performed in Galilee, in Cana.

Section 2. His Deity Is Disputed (5:1–10:42)

I. THE IMPACT OF HIS LIFE (5:1–6:71)

The Lord has presented himself as messiah to representatives of the Hebrew nation in Jerusalem, Judea, Samaria, and Galilee, with a mixed reception.

A. In Urban Jerusalem (5:1-47)

John turns now to the conflict that begins in Jerusalem and does not end until the blind nation has put its messiah to death.

1. The Impotent Man Challenged (5:1-15)

The Lord now sought out a man he intended to heal, and healed him, deliberately, on the sabbath day. This was a clear challenge to Jewish traditional religion, and therefore a stumbling block to the Jews' acceptance of the more spiritual aspects of his life and teaching.

In chapter 5 the conflict is centered in urban Jerusalem; in chapter 6 the conflict is centered in rural Galilee. The conflict in chapter 5 is centered around two challenges: the Lord's challenge to the impotent man (5:1-15) which was followed by the Lord's challenge to the impenitent men (5:16-47) who questioned his right to do as he did on the sabbath.

We look, first, at *the multitude* (5:1-4). John notes that this particular miracle took place at the time of "a feast of the Jews." There are a variety of views as to which feast is meant. Some take the view that it was the feast of Purim (March) or Passover (April) or Pentecost. One attractive view is that the feast is the feast of trumpets (the new moon of September), which heralded the new year. The Jews believed that on this day the Lord gave the law to Moses, on this day he created the world.

The location of the miracle was "the sheep market" or, more likely, the sheep gate. Of course, Jerusalem was probably already in ruins by the time John wrote, but he envisioned the scene as it was and how he remembered it. The sheep gate was in the northern wall of Jerusalem not far from the northeast corner (Nehemiah 3:1,32; 12:39).

Near here was a pool called Bethesda. The name has been variously translated as "house of mercy," "house of the portico," "house of the olive," and "house of the outpouring." It seems that there were two adjacent pools and the area that enclosed them was marked by four covered colonnades, with another one centered between the two pools. These formed cloisters, or covered alcoves, around the pool, in the shelter of which large numbers of sick people congregated. Some who have visited the area have described the waters as having a reddish color, probably from deposits of iron or other chemicals. The pool had the kind of reputation associated nowadays with a healing spa.

From time to time the water was "troubled" (5:4). There is some doubt about the validity of this verse. Perhaps it reflects the popular explanation of the time for the periodic disturbance of the water. That something happened periodically is evidenced by the fact that all kinds of sick people waited by the pool, watching for the first sign of the occurrence. The popular belief was that whoever managed to jump in first, when the pool was agitated, received healing of whatever disease he or she had.

The twin pools were part of an extensive reservoir system. Water was conducted into the pools from "Solomon's Pools" located southwest of Bethlehem. Probably, however, the pools also received an intermittent influx of water from some other natural spring.

Jesus knew all about this place and all about the people who thronged around. He knew the popular legends attached to the pool. He knew every person there, and all their hopes, frustrations, disappointments, and their anticipation.

That multitude represented humankind. There the sufferers lay, waiting, believing, despairing. There they were brought, there they were left—lying at the gates of a dead religion, so to speak—hoping against hope, bolstering flagging beliefs, passed by priest and people alike, longing for some kind of a miracle, perhaps fearful lest their religion prove powerless to meet their greatest need.

Now we must look at *the man* (5:5). He had been there a very long time. John says it was thirty-eight years, half a lifetime. It may be he had been brought there in his teens and left there to make the best of things. We can imagine how hope deferred had made his heart sick, how his expectations during his first months at the pool had given way to despair and then to dull acceptance of his fate. One by one, with the passing of years, his friends had left him. Now he was abandoned, evidently paralyzed. Unable to move, he had become a fixture. Days came and went; days became months; months became years. Others, stronger and more agile than he, were always ahead of him when the waters were "troubled." Yet he clung to his pathetic belief in the miraculous healing power of the pool.

But it was not for him. As for the thought that some priest or prophet would offer to help him into the pool—well, he knew enough about organized religion by now to know that it had its forms and rituals, its attendants, ministers, and devotees. But much good that was ever likely to do him.

How can we measure the misery of this man? He had no friends, no family. His companions were life's victims: blind people, lame people, people withered up inside and out. All their hopes had shrunk to the chance they had of outsmarting the others and being first in the pool. There would be the usual jockeying for position, all the intensity of people obsessed with their own physical condition and their pathetic hope of a healing; the sight, the stench of it all, must have been depressing. Here was institutionalized misery, unending poverty. Because this man could not work, cynicism no doubt had taken root in his mind. He had almost given up hope. He would watch the new arrivals, see how the others eyed them, made sure they were pushed to the back, or, if one was still too strong for that, see how they eyed that person with hatred and cursed him as a rival.

Had this man heard of Jesus? Had news of the healer from Nazareth filtered into this enclave of misery? Surely so. But, if this Jesus was that great a healer, why didn't he come here and heal them all?

Then one day Jesus came. Our attention is directed to *the master* (5:6-15) and to *the situation* (5:6-9a). The Lord "saw him" lying there, and knew all about him. He knew how long he had been there. He did not need to ask—just as he knew all about Nathanael and the woman at the well. The man's heart, character, and history were open to him.

Jesus then put the vital question to him: "Wilt thou be made whole?" Whatever may or may not be said about the sovereignty of God in human salvation, one thing is sure. The human will plays its part. Divine omnipotence never violates the sanctity of the will. God does not ravish; he woos. The Lord will neither heal nor save people against their will. And so the question was put to the man. It might well be that, having been so long in that situation, he had come to terms with it, had so acquiesced to it that he no longer wanted to face the challenge and competition of normal life. Perhaps, by now his place by the pool of Bethesda had so become the focus of his life that he had no will to change.

The man's answer showed at once that the delay in his healing was no fault of his. He had given up hope of being first into the pool, but if he had someone to help him, his hope would soon revive. It was lack of opportunity, not lack of will, that kept him where he was. There are many, in desperate need of salvation, who nonetheless are content to remain in their sin. So the question comes: "Wilt thou be made whole?"

The Lord, however, had a better answer than chance dependence on a cure that was half mythical and questionably reliable. "Rise, take up thy bed, and walk," he said. The man's "bed" was a light mattress or cotton quilt which could easily be rolled up and carried away.

The Lord spoke, with divine authority and with enabling power, directly to this man's will. It never occurred to him to disobey what, on reflection, must have seemed an impossible command. Faith surged in his soul, ability to respond flooded into his paralyzed limbs. He did what he was told and immediately "was made whole, and took up his bed and walked" (5:9). The Lord's word for "walk" was *peripateo,* which literally means "to walk about." Evidently the Lord wanted people to see this man. His healing was a sign. It is astonishing that there was not an immediate stampede to Jesus by all the other sick ones.

"And on the same day was the sabbath," John adds. There was no reason why the Lord could not have healed this man the day before or the day after. He chose to do it on the sabbath and then told the man "to walk about," carrying his bed, despite the sabbath.

Thus our attention is directed from the situation to *the sabbath* (5:9b-15). We note *the man's intelligence* (5:9b-11). It was not long before "the Jews" (the Jewish rulers) indignantly challenged him. "It is the sabbath day: it is not lawful for thee to carry thy bed" (5:10). The Lord did not tell this man to break the sabbath, just to defy a traditional religious scruple about the sabbath.

The rabbis had hedged the sabbath around with dozens of rules and regulations. They had turned sabbath-keeping into a chore. What God had ordained to be a blessing they had converted into a burden. Rule number thirty-nine forbade the carrying of a load from one dwelling to another. According to them, the man should either have stayed where he was until the sabbath was over (as though the man was not heartily sick of the place) or else should have left his bed there, taking a chance on its being stolen (which would be unthinkable for such a poor man). Jesus had more sense and more sympathy. He knew that this newly healed man, with legs eager for exercise, needed to walk. He mandated the obvious solution: "Take up your bed— and walk!" "And never mind the sabbath," he might have added. "The sabbath was my idea, not theirs."

When challenged by the religious authorities, the healed man showed his intelligence: "He that made me whole, the same said unto me, Take up thy bed and walk." It was obvious to him, if not to them, that the authority of the one who had healed him was superior to theirs. Surely a man who could heal with a single phrase must have some kind of understanding with God, which the religious authorities in Jerusalem did not have. This man had waited thirty-eight years and they had done nothing for him—nothing at all. They certainly had not demonstrated the kind of compassion or authority this unknown healer had demonstrated.

We note, also, *the man's ignorance* (5:12-13). He did not know who his benefactor was. And he said so, when challenged by the Jews. The authorities wanted to transfer their ire to the one who had dared to issue such a command. Nor could the healed man point out his benefactor, "For Jesus had conveyed himself away, a multitude being in that place" (5:13). The Lord had no intention of leaving this man in the lurch. He was simply following his usual policy of avoiding publicity. The man was not to be left in ignorance long.

We see *the man's innocence* (5:14-15). The Lord later found him in the temple, a good sign in itself, and absolved him of guilt. This man did not know where to find Jesus, but he knew where to find God. The man had gone to God's house to give thanks for his healing, or so it would seem.

But if the man did not know where to find Jesus, the Lord knew where to find him. He sought him out. He had something to say to him that had to be said. There was some unrevealed connection between this man's sickness and his sin. The Lord had healing for the one and forgiveness for the other. But the Lord never condoned sin. He issued a warning: "Behold, thou art made whole: sin no more, lest a worse thing come unto thee" (5:14). It is sobering to realize that sin could produce a worse condition than the one that had already overtaken this man. His sin, whatever it was, had overtaken him in his youth. It had robbed him of the best years of his life, and had left him a paralytic right on into late middle age.

Many human woes are the direct result of sin. In our day terrible diseases lurk in waiting for the promiscuous person and the pervert. It may be that many other ills could be directly traced to sin if we had all the facts.

Jesus left the man with his past forgiven and a new innocence awaiting him on the threshold of his future. He began life anew without guilt—and without guile.

The Lord had talked to the man about his sin as no one had ever talked to him about it before. The light dawned. The man was Jesus! With a complete lack of guile the man went back to the Jews to tell them that it was Jesus who had made him whole (5:15). He did not say that it was Jesus who had told him to carry his bed on the sabbath. He told them Jesus had made him whole, giving honor to his new-found Lord. Perhaps he thought that the name of Jesus would be enough to silence his critics. He was wrong. But we give him credit for being honestly wrong.

2. The Impenitent Men Challenged (5:16-47)

The healing of the impotent man on the sabbath and the subsequent identification by the man of Jesus as his benefactor turned the wrathful attention of the authorities on Jesus. That is what Jesus had intended should happen. He was about to challenge rabbinical traditions and soon turned the tables on them. Their attack on him became the ground for his outright challenge of their impenitence.

The section divides into three. We have the indictment against Jesus raised (5:16), then refuted (5:17-38), and then reversed (5:39-47).

The indictment raised (5:16) against Jesus was simply that, by healing the paralyzed man on the sabbath, he had profaned the sabbath. Further, by telling the man to walk about carrying his bed, he had aggravated his offense against the sabbath. The Lord had thrown down the gauntlet. They picked it up and threw it in his face. They "persecuted" Jesus and sought to slay him, John says. This was the opening barrage in a battle that would not end until he was crucified about a year and a half later.

Next we have *the indictment refuted* (5:17-38). The Lord denied that he had broken the sabbath. There follows one of those long, complex interchanges of charge and countercharge so characteristic of John's gospel. The Lord advanced three witnesses to his innocence of the charge brought against him: *the witness of his Father* (5:17-32), of his forerunner (5:33-35), and of his fruits (5:36-38). We begin here with the first of these. The underlying thought in the Lord's defense of his own behavior is that he had not desecrated the sabbath. Rather, they had distorted the sabbath. It was their beliefs, not his behavior, that were at fault. He called his Father to witness.

The Lord first spoke of *the Father and the sabbath* (5:17-18). It shook the Jews to the core of their being to hear this man refer to God as his Father in the most intimate and absolute of terms. "My Father worketh hitherto, and I work," he said, putting his own activity on a par with the activity of God (5:17). The Jewish sabbath was a divine and beneficent provision of rest, provided in the Decalogue (Exodus 20:8-11), based on God's creation rest (Genesis 2:1-3) and intended to give God's people a day for relaxation and rest. As far as God's sabbath rest was concerned, that rest was not the rest of inaction but the rest of divine satisfaction in a work well done. God's sabbath was soon broken by the introduction of sin into this world. God's creative rest having been thus disturbed, he began a new work, a redemptive work. That work was still going on, and Jesus was very much a part of it. That broken man by the pool of Bethesda was a prime exhibit of the ruin that sin had brought into the world. The healing of that man on the sabbath was part of God's work in this world.

The Jews ignored the part about God working and seized on the fact that the Lord had plainly made himself God's equal (5:18). "Therefore the Jews sought the more to kill him, because he not only had broken the sabbath, but said that God was his Father, making himself equal with God." The Jews rightly read the Lord's claims. He claimed to have the right to abolish the law of the sabbath because he, as coequal with God the Father, was his coworker in this world. From the point of view of these Jews, a more damning claim could not have been made. They were more determined than ever to kill him. That murder was three times attempted (John 5:17; 8:58-59; 10:30-31) and was finally accomplished (Mark 14:61-64). It was solely on the grounds that Jesus claimed to be God, something the Jews disbelieved and something John in his gospel is determined to demonstrate.

The Lord spoke next of *the Father and the Son* (5:19-24). The rage of the Jews at his claim to be equal with God did not deter the Lord. He was "the truth" and did not shrink from proclaiming that truth. He spoke now of the unique relationship he had with the Father. There was, for instance, the matter of *the Lord's jurisdiction* (5:19-21), the special sphere of authority in which he operated. Within this sphere there were things he could do and things he could not do. All was governed by the uniqueness of the relation of the three persons within the godhead.

For instance, as Son, there was *the question of his loyalty* (5:19) within the godhead, the loyalty of the Son to the Father (5:19). He said, "Verily, verily [we should note this solemn affirmation], I say unto you, The Son can do nothing of himself, but what he seeth the Father do: for what things soever he doeth, these also doeth the Son likewise." There was no independence, no friction, between the members of the godhead. But there was more to it than that. The Son of God had become the Son of man.

And, as man, though he still possessed all the attributes and properties of deity, he did not use them except at the behest of the Father. That is what is meant by the statement, "The Son can do nothing of himself." The thought of acting in independence of God was a foreign thought, a sinful thought, a satanic thought—the thought at the heart of sin. Satan had used this thought both in the temptation of Adam and Eve and in the temptation of the Lord in the wilderness.

The Lord could have put it like this: "While I, as God, am never anything less than God, so I, as man, am never anything more than man." He was here to make all that he was as man available to all that the Father was as God, so that all that the Father was as God might be available to all that he was as man. Independence was impossible. Perfect deity was enshrined in perfect humanity. This was something Jesus' opponents never grasped.

Let us think further of the awesome claims made by our Lord in this verse. He said he did the things he saw the Father do: "For what things soever he doeth, these also doeth the Son likewise" (5:19).

This means that to creation's remotest bounds, in the godhead's most distant and secret operations and councils, the Son knows what the godhead is doing. He knows it, not because this knowledge is communicated to him, but because he has an innate consciousness of it. The Father shows the Son all things—therefore the Son must have a mind coextensive with the mind of God, the mind of omniscience, in order to grasp what is being shown.

Perhaps an illustration will help. It is said that the mathematics of Einstein's theory of relativity are so difficult that they are understood by only a small number of scientists. When someone asked nuclear physicist Sir Arthur Eddington if it was true that only three people really understood the subject, the famous scientist replied, "I'm trying to think who the third person could be!" Well, Jesus knew. He invented those mathematics and all the concepts involved in them.

The Lord, even while on this earth, was omniscient.

There was the question not only of loyalty within the godhead but also of *the question of his love* (5:20): "For the Father loveth the Son, and sheweth him all things that himself doeth: and he will shew him greater works than these, that ye may marvel." The unity within the godhead is the unity of perfect love. The word for "love" is *phileo,* the word for ordinary love, the word that denotes personal affection, brotherly love, everyday, down-to-earth love, homey love.

This love enabled the Father to show the Son things he could show to no one else, and it enabled the Son to see things no one else could see. He looked at the man at the pool of Bethesda, for instance, and then he looked at the Father. The Father looked at the Son, and then at the man. So, sabbath or not, the Son, having seen the Father's approval, healed the man. Did this healing astonish the Jews? They would soon see greater wonders.

There were not only loyalty and love—there was *the question of his life* (5:21). "For as the Father raiseth up the dead, and quickeneth them; even so the Son quickeneth whom he will." The Lord claimed absolute power over the dead. He proved he had such power by raising three people from the dead. The Lord did not merely claim to be God's instrument for raising the dead, as, for instance, Elijah and Elisha. He claimed to be absolute Lord of the dead, with the right to raise them not just to physical life but to eternal life. It is hard to see how anyone could maintain that Jesus did not claim to be God. He did.

This, then, was the Lord's jurisdiction. His power and authority were coequal and coextensive with that of the Father. But following from all this was the matter of *the Lord's judgment* (5:22-24).

In the first place, the Son has been given *absolute monopoly* in the matter of judgment (5:22-23). The Lord has absolute power of life and death: "For the Father judgeth no man, but hath committed all judgment unto the Son: that all men should honor the Son, even as they honor the Father."

The fact that the Lord Jesus is the universal judge means that he has personal knowledge of all the countless human beings in all the ages of history. He has detailed acquaintance with the endless variety of circumstances of each and every individual. He knows the character of each one of us. He knows our motives, opportunities, hidden passions, mental ability, thoughts, desires, words, acts. He knows the lasting influence for better or for worse of our every act and look. Moreover, he has a perfect grasp of all the laws of God by which to judge the world. And he has the absolute right to pass eternal sentence, with no court of appeal and with no cases missed. In other words, the Lord was claiming, in no uncertain terms, to be God over all.

The purpose of this is to ensure that all people honor the Son even as they honor the Father. The Jews thought they honored God, but they dishonored Christ. The Lord put the lie to their self-deception: "He that honoreth not the Son honoreth not the Father which hath sent him."

Along with the Lord's absolute monopoly of judgment, however, is the Lord's *abundant mercy* (5:24) in judgment. Here we come across one of those great gospel texts so characteristic of John: "Verily, verily, I say unto you, He that heareth my word, and believeth on him that sent me, hath everlasting life and shall not come into condemnation; but is passed from death unto life."

We who believe in the Lord Jesus do not have to wait until we are dead and arraigned before the supreme court of the universe to find out what the verdict will be. We need only to consult our own hearts and this verse to find out now. All depends on whether or not we have heard the word of Christ and put our trust in him.

The Lord is still refuting the charge that he had no right to act as he did on the sabbath, and he is still calling on his Father as his witness. He has spoken of the Father and the sabbath, and the Father and the Son. Now he talks about *the Father and the sepulcher* (5:25-32). For, of all the issues that face humankind, none is more relevant, more pressing, more terrifying, than the issue of death.

The Lord draws our attention to *two realms* (5:25-26). He points, first, to *the Son's inherent lordship over the grave* (5:25): "Verily, verily, I say unto you, The hour is coming and now is, when the dead shall hear the voice of the Son of God: and they that hear shall live."

Even before his resurrection the Lord Jesus claimed to have power to raise the dead. This was no fantastic claim of a wild-eyed religious enthusiast. This was the sober statement of one who was God manifest in flesh, one who proceeded to demonstrate his ability to do what he said. When he spoke these words, there might perhaps have been some excuse for skepticism— not much perhaps because Jesus had already performed a number of notable miracles. He had changed water into wine (2:1-11) and he had healed a nobleman's son (4:46-54). He had healed a man possessed of an unclean spirit in the synagogue of Capernaum; he had healed Peter's mother-in-law and others (Luke 4:31-41). He had cleansed a leper and healed a paralytic (Luke 5:12-26). And he had just healed the man whose hopeless case had been evident for thirty-eight years—in itself an astonishing feat of power.

These are miracles that are recorded. There were others. But he had not yet raised the dead. So we can, perhaps, grant the Jews a few raised eyebrows when Jesus claimed to have this, the greatest of all powers, the power to raise the dead. There would be less excuse when, within a couple of months, he raised the son of the widow (Luke 7:11-17), and less still when about six months later he raised Jairus's daughter (Luke 8:41-56), and none whatsoever after the raising of Lazarus (John 11).

The Lord's claim, however, was far more comprehensive. The words "the hour" are better translated "an hour." What we have is a figure of speech (synecdoche) by which a part is put for the whole (as, for instance, in Matthew 27:4 where Judas said, "I have betrayed the innocent blood," meaning by "blood" the whole person). Here, the phrase "an hour is coming, and now is, when the dead shall hear the voice of the Son of God: and they that hear shall live," indicates a definite and special time. The Lord could say, concerning this definite and special time of resurrection, that it was not only coming but that it "now is" because, had the nation repented and received him as Savior and sovereign, "all that the prophets had spoken" would have been speeded up and fulfilled at that time. Peter hints at this in his pentecostal sermon (Acts 3:19-21).

The Lord's words, however, are not to be restricted to the coming literal resurrection of dead people from their graves at the sound of his voice—in itself a comprehensive claim to deity—but they include the giving of the life of God to people, spiritually dead, who likewise hear his voice. This is brought out emphatically, as we shall see, in the Lord's words to Martha at the time of the raising of Lazarus (11:25).

All this seems to have been received in stunned silence by the Jewish authorities. Indeed, they do not seem to have interrupted the Lord at all, from the time he began his defense of his sabbath-day activities (5:17) to the time he finished (5:47) except for a gesture of hostility at the beginning (5:18).

Having thus claimed his authority over one realm, the grave, the Lord now asserted his authority in another realm, *the Son's inherent life within the godhead* (5:26): "For as the Father hath life in himself; so hath he given to the Son to have life in himself." The tense of the verb carries us back beyond the beginning of time. We have life because we received it from our parents, who received it from their parents. Life is not spontaneously generated. There can be no life without antecedent life. Life is the monopoly of God. All the abundant varieties of life we discern on this planet are his invention. Each form of life is transmitted by divine law, each kind "after its kind"—as is so emphatically declared in Genesis 1, where the expression occurs ten times.

But the life the Lord Jesus has is not like that at all. He is "the only begotten of the Father" (1:14), begotten but not created. The Father has bestowed on the Son the divine characteristic of having life in himself: eternal, uncreated life. The very terms *Father* and *Son* imply coexistence. For instance, when my first child was born, I became a father. Before that time I was not a father. My fatherhood originated at the same time as the child's relationship to me originated. God could not be the Father without the Son; the Son could not be the Son without the Father. The Father and the Son enjoy the same kind of life.

We cannot grasp the eternal dimension because we are creatures of a time dimension. We express our mode of existence in three tenses of time. We say, "I was, I am, I will be." God does not express himself like that at all. He says, "I am, I am, I am." Because of our time-space limitation we cannot grasp the eternal nature of the godhead. We cannot comprehend one who had no beginning, one who is eternal and uncreated, one who has life in himself. Whatever it means for the Father to have life in himself, it means for the Son to have life in himself. The fatherhood of God the Father and the sonship of God the Son are of equal, eternal duration. Yet in some way, beyond human comprehension, the Father, as the Father, imparts the right to have life in himself to the Son, as the Son, and the Son as the Son receives the right to have life in himself from the Father as the Father. Neither the Father nor the Son was created. Neither the Father nor the Son existed without the other. The Father is not anymore God than the Son, and the Son is not any less God than the Father. Yet within the godhead itself there is a divine order, an eternal Father-Son love relationship. We obviously cannot explain it—but we had better believe it, because that is the way it is. The ultimate secret of the universe is God—one God, existing in three persons: Father, Son, and Holy Spirit. It is as such that God has been revealed in the Bible. By claiming to have "life in himself" the Lord Jesus was claiming to be the Son of God as emphatically, uncompromisingly, and clearly as language allows.

Now the Lord drew the attention of his silent auditors to *two resurrections* (5:27-32). We have, first, *the triumphant voice of the Son* (5:27-29). The Son of God has life in himself and, along with it, the power to impart life. He has been given the sole right to judge the world (5:22). But now his name is changed from "Son of God" to "Son of man." "And [the Father] hath given him authority to execute judgment also, because he is the Son of man" (5:27). The Lord is not going to judge mankind as God but as man, as one who has entered into human life, who has experienced its joys and sorrows, hopes and fears, trials and temptations, ups and downs—its daily round, its progress from cradle to grave. It is not to some alien angelic being untouched by the feeling of our infirmities that God has committed the judgment of the world. It is not even to Jesus as Son of God, in all his omniscient genius, but remote, as far removed from us as the creator is from the creature. He has committed judgment to a man, and there is something particularly appropriate about that.

Jesus has been here. He knows what it's like to be a boy, to be raised in a poor man's home, to work at the carpenter's bench. He knows what it's like to be tired, hungry, thirsty, and in pain. He has experienced the pressures and perils of life. He has been tempted with advancement and by adversity. He knows what it's like to have both friends and enemies. He has known both popularity and persecution. He has tasted the lash; he has experienced betrayal, scorn, and hate. He does not need to be told what it's like to be human, subject to human limitations. He knows, even though he is now seated on his Father's throne on high.

So there is something particularly fitting about his being given the authority to execute judgment.

Judgment is coming. The coming day of resurrection will be followed by a day of judgment. At this point in the process of divine revelation, the two resurrections and the two chief judgments are telescoped together: "Marvel not at this: for the hour is coming, in the which all that are in the graves shall hear his voice, And shall come forth; they that have done good, unto the resurrection of life; and they that have done evil, unto the resurrection of damnation" (5:28-29).

There are two resurrections. The first resurrection is "unto life." It is made up of saved people. It is in three stages. First came the firstfruits (Matthew 27:52-58). The full harvest comes next (1 Thessalonians 4:13-18). In due course will come the gleanings, the resurrection of various people who trust Christ after the rapture of the church in the period of the great tribulation, possibly including as well Old Testament believers not included in the firstfruits. There will be a judgment for believers. Paul says, "We must all appear before the judgment seat of Christ" (2 Corinthians 5:10). The question of personal salvation will not arise at this assize—this is "a resurrection of life": those appearing there have long since settled the matter of eternal life by their faith in Christ. What is at issue at this judgment seat is that of rebuke or reward, gain or loss, based on one's works since entering into new life (1 Corinthians 3:10-15).

The second resurrection is "unto damnation." It takes place at the end of the millennial reign of Christ. Those raised at that time will be the wicked dead of all ages. They will be summoned to the great white throne and will have no hope. Their names are not written in the lamb's book of life. For them there awaits "the lake of fire" (Revelation 20:11-15). (For a more complete discussion of these and other judgments, see John Phillips, *Bible Explorer's Guide*, Neptune, N.J.: Loizeaux Brothers, 1987.)

The point that John is making here, in his gospel, is that the Lord Jesus is the judge and that he acts as judge in his character as Son of man. The Jews, of course, were familiar with Daniel's prophecy of this (Daniel 7:9-14).

John has not quite finished with this aspect of the Lord's defense, the fact that the Father has invested in the Son all matters issuing out of the question of death. He has mentioned the triumphant voice of the Son, the voice that awakes the dead. Now he mentions *the total vindication of the Son* (5:30-32) by the Father. There are two kinds of testimony—first, the *autobiographical testimony* (5:30). The Lord said, "I can of mine own self do nothing: as I hear, I judge: and my judgment is just; because I seek not mine own will, but the will of the Father which hath sent me."

As Son of God, the Son did nothing of himself, nothing self-determined. That would be impossible. There is perfect harmony within the godhead. As Son of man, the role in which the Lord acts as judge, the statement raises other issues. As God, the Lord did not have to obey. Whom does God obey? God obeys no one. God is pre-existent and self-existent. He is omniscient and omnipotent. But when the Son of God became the Son of man he learned to do what God had never done. He "learned obedience" (Hebrews 5:8). Luke says of the boy Jesus that he went back to Nazareth with Joseph and Mary "and was subject unto them" (Luke 2:51).

When Jesus said, "I can of mine own self do nothing," he was referring to himself primarily as Son of man. It is an amazing statement. He was God behaving as man, perfect man. He learned, as man, to obey God, in order to demonstrate to man the truth about man: that man can do nothing without God.

But, if the Lord Jesus was always, as man, totally available to his Father, as God, then his Father, as God, was always totally available to his Son, as man. So the Lord goes on to say, "As I hear, I judge." As we have already seen, the mind of the Lord Jesus was coextensive with the mind of God. His judgment is identical with the judgment of God. Hence his judgment is flawless, omniscient, just. He does not seek his own will, only the will of the Father who sent him into this world. That is his autobiographical testimony.

But there is *another testimony* (5:31-32). "If I bear witness of myself, my witness is not true. There is another that beareth witness of me; and I know that the witness which he witnesseth of me is true." The word for "another" is *allos*, indicating another of the same kind. The Lord says that if he were simply testifying to himself his testimony would be invalid. A person does not witness his own signature. In any case, Jewish law required at least two witnesses. The "other" who gave certifying testimony to the Lord Jesus was either his Father or the Holy Spirit. When the Lord added, "I know that the witness he witnesses of me is true," he used the word *oida*. The absolute knowledge spoken of must be distinguished from the knowledge of experience.

The Lord is still refuting the Jewish claim that he had profaned the sabbath. He has called on his Father to be his witness. Now he calls on *the witness of his forerunner* (5:33-35), John the baptist.

The Jews might have found themselves out of their depth when the Lord appealed to God, his Father, as giving him the right to act as he did. They certainly were not prepared to admit that God was his Father. Far from convincing them, the claim infuriated them. The fact that it was true made no difference. They did not believe it.

But the appeal to John the baptist was different. That was answerable. "Ye sent unto John," said Jesus (the word *ye* is emphatic), "and he bare witness unto the truth." John the baptist's impact on the nation was tremendous. Everyone had heard of him. His message was clear: "The kingdom of God is at hand! The king is coming!" Thousands of people had responded to his message and had accepted the baptism of repentance at his hands. National excitement had run high. Popular expectation of the imminent appearance of the messiah reached a peak.

Then John announced Jesus to be that messiah, to be the lamb of God (1:29), and the Son of God (1:34). When John introduced Jesus as the Son of God this was not mere rhetoric or hyperbole. It was a sober statement of fact. Since the bulk of the nation acknowledged that John was a prophet, there was no more to be said. Either John was deluded or deceived, or was divinely inspired. Not even the authorities would have dared challenge John's prophetic call.

So Jesus said to the Jews, "Ye sent unto John, and he bare witness of the truth." John's witness should have been convincing. "But," the Lord added, "I receive not testimony from man: but these things I say, that ye [even ye] might be saved." The word *I* is emphatic, as is the word *ye*. The testimony of John the baptist was adequate for them, but the Lord himself had testimony from a much higher source than that which derived from a prophet, however illustrious and illuminated. Still, in hope of their salvation, the Lord accepted even the lesser witness of John.

John bore witness to the truth. Indeed, he was "a burning and a shining light." John, at best, was a lamp, one, indeed, which for a while the people were happy enough to have. But John's lamp had been extinguished by Herod. Not, however, before he had shed sufficient light on the times for the people to be able to recognize the one of whom he had so often spoken. The joy the Jews had in John's stirring promise of a soon-coming messiah did not last for long. The rulers were already disillusioned. They had anticipated a militant messiah, not someone like Jesus whose miracles they discounted, whose message they disbelieved, whose ministry they denied, and whose method they despised.

The Lord, however, had still another witness to his claims, *the witness of his fruits* (5:36-38). Let them look at the fruits of his life and ministry. He held those fruits up before them for close scrutiny. He mentions *the sufficient scope of his works* (5:36). "The works which the Father hath given me to finish, the same works that I do, bear witness of me, that the Father hath sent me." John uses the expression "the works" in his gospel to depict both the natural and the supernatural in the life of Christ—all ministered to the same end of demonstrating deity in humanity. The "many works" of Jesus (7:3; 9:3; 10:25,32,37; 14:10; 15:24) were all part of the one "work" he had come to do. All added up to an impressive proof that he had been sent into this world by the Father, not just born into this world like other people. So many and so varied were the works of the Lord Jesus, exhibiting his divine power over the elements, over inanimate objects and the ordinary forces of nature, over demons and disease, even over death itself, that unbelief was wholly without excuse.

The Lord adds a word about *the secret source of his works* (5:37-38). All came from his Father. We have already seen that the Lord Jesus never failed to bring his Father into the picture. The Jews, he said, did not know his Father: "Ye have neither heard his voice at any time, nor seen his shape. And ye have not his word abiding in you: for whom he hath sent, him ye believe not." John the baptist, the last in the line of the Old Testament prophets, had audibly heard the Father speak and had visibly seen the Holy Spirit (in form as a dove), but such manifestations of the deity were rare, and certainly the Jews had received no such divine visitations. All they would audibly hear of God or visibly see of God was before them, audibly and visibly, in the person of Jesus, the second person of the godhead.

These religious rulers of the Jews, so smug and complacent in their rites and rituals, feasts and fasts, sacrifices and sabbaths, traditions and teachings, so distorted and disbelieved the Bible that they were strangers to the truth of God: the truth embodied in Christ. God's word did not abide in them. Had they been really acquainted with all that the prophets had spoken (Luke 24:25-27) they would readily have recognized Jesus. But "whom [the Father] hath sent, him ye believe not."

The Lord has defended himself. The Jews did not like what he said, but it had to be said—and more. We have seen the indictment refuted by the Lord. We now see *the indictment reversed* (5:39-47) by the Lord. He lays bare the blindness, unbelief, and folly of the Jewish religious leaders. We will see that they never forgave him for the painful surgery he now performed on their souls.

We note, first, *the Lord's protest* (5:39-42). His first challenge to the Jews was that they should *search their Scriptures* (5:40-42): "Search the scriptures," he said, "for in them ye think ye have eternal life: and they are they which testify of me." The Jews did indeed search the Scriptures, after a fashion. Their zeal was such that they counted every letter, weighed every word, scrutinized every sentence. They hoped to find eternal life in the Scriptures, but they completely missed the mark. The Lord had already said to them that they did not have God's word abiding in them. All their study was in vain. They subjected each verse and word to painstaking investigation and came up with incorrect conclusions. They thought that because they had an intellectual knowledge of what they considered to be truth, they did not need anything more.

"Search the scriptures," Jesus said. The word he used was *ereunao*, a word used of a lion or a hound tracking by scent. He was telling them to go back and conduct another search, to retrace their tracks, pick up the proper scent, follow the trail to where it really led—to him. "They are they which testify of me," he said. To search the Scriptures and miss Christ is the greatest tragedy of all. There are millions who do it, however, to this very day. We must search the Scriptures. We are commanded to search the Scriptures. But the Bible is not an end in itself; it is a means to an end. It is a signpost pointing in the direction in which we must go, pointing directly to Christ. What folly to be taken up with measuring and studying and admiring the signpost and not to get its message and do what it says.

This is an important verse. Our Lord's appeal was always to the Scriptures. He never appealed to the body of Jewish tradition growing up around the Bible, which in time would become known as the Talmud and which was already well on the way not only to obscuring the Scriptures but also to replacing them. The Lord had nothing but the sharpest criticism for what the

Jews called "the oral law," for their traditions and erroneous interpretations. But he had nothing but the highest respect and love for the Old Testament Scriptures, which he knew enshrined the message of God. He held them in special sanctity, believed them implicitly, quoted them constantly, accepted their inspiration, infallibility, and inerrancy, and obeyed them implicitly.

Having directed the Jewish religious leaders back to the Scriptures, the Lord went on to tell them to *search their souls* (5:40-42). Their spiritual peril was dire. Although the purpose of the Bible is to direct people to himself, the Lord had to say to these Jews, "And ye will not come to me, that ye might have life" (5:40). We again note the use of the polysyndeton: "Search the scriptures; for in them ye think ye have eternal life: and they are they which testify of me. And ye will not come to me, that ye might have life." The use of the conjunction *and* marks each step in the sad process. What could be worse than to have access to the Scriptures, to study the Scriptures, yet to miss Christ and eternal life after all?

There is not only a mental problem involved in human unbelief. It was not just that their Bible study was defective and led to inadequate or erroneous conclusions. There is a volitional problem involved in human unbelief. "Ye will not come to me, that ye might have life." It is not so much a case of "I can't believe"—there was adequate evidence that the Lord was all he claimed to be; it is a case of "I won't believe." The will is where the battle is fought. It was so with the Jews. It is always so.

The Jews then were wholly unresponsive. They were also wholly unregenerate. "I receive not honor from men," Jesus said. "But I know you, that ye have not the love of God in you" (5:41-42). The problem was, of course, that these people had preconceived ideas about the messiah, what he would be like and what he would do and say. When Jesus did not meet those expectations they despised him. He was not here, however, to win the kind of honor they could give.

"I know you," he said. They did not know him, but he knew them, jointly and severally, as a group and as individuals, in their public attitudes and in their most private thoughts. "Ye have not the love of God in you." His insight read the state of their souls. Had there been any love for God in their souls they would have shown it long ago by their compassion for the poor man now set free from a thirty-eight year captivity to the consequences of his sin. They would have shown it by hailing Jesus for setting him free instead of carping and criticizing because he had upset one of their beloved religious taboos.

Now comes *the Lord's prophecy* (5:43-44), and a terrible one it is. The ground of this prophecy was their rejection of him: "I am come in my Father's name, and ye receive me not" (5:43a). Truth and error are opposite sides of the same coin. To refuse the truth is to embrace a lie. This is so in any realm, not just that of religion. If a man will not listen when someone tells him the right road, he will almost inevitably take the wrong road. A person who will not accept the truth of creation believes the lie of evolution. A man who refuses to listen to a doctor who prescribes the right remedy will fall prey to one who offers him the wrong remedy. Jesus came fully credited by the Father as Israel's promised messiah. The Jews refused to accept him, and as a nation refuse to accept him still.

So comes the inevitable consequence: "If another shall come in his own name, him ye will receive." The Jews never had a false Christ until they rejected the real Christ. Then they had a whole series of pseudo-messiahs who deceived them by the thousand. But the worst has not yet happened. The day is coming when the Jewish nation will wholeheartedly endorse the coming antichrist, the one who comes in his own name.

Indeed, there is something significant in the name the antichrist will assume. In the Greek language every letter of the alphabet is a number. By substituting the letters for numbers, it is possible to assign a numeric value to any Greek word. The antichrist's name, written thus in Greek, will yield the number 666, a number associated with human failure. The significance of the Lord's statement, "If another shall come in his own name, him ye will receive," becomes even more significant when it is remembered that the name *Jesus* in Greek yields the number 888, the number eight being associated in Scripture with resurrection and a new beginning.

The Lord added an explanation for their stubborn unbelief: "How can ye believe, which receive honor one of another, and seek not the honor that cometh from God only" (5:44). At issue was the question of their inability to believe in Jesus as the Christ. The problem was, the Jews were looking to the wrong place and for the wrong kind of honor. The word is *doxa,* also used by the Lord in verse 41 in repudiating the honor of men. The word can be translated "praise" or "glory." What the Jews were looking for in the Christ was the kind of glory they gave one to another, worldly glory. They wanted a Christ who would smash the power of Rome, make Jerusalem the capital of a new world empire and them a new imperial nobility with authority over the nations. No wonder they could see no glory in Christ, one who taught them to forgive their enemies, go the second mile, and to love and pray for those who despitefully used them. What kind of messiah was that? The Lord Jesus had the honor that came from God, but they were blinded to that by their carnal notions of glory.

This long defense is concluded with *the Lord's proclamation* (5:45-47). He returns to the matter of their certain judgment for rejecting him, bringing Moses into the picture. Next to Abraham the Jews venerated Moses as the greatest saint in their catalog, as a star of the greatest magnitude in the Hebrew firmament.

He mentions *Moses' accusation of them* (5:45): "Do not think that I will accuse you to the Father: there is one that accuseth you, even Moses, in whom ye trust." The chief witness for the prosecution would be Moses, the one whose law they venerated and whose name was exalted high above all by their religious leaders. Not only was the law of Moses, which they broke repeatedly, their condemnation (Romans 2:17-29), but Moses himself would rise up in the day of judgment and condemn them for using him as their excuse to persecute Christ.

Our Lord mentions, finally, *Moses' accreditation of him* (5:46-47). He said: "For had ye believed Moses, ye would have believed me: for he wrote of me. But if ye believe not his writings, how shall ye believe my words?"—and let every liberal theologian addicted to attacking the book of Genesis make note of that. The writings of Moses were full of types that depicted Christ: the ark of Noah, the offering of Isaac, the ladder of Jacob's dream, the story of Joseph, the Passover lamb, the manna from heaven, the riven rock, the serpent on the pole, to mention just a few. The writings of Moses contained one outstanding messianic prophecy known by heart by every Jew (Deuteronomy 18:15).

Jesus could well say, "Moses wrote of me." He wrote of him repeatedly. But these people discounted all these types and prophecies of Christ. The indictment was clear, the consequence inevitable. To disbelieve the writings of Moses was to make any genuine faith in Christ impossible. Their case was hopeless if Moses, the great intercessor of the Old Testament (Exodus 32:30–33:17), became their great accuser. Their doom was sealed.

B. In Rural Galilee (6:1-71)

Chapter 6 finds us back in Galilee. It contains all that John has to say about a year's Galilean ministry in the life of the Lord. The healing of the man at the pool of Bethesda took place in the spring of A.D. 28; the feeding of the five thousand took place in the spring of A.D. 29. Some two dozen incidents recorded in the synoptic gospels are wholly ignored by John. He picks up the story after the return of the twelve from their mission to "the lost sheep of the house of Israel."

1. Christ's Claims Revealed (6:1-40)

In this long chapter the Lord's claims are revealed (6:1-40) and resented (6:41-71). His claims are revealed first *in his power* (6:1-21) and then in his preaching (6:22-40). He revealed his claims in power, first *publicly in the breaking of the bread* (6:1-15) and privately by walking on the waves (6:16-21).

We begin with the public manifestation of the Lord's claims in the miracle of the feeding of the five thousand, one of the chosen "signs" of John's gospel. Our attention is drawn, first, to *the throng* (6:1-9). The scene is the eastern shore of the sea of Galilee, called here the sea of Tiberias. Herod Antipas had recently founded a Roman city on the western shore of the lake, naming it after the Emperor Tiberius. Religious Jews refused to set foot in this more than half-pagan city. In time it gave its name to the lake.

Herod had already murdered John the baptist, and an attempt had been made by enthusiasts to use Jesus as the leader in a new revolt against Herod and Rome. That, and the return of the twelve, made a temporary retirement desirable, so Jesus entered into a boat and crossed over to the less populated side of the lake. The crowds, which dogged his footsteps, eager to see more miracles, took note of his departure and hurried around the lake. Though theirs was the longer journey they made haste and were there waiting for him when his vessel was run up on the shore. So much for his needed rest.

With the crowds still thronging all about him the Lord headed for the mountains which rise sharply to the eastern side of the lake—now known as the Golan Heights. The multitudes followed, full of eager expectation "because they saw his miracles which he did on them that were diseased," John says (6:2). The Lord found a suitable spot, where the crowds could also find a place to sit down, and seated himself while the people gathered and settled down.

"And the passover, a feast of the Jews, was nigh" (6:4). Three Passovers are mentioned in John (2:13; 6:4; 11:55). This was the second one. The Lord went up to Jerusalem for the first one and the third, but for this one he remained in Galilee. It is likely that the regular crowds who followed him may have been swelled on this occasion by the throngs of pilgrims headed for Jerusalem to keep the feast.

Thus it was that great throngs *sought him* (6:1-4). The Lord was still riding the crest of popularity in rural Galilee. The crowds also *stirred him* (6:5-9). We learn from parallel accounts in the other gospels that they stayed all day listening to his teaching. "The day began to wear away," says Luke (9:12). "The day was now far spent," says Mark (6:35). "When it was evening," says Matthew (14:15). The Lord's heart went out in tenderness for this throng which comprised five thousand men besides women and children. The children were getting tired, the disciples impatient; all were hungry. Doubtless Jesus was hungry too, though he never performed a miracle to satisfy his own needs.

The Lord saw in this situation an ideal opportunity to put his disciples to the test. "Whence shall we buy bread, that these may eat?" he said, singling out Philip. Philip came from the neighboring town of Bethsaida (1:44). It would require a merchant of no small means with stock on hand sufficient to supply the needs of such a multitude on this short notice. The Lord, of course, was testing Philip, as John hastens to record. He already knew what he intended to do (6:6).

Instead of referring the problem back to Jesus in simple faith, Philip did some mental arithmetic in view of *the scope of the problem* (6:5b-7). He was staggered. "Two hundred pennyworth of bread is not sufficient for them," he said, "that every one of them may take a little" (6:7). The crowd by this time was aware that the master had stopped teaching and was now talking to one of his disciples. Were they eagerly and expectantly looking for something to happen?

Since a working man was content with a penny as fair wages for a day's work (Matthew 20:2), Philip estimated that it would take the best part of two-thirds of a laborer's annual wages to buy the bare minimum of what would be required—and that would be by no means enough to give everyone a satisfactory meal. The entire idea of buying enough bread was ridiculous.

The number two hundred is of great significance in the Bible. As indicated here, it is the number of insufficiency. Trace it out in the story of Achan (Joshua 7:20-21) and Absalom (2 Samuel 14:26-27; 15:11), in the story of the apostate Micah of Mount Ephraim (Judges 17:1-5), and in the prophecy of the armies that will engage in battle in the end times (Revelation 9:16).

In the meantime Andrew had been looking around. He had spotted a lad (*paidarion*, "a little boy") preparing to do something about his own hunger. He had come prepared! Doubtless his mother, when giving him permission to go presumably with friends or relatives and listen to the great teacher, had packed him a little lunch. Perhaps Andrew had approached him saying: "Look, son, would you consider sharing your lunch with Jesus?" He brought the boy and his small provision along with him. Andrew, too, had been doing some mental arithmetic: "There is a lad here, which hath five barley loaves, and two small fishes: but what are they among so many?" he asked (6:9). His arithmetic was done in view of *the smallness of the provision* (6:8-9). The idea of feeding all those people was wholly illogical both to Philip and to Andrew. Barley was the food of the poor. The loaves were small flat barley wafers; the fish were about the size of sardines. The meal was barely sufficient for one small hungry boy and would have provided no more than a few mouthfuls for a hungry man.

Thus the stage was set for a miracle. There were the hungry people, thousands of them, men, women, and children. There were the worried disciples, helpless in the face of an enormous need. There stood that anonymous little boy, willing to give up his lunch for Jesus. And there stood the incarnate Son of the living God about to demonstrate what can happen when anyone is surrendered to God. We have next *the thrill* (6:10-13). Jesus took what was given to him and transformed what was given to him. First he had the people sit down ("there was much grass in the place," that detail corresponding with the date; Passover time was early in the spring. This Passover has been calculated as having fallen on April 16, A.D. 29.)

"And Jesus took the loaves; and when he had given thanks, he distributed to the disciples, and the disciples to them that were set down; and likewise of the fishes as much as they would" (6:11). There was plenty for everyone.

How did he do it? We must remember that when Jesus came down to earth he did not come to behave as God, although he was never less than God. He came to behave as though he were never more than man, God though he was. So, he did a very human thing. He took the loaves and gave thanks. He was acknowledging his human dependence on his Father. He had already stated the principle: "I can of mine own self do nothing" (5:30). He had declared, "What things soever he [the Father] doeth, these also doeth the Son likewise" (5:19). Although he was the creator, as man he was willing to let the Father be in him what he now intends the Holy Spirit to be in us: the source of all his power. On whom did the Lord Jesus count, as he prepared to perform this astounding miracle? He looked to the one to whom he gave thanks: his Father.

So the thrilling miracle took place. There was "bread enough and to spare." When everyone was full and more than full, the Lord sent the disciples through the seated ranks of the people to gather up the leftovers. "Gather up the fragments that remain, that nothing be lost" (6:12). John, who was one of the twelve kept busy that day, still marveled at the miracle: "They gathered [the fragments] together and filled twelve baskets [stout wicker baskets] with the fragments of the five barley loaves, which remained over and above unto them that had eaten" (6:13). Even when omnipotence spreads the table, God takes no pleasure in waste.

There was a sequel to all this. Our attention is directed to *the throne* (6:14-15). It did not take the people long to decide that this was the kind of king they wanted: one who would supply their material needs. "This is of a truth that prophet that should come into the world," they said (6:14). Luke adds an extra detail. He tells us that the Lord had spoken to the people that day "concerning the kingdom of God" (Luke 9:11).

They were ready then and there to make him a king. Here was a ready-made force of five thousand men, the nucleus of an army, ready to rise up and follow him to Jerusalem, to Rome, to the uttermost parts of the earth. But their vision was not his. Their concept of the kingdom was secular and material. His was spiritual. "When Jesus therefore perceived that they would come and take him by force, to make him a king, he departed again into a mountain himself alone" (6:15).

Christ's power had been seen publicly, in the breaking of the bread. Now, this power is seen *privately, in the walk upon the waves* (6:16-21). This next mighty demonstration of divine power was of a more or less private nature, though not altogether unnoticed by others (6:25). We learn from the synoptic gospels that the Lord sent the disciples away, no doubt to get them out of harm's way. He had to consider the ambition of Judas Iscariot, the impetuosity of Simon Peter, the zealotry of Simon the Canaanite, the tempers of James and John. It would never do for these disciples to fall in with the wishes of the crowd and try to force his hand into accepting a crown he did not want and had no intention of accepting. So he sent his disciples away and, by sheer force of character, sent the excited multitudes home. He headed for a more secluded spot on the mountain.

Meanwhile the disciples were no doubt talking among themselves and thinking that things were getting somewhere at last. And about time too, some of them might have felt. Going around preaching and healing sick people was all well and good but it was time for the real action to begin. Now that the master had seen the enthusiasm of the Galileans, he would be able to make his plans accordingly and lead a triumphant entry into Jerusalem, head a popular national uprising, put forth his mighty power, overthrow Rome, and bring in the kingdom.

There is something almost symbolic in the fact that "the disciples went down" to the lake. That is the only way they could go when they were so much out of fellowship with the Lord. He had deemed it advisable to send them away. So we note the *direction* (6:16-17a). They were on the way down.

They entered the small ship moored on the seashore and headed out across the lake in the direction of Capernaum where Jesus now had his home. In their self-confidence they had no thought of disaster. If there was one thing Peter could do, it was sail a boat. His fishing partners were with him. This would be a swift and easy passage to the other side. But they were about to have a sudden awakening. There was stormy weather ahead, literally and symbolically, both for them and for the cause of Christ.

We notice, too, the *darkness* (6:17b,c): "And it was now dark, and Jesus was not come to them." That is where the majority of people in this world are: alone, in the dark, without Jesus. That is a terrible place to be. They have been launched on the seas of time. They are cast on their own resources. The darkness overtakes them. And Christ is not on board their life's little vessel. There may be others with them, persons of ability in their own field, but just as much in the dark as anyone else. Terrors that are real enough in themselves can assume new dimensions of menace in the dark.

We should remember that most people in this world live and die in the dark. They are without God, without Christ in this world, and without hope in the world to come. Imagine dying in your sins never having heard of Jesus, never having heard John 3:16 or Romans 10:9. Imagine being born in heathen darkness, duped by a false religion, deprived of even a single verse of Scripture, a stranger to the grace of God.

The darkness gave way to *dread* (6:18-20). We note first *the tempest that overtook them* (6:18). "And the sea arose by reason of a great wind that blew" (6:18). Satan was behind that storm. He is "the prince of the power of the air." Angelic beings control the forces of nature (Revelation 7:1-3) and Satan himself has power over them (Job 1:9-12,16,18-19). The storm that descended without warning on the lake of Galilee was symbolic of the storms of life that overtake us on our journeys across time's uncertain seas. Those storms come upon us, often before we are aware. They do great damage, leaving ruins and wreckage behind: broken homes and broken hearts, disease and despair, death and loss. And, with so many, Christ is not on board the frail vessel.

Often thoughtless and vicious people attribute these things to God. The whole subject of good and evil coexisting in the universe, however, raises far more questions than can be answered here.

We note *the terror that overwhelmed them* (6:19). Strange to say, it was not so much the terror of howling wind and heaving waves, but of the Lord's supernatural appearance. They were about halfway across the lake, having gone "about five and twenty or thirty furlongs," John says. He had grown up on that lake, knew its dimensions by heart, and he was on board that night. From the vicinity of Bethsaida, the distance across the lake to their destination at Capernaum was about five miles. They had rowed about three.

We can imagine their terror when they saw a figure walking on the water toward them—Jesus?—his hair and garments streaming in the wind, spray blowing all about, now hidden for a moment in a valley, now striding atop a mighty billow, and all the time coming nearer and nearer. John's brief comment was, "They were afraid"—far more afraid of this unexpected phenomenon of the darkness and storm, we can be sure, than they were of the raging elements. They were used to storms at sea. Those, unwelcome as they were, hurtful as they were, could be labeled (or mislabeled) "natural phenomena." But to see someone, even their Lord, walking toward them across the wildly tossing waves was something to make the hair stand on end and the blood run cold.

Then, too, there was *the tenderness that overshadowed them* (6:20). Across the waves, above the scream of the wind, came that well-known voice with its words of reassurance: "It is I; be not afraid." His eye had seen them, his thoughts had surrounded them, his heart had gone out to them. He had not abandoned them. Although he knew all about the storm, he had not prevented it from overtaking them, although he could have— and there is a lesson in that. They were in his will. He had sent them on that voyage. He knew of those malicious, unseen powers that would seize on his seeming absence as an opportunity to do them harm. It was all part of his permissive will, all a means to an end, all intended to strengthen their faith in him and give them a greater knowledge of him. No, that storm did not overtake them by chance.

Nothing overtakes us by chance. "All things work together for good to them that love God, to them who are the called according to his purpose" (Romans 8:28).

We note also what happened to the *distance* (6:21). First "they willingly received him into the ship." The Lord never violates our human will, never intrudes, never forces himself on us. In this case, we can be sure that the disciples were glad to have him on board. We marvel at those men and women who choose to face life's treacherous seas without him.

Then John adds something astonishing: "And immediately the ship was at the land whither they went." That statement is watered down by some: "In no time the boat reached the land." The idea is, with Christ on board and in charge, all will be well; and he is such an absorbing center of attraction that the journey seems less.

I prefer to let the comment stand. The Lord annihilated distance, abolished time. I see it as another miracle, a harbinger of that life in another dimension which awaits us when our days on earth are done. He had just demonstrated his ability to defy the "natural laws" that normally regulate the way a solid passes through liquid. Nor was it a great thing for him to suspend other laws of space, matter, and time. No great thing at all—he invented those laws. Who can explain how he turned water into wine, or how he was able to cleanse leprosy with a word, or how he could bring Lazarus out of the tomb all wrapped up with grave clothes like an Egyptian mummy? So it is no great thing that, one moment the ship was three miles off shore and the next moment, immediately "the ship was at the land whither they went."

We have seen how Christ's claims are revealed in his power. Now we will consider how these claims are revealed *in his preaching* (6:22-40).

The two miracles just performed by the Lord now become the basis for a long and difficult discourse, interrupted from time to time by the questions and increasingly hostile comments of the Jews. We must not minimize the complexity of this discourse. Many misunderstood the Lord's teaching and abandoned him as a result. To this day the Roman Catholic Church bolsters one of its most daring blasphemies by appeals to this discourse. The structural analysis, if followed out step by step, will show how the parts make up the whole.

We begin with *the astonishment of the multitudes* (6:22-25). Their astonishment centered in *a missing Christ* (6:22-24a). The last the crowd had seen of this miracle-worker was the night before, when he had sent his disciples off across the lake and told them to go home. Looking back they had seen him heading for the hills. They confidently expected to reassemble the next day, find him, and doubtless try to persuade him to lead a popular revolt. But he was gone. They had seen him left behind by the disciples. There was no other boat available for him to use to cross the lake. Anyway, the violent storm of the night before would have made any attempt to cross it a hazardous if not foolhardy business. But where was he?

By the next morning other boats had landed on the eastern shore, or had been driven there by the storm, but that did not explain his disappearance. So we have, also, *a mystified crowd* (6:24b-25). They scoured the vicinity where he had last been seen, failed to find him, saw no signs of his disciples coming to get him, and eventually concluded that somehow or other he must have gone to the other side of the lake. They set off as fast as they could to find him. "And when they had found him on the other side of the sea, they said unto him: Rabbi, when camest thou hither?" (6:25). The Lord did not satisfy their curiosity.

Instead, we have *the assessment of the master* (6:26-29). First he put an unerring finger on *their carnal nature* (6:26). "Your thoughts rise no higher than your physical needs," he said. "That's why you come running after me. Even the sign I gave you was lost on you." They failed to get the message of the miracle; they did not even know that there was a message to it. All they knew was that when they went hungry he had fed them.

Once the Lord explained to them the significance of the sign, they would not like it at all. They would leave, thoroughly disappointed that he did not perform another gratifying miracle for them.

Then the Lord put his finger on *their crying need* (6:27-29). "Do not labor for the meat that perishes, but for the meat that endures to everlasting life," he said. At once this opened a discussion on the way to receive this sublime possession. We should contrast the warning "Labor not" with the promise, "that meat . . . which the Son of man shall give." This discussion in many ways parallels the Lord's conversation with the woman at the well. There it was water about which he spoke; here it is bread. In both cases he spoke in metaphors and in both cases he was misunderstood. His listeners insisted on taking his words literally.

Eternal life cannot be earned. It is not achieved by our good works. As the hymnwriter puts it:

> Not the labor of my hands
>   Can fulfill Thy Law's demands,
> Could my zeal no respite know,
>   Could my tears forever flow,
> All for sin would not atone,
>   Thou must save and Thou alone.

It is "the Son of man" who gives everlasting life, "For him hath God the Father sealed," Jesus said (6:27). The Lord carefully kept away from the term *Christ* or *messiah*. He had to defuse their nationalistic and militant hopes of yesterday. "Son of man" was a title familiar to the Jews from its Old Testament usage. It linked the Lord to their humanity, as one who knew and understood their deepest needs, but it was free from the overtones associated with the title Christ. The Lord was "sealed," that is divinely authorized at his baptism, to administer eternal life (1:32-34).

Human beings crave to do something for their salvation. Until we are born again, we feel a repugnance, born of our fallen nature, to accept salvation solely as a gift. So the Jews demanded, "What shall we do, that we might work the works of God?" (6:28). A similar spirit animated Naaman the leper. He was furious when Elisha sent word to him that all that was required was a simple act of faith: he was to dip himself in the Jordan. He was well served by his attendants, who were able to talk sense into him: "If the prophet had bid thee do some great thing, wouldest thou not have done it? how much rather then, when he saith to thee, Wash, and be clean?" (2 Kings 5:13). The unregenerate want salvation on their terms, not God's, and in some way that ministers to human pride. All false religion has its answer to the question, "What shall we do, that we might work the works of God?" "Fast!" says Islam, as it sets apart the month of Ramadan for that purpose. "Do penance," Roman Catholicism said for centuries, "earn indulgences, say masses." "Torture your body, perform prodigies of physical endurance," says Hinduism. "Keep the law according to the tradition of the elders," said the rabbis.

"Jesus answered . . . , This is the work of God, that ye believe on him whom he hath sent" (6:29). That is all God requires: faith and trust in his Son. Belief in Jesus as the Son of God and Savior is the one thing God wants from us. Irritated with that answer, the Jews demanded a sign.

Next comes *the appeal to the manna* (6:30-31). "What sign showest thou?" they demanded (the emphasis is on the word *thou*). They evidently were not satisfied with the astonishing sign he had given them only the day before, feeding them by the thousand with a child's lunch. More, if they had asked the disciples (which probably they did, when Jesus refused to answer them about how he had crossed the lake), the disciples would have told them about Jesus walking on the waves. What greater sign could there have been than that?

But miracles breed a craving for more miracles. Even spurious miracles and satanic miracles are more satisfying to those who have acquired that craving than no miracles at all.

"What sign showest thou? What dost thou work?" How could they ask such a question, when the land rang with his exploits? Never before in all their history, not even in those rare periods when miracles marked a transition point in time—in the days of Moses and Elijah and Daniel—had anyone demonstrated such mastery over the forces of nature and performed so many and such varied miracles.

Then they pointed back to what had been a comparable miracle in the life of Moses, the daily miracle of feeding the wandering Hebrews with bread from heaven. Why didn't he do something like that? "Our Fathers did eat manna in the desert; as it is written, He gave them bread from heaven to eat" (6:31), loosely quoting Psalm 78:24. They evidently expected the messiah to duplicate that miracle. In effect they were saying: "So you fed five thousand with some loaves and fishes! What's so wonderful about that? Why don't you feed us all for forty years?" It was a statement of insulting unbelief, challenging him to do something as great as what Moses did.

There follows at once *the announcement of the mystery* (6:32-40). The only answer to such taunts was to couch truth in symbolism, to force them to think beyond the material to the spiritual, beyond the temporal to the eternal. We see, first, *their mistake revealed* (6:32-34). They had referred to the manna, to "bread from heaven." Very well, that is what he would talk to them about. But first, he must correct an error: "Verily, verily, I say unto you, Moses gave you not that bread from heaven; but my Father giveth you the true bread from heaven" (6:32). It was not Moses but God who performed that former miracle. Moses was an instrument in God's hand, and he would be the first one to repudiate the use they were making of his name. Moreover, the one who really performed that former miracle was now performing an even greater one. Manna was perishable bread, fit only to sustain the physical. "My Father," he said, "giveth you the true bread from heaven. For the bread of God is he which cometh down from heaven, and giveth life unto the world" (6:33). The manna came down from heaven. He, Christ, had come down from heaven. The manna was heaven-sent bread; he was the heaven-sent true bread.

As yet the Jews had not made the transition in their minds from the manna to the metaphor. Some of them never did. They said, "Lord, evermore give us this bread," just as the woman at the well, likewise mistaking the literal for the symbolic, had said, "Sir, give me this water, that I thirst not, neither come hither to draw" (4:15).

The Lord answered in the first of his famous I AM sayings

(6:35; 8:12; 10:7,11; 11:25; 14:6; 15:1). In this saying we have *their messiah revealed* (6:35-40). He was *the bread of life* (6:35-36). "Jesus said unto them, I am the bread of life: he that cometh to me shall never hunger; and he that believeth on me shall never thirst" (6:35). This is the key statement of the discourse. All the imagined difficulties in the startling symbolism that followed, and which so startled and horrified the Jews as well as many of the Lord's own followers, are resolved when we see that the Lord is equating believing and receiving with eating and drinking. The natural physical acts of eating and drinking bread and water are the symbolic vehicles for describing the way we receive Christ into our lives, the one who imparts and sustains our spiritual lives just as bread and water sustain our physical lives.

Nor must we ignore the I AM at the heart of the statement. Later, in his controversy with the Jews, the Lord will plainly announce himself to be the I AM of the Old Testament (Exodus 3:13-14). Here, and in the six other I AM assertions in John's gospel, the Lord showed how that mysterious name for God was amplified in him. He could say I AM the bread of life; I AM the light of the world; I AM the door of the sheep; I AM the good shepherd; I AM the way, the truth, and the life; I AM the true vine.

A personal response was needed (6:35). A hungry person can sit down at a table, turn up his nose at what is set before him, push back from the table, and leave as hungry as he came. Evidently his hunger has not yet reached the point where he is starving. Not until a person eats does food do him any personal good. A personal response to Christ's claim to be the true bread, the bread of God, the bread of life, is needed. Not until Christ is personally received by an individual, into his or her life, can Christ impart the life of God. But here *a personal response was neglected* (6:36): "But I said unto you, That ye also have seen me, and believe not." The Jews had asked, "What sign showest thou?" The Lord's answer was, "I am the sign. You have seen me. You have seen the sign. You refuse to believe." That was why the situation was so hopeless. If people will not eat the life-giving bread when it is set before them, deny its existence, refuse to believe it is there, argue about it, by what sign can you demonstrate to them the existence of that bread?

The Lord now discusses *the basis of life* (6:37-40). But he is by no means through with the analogy of bread. He has much more to say about that. But first, given the seriousness of refusing the bread of life, he must talk about the basis of life.

The matter of *sovereignty* (6:37) is involved in the case of all those who do trust in him: "All that the Father giveth me shall come to me; and him that cometh to me I will in no wise cast out." These verses seem to be addressed to the Lord's own disciples rather than to the crowd.

God does not act in an arbitrary way nor in defiance of the human will when he draws people to Christ. Someone once tried to persuade me that God has chosen some people for salvation and chosen other people for damnation. Such an idea is monstrous. God does not arbitrarily and sovereignly damn the greater part of the human race into an existence they did not seek, on terms they did not select (so-called "total depravity"), under impossible handicaps they did not choose (depraved in will and "dead in trespasses and sins"), dominated by forces they cannot control (the world, the flesh, and the devil), into a ruined family (Adam's) they did not themselves plunge into original sin, just in order arbitrarily to send people to hell for not choosing a salvation offered only to the "elect." That may be some people's idea of God and some people's view of salvation, but such concepts make God out to be a tyrant worse than any in the history of the human race. However, such is not the God of the Bible and such is not the kind of "salvation" offered us.

"All that the Father giveth me shall come to me," Jesus said. That is divine truth. So is this: "Ye will not come to me" (5:40). So is this: "Come unto me, all ye that labor and are heavy laden, and I will give you rest" (Matthew 11:28). So is the closing invitation of the Bible: "Come! Come! Come!" God does not invite people to come and then make it impossible for them to come.

Whatever is to be said about the sovereignty of God in human salvation, God never sets up arbitrary, impossible, and wholly unobtainable terms for our coming to Christ. Nor does he violate our moral accountability by ravishing anyone's human will in certain cases (by so-called "irresistible grace"). The solution to the problem suggested by some, built around such texts as John 6:37, lies in the omniscience of God and in the timelessness of his mode of being. God knows all those who will accept Christ and he knows them because he knows everything. Moreover, God dwells in an eternal present tense (hence he describes himself as the I AM). So, from God's standpoint of events, his choosing and our choosing are simultaneous acts. They both occur at the same moment in God's eternal present tense of "time."

What John is saying here is that the God who knows "all those who will come to Christ" gives them all to Christ. And, in infinite grace, the Lord receives them one and all, no matter who they are or what they have done: "Him that cometh to me I will in no wise cast out" (6:37).

The sovereignty of God in salvation results in the *security*

(6:38-40) of the believer. The Lord came down from heaven expressly to accomplish God's eternal purpose on earth with regard to the human race. He did not come to act in independence of his Father but to act in compliance with the Father's perfect will. "And this is the Father's will which hath sent me, that of all which he hath given me I should lose nothing, but should raise it up again at the last day." Such was *the Father's will for the Savior* (6:39).

The idea that a person once saved can be lost again is foreign to Scripture. "All which he hath given me" are to be kept secure, Jesus said. Not just the victorious ones or the virtuous ones, but all! The concept brings peace to the heart and joy to the soul. The goal of our salvation is realized in the redemption of our bodies and our entrance into a glorified life beyond our power to imagine or describe. The accomplishment of this preordained goal has been entrusted to Jesus by the Father.

The truth is restated, only this time in terms of *the Father's will for the saved* (6:40): "And this is the will of him that sent me, that every one which seeth the Son, and believeth on him, may have everlasting life: and I [emphatic] will raise him up at the last day." The sepulcher does not have the last say; the Savior does. "I," he says, "the incarnate Son of the living God, creator of heaven and earth, in whom resides all the fullness of the godhead, bodily, to whom all power is given in heaven and in earth, *I* will raise him up at the last day." No one trusts in Christ in vain. Eternal life, the present possession of every believer (3:16; 5:24) is yet to be consummated in the restoration to each believer of a perfect and transfigured personhood. We are to be complete—body, soul, and spirit—beyond the reach of sin and death, bathed eternally in "joy unspeakable and full of glory," our deathless humanity as radiant as was our Lord's on the mount of transfiguration.

2. Christ's Claims Resented (6:41-71)

At this point there seems to have been an interruption caused by the arrival of some new people, necessitating an end to the Lord's private words to his disciples and a renewal of his controversy with the Jews over his claim to be the "bread of God." This section is taken up with *the resentment of the Lord's foes* (6:41-59). John begins with *their murmuring* (6:41-51). There were two reasons why they objected to the Lord. First there was *the preliminary reason* (6:41-42). Here he was, claiming to be "the bread which came down from heaven," claiming, in short, to be from heaven, to be God—but how could that be? "Is not this

Jesus, the son of Joseph, whose Father and mother we know? how is it then that he saith, I came down from heaven?" They murmured at him, John says. Interestingly, the word for *murmured (gonguzo)* is the same one used in the Septuagint for the murmuring of the children of Israel in the wilderness (see Exodus 16:2,7,8,9,12 and 1 Corinthians 10:10). Probably the Jews (doubtless, representatives of the dominant religious party) had been murmuring *about* what he had been saying before now murmuring *at* him.

"We know who this man's parents are" they said. "Joseph is his father. How can he say: 'I came down from heaven'?" Evidently it was assumed that Joseph was the Lord's father which, of course, made him an illegitimate child and the subject under the mosiac law of extreme religious discrimination. The only way Jesus could describe his birth was to say he had come down from heaven. The Jews, however, regarded such a claim as pretentious and blasphemous.

The profounder reason (6:43-51) for their murmuring is to be found in what he had to say about his Father, his facts, and his flesh. The more they objected to what he was saying, the more obscure his words became.

There was, then, *the matter of his Father* (6:43-46). The Lord picks up what he had just been saying privately to his disciples and repeats it for the benefit of his larger audience, including the newly arrived, highly suspicious, and critical religious leaders: "No man can come to me, except the Father which hath sent me draw him: and I will raise him up at the last day." The expression "at the last day" is found only in John (6:40,44,54; 11:24; 12:48). Coming to Christ from the human side requires an action of human will and from the divine side an action of *God's will* (6:44). It does not limit but rather defines the nature of the human will. The drawing power is God's love, put forth in power (3:16) but not riding roughshod over anyone's will. The fact is that the Father draws all people into the sphere of his love, though all do not respond. Those who do respond are regenerated and will be raised up by Christ at the last day for an eternity of bliss.

The Lord turns from God's will (6:44) to *God's word* (6:45-46) and quotes a passage from Isaiah 54:13 (Jeremiah 31:34). The prophecy is directed to the restored city of Jerusalem. A kingdom age prophecy, anticipating the millennial reign of Christ, that passage assures the people, "All your children shall be taught by the Lord." That, of course, did not happen after the return from the Babylonian captivity, although Ezra and the scribes made a valiant effort to re-educate the returned pioneers in the things of God, as did the postexilic prophets Haggai and Zechariah. Things soon began to degenerate, calling for the ministry of Malachi. By the time of Christ, those teachings had degenerated into rabbinic traditions that effectively annulled the truth of the word of God. The Lord here treats the prophecy as messianic and, had the Jews accepted Christ, the promise of Isaiah would have been fulfilled. Since the Jews rejected Christ, the prophecy was again postponed, this time as millennial.

Some think that Isaiah 54 was included in the regular synagogue liturgy for this time of the year. If so, the Lord's quotation was an appropriate reminder to his hearers that the time was at hand when the prophecy could be fulfilled. The Lord makes the application: "Every man therefore that hath heard, and hath learned of the Father, cometh unto me" (6:45).

The Jews had mistakenly identified Joseph as the father of Jesus and made it the basis for their unbelief. By this constant reference to God as his Father the Lord endeavored to set the record straight and also open up a channel for belief. Now he adds, "Not that any man hath seen the Father, save he which is of God, he hath seen the Father" (6:46). The second use of the pronoun *he* is emphatic. Before his incarnation, as a member of the triune godhead, Jesus had seen the Father. The Lord's words are a clear claim to deity and mark the fact that the incarnation did not change the Lord's personality. The man Jesus, mistakenly identified by the Jews as the son of Joseph, was the same one who had existed eternally as God the Son. His becoming human had not changed either his identity or his personality.

There was *the matter of his facts* (6:47-50) which he conveyed to his incredulous audience with fearless integrity, wholly disregarding how unpalatable and indigestible they were. Facts, after all, are facts, and facts are stubborn things. They refuse to go away.

The Lord first stated *the basic fact* (6:47): "Verily, verily, I say unto you, He that believeth on me hath everlasting life." We can imagine the Jews shaking their heads over such an assertion. The thing that blinded them was that they knew his family. They knew the village where he had grown up. They had known him as a schoolboy and as the village carpenter. They knew his mother and his human brothers and sisters. They knew the house he had grown up in. Now he was running all over the country stirring people up and making these statements they considered to be outrageous.

But how could they account for his miracles? We know from

elsewhere in the gospels that they described him as mad or demon possessed. The basic fact, however, was much simpler. He was speaking the truth, and they had better believe it. The Lord uses his "verily, verily" to affirm the sober truth of what he was saying.

Then there was *the broader fact* (6:48-50). The Lord brings them back to the great truth he has been proclaiming all along in this discussion: "I am that bread of life. Your fathers did eat manna in the wilderness, and are dead. This is the bread which cometh down from heaven, that a man may eat thereof, and not die." Perhaps for the benefit of those who had recently joined the crowd he restated his I AM claim to be the bread of life. The bread which came down from heaven in the old dispensation did not ward off death. All it did was prolong physical life for a while. He, on the other hand, was offering eternal life.

But what brought things to a head with his listeners was *the matter of his flesh* (6:51) and what he had to say about that. "I am the living bread which came down from heaven: if any man eat of this bread, he shall live forever: and the bread that I will give is my flesh, which I will give for the life of the world." It is important to understand what the Lord means here by his "flesh." It is not his literal body; such a concept is ludicrous. His flesh is the metaphor he uses for his human nature, the totality of his life on the side of his humanity. The giving of his flesh is a reference to his sacrificial death, a death both voluntary ("I will give") and vicarious ("for the life of the world").

That the Lord's reference to his flesh must be understood in this way is clear from Hebrews 10, where God speaks of our present unhindered access into his presence: "Having therefore, brethren, boldness to enter into the holiest by the blood of Jesus, By a new and living way, which he hath consecrated for us, through the veil, that is to say, his flesh" (Hebrews 10:19-20). In that passage the Lord's flesh is identified with the temple veil. That veil represented all that Jesus was as God incarnate. It was made of fine, twined linen symbolizing his sinlessness and righteousness. It was dyed blue, scarlet, and purple. The blue symbolized his deity: he came from heaven; he was the Son of God. The scarlet symbolized his humanity: he was "the last Adam, the second man" (the name Adam means "red"). The purple symbolized deity in humanity. If you take a quantity of blue dye and an equal quantity of red, and then mix one into the other, you have purple. Jesus was "God manifest in flesh." So the veil represented all that Jesus was and is as deity in humanity.

The veil in both the temple and the tabernacle hung between

the holy place, where the priests ministered, and the holy of holies, where God was enthroned in the shekinah glory cloud on the mercy seat between the cherubim. That veil had one message: "Keep out!" It was an impassable barrier between human beings in their sinful estate and God in his holiness. The veil represented the flawless life of Jesus, and that life is our greatest indictment. It demonstrates that the life of sinless perfection which God has every right to demand of us and which we cannot live, has been lived by the man Christ Jesus. Thus that life condemns us (Romans 8:3). The greatest tragedy would have been for the Lord Jesus to come to earth, live a sinless life, set before us a peerless example of life as God intends it to be lived, and then to return to heaven. That is the lesson of the unrent veil.

But the veil was rent. The literal veil in the temple was rent when Jesus died (Matthew 27:51), opening the way into God's presence in the holy of holies. It was rent because "the veil, that is to say, his flesh" was rent upon the cross. When at last the Lord Jesus surrendered his life, when *that* veil was rent, everything that barred us from God was removed.

The Lord Jesus, then, said to the Jews: "The bread that I will give [pointing forward to his impending sacrifice at Calvary] is my flesh [his unique and sinless life as God manifest in flesh], which I will give [a repetition of the all-important fact of his death] for the life of the world [for the salvation of humankind, in order to impart to human beings the life of God, eternal life]." What we have to do is "eat of this bread," that is, personally take and appropriate this bread: personally accept Christ into our lives as a deliberate, volitional act.

Now, the opposition of the Jews broke out into the open. It was no longer murmuring but outright hostility, based on *their misunderstanding* (6:52-59). We note, first, *the problem* (6:52): "The Jews therefore strove among themselves, saying, How can this man give us his flesh to eat." They did not recognize that he again was using that figure of speech (synechdoche), in which a part is put for the whole. "Flesh" here is used for the Lord himself. Or we can view it as a metaphor, where one thing is declared to be something else. Both are common figures of speech in Scripture and also in everyday life. To take a figure of speech literally, or to take what is literal as a figure of speech, is a common error in Bible interpretation. The Jews failed to grasp the fact that the Lord was using a figure of speech and concluded that he was suggesting some form of cannibalism: the literal eating of his flesh.

The Lord then expanded *the proclamation* (6:53-58). He ignored their mistake and spoke further of the bread: "Verily, verily, I say unto you, Except ye eat the flesh of the Son of man, and drink his blood, ye have no life in you. Whoso eateth my flesh, and drinketh my blood, hath eternal life; and I will raise him up at the last day. For my flesh is meat indeed, and my blood is drink indeed. He that eateth my flesh, and drinketh my blood, dwelleth in me, and I in him" (6:53-57).

The Roman Catholic Church has used these verses to formulate its dogma of transubstantiation. That dogma claims that eating the flesh and drinking the blood of the Lord means to partake of his real body and blood in the holy communion. What is clearly a figure of speech is taken as literal. It is evident that the "coming" and "believing" of verse 35 mean the same as the "eating" and "drinking" of verses 51 and 54, since they have the same blessing attached to them. When we come to Christ and believe in him we receive into our souls the benefits of his body and blood offered for us on the cross of Calvary.

Quite apart from the fact that John 6 has nothing to do with the Lord's supper, which was not instituted by the Lord until just before his crucifixion (Matthew 26:26-28), the Lord's teaching in John 6 is figurative throughout and cannot be used to support Catholic dogmas. The Jews used the expression "eat, drink" in a figurative way to denote the operation of the mind in receiving and "inwardly digesting" truth (Deuteronomy 8:3; Jeremiah 15:16; Ezekiel 2:8-10). We speak of people devouring a book or chewing on a piece of information or swallowing an outrageous lie. To take an obvious figure of speech as literal and then to build a doctrine on that literal interpretation is a travesty of spiritual truth.

The theory accepted by Rome as dogma is that the bread and wine are changed into the body and blood of Christ. It is an attempt to explain the statements of Christ in Mark 14:22,24, where he says, "This is my body" and "This is my blood." Rome insists that the word *is* must be taken literally. The devout Catholic believes that the wafer has ceased to be a wafer. It may still look and taste like a wafer, it may mold like a wafer, but it is no longer a wafer. There has been effected a real change of the substance of the wafer and the wine into the body and blood of Christ when the priest speaks the holy words of Christ (James Doyle, Bishop of Kildare and Leighin, *An Abridgment of Christian Doctrine*, p. 81, cited by T. C. Hammond, *The One Hundred Texts*, London: The Society for Irish Missions, 1939, p.407). The theory of transubstantiation "carries with it many serious consequences. If Christ is substantially present, it is natural that the elements should be adored. It can also be claimed that he is received by all who communicate, whether rightly to salvation or wrongly to perdition" (*Evangelical Dictionary of Theology,* Grand Rapids: Baker Book House, p. 1108).

The Jews, who first heard the Lord give this teaching, were likewise inexcusable in their misunderstanding. The Lord, however, ignored their mistake. He gave a final summary: "This is that bread which came down from heaven: not as your Fathers did eat manna, and are dead: he that eateth of this bread shall live forever" (6:58). It is almost as though the Lord said, "Take it or leave it." The time had come to begin winnowing the chaff from the wheat.

This turning point in the ministry of the Lord was so important that John mentions *the place* (6:59): "These things said he in the synagogue, as he taught in Capernaum." This city had become his Galilean headquarters. There he now made his home. There, too, he performed many of his miracles, including the healing of a servant of that Roman centurion who had built the synagogue (Luke 7:1-10).

But it was not only the Lord's foes who were disturbed by this kind of teaching. The iron went much deeper than that into his soul.

Our attention is now directed to *the resentment of the Lord's followers* (6:60-71). That resentment revealed itself first in *dissension among his disciples* (6:60-65). The misunderstanding of the multitude was bad enough, the active ill will of the religious authorities was an ominous portent of the future, but the murmuring among many who had attached themselves hopefully to this miracle-working prophet, in expectation of a soon-coming material kingdom, was the worst of all. It is likely, however, that the Lord deliberately provoked this crisis to weed out those who were after only the loaves and fishes. We note, first, *what he exposed* (6:60-61). Many of his followers, unable to follow his metaphoric style, said, "This is an hard saying; who can hear it?" The Lord read their thoughts. He said, "Does this offend you?" Even those who grasped the metaphor were outraged. The Lord made himself greater than Moses. He claimed to come from heaven. He claimed to be one with God. He was pointing to his death as the way to life. The discourse, where it was not unintelligible, was downright offensive. "Who can listen to this kind of talk?" they said. The Lord had exposed their hearts.

We note *what he explained* (6:62-63). He explained *the supernatural* (6:62) nature of things: "What and if ye shall see the Son of man ascend up where he was before?" Here the Lord emphatically declared that he was in heaven before his incarnation and he would go back to heaven after his resurrection. It is a declaration of his unchanging personality. Before his birth, during his earthly life, after his ascension, it is the same person, the same personality.

Some have rephrased the question like this: "If therefore you should behold the Son of man ascending up where he was before, will you be offended then?" The Lord's whole life was a supernatural life. His birth was supernatural, his life was supernatural, his miracles were supernatural, his death was supernatural and attended by the supernatural, his resurrection was supernatural, and his bodily ascension into heaven was supernatural. The Lord points to the supernatural nature of his coming ascension as proof of the supernatural nature of his incarnation.

But there was more to it than the supernatural; the Lord explained also *the spiritual* (6:63) nature of things: "It is the spirit that quickeneth; the flesh profiteth nothing: the words that I speak unto you, they are spirit, and they are life." We are reminded of the Lord's words to Nicodemus: "That which is born of the flesh is flesh; and that which is born of the Spirit is spirit" (3:6). The Lord's words are life-giving. They are "spirit." They can engender spiritual life; they can "quicken," make alive, impart the life of God. It is his Spirit in the human spirit which imparts eternal life, and that Spirit resides in his word. Even if a priest could give the Lord's flesh to a communicant, it would profit nothing. The life-giving principles reside in the Spirit, in his word, which is "God breathed."

Then we are told *what he expected* (6:64): "But there are some of you that believe not. For Jesus knew from the beginning who they were that believed not, and who should betray him." There were two circles of disciples. There was the outer circle, made up of these who were very interested in him. They had been attracted by his miracles and were impressed by teaching marked by such authority—so different from that of the scribes. We could say, perhaps, of these people that they were more or less convinced in their minds that Jesus was the messiah, but they had made no real, life-transforming, faith-energized heart commitment to Christ. The Lord read their hearts. His knowledge was omniscient. He "knew from the beginning who they were that believed not." They may have fooled others, they may have fooled themselves, but they did not fool him.

Then there was that inner circle of disciples, the twelve, those who had made a heart commitment to Christ. But even there the Lord was not deceived. He "knew from the beginning . . . who should betray him." From the first day that Judas joined the apostolic circle of fellowship, Jesus knew he would betray him. This is the first intimation of the future treachery of Judas. Judas was able to deceive the other disciples right up to the end. Christ was not deceived.

We are told *what he expanded* (6:65): "And he said, Therefore said I unto you, that no man can come unto me, except it were given unto him of my Father." The Lord here draws the line between those who were drawn to him by divine constraint and those who were drawn to him by mistaken ideas concerning him—those, for instance, who were drawn by his miracles, or drawn by expectation of a prominent place in the kingdom they believed he was about to establish on earth. People come to Christ for all kinds of reasons. Some, even today, come to Christ hoping for a miracle of healing or for some "gift." Many come to Christ under the pressure of a fervent evangelistic appeal, and many of them experience a psychological conversion and nothing more. Some have even baser ulterior motives. Judas was the prime example of those who came hoping to gain some material advantage. People who come to Christ for any reason other than the spiritual reason that they are drawn to him by God soon fall away, and some of these, like Judas, who was much more enlightened than most, become apostate and even active enemies of Christ.

John now goes on to show how resentment of Christ revealed itself in *desertion among his disciples* (6:66-71). John recalls *the cry of Jesus* (6:66-69). "From that time many of his disciples went back, and walked no more with him" (6:66). They not only ceased following him but they gave up whatever they had received from him. They went back to their old ways of life. His teaching had sifted them.

At least the twelve remained. These too he intended to put to the test. "Will ye also go away?" he asked. Then Peter spoke up: "Lord, to whom shall we go? Thou hast the words of eternal life. And we believe and are sure that thou art that Christ, the Son of the living God" (6:68-69). This confession of Peter is not the same as the one he gave at Caesarea Philippi (Matthew 16:16). It precedes it by a number of months. Peter had grasped the spiritual dimension of the Lord's teaching, that by believing in him they could have eternal life, that Christ's words indeed were "spirit" and "life" (6:63). Peter had taken the Lord's words at their face value. He had grasped the metaphor; he had seized the inner truth.

"To whom shall we go?" he said. Who, having heard Christ, would want to go to Buddha or Confucius or Mohammed or Krishna? Who, having heard Christ, would want to listen to Darwin or Marx or Lenin? Who, having heard Christ, would want to go to Plato or Philo or Marcus Aurelius? "Thou hast the words of eternal life. We believe and are sure that thou art that Christ, the Son of the living God." Well said, Peter. To turn away from Christ to the dead founder of one of the world's false religions, or to the lifeless sophistries of a pagan philosopher, or to one of the modern proponents of today's humanistic creeds, is to exchange light for darkness, life for death, hope for despair, heaven for hell. There is no one else to whom we can go.

"And we," says Peter (the pronoun is emphatic: we who are closest to you), "We believe and are sure [have come to know— *ginosko*, by experience, by becoming acquainted with you, through a learning process, by perceiving] that thou art that Christ [the promised messiah of Israel], the Son of the living God." Faith could soar no higher. At least Peter and the inner circle of disciples were convinced. They would not go away. There was nowhere else to go.

All were convinced, except one. John, who seems of all the twelve to have been particularly outraged by the activities of the traitor, is careful to show that the Lord's all seeing, inerrantly sifting eye had already seen through Judas. He therefore records *the crime of Judas* (6:70-71). The Lord's statement is a terrible one and solemn indeed: "Jesus answered them, Have not I chosen you twelve, and one of you is a devil? He spake of Judas Iscariot the Son of Simon: for he it was that should betray him, being one of the twelve."

That one of his disciples was to be a traitor was foreknown to the Lord before the beginning of time, before the fall of man made necessary a plan of redemption, before Judas, the son of Simon, was born in Kerioth in the land of Judea. Jesus knew it, too, from the prophecy of Psalm 41:9. He deliberately chose Judas to be one of the twelve. It was love unbounded that led the Lord to choose the man who would one day betray him with a kiss—love for the soul of Judas. He would have saved him if only he had been willing. He drew him to himself to show him his love and concern, to set before him the hope of a home on high, to lay siege to his heart, to appeal to his mind, to knock loudly at the door of his will, to awaken his conscience. It was all in vain. Judas hardened his heart again and again.

The Lord openly describes him as a devil *(diabolus)*. G. Campbell Morgan takes that at face value and maintains that Judas was not a man at all, but a devil masquerading as a man. The word means "accuser" or "slanderer" and is one of the two chief names given to the evil one. The other prominent name is Satan, which means "adversary." It is of interest that here, when Peter makes his great confession, the enemy is at once revealed and called the "devil," the accuser. On the next occasion when Peter makes his great confession, at Caesarea Philippi, the enemy is again revealed, only on that occasion he is "Satan," the adversary.

And what about Simon of Kerioth, the father of Judas, whose name is introduced here? Was he, perhaps, partly to blame for the sly, avaricious, heartless, conscienceless, and unscrupulous behavior of his son? What kind of father was he? What kind of example did he set before his growing boy? What was he like at home? How did he treat his wife? How did he do his job? Was he a religious man? What kind of friends did he invite to his home? Was he partly to blame? Is that why his name is introduced? Or is his name introduced to evoke our pity that a man should have a son so lacking in conscience that he could find it in his heart to betray the Christ with a kiss?

Thus ends another section of John's gospel. Matthew and the other synoptic writers tell us much more about the Lord's Galilean ministry. John has no more to say. He has introduced the traitor. He will now begin to paint in the darker portions of his picture, drawing us ever nearer to the cross.

II. The Implications of His Life (7:1–10:42)

John has set before us the impact of Christ's life, both in urban Jerusalem and in rural Galilee (5:1–6:71); now he wants to show us the implications of that life (7:1–10:42). In this section of the gospel we have three movements: the Lord's exposition of the word of God (7:1–8:1), the Lord's exposure of the wickedness of men (8:2–9:41), and the Lord's explanation of the way of life (10:1-42).

A. His Exposition of the Word of God (7:1–8:1)

Our Lord's exposition of the word of God revolves around three centers of opposition. We have the animosity of his family (7:1-10), the arguments of the Jews (7:11-29), and the antagonism of the rulers (7:30–8:1). These three spheres of controversy enable the Lord to make increasingly clear the implications of his life as God incarnate on planet earth.

1. The Animosity of His Family (7:1-10)

We begin with the animosity of his family. We note, first, *the date* (7:1-2). After the feeding of the five thousand and the discourse on the bread of life, the Lord continued to minister in

Galilee up until the time of the annual feast of tabernacles, the happiest of all the Jewish feasts. The Lord well knew what hatred and opposition awaited him in Jerusalem.

The feast of tabernacles began on the fifteenth day of Tisri, the Jewish month corresponding with our September-October (we cannot correlate Jewish months with ours exactly because the Jews used a lunar calendar, the first day of each month coinciding with a new moon). This feast was a kind of harvest or thanksgiving festival. It was midway between Passovers. People flocked in great numbers to Jerusalem for this feast, built temporary shelters all around the walls of the city, and came prepared for a great deal of fun and fellowship. Along with Passover and Pentecost, this was one of three pilgrimages in the Hebrew religious calendar. There is an interval of six months between chapters 6 and 7 of John, months John passes over in silence.

Next comes *the debate* (7:3-8) and the Lord has to listen to *advice from his brothers* (7:3-5). They were almost insolent and certainly presumptuous in their comments. "You ought to go up to Jerusalem and do your miracles there," they said. They considered him to be wasting his time in the backwoods of Galilee, healing peasants and wayfarers. Jerusalem was where the action was. Jerusalem was where the people lived who really mattered. He should go to the capital and build a real following there instead of among the handful of assorted Galileans he now had. "You need more publicity," they said. It was silly, in their estimation, to be shrinking from the public eye, when what he needed to do was step boldly onto center stage in Jerusalem. If he was the messiah, the thing to do was to strike fire into the dry tinder of incipient national revolt, fan the flames, and spread the conflagration throughout the nation. That was the way a messiah worth his salt ought to act. He would never get anywhere running timidly from place to place in Galilee. In any case, Jerusalem was the place to proclaim and prove himself to be the messiah, not in Cana or Capernaum, not in Nazareth or Nain.

John explains what was behind this piece of gratuitous advice: "For neither did his brethren believe in him" (7:5). The incredible fact is that these brothers of his had lived in the same Nazareth home and failed to see that he was anything more than an ordinary human being. He was "holy, harmless, undefiled, separate from sinners" (Hebrews 7:26). He was good beyond all goodness known to the children of Adam. He was loving and kind, patient and pure, wise and capable beyond all others. Yet they failed to recognize him for who and what he was. It is a remarkable tribute to the genuineness of his perfect humanity—and a sad tribute to their blindness.

Even his astounding miracles failed to convince them. His teaching did not stir them. His claims did not impress them. His character did not interest them. All they could say was that if he was indeed the messiah, he had a strange way of going about claiming his kingdom. They had a much better idea how things should be done.

The Lord had a word of *admonition for his brothers* (7:6-8). He knew far better than they the spiritual climate of Jerusalem. The hostile religious leaders of Jerusalem wanted to kill him. "My time is not yet come," he said, working according to a divine timetable. He was not going to be high pressured by these unbelieving brothers of his who so presumed upon their kinship as to tell him what he ought to do.

Not many people live in moment by moment awareness of God's leading in their lives. Certainly the Lord's brothers knew no such walk with God. "Your time is always ready," he said. They came and went at the dictate of their own desires. They were not living in harmony with heaven. It made no difference if they went to Jerusalem today, tomorrow, or next week. Their steps were not ordered of the Lord.

They were governed by this world, its principles, policies, priorities. He was governed by that world. The world could not hate them, because they were in fellowship with it. They approved its ways of thought and action. "The world cannot hate you," he said, "but me it hateth, because I testify of it, that the works thereof are evil" (7:7). The Lord understood the true nature of things. This world and its system is the enemy of God. It is the devil's lair for sinners, it is his lure for saints. As the word is used here, and in many other places in the New Testament, the "world" is simply human life and society as opposed to God. Its science, politics, economic and social systems, philosophies, pleasures, religions, goals, and organizations are opposed to God, indifferent to the world to come. Its prince is Satan; its motivating factors are the lust of the eye, the lust of the flesh, and the pride of life. Simply by living in this world, in the power of that other world, the Lord testified of it "that the works thereof are evil." When we are tempted to compromise with the world we need to remember that the hand it reaches out to us is stained with the blood of Christ.

As for the Lord Jesus, he was in the world but he was not of the world. "You go on up to the feast," he said to his brothers. "I am not going yet; my time is not yet full come" (7:8). The Lord had not yet received inner assurance from his Father in heaven that it was time for him to go. There was the ever-present possibility that the marching, singing bands of pilgrims might again try to make him a king by force if he joined them. But there was no need for his brothers to miss any of the good cheer of the journey or any of the joys of Jerusalem. Further, he knew he would eventually appear suddenly in the temple, as foretold by the Old Testament prophet Malachi (Malachi 3:1).

Then came *the departure* (7:9-10). The Lord remained for a while in Galilee. He waited until his brothers were gone, taking their worldly ideas of the kingdom with them. "Then went he also up unto the feast, not openly, but as it were in secret" (7:10). When the Lord went to Jerusalem in John 2:13 it was as a prince, to cleanse his Father's house and demonstrate his messianic zeal. When he went up in John 5:1 it was as a pilgrim. This time he went up as a prophet to make an important pronouncement to the hearts of all.

2. The Arguments of the Jews (7:11-29)

The general feeling of indecision and hostility toward Jesus can now be seen at work among the Jews; these seem to be the Jewish parties in the group of Galilean worshipers. First we see them *arguing about him* (7:11-13). Jerusalem was full of pilgrims from all parts of the world, and one major topic of conversation was the miracle-working prophet from Galilee. There was general murmuring or muttering among them. Some were sure that at least Jesus was a good man. Very likely there were those in the crowd who had been healed by him, or who had relatives or friends who had been healed by him, or who had seen Jesus heal people. There would be those in the throng who had heard him. Some would recall snatches of the sermon on the mount or bits and pieces of his teaching given at various times. "He is a good man," some said.

"Nothing of the kind," said others. "He is a deceiver; he goes around leading people astray. His claims are extravagant, absurd. He even claims to be God—and we know that can't be true because we know his parents. Why, up until recently, he was just the village carpenter at Nazareth."

So the arguments went, and visitors from distant places would go from this group to that one, pulled this way and that. But all such discussions were muted. "No man spake openly of him for fear of the Jews" (7:13). That was one thing everybody acknowledged: it was not safe to speak too loudly either way. The religious authorities, although not yet organized in their opposition, certainly wanted to dampen any discussion. The best thing was to ignore this irritating young prophet. The displeasure of the Sanhedrin was not something the common people were anxious to court.

Arguments about him soon blossomed into *astonishment at him* (7:14-19), sparked by *his sudden appearance* (7:14-15). The feast of tabernacles lasted a week, with an extra day, an eighth day added, "the great day of the feast." Halfway through the week, word flashed around the city. The prophet had come, was in the temple courts, and, with total disregard for the authorities, was boldly teaching. The people flocked to hear him.

John tells us what impressed them most. "The Jews marveled, saying, How knoweth this man letters, having never learned?" There he stood in a homespun peasant's robe, speaking with a north country accent, a village boy from Nazareth (of all places), teaching with skill and ease. He was certainly not the product of any rabbinical school. He had been enrolled as a student under none of the lettered teachers of Jerusalem. How could he know anything? He had no "letters," no learning.

That kind of intellectual snobbery is with us still. It flourishes in religious circles. Most Bible institutes, colleges, and universities would not dream of putting anyone on the faculty who was not a product of the academic system. He may be a Spirit-taught, God-anointed Bible teacher with vast knowledge of the Scriptures and skill in expounding them that is evident to those who hear him. He may have written a score of books that are blessed of God, avidly used by thousands, even as required texts in those schools. No matter. He is not qualified to be on the faculty—he does not have any degrees. Accrediting associations will not recognize a person taught of God who has not met their criteria. Here we see worldliness in a particularly outrageous garb.

The scholars and accredited teachers of Jesus' day left their impress on their students. They had their individual styles, methods of exegesis, accepted interpretations. And there in the temple, speaking with ease and authority, speaking with convincing power and evident mastery of the Scriptures, was a man who had not attended their schools. He did not have a diploma or certificate to preach. (As if people cannot master the Bible on their own!) It would be true to say that Jesus knew the Scriptures far better than Hillel or Shammai or Gamaliel or any of the celebrated rabbis of the day.

We note, too, *his serious appeal* (7:16-18). The Lord told them how it was he could teach as he did. He was taught by God. "My doctrine is not mine," he said, "but his that sent me" (7:16). His was the mind of omniscient genius but on the purely human level it was a mind saturated with the word of God. We can be sure that Jesus could read the Hebrew Scriptures flawlessly. He knew the kind of exegesis common in the rabbinical schools. He had attended the synagogue since he was a child. But he knew the author of the Scriptures. He knew not only the letter of the law and the prophets, he knew the spirit and intent of every line. He had been filled with the Holy Spirit from his mother's womb. He had been anointed by the Holy Spirit. His teaching was not his own; he had received it from heaven. Diligent work in memorizing the Scriptures, in applying sound hermeneutical principles to the sacred text, in formulating his theology, had all been done under the guidance of the Spirit.

They could put his teaching to the test: "If any man will do his will, he shall know of the doctrine, whether it be of God, or whether I speak of myself" (7:17). Everyone's teaching stands or falls by the fruit it produces in the lives of those who embrace it.

Take for instance the theory of evolution, propounded by Charles Darwin, popularized by T. H. Huxley, and accepted as true today by millions. Let us put it to this test. "If any will embrace it and translate it into action, he shall know of the doctrine, whether it be of God." When reduced to its lowest common multiple, the theory of evolution applauds the survival of the fittest. It is the theory that might is right. Away with the weak, the infirm, the deformed. Let the law of the jungle hold sway. It is the theory that underlies many of the social and political philosophies of our time. Hitler embraced it. It is at the heart of Nazi philosophy. The theory of a master race, "blitz-krieging" across Europe eradicating the despised of the human family (Jews, Slavs, blacks, gypsies), draws its inspiration from the theory of evolution. Hitler reveled in the vision of magnificent blonde Aryans, armed and uniformed, striding in jack boots on the bodies of the slain. Behind the panzer divisions, the U-boat wolf packs, the Luftwaffe, was the philosophy of Nazism. Behind the political philosophy of Nazism with its Gestapo, concentration camps, and gas chambers was the theory of evolution. Behind Marx and Lenin and communism is the theory of evolution. Behind secular humanism with its attack on Christian morality is the theory of evolution. No matter how the theory may be bolstered by those brainwashed by our colleges and universities, the theory stands condemned by its fruits.

"Put my teaching to the test," Jesus challenged his listeners. And that is the answer to those who say that Christianity has failed. Here and there a man, a woman, a teenager, a boy, a girl, dares to stake all on Christ. What happens? It works. The Lord's teaching, when put to the test, makes the drunken sober, the profligate pure, and the crooked straight. It cleanses society, redeems the individual, transforms lives, makes people godly and Christ-like. That claim can be made by no other philosophy, theory, or religion on earth.

"Those who bear their own message seek their own glory," Jesus added (7:18). This, too, is illustrated in the case of Charles Darwin, whose theory of evolution closely paralleled the work of Alfred Russel Wallace. Darwin had vacillated for months before publishing *On the Origin of Species*, afraid of ridicule from the scientific community on the one hand and rejection by the Christian community on the other. Worried that his rival might publish his own findings first, Darwin finally plucked up enough courage to condense his research and publish his own book. By then, he was concerned lest credit for evolutionary theory go to Wallace instead of to himself as well.

In contrast, Christ said of his teaching: "He that seeketh his glory that sent him, the same is true, and no unrighteousness is in him." Again and again John reminds us that Jesus always gave credit to his Father, the one who sent him.

The Lord followed with *his sad appraisal* (7:19-20). He looked into the faces of the people who thronged about him. He read their hearts and saw the future. What a terrible accusation he levied at them: "Did not Moses give you the law, and yet none of you keepeth the law? Why go ye about to kill me?" (7:19). Reading such an accusation we must remember that there was not a Jew who did not venerate Moses. The law itself had become a fetish with many of them. They regarded themselves as its custodians and interpreters. They elaborated its precepts, delved into mazes of legal minutiae, hedged it around with elaborate detail—and failed to keep it, Jesus pointed out. The evidence of that was terrible indeed. They were plotting his death. He knew it, and told them so. Their plots would be successful. He knew that too.

Furiously they denied it. How terrible was the accusation they levied at him: "The people answered and said, Thou hast a devil: who goeth about to kill thee?" (7:20). That was a fearful thing to say to the Son of God. They were astonished at the claims he was making for himself. He was either insane or demon possessed, in their estimation. They dared him to name names to his accusation that they were going to kill him.

Arguing with him and astonishment at him now give way to *anger with him* (7:21-24). Again John brings us back to the underlying cause of Jewish hostility toward Jesus: his refusal to bow to their rules and regulations concerning the sabbath.

The Lord reminded them once more of the healing of the man at the pool of Bethesda some considerable time before.

Evidently his performing that miracle on the sabbath was a continuing sore point, the basis of their subsequent hatred. "I have done one work, and ye all marvel," Jesus said (7:21). It was not just the miracle that astonished them, not even the fact that he had taken on the whole religious establishment by performing it on the sabbath. It was the fact that he had done this miracle on the sabbath deliberately, without apology, with forethought and obvious intent, and that he had claimed divine authority for doing so. The Jews never forgave him for that or for his other sabbath miracles.

Jesus next raised another matter related to their sabbath myths. He said, "Moses . . . gave unto you circumcision." That is, Moses formalized circumcision as a requirement under the law although the rite itself had its roots in the abrahamic covenant. The mosaic covenant was a later addendum to the abrahamic covenant; it was a temporary addition to the original covenant, made necessary by the sin of the covenant people, and it did not take precedence over the abrahamic covenant (Genesis 17:10; Leviticus 12:3; Exodus 12:44).

Here, then, was the case cited by Christ. A child was to be circumcised on the eighth day. But what if the eighth day fell on a sabbath? In that case it would conflict with the fourth commandment, which forbade work on the sabbath. Yet the rule about circumcision took precedence over the law of the Sabbath. So, a priest who circumcised Hebrew boys on the sabbath worked—without sin.

Further, the rule that required circumcision, although part of the original abrahamic covenant, was concerned primarily with ritual cleansing. The law of circumcision was carried out, sabbath or no. If the law of the sabbath could be suspended to carry out minor surgery of a ritual nature, how much more appropriate it was for him to heal a man on the sabbath who had been wholly paralyzed for thirty-eight years (7:22-23).

The Jews were passing judgment on him because he had performed a miracle on the sabbath. However, they were wrong and he was right. What was at fault was not his understanding of the sabbath, but theirs. "Judge not according to the [outward] appearance, but judge righteous judgment" (7:24). How patient and painstaking Jesus was with these narrow-minded, hard-hearted, and stubborn-willed people. They had murder in their hearts; he had mercy in his.

Now comes *ambivalence toward him* (7:25-29). The Jews were at odds one with another and could not make up their minds about him. Two questions predominated. First there was *the question of identification* (7:25-27). The citizens of Jerusalem were

perplexed because they knew the authorities wanted to kill this
man: "Is not this he whom they seek to kill?" (7:25). These
people were acquainted with the plots of the hierarchy but did
not seem to be in full approval with them yet. Their words,
however, were an unconscious confirmation of the Lord's charge:"Why go ye about to kill me?" They expanded their surprise:
"But, lo, he speaketh boldly, and they say nothing unto him. Do
the rulers know indeed that this is the very Christ?" (7:26).
Could it be that the Sanhedrin had changed its mind and had
now decided that Jesus of Nazareth was the messiah of Israel?
How else could his bold preaching in the temple be explained?
He was preaching fearlessly, under the shadow of the Sanhedrin
headquarters. It would be like Martin Luther preaching to the
crowds in Vatican Square. The indecision of the authorities was
not rooted in any doubts they had about the desirability of
getting rid of this unwanted provocateur, but in a lack of method and opportunity. The last thing they wanted to incite was a
popular uprising by the masses.

But it was not only the masters of Israel who were indecisive.
The same was true of the multitudes. Some were saying, in
effect, "We know where this man comes from, but nobody is
going to know how or from where the messiah will come"
(7:27). The rabbis taught that the messiah would come from
Bethlehem and would then be hidden, nobody knowing where,
only to appear suddenly. Isaiah had written, "Who shall declare
his generation?" (53:8), hinting at a possible mystery concerning
the messiah's parentage. There is deep irony in all this. The
Jews were sure they knew all about this "Jesus of Nazareth." He
was just a village carpenter who had lived in that unpretentious
northern town for decades. How could he possibly be the
Christ? They did not even have the facts right. Jesus was from
Bethlehem, he had been hidden, under their very noses, in the
least likely place to produce a messiah (Nazareth), he had "suddenly come to his temple," and, as for his origins, although
Mary was his mother, Joseph was not his father. Nobody knew
from whence he really was. He had told them often enough but
they did not believe it.

The Lord hastened to enlighten them. He raised at once *the
question of the incarnation* (7:28-29). That solved their difficulties: "Ye both knew me, and ye know whence I am: and I am not
come of myself, but he that sent me is true, whom ye know not.
But I know him: for I am from him, and he hath sent me." "Ye
know . . . Ye know not!" They knew some of the facts, some of
the more obvious, outward facts. But what they did not know
obliterated what they did know. There was one God in heaven,

the one who had sent him into this world, the God he knew, the God they did not know. Of course they were ignorant of Jesus' divine origin. He came from God and they did not know God.

Jesus proclaimed this boldly. John says, "Then cried Jesus." The word suggests he cried aloud. He lifted up his voice. He wanted them all to hear. Moreover, he was "in the temple," the heart and soul of Jewish national religious life. If God was to be known, it was not to be in some pagan shrine but here, in Jerusalem, in the temple. Originally in the tabernacle and then, later, in the temple, God had manifested his presence. The structure itself and the sacrifices and services connected with it were all designed to make God known. Yet, right there, the one place in all the world where God could be known, Jesus lifted up his voice to tell the people that they did not know him because they did not know God. And they thought they had a monopoly on God.

3. The Antagonism of the Rulers (7:30–8:1)

Even while the debate was heating up in the temple courtyard the Sanhedrin was coming to a decision and nerving itself to take action. The news that the people were speculating as to whether or not they had changed their minds about Jesus seems to have tipped the scales.

We note, first, *a looming danger* (7:30-36). To begin with, *a forcible attempt* (7:30-31) was made to take him. "They sought to take him," John says. However, the immediate attempt came to nothing "because his hour was not yet come." It was not God's sovereign will that he should be arrested at this time. Another half year was to elapse before God would allow them to have their way. At this time, rather, "many of the people believed on him, and said, when Christ cometh, will he do more miracles than these which this man hath done?" (7:31). The rank and file of the people were more than half inclined to believe that Jesus was the promised messiah.

This information stiffened the Sanhedrin's resolve. They instigated *a formal attempt* (7:32-36) to take him. The Pharisees and the chief priests joined forces. The chief priests were drawn from the ranks of the most wealthy and influential priestly families, from whose ranks the high priest was selected. They were the backbone of the Sadducees, the majority, aristocratic party in the Sanhedrin. Men like Annas, his son Eleazar, Caiaphas, and others of this hierarchical family were prominent members of this elite caste. Normally the Pharisees were at odds with the Sadducees. Now they seemed to have closed ranks.Both parties felt threatened by this unwanted messiah. Accordingly, as John puts it, "They sent officers to take him" (7:32).

These officers were members of the temple police, charged with the maintenance of law and order within the precincts of the temple. They were Levites. Their commanding officer, called "captain of the temple," wielded considerable power, second only to that of the chief priest. For this reason he was usually chosen from one of the leading chief-priest families.

John does not tell us at what exact moment the officers arrived. Jesus was not disturbed. His times were in God's hands. He went on teaching, doubtless knowing that the police were on the way. Quite possibly they arrived in time to hear much of what he was saying.

The Lord continued to speak of *his duration on earth* (7:33). "Yet a little while am I with you," he said, "and then I go unto him that sent me." The Lord knew that his time on earth was short, a bare six months. This knowledge was based not only on his spiritual intuition and omniscience. It was something that a diligent student of Scripture could figure out for himself from Daniel's prophecy of the seventy weeks (Daniel 9:24-27). The messiah was to be "cut off" after the lapse of sixty-nine "weeks" of years (483 years) from the date of the decree of Artaxerxes, in the twentieth year of his reign (445 B.C.), permitting Nehemiah to return to Jerusalem and build it (Nehemiah 2:1-8). The computation is not simple, but we can be sure that Jesus figured it out. The exact date was known to him. He was to be crucified within a week of his triumphal entry into Jerusalem and that date had been foretold by Daniel's prophecy.

So, he spoke to the people of the shortness of the time he had left. He spoke to them also of *his departure from earth* (7:34-36). "Ye shall seek me, and shall not find me: and where I am, thither ye cannot come" (7:34). He was going back home to his Father in heaven. If their unbelief made it difficult for them to find him, when he was physically present on earth, it would make it impossible for them to find him once he had returned on high.

Of course the Jews misunderstood him (7:34-36). They bandied his words back and forth among themselves. Some scornfully supposed he was talking about going to the Jewish diaspora in other lands, others that he was proposing to carry his mission to the gentiles! There was no knowing what this strange prophet was going to do next. But going to the gentiles was, to these Jews, the last straw.

We must remember that the Lord's death and resurrection were still in the future. We read these words with subsequent events in mind. We know where he was going: home, by way of the cross, the resurrection, and the ascension. We know about the coming of the Holy Spirit at Pentecost. We have a completed New Testament in our hands. These Jews were still in the dark about what is common knowledge to us. We can surely sympathize to some extent with their bewilderment. "What manner of saying is this that he said, Ye shall seek me, and shall not find me: and where I am, thither ye cannot come?" (7:36). As far as the Jews were concerned, all this talk about going where they could not find him, especially if it meant going to the gentiles, was irrational. No true messiah could possibly entertain such irresponsible notions as that. "What kind of talk is this?" they asked. It was nonsense—yet a vague feeling persisted that perhaps there was more to it than they understood. So, there was a looming danger.

John tells next of *a last day* (7:37-39), that great day of the annual feast of tabernacles. The last day of the feast was a special day. It was "an holy convocation . . . a solemn assembly" kept as a special sabbath (Leviticus 23:36; Numbers 29:35). At this feast the people thanked God for the harvest. To the instructions for keeping the feast given in the Old Testament the Jews had added another ritual, a rather attractive ritual, one that acknowledged their indebtedness to God for sending the rain without which there would be no harvest.

Each of the first seven days of the feast, at early dawn, the priests and people joined in joyful procession and made their way with a golden pitcher to the pool of Siloam. They filled the pitcher and returned to the temple. They then poured out the water at the west side of the altar as the temple choir burst into the great *hallel* (Psalms 113–118). Some think that this ritual was to commemorate the water that Moses brought from the riven rock (Exodus 17:1-7) and which typified Christ (1 Corinthians 10:4). Probably it symbolized God's gift of rain (Zechariah 14:16-19), with an element of thanksgiving for the rains of the previous year and an element of petition for rain in the year to come.

On the eighth day of the feast this daily libation of water seems to have been omitted. This would make all the more pointed the Lord's words, when "In the last day, that great day of the feast, Jesus stood and cried, saying, If any man thirst, let him come unto me, and drink. He that believeth on me, as the scripture hath said, out of his belly [innermost man] shall flow rivers of living water" (7:37-38). The reference is not to a single verse of Scripture but to the general theme of several Old Testament passages, such as Isaiah 12:3; 55:1; 58:11; Ezekiel

47:1; Joel 3:18; Zechariah 13:1; 14:8. As Israel in the Old Testament drank from that life-giving stream flowing from the riven rock, so Christ offers those who believe in him an ever flowing, never failing, soul satisfying, thirst quenching inner supply of living water.

When Christ spoke to the woman at the well, he himself was the well of living water, a well that would meet her every need. Now, speaking to the Jerusalem throngs, he refers to the Holy Spirit as a river of living water, indeed, to rivers of living water, an overflowing supply able to minister to the needs of others. John makes this clear: "This spake he of the Spirit, which they that believe on him should receive: for the Holy Ghost was not yet given; because Jesus was not yet glorified" (7:39).

As Moses smote the rock, so it was that our Lord was smitten. He returned at length to his home on high and sent the Holy Spirit to take his place on earth. The Holy Spirit filled the disciples. On the day of Pentecost the rivers began to flow. The church was born. Thousands were saved. That ever flowing river flows still. Those who come to Christ are indwelt by the Holy Spirit, who is abundantly able to fill them and pour out his blessing to others.

Over the years, my ministry in Canada and the United States has taken me on countless occasions into the province of Ontario. Whenever my travel plans allow, I drive up to Buffalo, New York, and then on to Niagara Falls. I never cease to be amazed at the sight of the Niagara River pouring its thundering waters over the rim of the falls into the gorge below. No matter how often I return, the water is still cascading out of Lake Erie into the Niagara River, over the falls, down the gorge, and on into Lake Ontario. And it has been doing that for many thousands of years.

There is a place on the Canadian side of the falls where the visitor can descend in an elevator deep into the earth and then along long corridors hewn through rock to a spot where the thunder and roar of the falls make conversation difficult, where the spray from the falls would drench visitors in a moment were they not wearing oilskins, and where the sight of the water, falling in an endless avalanche, takes one's breath away.

Day after day, year after year, century after century, still the water flows. It drives the mighty turbines that supply power to cities both in Canada and the United States. It knows neither measure nor end. So it is with the Holy Spirit. What were a few jars of water from Siloam, poured out at the altar in Jerusalem, compared with the flow of the Niagara? What were Judaism and its ceremonies compared with Jesus and the Spirit?

All this provoked *a lively debate* (7:40-44). There were three kinds of listeners, then as now. There were *those who heeded the message* (7:40-41a): "Many of the people therefore, when they heard this saying, said, Of a truth this is the Prophet. Others said, This is the Christ." The verb for "said" in both cases implies a repeated expression of opinion. What was it about this promise of living water that prompted reactions by so many? Was it the comparison with the water ritual of the feast? Was it the authority with which the Savior spoke? Was it the realization of some profound thirst of soul to which his words appealed? What is it about the gospel that quickens a response in human hearts?

But not all of them believed. There were *those who hindered the message* (7:41b-43) by their argumentative spirit. "Shall Christ come out of Galilee?" they said. "Hath not the scripture said, That Christ cometh of the seed of David, and out of the town of Bethlehem, where David was?" Their unbelief was based on ignorance and half-truth (as so much unbelief is). They were right in their eschatology as far as it went, but wrong in their final conclusion because they did not have all the facts and were too comfortable in their error, or too lazy, to find out the truth. The Scriptures they used to support their unbelief were the Scriptures that helped establish the claims of Christ to be their messiah. He had been born in Bethlehem and he was the Son of David. Nearly all unbelief is bolstered by the same methods of pseudoscholarship.

But there is always a hard core of unbelievers, *those who hated the message* (7:44). "And some of them would have taken him; but no man laid hands on him." It is certain that by now the officers of the Sanhedrin were on the scene. But neither they nor those in the crowd who now joined the people of Jerusalem (7:30) and the Pharisees (7:32) in rejecting Christ dared lay hands on him. Indeed, the officers of the Sanhedrin were impressed by the words of Jesus.

Next comes *a legal defense* (7:45-52). The Sanhedrin now received the testimony of two very different kinds of witnesses, both sets of testimony being equally unwelcome to those who had already made up their minds and were no longer interested in finding out the truth. They had already discovered the truth about Christ to be uncomfortable.

The first defense was *the testimony of the soldiers* (7:45-49), the official, armed Sanhedrin police who now returned empty-handed from their mission to arrest Jesus. "Why have ye not brought him?" their superiors demanded. It seemed incredible to them that a body of armed men could not apprehend one unarmed man right on their own territory, the temple courts.

The answer they received was revealing. "Never man spake like this man," the officers said (7:46). They were astounded by the gracious and God-exalting words of Jesus, and their response has become almost a proverb. Those words have rung down the centuries. Their tribute to Christ has a remarkable ring: "Never man spake like this man."

It was not merely that Jesus was a great orator. It was not simply that he voiced truth in a memorable form. It was not just that he spoke with authority. It was that he spoke the words of God. Whether it was the sermon on the mount or one of his parables, each was a miracle in words; whether he was speaking with that voice that wakes the dead, answering his critics, or instructing his disciples, it was true that no one spoke as he did.

The baffled authorities poured scorn on their militia. "Are ye also deceived: Have any of the rulers or the Pharisees believed on him?" Then, in their contempt for the common people, they added, "But this people who knoweth not the law are cursed" (7:47-49).

What did the common people know of the scope and subtlety of the oral law and the traditions of the elders? Nothing. They were an ignorant crowd who broke the rabbinical rulings everyday. Such untaught people might imagine that the claims of Jesus had some validity. But what can you expect from such dolts? Name a single man of learning and repute who has been deceived by this so-called messiah.

Their argument was annulled at once by *the testimony of the senator* (7:50-52; compare Acts 5:21), and one of the more influential ones too, a man who was a Pharisee, the leaders in this official attitude of hostility to Christ. At this important moment Nicodemus spoke up. John identifies him: "Nicodemus saith unto them (he that came to Jesus by night, being one of them,) Doth our law judge any man before it hear him, and know what he doeth?" (7:50-51).

A spokesman from within their own ranks was an unwanted and disagreeable thorn in the flesh. It must have cost Nicodemus a lot to make even this moderate statement in defense of Jesus. But the irony of that long talk with Jesus, on the occasion of the Lord's first visit to Jerusalem, had gone into his soul. He had sat silent listening to many a vicious attack on the one he was convinced was the messiah. He could stand it no longer. At least he must demand fair play. He challenged his fellow Sanhedrinists. Weren't they breaking the law themselves, passing judgment before the hearing (Exodus 23:1; Deuteronomy 1:16)?

But the others were in no mood to listen to lectures about the law or to hear any voice raised in favor of this Jesus of Nazareth. They turned on Nicodemus in scorn. "Art thou also of Galilee?" No greater insult could be hurled at a patrician like Nicodemus. "Search, and look: for out of Galilee ariseth no prophet," they said (7:52). They were wrong. Elijah, the greatest of all the prophets, came from Gilead. Jonah came from Gath-Hepher, a stone's throw from Nazareth. It is of interest that at one time the Jews thought that Jesus was Elijah (Matthew 16:14) and also that the Lord had likened himself to Jonah (Matthew 12:38-40).

Thus all the attempts recorded in this chapter, made on the life of Christ, were foiled. His hour was not yet come.

The chapter ends with *a lonely departure* (7:53–8:1). The chapter division that occurs at this point is regrettable. As it stands, the chapter reads: "And every man went unto his own house." We should ignore the chapter division and move on to the next verse. The statement then reads: "Every man went unto his own house. Jesus went unto the mount of Olives." Jesus is thus, by the Holy Spirit, set in another contrast with them. Everyone else went home. The priests and Pharisees went home; Nicodemus went home; the captain of the temple went home; the officers went home; the people of Jerusalem went home. Lights were kindled, fires were lit, supper was put on the table, people washed their hands, changed into more comfortable clothes, reclined on their couches, played with their children, yawned, snuffed their candles, and went to bed. Jesus went to the mount of Olives. "The foxes have holes," he once said, "and the birds of the air have nests; but the Son of man hath not where to lay his head" (Matthew 8:20). Shame on you, Nicodemus. Why didn't you invite him home with you?

B. His Exposure of the Wickedness of Men (8:2–9:41)

We are still considering the implications of the Lord's life (7:1–10:42). We have looked at his exposition of the word of God (7:1–8:1). Now we must look at his exposure of the wickedness of men. We shall see him convicting them (8:2-11), contradicting them (8:12-59) and confounding them (9:1-41). Let us look first at the Lord convicting them (8:2-11).

1. Convicting Them (8:2-11)

The story that begins John 8 has been attacked by the critics. Gallons of ink have been spilled trying to prove that John did

not write this story. Editions of the Bible that place it in heavy
brackets have appeared, as if these verses were a questionable
footnote. Commentaries ignore it, apologize for it, put it in the
back of the book. We shall let it stand where it is and treat it as
part of the inspired word of God. The story vouches for itself. It
rings true. The words in which it is told harmonize with the
gospel narratives. It follows on logically from the preceding
events in John.

As we approach this story, so characteristic of Jesus, so fitting
in its context, we note first *the time* (8:2a). It was "early in the
morning." The last view we had of Jesus was the night before,
when he made his way at nightfall to the mount of Olives.
Perhaps he dropped in on Lazarus and his sisters. Perhaps he
spent the night in Gethsemane praying. Perhaps he spent the
night under the stars, looking at the slumbering city, thinking
over the events of the past day, the last day of the feast, and
preparing himself for the encounter he now must face.

Early in the morning he was back in the temple. If the authorities thought they could scare him off, they were mistaken.
Dawn found him in his Father's house. Although he may have
had no place to go for the night, he was in his Father's house at
break of day.

Our attention is drawn next to *the temple* (8:2b). "He came
again into the temple." If you wanted to find Jesus when he was
in Jerusalem, that was the most likely place to look. That is
where Mary and Joseph had found him many years before
(Luke 2:42-46). No doubt many of the pilgrims from Galilee
and various parts of the world, preparing to go home (now that
the feast was over), would come to the temple for one last look
before leaving. Some would be sure to linger to hear this remarkable prophet one more time. "And all the people came
unto him," John says.

We are told of *the teacher* (8:2c): "And he sat down, and
taught them." Authoritative teachers invariably sat down to
teach and their students gathered around them. In the temple
that day Jesus had the crowds. Perhaps some of the temple
officers stopped by to hear this marvelous teacher once again.
Perhaps they had hurried home that night to tell their wives
and children. Perhaps their families mingled with the crowds
that thronged around the Savior.

But then came *the trap* (8:3-6), and a sad but subtle trap it
was. Mention is made of *the scribes* (8:3a). A woman was hauled
into the temple and brought to Jesus by the scribes and Pharisees. Critics make a great deal out of the fact that the scribes
were involved. "John never mentions the scribes," they say.

Well, he does here. Why should he be obliged to mention them
more than once? Why should their mention here be proof that
John did not write this story? The scribes were experts in the
Scriptures. Their order, which had risen to prominence after
the Babylonian captivity, took charge of copying, teaching, and
explaining the law (Ezra was one of the most noted of them).
Before the exile this work was done by Levites but it gradually
became monopolized by a specially trained body of laymen.
They not only copied the written law but they were custodians
of the traditions of the elders, those added rules and regulations
comprising the ever growing oral law.

The synoptic gospels mention the scribes often. Many were
Pharisees. They were frequently denounced by Christ for their
hypocrisy. They are mentioned by John here in company with
the Pharisees, doubtless because of their connection with the
situation now to be presented to Jesus. In the synoptic gospels
the scribes are seen as inveterate enemies of Christ.

The scribes and Pharisees brought *the sinner* (8:3b) to Jesus.
They "brought unto him a woman taken in adultery; and . . . set
her in the midst." Adultery was a serious breach of the law.
Perhaps the guilty woman had been brought before the Sanhedrin first. The wily scribes and Pharisees at once saw in this case
an opportunity to bait a trap for the upstart teacher. With
callous lack of feeling they hauled the woman into the public
arena of the temple court, pushed through the throngs now
surrounding the seated teacher, and stood the woman in front
of Jesus. To be thus publicly exposed, before the hostile eyes of
the nation's religious leaders, before the curious eyes of the
crowds, before the eyes of this holy teacher from Nazareth, who
many thought was the messiah, must have been excruciatingly
painful.

With evident relish her accusers told *the story* (8:4). "They say
unto him, Master, this woman was taken in adultery, in the very
act." This charge was already prejudicial, grossly unfair, since it
takes two to commit adultery. To be caught red-handed meant
that her partner must have been caught in the act too, but she
alone was brought into court. It should have been easy enough
to identify and apprehend her companion. These evil men,
however, were not interested in justice, but only in setting a trap
for Jesus. The way they underlined the poor woman's offense
("in the very act") shows how coarse-minded they were.

But they were not finished yet. They wanted to use *the Scripture* (8:5-6a) to put a noose around her neck, so to speak, and,
what was even more desirable from their point of view, to put a
noose around Jesus' neck. "Now Moses," they said, "in the law

commanded us, that such should be stoned: but what sayest thou?" The laws to which they referred are found in Deuteronomy 22:22 and Leviticus 20:10. Stoning was the usual method of carrying out an execution under the mosaic law. The Lord of course was quite familiar with the severity of those parts of the mosaic law designed to safeguard the sanctity of sex, the holiness of marriage, and the moral purity of the nation.

"But what sayest thou?" That was the trap. "This they said, tempting him, that they might have to accuse him" (8:6a). Only yesterday they had been frustrated by the failure of their temple police to arrest him. Now providence had delivered into their hands a perfect way to see how this man would speak. He could not set aside the law of Moses and set the woman free. (He is incarnate truth.) Nor could he insist on the full penalty of the law, and order the woman stoned. (He is incarnate grace.) If he ordered them to free a woman taken in a capital offense, he would lose the support of the people. If he ordered them to execute her, he would be assuming authority that belonged to the Romans and they could denounce him to Pilate.

But, as Jesus himself once put it, "a greater than Solomon is here." If they thought they could snare incarnate omniscience like that, they were in for a rude awakening.

Our attention is drawn to *the Savior* (8:6b). The Lord did not answer them. In kindness, he refrained from looking at the poor woman. Nor did he spare her accusers a second glance, although he could read the secrets of their souls. Instead, "Jesus stooped down, and with his finger wrote on the ground." This is the only time we read of Jesus writing and we do not know what he wrote. We can be sure, however, that accused and accusers alike looked eagerly to see what it was.

Now comes *the truth* (8:7-9). "They continued asking him," John says. In their self-righteousness they persisted. The fact that he bent over to write in the dust perhaps convinced them he could not look them in the eye. They had him at last, this upstart preacher.

Having finished his writing, he straightened up and looked them in the eye, from the oldest to the youngest. "He that is without sin among you, let him first cast a stone at her," he said. His answer did not lower the standard of the law nor did he allow his infinite love to run away with his sense of right and wrong. Rather he upheld the law in such a way that he put the onus back on them. He "knew what was in man" (2:25). He knew that in the presence of divine holiness and omniscience not one of them would dare lay claim to being without sin.

The word Jesus used, *anamartetos*, occurs only here in the

New Testament. The root is the word *harmartia*, which has to do with failing to miss the mark. It has to do with a breach of the law resulting from such failure. In the New Testament it is always used in a moral sense for a sin, whether by omission or commission, in thought, word, or deed.

The words "cast a stone" can be rendered "cast the stone" and refer to the heavy stone used for execution. Under the law this stone had to be cast by the witnesses. There is no place in the incident where the actual witnesses are produced, so these men have to act as witnesses. The law further required that the witnesses themselves be free from the same crime, lest by stoning the condemned person they become liable to a similar death (Deuteronomy 17:7).

The Lord thus opened up their consciences while at the same time giving a gleam of hope to the woman who was the center of this unhappy scene. He then bent down again and resumed writing in the dust.

The arrow of conviction went home. "They which heard it, being convicted by their own conscience, went out one by one, beginning at the eldest, even unto the last."

Again we wonder what Jesus was writing in the dust. Meanwhile, the eldest went out first. He had the longest list of sins on which to meditate. "And Jesus was left alone, and the woman standing in the midst" (8:9). The convicting arrow had penetrated everyone's soul. Even the people in the courtyard left the scene. Now it was just Jesus and the woman, alone.

Finally, we have *the terms* (8:10-11). Clearly the Lord was not free to mitigate the seriousness of this woman's sin. First of all *he faced her* (8:10): "When Jesus had lifted up himself, and saw none but the woman, he said unto her, Woman where are those thine accusers? hath no man condemned thee?" The crowd had gone away but the condemnation had not gone away. Her human accusers had vanished, spurred on by guilty consciences of their own. But the true judge was still there in all his purity. He alone had the right to cast that first stone. So he looked at her and she looked at him. All around was the silence of the deserted temple.

No one could have invented this story. No one but Jesus could have emptied the temple courts like that.

Then *he forgave her* (8:11). He set before her *a new Lord* (8:11a). "Hath no man condemned thee?" he asked. "No man, Lord," she said—and in that simple statement she made Jesus the Savior and sovereign of her life. Years later Paul put it like this: "If thou shalt confess with thy mouth the Lord Jesus . . . thou shalt be saved" (Romans 10:9). "Lord." She put him on the throne of her heart. She put herself under his authority. The law could only condemn her to death. This man offered her hope when hope was dead. He had not come into the world to judge the world, but that the world through him might be saved (12:47). He would not dismiss her sin; he would die for her sin.

He set before her *a new life* (8:11b,c). He said, "Neither do I condemn thee: go, and sin no more." He did not condone sin; he conquered sin. With a new Lord and a new life, she went on her way.

The Lord's commands are always his enablings. He imparts the power to do what he says. She experienced what Henry Drummond once called "the expulsive power of a new affection." What the law could not do, the Lord could accomplish by a few words from his understanding heart. Everyone else left the temple courtyard that day with a guilty conscience; the woman left it with joy in her heart.

2. Contradicting Them (8:12-59)

John now continues his discussion of the Lord's growing controversy with the Jews. In this section we see him contradicting them. We can divide the section into four parts: Jesus and *his witness* (8:12-19), his world (8:20-24), his word (8:25-45), and his walk (8:46-59). The first of these parts sets Jesus before us as *the light of the world* (8:12): "Then spake Jesus again unto them, saying, I am the light of the world: he that followeth me shall not walk in darkness, but shall have the light of life." This second great I AM saying of Jesus was evidently given on a subsequent occasion, perhaps when people began to recongregate in the temple courts. As yet the rulers were not wholly blinded by their hate, and the rank and file of the common people were vacillating. In the court of the women where Jesus was speaking stood a great golden candelabra, the lamps of which were lighted on the night of the feast of tabernacles, and perhaps on other nights. It symbolized the shekinah glory light which had guided Israel on its wilderness journeys and which had shone for centuries in Solomon's temple. It had departed from the city prior to the Babylonian invasion and has never lighted the second temple. Like the copper shields made by King Rehoboam to replace the golden ones that formerly adorned the temple and which were stolen by the Egyptians, the Jews tried to keep up appearances with a makebelieve shekinah (1 Kings 14:25-28).

It is against this background that the Lord Jesus proclaimed himself to be the light of the world. A glory and a light far greater than the one that shone in the first temple had come here. But it was withdrawn from Judea and from Jerusalem when the Jews consummated their rejection of Christ (Matthew 23:38). Now it shines in splendor in the church—for this age at least. It will one day be restored to Israel (Haggai 2:6-7).

Light is a characteristic of God (1 John 1:5). It was the first thing God created (Genesis 1:3-4). "He that followeth me shall not walk in darkness," Jesus said, "but shall have the light of life." Those who followed the Pharisees, the priests, and the scribes walked in darkness. Those who follow Confucius or Buddha or Krishna or Muhammad walk in darkness. The end of their road is the darkness of death. The person who follows Jesus walks in the light, and the end of that road is the light of life.

Next we have Jesus and *the lies of the world* (8:13-19). The Lord's statement was instantly challenged by his enemies. They gave the lie to his claim. "The Pharisees therefore said unto him, Thou bearest record of thyself; thy record is not true" (8:13). A homespun proverb says, "There are none so blind as those who will not see." The Lord had asserted a great fact about the true nature of things. What the sun was to the earth (the source of physical light) he was to the world (the source of spiritual light). It was a statement of fact by one who knew the ultimate nature of things, by one who could not lie. The reality of light is affirmed by the fact that it shines. It needs no other witness. If a person denies that it shines, no more can be said. Jesus proclaimed a self-evident truth. That he was the light of the world was affirmed by his character, conduct, and conversation. But they called him a liar. There remained no more to be said. The light shone; they said it didn't.

Yet with infinite patience he sought to reason with them. He presented proof along two lines. We note, first, *the Lord's testimony* (8:14-16). "Though I bare record of myself," he said, "yet my record is true." It was impossible for him to lie. His character was the only credential he needed. "For I know whence I came, and whither I go; but ye know not whence I come, and whither I go" (8:14). The Lord was contrasting his own knowledge of his being with their ignorance of his being. He knew what he was talking about. He knew where he had come from and where he was going. He had come out of eternity into time; soon he would leave time for eternity. He had perfect knowledge of his eternal existence. There are truths about God that only God can affirm. They were ignorant of both his true origin and destiny.

"Ye judge after the flesh," he added. "I judge no man. And yet if I judge, my judgment is true: for I am not alone, but I and the Father that sent me" (8:15-16). It was impossible for them to form any valid opinion about him because of their carnality. As he had once said to Nicodemus, "That which is born of the flesh is flesh" (3:6). They judged superficially, according to the only criteria they could grasp: outward appearances. It would make as much sense to ask an ant to define the nature, person, and personality of a human being as to ask an unregenerate man to define the nature, person, and personality of Christ.

He contrasts his spirit with theirs. Ignorant of the facts, they were sitting in judgment on him. He was not being judgmental of them, even though he had all the facts. He was absolute in his knowledge and comprehension, beyond all possibility of making a mistake because of his perfect harmony of mind, heart, and spirit with the one who had sent him. Even so, he withheld judgment because he was here to save, not to condemn. Love, not law, was the motivating factor in his attitude toward his enemies. That was the Lord's testimony.

He did not, however, ignore *the law's testimony* (8:17-19). Because of human failings, the law required two witnesses to establish adequate testimony (Deuteronomy 19:15). "It is also written in your law, that the testimony of two men is true. I am one that bears witness of myself, and the Father that sent me beareth witness of me." A single witness might not have fully observed the incident; spite, hatred, malice, jealousy, revenge, or prejudice might influence his judgment; he might make an honest mistake. Two independent witnesses would not be so likely to provide false witness. In the subsequent trial of the Lord before the Sanhedrin, the authorities had to sift through the testimony of many false witnesses before they found two whose stories were close enough to make the semblance of a case (Matthew 26:59-61).

If the testimony of two men established a fair witness, the testimony of God the Father and God the Son established a testimony beyond question. That was the Lord's point.

The Jews instantly rejected the Lord's assertion that his Father was the second witness. To them, that was unacceptable; "Where is thy Father?" they asked. Jesus answered, "Ye neither know me, nor my Father: if ye had known me, ye should have known my Father also" (8:19). That is obvious enough. Just because I do not know a person is no proof that he or she does not exist. If the Jews had known Jesus they would have known his Father too, because he was always talking to him and about him.

The Lord changed the subject. He began to talk about *his world* (8:20-24), the world from which he came, the world in which his Father lived. His Father was an enigma to them but real to him. We are told by the Holy Spirit just where Jesus was when this conversation took place. He was "in the treasury, as he taught in the temple." The treasury was the most accessible and public part of the temple. It was actually very close to the hall Gazith, where the Sanhedrin held its sessions.

They were standing on *the portals of his world* (8:20a,b). If there was one place where heaven came down to earth, it was there at the temple in Jerusalem. There the sacrifices and offerings were made. There the priests ministered at the altar and cleansed themselves at the laver before going into the holy place to trim the lamps, offer incense on the golden altar, and eat the bread on the table. There hung the veil, a constant reminder that beyond was the holy of holies with the sacred ark, the mercy seat, the winged cherubim. There, in former times, God had sat enthroned in the shekinah glory cloud. If ever there was a place on earth associated with the true and living God it was that temple on mount Moriah. Jesus called it "my Father's house." Had the Jews entered into all the truth of that temple they would have welcomed Jesus.

He was in the court of the women. In Christ, God had come out from the holy of holies, so to speak, to meet the people in the one place to which even the women could come. If Jacob could say of Bethel, "This is none other but the house of God, and this is the gate of heaven" (Genesis 28:17), surely it could be said of the temple in those days when Jesus took up his place in its courts. The Jews were too blind to see it. When Jesus was there, they were standing at the portals of his world.

We notice, too, *the protection of his world* (8:20c). "No man laid hands on him; for his hour was not yet come." He had taken up his stand alongside the stronghold of the enemy. The world at large may not know the strategic importance of the place where God puts his name and where he makes appointments to meet his own. His own people, indeed, may depreciate its importance and neglect the place of prayer. But the enemy knows its importance. He occupies that place whenever he can. In Jesus' day the Sanhedrin (made up of men who for the most part were worldly, carnal, religious, but lost—tools of Satan) was entrenched in the sanctuary. Jesus had invaded what they considered their territory. He was teaching "in the temple." He had invaded ground that belonged to his Father but which was firmly held by the foe.

No matter, they could not harm him. They could have secret

meetings to plan his death. They could gnash their teeth with rage and send out their militia to arrest him, to no avail. Twelve legions of angels were his bodyguard. No power in earth or hell could touch him. His hour was not yet come.

Then, too, we note *the pathway to his world* (8:21-22). The Lord mentions first *its godly direction* (8:21a): "I go my way." In this, of course, he was unique. Of all other human beings, the prophet could write: "All we like sheep have gone astray; we have turned every one to his own way . . . " (Isaiah 53:6), a way the prophet at once labels "iniquity." Not so Jesus. His way was God's way. He could say, "I do always those things that please him [the Father]" (8:29). From the cradle to the cross the sole direction of his life was heavenward and homeward, with every step being marked by obedience to his Father. Only he could say "Follow me" and know that his way was the good and right way and would lead us unerringly home.

He mentions *its great divide* (8:21b-22): "And ye shall seek me, and shall die in your sins: whither I go, ye cannot come." The primary reference is to the Lord's physical presence on earth and to his offer of himself to the nation of Israel as messiah, able and willing to set up the long promised millennial kingdom. The Lord's words have been literally fulfilled in Jewish history.

Taken beyond the immediate meaning, however, the Lord's words are a revelation of the doom of those who reject Christ once too often. A classic Old Testament example, given for all time, is that of King Saul. He "sinned away the day of grace" and God's Spirit thereafter left him to himself and at the mercy of an evil spirit. After the death of Samuel, Saul's history was one of ever increasing sin. The chief occupation of his wicked life was persecuting David, the Lord's anointed. At the end he acutely needed a word from God but was confronted with a silent heaven. Finding the door of heaven barred against him, he went to a witch at Endor and knocked on the door of hell, hoping for some word from beyond to guide him in his distress. God simply opened that door and Saul walked through it to his doom.

Well may those persons beware who trifle with God's grace. How terrible will be the end of those, brought up in a Christian home, taught the truth of God from infancy, who rebel against it and who persistently resist the Spirit of God until at last he goes away to return no more. How desperate the closing hours of such a life. "Ye shall seek me, and shall die in your sins."

The Jews did not understand. They said, "Will he kill himself? because he saith, Whither I go, ye cannot come." The blindness of centuries was already on them. The impossibility of a person finding heaven after rejecting Christ is an awesome truth. The Lord sheds light on it in Luke 16. "Between me and thee," Abraham said to the rich man in hades, "is a great gulf fixed." The Bible closes on a similar note. The character of the dead is fixed, hardened as concrete, at death. The terrible sentence is, "He that is unjust, let him be unjust still: and he which is filthy, let him be filthy still" (Revelation 22:11). The same eternal unchangeability of character is also ascribed to the righteous and holy. As the tree falls, so it lies. No change is possible once the portals of death are crossed.

In speaking thus of his world, a world to which they, with all their religion and self-righteousness, were strangers, Jesus spoke of *the passport for his world* (8:23-24). *The need* (8:23) for such a passport was evident: "Ye are from beneath; I am from above: ye are of this world; I am not of this world." That stated the need in terms of this life and the next life. As far as the life to come was concerned, he and they were worlds apart, as far, indeed, as beneath is from above, as hell is from heaven.

The thought is underlined for us in the opening stanzas of the Bible. In the creation record the Holy Spirit states that on the second day of creation God separated "the waters which were under the firmament from the waters which were above the firmament" (Genesis 1:7). "And it was so" is the Spirit's added comment. What was it that separated the surging seas beneath from the lofty clouds of the sky? It was the atmosphere—an atmosphere which separates those who love the Lord and those who don't.

Saved persons love the atmosphere of heaven, of the prayer meeting, of the Bible class. The lost love the atmosphere of the bar, of the pool room, and the company of other unsaved people. The Lord is from above and those who love him are made to sit "in heavenly places" (Ephesians 1:3,20; 2:6). Not so the lost. They are "from beneath." Water seeks its lowest level. That is its nature. The lost are on their way down.

Jesus said, "Ye are of this world; I am not of this world." The Lord was from heaven. They belonged to earth, a planet under the reign of the enemy. No wonder some kind of new allegiance was required if ever they were to get to heaven.

The nature (8:24) of the passport is clear as well: "I said therefore unto you, that ye shall die in your sins: for if ye believe not that I am he, ye shall die in your sins." The passport to heaven is Christ. He alone can save men and women from their sins. Sin has wrecked and ruined this world and God has no intention of allowing it to wreak its havoc in his. Belief in Christ opens the door to heaven. The text is forceful. The word *he* is in italics, indicating that it has been supplied by the translators and can be left out. "Ye believe not that I am!" That is what Jesus said. They refused to believe his claim to be the I AM of Old Testament revelation, the covenant making God, the source of life. To refuse to believe in him, to give him his proper place and title, is to close the door of heaven irrevocably for all eternity.

Earlier the Jews had brought to Jesus a woman taken in adultery, quoting Moses. They revered him as much as Abraham, the founding father of their nation. Moses it was who brought home to Israel this greatest name for God in the Old Testament: "I AM" (Exodus 3:13-14). The Lord's use of this name was an unequivocal claim to be God.

Nothing less will do in our acceptance of him. We may call him great and good but until we call him God we have missed the mark and are still without our passport to that land where his deity is the most obvious fact in the universe.

The discussion with the Jews now comes to a turning point. He has talked to them about his witness and about his world. Now he talks to them about *his word* (8:25-45). This segment divides into two: what he has to say to them about his *identification with his Father above* (8:25-32) and what he has to say to them about his identification with their father Abraham. The Lord identifies himself with both. We begin with things the Lord had to say to his adversaries about his Father.

They could not have missed the plain identification Jesus had just made with the great I AM of Old Testament revelation. His statement provoked an immediate and, one suspects, an incredulous response. *Those who tested him* (8:25-29) asked: "Who are you?" He replied with *a word about his Father* (8:25-27).

We must not leave this statement isolated from the marvelous context of the Lord's supernatural life and ministry. He had performed countless miracles. He had cleansed lepers, cast out demons, raised the dead, fed the hungry multitudes, and walked on the waves. He had taught them with authority. How insolent they were to challenge him still, demanding some further statement of his identity.

The Lord referred them to *his previous testimony* (8:25b): "Even the same that I said unto you from the beginning." It has been said that this is perhaps the most difficult clause to translate in this whole gospel. The *New English Bible* translation ("Why should I speak to you at all?") best conveys the sense put on the words by the Greek fathers, but that construction does not really fit the context. Far from not wanting to speak to them at all, the Lord told them he still had much to say to them, especially about judgment. Espousing the view of the Greek fathers (who, at least, can be presumed to know the Greek text), some take the view that the Lord was really saying, "How can your question be answered?" The very fact that they asked such a question proves that it would be in vain to answer it. How do you describe a sunset to someone born blind? Words are inadequate. How do you describe a symphony to someone born deaf? Sign language is inadequate.

If the text is allowed to stand as it appears in our version, the Lord has just declared the essential need that people believe in him as the I AM. When they challenged him, he replied, "Just what I say I am," that is to say, "My person is my teaching." His miracles were proof of that.

In continuing with *his present testimony* (8:26-27) the Lord says that there were *things he could not unveil* (8:26) because there were *things they could not understand* (8:27). He said, "I have many things to say and to judge of you: but he that sent me is true; and I speak to the world those things which I have heard of him" (8:26). Up to now the Lord Jesus had revealed himself to them. From now on he would still do that, but he would also reveal what *they* were. Since the revelation of their hearts would be painful and unpalatable, they would dislike it. Truth, however, was truth, whether they liked it or not. Moreover, it did not originate with him. It originated with his Father in heaven. However, "They understood not that he spake to them of the Father" (8:27). The Jewish leaders did not want to believe that he was God and were enraged when he said that he was (5:18), even when his miracles proved that he was. How could he talk to them about anything except judgment when, in spite of the clearest statements of fact, an amazing and continuous outpouring of miracles, his authoritative teaching, couched in compelling and unforgettable form, they still asked "Who are you?"— especially when their unbelief would involve them in the crime of all crimes, his death.

He gave them next *a word about his future* (8:28-29). We notice *what the cross reveals* (8:28a). "Then said Jesus unto them, When ye have lifted up the Son of man, then shall ye know that I am he." Again *he* is in italics (that is, added by the translators): "Then shall ye know that I am." The cross would reveal once and for all who he really was. Matthew describes the Calvary miracles, the darkening sky and the rent rocks, the opening of the graves, and the tearing in two of the temple veil. He records the testimony of the centurion and of those who were with him. "Truly this was the Son of God," they said. Luke adds his voice, "And all the people that came together to that sight, beholding the things which were done, smote their breasts, and returned"

(Luke 23:48). There was no doubt that a terrible crime had been committed, against which heaven and earth alike proclaimed their protest. Moreover, all this was only preliminary proof: "Then shall ye know that I am." Three days later he rose from the dead and put an end to all doubt—except that the authorities still refused to believe. "A man convinced against his will is of the same opinion still."

We notice, too, *what the Christ reveals* (8:28b-29). We see *the Son's absolute dependence on his Father* (8:28b): "Then shall ye know that I am he, and that I do nothing of myself; but as my Father hath taught me, I speak these things" (8:28). God knows everything. Many of the things Jesus knew, he learned the same way we learn: from his education at home and at school, from reading, meditation, and study of the word of God. Other things he learned directly from his unbroken communion with his Father. As God, he was never anything less than God; as a human being, he was never anything more than human. He was man as God intended man to be, indwelt by God and wholly dependent on God. "I am here, Father, to make all that I am wholly available to you." He was at the disposal of God at all times, in all places, under all circumstances. That is why Jesus constantly made statements like the one in this verse: "I do nothing of myself . . . as my Father hath taught me, I speak . . . "

The essence of the fall, of all sin, is independence of God. It was by this "one man's obedience" that God at last was able to demonstrate on earth what God had in mind in making humankind. Jesus is not here defining his deity—he never ceased to be God. He is defining his humanity. He had just defined his deity in the words I AM. The Jews had instantly reacted against a humanity at one with deity.

Next we see *the Father's abundant delight in the Son* (8:29), evidenced by his constant presence and pleasure in him: "And he that sent me is with me: the Father hath not left me alone; for I do always those things that please him." There was not a moment in the life of the Lord Jesus when he did not bring joy and delight to his Father's heart. There was no such thing as the secularization of the Lord's life. Everything he did was motivated by one sovereign principle: he was here to please his Father. It made no difference if he was helping his mother mop the floor as a boy, or if he was learning the Greek alphabet in school, or sawing a piece of wood to make a plow as the village carpenter, or preaching the sermon on the mount, or raising the dead, or weeping in Gethsemane, or dying on a Roman cross, or lying still and cold in death in Joseph's tomb. He always did those things that pleased the Father. Moment by moment, situation by situation, from the cradle to the grave (except for those three dread hours when he who knew no sin was made sin for us) he enjoyed the conscious presence of his Father. And his Father was delighted with him, something which of itself sets Christ apart from all people who have ever lived.

Thus John draws our attention to those who tested him, and to the interplay of his unrivaled claims and the Jewish leaders' refusal to believe.

But John draws our attention also to *those who trusted him* (8:30-32). There was *an easy profession of faith* (8:30): "As he spake these words, many believed on him." After all, these extraordinary claims had the ring of truth about them. The one who made them either had to be mad—or saner than anyone in the world. The wholesomeness, balance, and sanity of the Lord as attested by his life and teaching were incontrovertible. It could not be denied that he was good beyond all others. He was wholly convincing to many.

"Many believed on him" or, as some have rendered it, "put their faith in him." The phrase suggests faith in the fullest sense. They cast themselves on him, so to speak. The words imply energetic faith in a person, something to be distinguished from mere acceptance of certain statements as true. The phrase is characteristic of John's gospel. The only place where it occurs in the other gospels has to do with the faith of a child (Matthew 18:6; Mark 9:42). So, many believed in him. They made that soul saving transfer of trust to him. That is how easy it is to become one of his. But the simplicity of this life transforming transaction has its perils.

The Lord immediately warns that *an essential proof of faith* (8:31) is necessary: "Then said Jesus to those Jews which believed on him, If ye continue in my word, then are ye my disciples indeed." The words "believed on him" can be rendered "believed him," indicating a type of belief inferior to that mentioned in the preceding verse. The Lord's remark is addressed to "those Jews" who had believed him, indicating some members of the hierarchy, perhaps, or some of those who were still held back by their preconceived notions of what the messiah would be like and should do. They believed him, but did not believe *in* him. The Lord, however, was gracious. He acknowledged their belief, however feeble, inadequate, or opinionated. He puts the emphasis on the word *ye.* "If ye continue in my word, then are ye my disciples indeed [truly]." They must truly trust him, not just assent mentally to his claims. The essential proof of genuine, saving faith would soon be evident by their continuing in his word. His teaching would become their rule of faith, the law of their lives.

The Lord speaks, too, of *an emancipating practice of faith* (8:32): "And ye shall know the truth, and the truth shall make you free." How well the Lord read their hearts. There had been some discussion, and it had resulted in favorable response. The Lord at once sifted the wheat from the chaff. Of what value some of that favorable reaction was will be seen at the end of the chapter, when they finally took up stones to kill him.

The Lord here gives brief instructions for true discipleship, as he points out an *identification with their father Abraham* (8:33-45). They must know and obey the truth, the truth as it was in him, and that truth would set them free. Falsehood enslaves; truth liberates. The freedom the Lord had in mind would embrace mind and morals alike. Their intellectual horizons would be broadened and they would be set free from sin's shackles.

The Jews reacted at once to this statement, as we shall see. The Lord had just promised emancipation for all who trusted in him. The immediate response of the Jews was ludicrous. We observe *their boast* (8:33). "They answered him, We be Abraham's seed, and were never in bondage to any man: how sayest thou, Ye shall be made free?" (8:33). Why, their whole history had been one of bondage. They had been slaves in Egypt when Moses came to set them free. For the greater part of the time of the judges they had been in bondage to one or the other of the petty Palestinian principalities they had never driven out of the land. The northern tribes had been carried away into captivity by the Assyrians. The tribe of Judah had been exiled to Babylon. Their return to the promised land had been under the sufferance of a Persian king. They had writhed under the heel of Greek, Syrian, and Egyptian for centuries until at last the Romans had taken over. Their boast, therefore, was one of obvious self-deception. They shrugged those servitudes off as temporary chastisements. Because they had rarely submitted tamely to the periods of servitude, they imagined themselves free. The covenant promise to Abraham guaranteed him the lordship of the earth. How then could they regard themselves as in bondage, all the facts to the contrary notwithstanding? It was a foolish boast, the essence of deluded national and spiritual pride.

The Lord again, and more pointedly now, emphasizes *their bondage* (8:34-36). He exposes the true nature of their slavery: "Verily, verily, I say unto you, whosoever committeth sin is the servant of sin" (8:34). The Lord, we must remember, is here talking to the Jews who "believed" (8:31) and who now prove that they are not true believers at all. To "commit sin" here does not refer to an isolated act but to living a life of sin. All who live that way are in bondage and under the power of Satan, the slave master of all sinful people. How real that bondage is we all know from personal experience. Times without number we find ourselves bound by some enslaving habit and we promise to break free, only to be entangled again.

Nor does a slave have any permanent standing in the master's house (8:35a). At any time he can be sold and hauled away to a worse captivity. This was the haunting horror of every slave in the south before emancipation. A change in the master's fortunes, a dislike taken to a slave, or an attractive offer from another slave owner could lead to a slave's sale. Marriage, children, personal preference, prayers, and supplications made no difference. A slave was a slave and had no rights, no status, no say in his fate. Such are all who are slaves of sin.

In contrast with their slavery, Jesus set his sonship. He is the eternal one: "But the Son abideth ever" (8:35b). We think of Isaac and Ishmael in the house of Abraham. Ishmael was the son of the bond woman, slave-born, with no lasting standing in Abraham's house. Isaac, by contrast, remained in the house and was his father's heir. A much greater than Isaac, Son of a much greater Father than Abraham, was now speaking. He would remain in the house forever. As for the Jews and their boast of freedom, even at that moment God was preparing to cast them out of the house into a bondage that would last for millennia.

The Son is also the emancipating one. Jesus held out hope even yet: "If the Son therefore shall make you free, ye shall be free indeed." Jesus can break sin's fetters. Countless are the testimonies of those, down through the centuries of the Christian era, who have been set free by Jesus from filthy and lying tongues, from passion and lust, from the most binding and horrible of habits.

The Lord, however, was not yet through with the Jews and they were by no means through with him. He speaks next of *their blindness* (8:37-41a). Their claim to be "Abraham's seed" was *partially accepted* (8:37) by the Lord. "I know that ye are Abraham's seed," he said. As far as their physical descent was concerned, that was so. They were Hebrews. But that made their rejection of him only the more culpable: "But ye seek to kill me, because my word hath no place in you." Abraham was "the Friend of God" (James 2:23) but they, lineal descendants of Abraham, had made themselves the enemy of God's Son. The reason? His word had "no place" in them. It could find no entrance.

Their claim to be Abraham's seed was *potently analyzed* (8:38-41a) by Christ. In a frank exposure of their unbelief he said: "I speak that which I have seen with my Father: and ye do that which ye have seen with your father." He contrasted his Father with their father, his words with their deeds. He revealed his origin, and they revealed theirs. His Father was God; their father was the devil. He revealed God in his manner of life; they revealed the evil one in theirs. Far from being the spiritual seed of Abraham, they were the spiritual seed of the devil.

The Jews do not seem, at first, to get the point. "Abraham is our father," they repeat (8:39), a claim Jesus now categorically denies: "If ye were Abraham's children, ye would do the works of Abraham."

About one quarter of the book of Genesis is devoted to the story of Abraham. Although Abraham was born and raised a pagan idolater, when God's word came to him he obeyed it. He turned his back on his old way of life and became a pilgrim and stranger on earth—and a citizen of heaven. He learned to trust and obey. His spiritual pilgrimage began with a great demand on his faith, that he give up his father, and it climaxed with an even greater demand on his faith, that he give up his son. Abraham staked everything on the dependability of God and the reliability of his word. "My word has no place in you," Jesus said, in effect, to the Jews. "So do not boast that you are Abraham's heirs. Abraham is not your father." No, indeed. Their father, the one whose works they were doing, was certainly not Abraham.

Now the Lord makes a shocking charge: "But now ye seek to kill me, a man that hath told you the truth, which I have heard of God: this did not Abraham. Ye do the deeds of your father" (8:40-41a). Their murderous behavior was coming from the devil. He knew them better than they knew themselves. Perhaps he could see the evil one leering at him over the shoulders of his enemies, just as he could detect the devil's voice in what they were saying.

John now tells of the Jews and *their blasphemy* (8:41b-43). The Jews had no doubt now that the Lord was accusing them of being children of the devil. The truth had sunk home at last and they were stung enough to make *their terrible accusation* (8:41b,c). They said, "We be not born of fornication; we have one Father, even God" (8:41). The intimation, if indeed this was the thrust of their jibe, was appalling. He had accused them of being children of the devil. They intimated that there was something suspicious about *his* birth. Who was his father anyway? Who was he to cast slurs on their parenthood, when they, at least, were not born of fornication?

As for them, God was *their* Father. Did not the Bible itself proclaim that fact? Did not God himself call Israel his firstborn? Did he not say, "I am a father to Israel?" (Jeremiah 31:9), in one of the rare places in the Old Testament where God is called a Father?

The Lord swept aside their claim to be children of God and laid bare *their terrible accountability* (8:42-43). He said, "If God were your Father, ye would love me: for I proceeded forth and came from God; neither came I of myself, but he sent me. Why do ye not understand my speech? even because ye cannot hear my word." They were devoid of the Father's character; there was nothing of God to be seen in them. Their hearts were dead—they had no love for him; their ears were deaf—they could not hear what he was saying to them. But he had proceeded from the Father. The origin of his being was in the being of the Father.

The reference seems to be to his eternal generation. There never was a time when God and the Son did not eternally exist. The point here is that the eternal, uncreated, self-existing Son of the living God came forth from the Father, entered into a space-matter-time universe by way of a virgin's womb in accordance with the determinate counsel and foreknowledge of God, to act on earth as God manifest in flesh, in a way that would demonstrate his unfailing communion and cooperation with his Father in heaven. That is true of no other individual. It was certainly not true of the Jews who were seeking to kill him.

We see next the Jews and *their birthmark* (8:44-45). Without any more attempts to soften the message, *the terrible truth was exposed* (8:44a) by Jesus. "Ye are of your father the devil," he said. He was never guilty of name-calling. He loved these people, loved them even though he knew they would kill him. Because he knew their thoughts, their peril, he told them the unpalatable, sober, startling truth. They would never forgive him for saying that. But say it he did, and we can be sure he said it with a sob in his voice and with great sorrow in his heart. He would have saved them, but they would not let him.

The Lord's own commentary on the devil's children in this world is found in his interpretation of the parable of the wheat and the tares (Matthew 13:24-30,36-43). Not all people are children of the devil, just certain people, a special class of people whom the devil introduces among God's people in this world. Wherever the divine sower goes, planting his children in this world, Satan goes planting his counterfeits. Usually they are religious leaders, masters of deceit, spiritually begotten of the devil, sowers of apostasy, enemies of the gospel, disguised to look like good people, at least to the spiritually undiscerning.

Their picture is drawn at length in 2 Peter, in 2 Timothy, and in Jude.

The terrible truth was expanded (8:44b,c). "The lusts of your father ye will do." As a man expresses his inner desires through the members of his physical body, as Christ now expresses his life corporately on earth through the members of his mystical body the church, so Satan expresses his diabolical body life through those who have become his physical instruments for making real his nefarious designs in human history.

In this remarkable passage, the Lord unveils the devil as only he could, who knew him so well, as that personal, powerful spirit of all evil. He said, "He was a murderer from the beginning, and abode not in the truth, because there is no truth in him." A murderer is one who deliberately kills. A liar is one who deliberately deceives. All death on this earth is laid at the devil's door. He is responsible for it. He is a mass murderer, the murderer of our race. He is the author of death, the reason for every graveyard. He hates the human race. The Lord warned our first parents that this murderer was abroad. He gave them a hedge about them to protect them from him: his word. He told them to trust and obey. He warned them against opening the gate: "Thou shalt surely die."

The devil is a liar: "He abode not in the truth." That takes us back beyond the beginnings of human life, to the time when Lucifer, the son of the morning, the anointed cherub dwelling in the light of God's presence, entertained rebellion in his heart and was cast out of heaven along with the angels he had successfully deceived (Isaiah 14:9-14; Ezekiel 28:12-15). "There is no truth in him," Jesus said. The devil's moral being has been distorted. He retains much of his former brilliance of intellect and power of will, but it is warped and bent and twisted so that he is incapable of speaking the truth. His first words on earth were a lie: "Ye shall not surely die . . . ye shall be as gods. . . ."

He is the antithesis of Christ. The Lord is introduced in this gospel as being "full of grace and truth." Satan, the spiritual father of these Jews, is the opposite.

The terrible truth was explained (8:45): "And because I tell you the truth, ye believe me not." Of all people, these religious leaders should have warmed to his grace and welcomed his truth. But instead, hatred and murder were in their hearts; theirs had become a false religion.

We have been considering Jesus and his witness, his world, and his word. This section concludes with *his walk* (8:46-59). Two things are brought out: *his essential sinlessness* (8:46-50) and *his eternal sonship* (8:51-59).

Jesus begins with *the challenge* (8:46-47), with *the absolute transparency of his walk* (8:46). "Which of you convinceth me of sin? And if I say the truth, why do ye not believe me?" He challenged them to point the finger at a single sin in his life. He dared them to take the entire mosaic law in all its 613 commandments and test his life by its letter and spirit, by its sum and substance, by its precepts and principles. He challenged them to take the prophets and the writings as well, the whole Old Testament, and to lay that infallible plumbline alongside his life to see if they could detect the slightest deviation from the upright and the true. He challenged them to go to his home, to cross-question those who had lived with him, his mother, his siblings, to see if he had ever been anything less than perfect. He dared them to go to Nazareth and talk to anyone and everyone who had done business with him to see if he had ever been anything but honest, diligent, generous, and exemplary. He challenged them to go to Nazareth and Nain, to Cana and Capernaum, to Bethesda and to Bethsaida, to trace his footsteps for the past years of public ministry and talk to man, woman, and child to see if they could find the slightest flaw in his conduct.

Had he ever done anything he ought not to have done? Had he ever not done something he ought to have done? Had he ever said anything untrue or taught anything false? Had he ever behaved lustfully or lost his temper or spoken covetously? Had he ever promised anything he had not performed? Could they find any inconsistency in his public or private life? Let them ask friends and foes. Let them take the sermon on the mount and sift his life, whether by the test of law or the test of love.

Surely no man, woman, boy, or girl would dare to issue such a challenge, especially to those who disliked them and wished them ill. But Jesus dared. He knew that not even the omniscient mind of an omnipresent God could find a single sin in him. That being so, he said, if I speak the truth, truth backed by an impeccable life, why don't you believe me?

There was also *the absolute trustworthiness of his word* (8:46b-47): "He that is of God heareth God's words: ye therefore hear them not, because ye are not of God." Confronted with truth incarnate, the only reason they could not recognize it—though he spoke with the thunder of a life that silenced all accusing voices—was because they were not of God. When he spoke, God spoke. They failed to hear God's voice when he spoke.

Now comes *the charge* (8:48-50), and a very wicked charge it was. "Then answered the Jews, and said unto him, Say we not well that thou art a Samaritan, and hast a devil?" (8:48). The only thing of which they could accuse him, which to their warped minds could be said to be sin, was that he had been to Samaria. Since no self-respecting religious Jew would go to Samaria and visit in the homes of Samaritans, who were regarded as aliens and enemies, they concluded he was a Samaritan.

Jewish hatred of the Samaritans was bitter, based on past history, and aggravated by Samaritan claims to be the true Israelites. F. F. Bruce has recorded a legend that Cain was the product of the devil's seduction of Eve and has suggested that possibly the Samaritans accused the Jews of being descendants of Cain, not of Seth. That particular calumny, if it had circulated, must have been especially galling to the Jews. They detested all Samaritans and for these Jews to accuse Jesus of being a Samaritan was particularly vicious—or so they thought. As for Jesus, he loved Samaritans as much as he loved Jews.

Much more serious was the sneer, "Thou art a Samaritan, and hast a devil." To accuse the incarnate Son of God, the holy one of Israel, the sinless Christ, of being demented was an indication of how furious they were and of how completely they were under the control of the devil.

The Lord ignored what they said about his being a Samaritan but took instant issue with their statement that he was demon possessed: "I have not a devil; but I honor my Father, and ye do dishonor me. And I seek not mine own glory; there is one that seeketh and judgeth" (8:49-50). If the Jews thought they could goad him into a display of temper, cause him to flare up in angry resentment, or lash back at them for their provocative remark, they were mistaken. No such sinful reaction was possible from him. With stately dignity he denied the charge that he had a demon. Then quietly but firmly he again asserted the fact that he was here to honor his Father and not himself. They could dishonor him if they so desired. He sought no glory for himself but there was one who did seek his glory and who rightly judged.

He was not put out by their slanders. He could trust his Father to take care of his reputation. What they thought was quite without value.

The Lord turned now from the question of his essential sinlessness to the question of *his eternal sonship* (8:51-59). They had accused him of being possessed by an evil spirit. The opposite was really the case.

There were two areas over which the incarnate Son of God claimed to be absolutely triumphant: over the tomb and over time. Only one who was truly God manifest in flesh could make the kind of claims he now made in the closing part of this long dispute with the Jews.

First, he claimed to be *triumphant over the tomb* (8:51-55). There was no equivocation about it. The statement was plain and unmistakable. It was preceded by the Lord's solemn affirmation, "Verily, verily." He said, "Verily, verily, I say unto you, If a man keep my saying, he shall never see death" (8:51). It is impossible to imagine anyone in his right senses making a statement like that—except Jesus. He made it because it was true, a fact. Those who trust in him will escape death.

A number of years ago, a preacher friend of mine was having an evangelistic campaign on the island of Jamaica. One day there arose a storm at sea and off the coast of the island a ship found itself in distress. It sent out an sos signal to the land, and just as the sun was going down a lifeboat put off from shore, braving the perilous waves, in a desperate race against time, to see if the sailors on that stricken ship could be saved. Darkness came on, and all night long on the island, people watched and waited to hear the news. The next morning my friend set off for town to see what had happened. He did not have to wait long. A newsboy was standing on the corner of the street selling newspapers. Right across the front page, in a banner headline was the one word, SAVED.

My friend was curious. He bought a paper, pointed to the word *saved,* and said to the little boy, "Say, Sonny, what does that word mean?" The boy looked at him in astonishment. "Why, mister," he said, "it means those people never died!"

That is what can be said of those who leave this life, for the shores of eternity, trusting in Christ for salvation. "Those people never died!" We have Jesus' word for that. "If a man keep my saying, he shall never see death." What happens when a believer comes to the end of life's journey and faces the inevitable exodus through the dark portals of death that await us all? In Paul's expressive phrase, that person is "absent from the body . . . present with the Lord" (2 Corinthians 5:8). A believer, lying on his deathbed, opens his eyes and looks into the faces of his loved ones gathered around. He closes his eyes. He opens them to gaze straight into the face of Jesus. He does not see death. He sees *him.*

The Jews were outraged by this claim. We note, first, *how terribly they disbelieved it* (8:52a): "Then said the Jews unto him Now we know that thou hast a devil." The Lord had revealed to them one of the greatest truths ever uttered. Their response was: "Now we know you are demon possessed." Such is the insanity of unbelief.

We note, too, *how totally they disbelieved it* (8:52b-55). This is revealed first in *the argument they raised* (8:52b-53): "Abraham is dead, and the prophets; and thou sayest, If a man keep my saying, he shall never taste of death. Art thou greater than our father Abraham, which is dead? and the prophets are dead: whom makest thou thyself?"

"Who do you think you are?" they asked. They must have stared at him in amazement. When Paul proclaimed a parallel truth at Athens, the truth of resurrection from the dead through Christ, there was a similar reaction (Acts 17:32).

Why, everyone dies, the Jerusalem Jews exclaimed. What about Abraham? The founding father of the Hebrew nation, a man who was called "the friend of God," the man to whose bosom all the faithful go—what about him? If ever a man deserved not to die, it was Abraham. Did he, Jesus of Nazareth, imagine he was greater than Abraham? And what about the prophets? What about Isaiah and Jeremiah and Ezekiel and Daniel? What about Elijah? True, he did not die but even he made no such preposterous claim as to give eternal life to those who would believe in him. Imagine Elijah going around saying, "Whoever keeps my word will never see death."

Who do you think you are anyway? That, indeed, was the crux of the matter. Who was he? Who did he claim to be? Settle that question, and all other questions cease. The Jews stood him alongside the greatest men in their history and compared him with them. That was as far as they were willing to go (Matthew 16:13-14). But faith goes further than that. Faith says, "Thou art the Christ, the Son of the living God" (6:69). As long as the Jews were unwilling to concede his deity, no wonder they were scandalized by the things he said. Once confess his deity, and all things are possible, even the fact that his followers do not experience death.

Death is separation. It separates man from man and it separates man from God for all eternity. Death is not extinction of being. The death of unbelievers is a terrible reality. They die in utter loneliness and go out into the horror of a great darkness to be cut off from God in their sins while the endless ages roll. The death of believers, on the other hand, is a warm welcome home, to be with God and his Son for ever and ever, in a tumult of bliss, in "joy unspeakable and full of glory." Physical death, only a temporary measure pending the coming resurrection, is swallowed up in life abundant and free.

How totally they disbelieved is revealed, too, in *the answer they received* (8:54-55). This answer was threefold. It contained a statement about *God's inerrancy* (8:54a,b): "Jesus answered, If I honor myself, my honor is nothing: it is my Father that honoreth me; of whom ye say, that he is your God." That was a positive affirmation of his deity, a deity that substantiated his claim to protect his own from seeing death. Their God was his Father; their father was the devil; his Father was God.

It would be impossible for the Jews now to mistake what he was saying. As for himself, he was not making this claim to deity in a spirit of self-exaltation; he was simply doing what pleased his Father, who would indeed glorify him and vindicate his claim. If a person bears testimony to himself, that is no testimony at all. Their God, his Father, however, was the one who endorsed his claim. There was no room for error or self-deception.

There was a statement about *their ignorance* (8:54c-55a): "Ye say, that he is your God: yet ye have not known him; but I know him." He was not self-deceived; they were. They imagined they knew God but in reality they were strangers to him. Were they Abraham's seed (8:33)? They were the serpent's seed (8:44). They did not know God at all. They might take their seats in the Sanhedrin, they might don the robes of the rabbi, they might be the rulers of the Jewish religious establishment, they might delight in the praise of men, they might set themselves up as interpreters of the law and as guardians of the temple, they might extend their authority at home and abroad in the synagogues and throughout the Diaspora, but they did not know God.

There was a statement concerning *his integrity* (8:55b): "I know him: and if I should say, I know him not, I shall be a liar like unto you: but I know him, and keep his saying." There are two words for *know* in this verse. In describing their ignorance ("ye have not known him") the Lord used a word that carries the idea of knowing by experience or by effort, by acquiring knowledge, by becoming acquainted (*egnokate*). For all their learning they still did not know God. In proclaiming his own knowledge of God ("I know him") he used a word (*oida*) that conveys the idea of knowing without effort. Their efforts to know God were objective; his knowledge of God was subjective. Their knowledge of God was progressive; his knowledge of God was absolute.

It was part of the integrity of his character that, at the cost of his life, he should tell them the truth about himself. They might treat his witness with incredulity and violence. But he had to tell them the truth, or he would be as false as they were. Further emphasizing that contrast, he added, "But I know him, and keep his saying [word]."

His claim to be triumphant over the tomb led naturally to the next claim, that he was *triumphant over all time* (8:56-59). There are three movements in the closing drama of this confrontation with the Jews. Twice they had injected Abraham into the argument. Now the Lord has something to say about him. He mentions *the rejoicing of the Hebrew patriarch* (8:56): "Your father Abraham rejoiced to see my day: and he saw it, and was glad." They had been boasting about Abraham and their descent from him. They had been standing Jesus alongside Abraham and daring him to make himself greater than their most revered patriarch. Indeed, Jesus continued, Abraham had not only looked forward to seeing his day, he had actually been given a sight of it—he had seen it and had rejoiced.

At some point in his history Abraham had not only seen the day of Christ in a messianic sense, he had been given a vision of something more personal and intimate than that. "He rejoiced to see my day," Jesus said. When it was that Abraham received this Pauline-type vision (2 Corinthians 12:1-5) we are not told. Perhaps it was when God first called him. Perhaps it was when God confirmed to him the promise of the coming seed. Perhaps it was on Moriah when he so graphically prefigured the tragedy of Calvary and the resurrection that lay beyond. Perhaps it was when he met Melchizedek if, as some believe, Melchizedek was one of the types of Christ. Maybe it was when he was visited by angelic guests just before the fall of Sodom. The Lord did not enlarge on the subject. He simply told the Jews a truth that they then treated with the same scandalized outrage they treated everything else he had to say in this dialogue. He told them that Abraham, the one they called their father, actually saw his day and rejoiced. The word for "rejoiced" is *egalliasato* which means "leaped for joy."

Next comes *the reaction of the Hebrew people* (8:57): "Then said the Jews unto him, Thou art not yet fifty years old, and hast thou seen Abraham?" They thought they had him now. It was two thousand years since the time of Abraham. This may have been an indication of how old Jesus looked, although he was actually only thirty-three. (The age of fifty marked the attainment of maturity among the Jews; the priests who served under the Old Testament economy retired at the age of fifty.) He was still younger than many of them. So how could he have seen Abraham, or Abraham have seen him? The whole idea was ridiculous.

Now comes *the revelation of the Hebrew prophet* (8:58-59) whose day Abraham had rejoiced to see, the one to whom all the other prophets bore witness. And what a revelation. Here we have an unmistakable declaration of deity in humanity. Three swift steps climaxed this drama, all of which were still vivid in John's mind as he wrote to quell whatever questioning was arising in his day about the deity of Christ.

There was *a clear disclosure of his deity* (8:53): "Jesus said unto them, Verily, verily, I say unto you, Before Abraham was, I am." That was the third time he had said it (8:24,28). Now he couched his claim to be the I AM in terms not even the dullest could misunderstand.

It is worth remembering that I AM was the greatest name for God known to the Jews and was treated with utmost reverence by them. It was known as the ineffable name. They would not speak it. It is said that when a scribe was copying the Scriptures and came to this name for God he would take a new pen just to write that name. It is said that when a reader in the synagogue came to this name in the sacred text, he would not read it; he would bow his head in worship, and the congregation, knowing he was thinking the ineffable name, would bow in worship too.

We can imagine, then, the horror with which the unbelieving Jews heard Jesus make this statement. He looked them calmly in the face and said, "Before Abraham was, I am." Not "Before Abraham was, I was"—although that would have been true. He was stating that he, Jesus, was the Jehovah of the Old Testament. Not simply that he had priority over Abraham because he had existed before Abraham existed or the Hebrew nation existed, but that he had pre-eminence because he had always existed. He belonged to eternity, not to time. There never had been a time when he had not existed. He was eternal, as God is eternal. These are the words of the most daring and deluded blasphemer—or they are the words of God manifest in flesh.

This disclosure of his deity was followed by *a clear denial of his deity* (8:59a): "Then took they up stones to cast at him." The time for argument was over. They were outraged beyond words. There was only one thing to do with such an audacious, brazen blasphemer—they must put him to death. We can have no doubt that the devil was behind this attempt on his life. With the backing of Leviticus 24:16, as they supposed, they took up stones to stone him.

The word for "stones" literally means "heavy stones." There were plenty of these at hand. Herod's workmen were still employed in the temple reconstruction. Thus would the Jews murder their messiah and put an end once and for all to the life and ministry of the Son of God.

It is significant that this section begins with Jesus defending a woman with the words, "He that is without sin among you, let him first cast a stone at her" (8:7) and ends with the enraged Jewish leaders actually picking up stones to hurl at him, to give him the death from which he had saved the woman.

But it was not to be. The Savior was not to die in that way. The incident concludes with *a clear demonstration of his deity*

(8:59b): "But Jesus hid himself, and went out of the temple, going through the midst of them, and so passed by." Again there is a blending of the human and divine in this escape. He could, of course, have called down fire from heaven. He could have turned them into stone. Instead, he resorted to a human expedient. He "hid himself" or "was hidden," perhaps by his friends who maybe crowded around and concealed him. Be that as it may, he was also protected by his deity; he passed right through them on his way out of the temple. Not a stone was cast. Not even their fury or all the devil's urging could nerve those arms to throw the stones they had in their hands. Thus ended an eventful and tragic day.

They had asked question after question, not wanting answers, but only to argue: "Where is thy Father?" (8:19), "Who art thou?" (8:25), "Will he kill himself?" (8:22), "Whom makest thou thyself?" (8:53). They had called him a liar (8:13), an illegitimate son (8:41), a Samaritan (8:48), a demoniac (8:48,52). Finally they had taken up stones to make an end of him (8:59). And who were they? The world has forgotten their names; not a single one is recorded.

3. Confounding Them (9:1-41)

In section one of this part of John's gospel the Lord's deity is declared (1:19–4:54). In section two that deity is disputed (5:1–10:42). We have studied the impact of the Lord's life in urban Jerusalem (5:1-47) and in rural Galilee (6:1-71). We have been considering the implications of his life (7:1–10:42). We have been contemplating his exposition of the word of God (7:1–8:1) and his exposure of the wickedness of men (8:2–9:41), an exposure that climaxed as we have just seen, in his forthright claim to be God and in an immediate attempt by the Jews to stone him to death. We have seen the Lord convicting the Jews (8:2-11) and contradicting the Jews (8:12-59). We have watched the storm clouds gather ever darker in the sky. But the Lord has not finished with his enemies yet. In this section we see him confounding the Jews (9:1-41). First we see the Lord *delivering the blind man* (9:1-34) Their violent display of hostility in the temple did not deter him. It only led him to give them another demonstration of his deity, a deity they rejected and would continue to reject until at last they had him nailed to the tree.

We begin, then, with *the case* (9:1-5): "And as Jesus passed by, he saw a man which was blind from his birth" (9:1). Obviously this case was *difficult* (9:1); John seems to have chosen some of the Lord's hard cases for illustrations. This case is sign number seven in John's choice of signs. It is a dividing point in the Lord's dealings with the Jewish people.

Something about this poor man's need arrested Jesus. His was a congenital disease, the only one recorded in the gospels. The man was born blind. He had never seen the light of day, the silver gleam of Galilee, or a sunset over Carmel. He had never seen a daisy, a bird, a human face. He had grown up from babyhood through boyhood to manhood in the impenetrable darkness of the totally blind.

This case was also *debatable* (9:2-3a). The disciples wanted to know: "Master, who did sin, this man, or his parents, that he was born blind?" Jesus said, "Neither hath this man sinned, nor his parents." The supposition was that all such disability was the result of sin.

The Lord swept both those suggestions aside. This man's blindness was not punishment for sin. The Lord does not say that no human disabilities are the result of sin. He says that such was not the case in this man's life. There was a higher cause.

It was a *deliberate* (9:3b-5) case, planned in heaven with a specific divine purpose in mind. Its first was *to reveal God's touch* (9:3b) in a human life: "That the works of God should be made manifest in him." No matter how contrary appearances may be from our limited perspective, we must take our stand on a threefold proposition:

God is too loving to be unkind.

He is too wise to make any mistakes.

He is too powerful to be thwarted in his infinite purpose.

Doubtless many people questioned the goodness of God in the face of this man's congenital disability. On the surface of things he seemed condemned to a life of blindness and beggary, robbed of much that adds ease and pleasure to life. Arguing from his blindness they could build a case for agnosticism, atheism, even for those blasphemous tirades against God heard at times on university campuses and among people who consider themselves to be intellectuals. The answer to all such bitter philosophies is to be found in the book of Job, and is further illustrated by the case of this blind man. In the book of Job we find Job, his wife, and his friends debating the calamities that had overtaken Job—and all of them were wrong because all were arguing from incomplete data.

This man's blindness was the touch of God in his life—not punitive, not arbitrary. It was part of a plan unknown to anyone but God and his Christ, a plan intended to bring Christ into this man's life and ultimate praise and glory to God.

It was also intended *to reveal God's timing* (9:4) in a human life: "I must work the works of him that sent me, while it is day: the night cometh, when no man can work." In other words, this man's blindness was timed by God to coincide with the Lord's earthly ministry. God has other timings in his providential dealings with other persons. Although those marvelous conjunctions of our need and God's purposes are often obscured to us, they are clear to him. Perhaps part of eternity will be devoted to unraveling for us some of the marvels and mysteries of God's ways. If we cannot see those ways, the fault lies with us, not with God. This is brought out by David: "He made known his ways unto Moses, his acts unto the children of Israel" (Psalm 103:7). If the rank and file of the children of Israel could not see beyond their circumstances it was because they did not know God as well as Moses knew him. Moses could see farther than they. They could see only the *what* of their circumstances; Moses could see the *why.*

The Lord Jesus lived his life moment by moment in conscious cooperation with the known will of his Father. He understood the reason for this man's disability. It had been planned to coincide with the messiah's earthly ministry, when God was at work in a unique way on earth. The "day," to which the Lord referred, was the time of his personal sojourn on earth, the time when all kinds of miracles were performed. The "night" is the present time of his withdrawal from earth.

The case of the man born blind was also intended *to reveal God's truth* (9:5) in a human life: "As long as I am in the world, I am the light of the world." This man's blindness becomes the background against which Jesus was able to make another of his I AM statements. "I am the light of the world." He had made the statement once before (8:12), but this circumstance enabled him to repeat it. In the former instance the background related to a moral problem, the woman taken in adultery; here the background is a mental problem, the problem of pain and suffering and God's seeming indifference. Here the definite article is omitted, so the statement could read: "I am light to the world." The Lord then proceeded to give physical sight to this man in order to demonstrate God's active involvement in the mysteries of life. Only through Christ can final answers be found to what otherwise appear to be tragedies.

John now describes *the cure* (9:6-12) and its aftermath. He tells us how *the man was healed* (9:6-7). First came *the clay* (9:6). In healing this man, Jesus performed "work," according to the rabbinic definition of work. He spat on the ground, made clay, and placed it on the blind man's eyes. We don't know why he did this. Sometimes the Lord healed people by a simple word of command. Sometimes he employed means. But with or without means, God is the one who heals.

The clay was applied; *the command* (9:7) followed: "Go, wash in the pool of Siloam, (which is by interpretation, Sent). He went his way therefore, and washed, and came seeing." The miracle happened. He saw. He was healed.

Then, *the man was heard* (9:8-12). His voice was raised in testimony and praise of the one who had given him sight. We note *what the multitudes said* (9:8-10). There was a mixed reaction to the miracle. Those acquainted with the man could hardly believe the evidence of their own eyes. "Is not this he that sat and begged?"

That's a second fact about the man: the man who was blind, was blind no more; the man who had begged, begged no more. A genuine work of grace always turns persons into useful members of society, as well as opens their eyes to divine truth. Still puzzling over the transformation, some people said, "He is like him." Others said, "This is he." So they appealed to him. "I am he," he said. "How were your eyes opened?" they demanded.

That's another thing about a miracle of grace. People want to know what happened. A transformed life is a powerful testimony.

We note also *what the man said* (9:11-12): "A man that is called Jesus made clay, and anointed mine eyes. . . . " Then they said, "Where is he?" "I know not." It is remarkable that this man was so ignorant of Jesus. He did not know who he was or where he was. It is instructive of the fact that we do not have to know much about Jesus in order to be saved. All this man knew was his name—astonishing in view of the impact of Christ's ministry on the whole country, not to mention the debates about him going on all over Jerusalem. All he knew was his name: Jesus, the one who saves. That is the gospel reduced to bare minimum.

One does not have to be a theologian in order to experience salvation. One does not have to have thorough knowledge of who Jesus is. Nor does a person have to know where he is: at God's right hand. We need only to know his name and be willing to respond in faith.

The discussion in Jerusalem swirling around the blind man's cure soon came to the ear of the Pharisees. Now comes *the clash* (9:13-29) between them and the new convert.

We note their threefold attack. First they *attacked the man's faith* (9:13-17). John draws attention to *their question* (9:13-15). They asked how he had received his sight (9:13-15), the question being all the more urgent from their point of view because Jesus had performed this miracle on the sabbath (9:14). He had repeated the offense that had embroiled him in controversy with the Pharisees the last time he was in Jerusalem (5:1-9).

Next comes *their quibble* (9:16). "This man is not of God, because he keepeth not the sabbath day. Others said, How can a man that is a sinner do such miracles? And there was a division among them." On one side of the fence were those ruled by legalism. Their stance was that this man could not be of God because he does not keep the sabbath. Unless he would subscribe to their convoluted interpretations of the law, he could not be of God. On the other side were those who were ruled by logic. Their position was that anyone who could perform a miracle of this magnitude could not possibly be a sinner but was evidently of God.

Some have seen in this difference of opinion among the Pharisees a reflection of the two popular rabbinic schools of the day. The followers of Shammai would argue from established principles: "A man who breaks the Sabbath is a sinner." The followers of Hillel would argue from evident facts: "A man who performs obvious good works is not a sinner."

John pinpoints *their quandary* (9:17): "They say unto the blind man again, What sayest thou of him, that he hath opened thine eyes? He said, He is a prophet" (9:17). "What do *you* have to say about him? It was your eyes he opened." They were hoping to get more details. One group was hoping to intimidate the man and get him to say something derogatory about Jesus. The other group hoped that in his gratitude the man would be more positive in what he had to say about him. Under all this bullying the man himself, who seems to have been made of sterner stuff than his parents, came to his own conclusion. "He is a prophet," he said. That was not the answer the legalists wanted. It put them in a quandary indeed.

Having attacked the man's faith, the Lord's enemies next *attacked the man's family* (9:18-23). Here they were more successful. There was still a loophole. Maybe the man had not been born blind after all. His own testimony could be challenged, since nobody can remember facts connected with their birth. Maybe he had contracted blindness by disease or accident in very early childhood. So they summoned the man's parents. "Is this your son, who ye say was born blind? how then doth he now see?" they demanded. Intimidated, the man's parents answered with caution: "Yes, he is our son and, yes, he was born blind. Yes, obviously he can now see, but no, we cannot tell you how it is he can now see. We don't know how it happened or who made it happen." They shrank from incurring the wrath of the most powerful party in Jerusalem. They referred the authorities back to their son. "He is a grown man. Ask him. He's old enough and able enough to answer your question." We should read this verse emphasizing the pronouns: "*We* know that this is *our* son, and that *he* was born blind: But by what means *he* now seeth, *we* know not; or *who* hath opened *his* eyes, *we* know not: *he* is of age; ask *him: he* shall speak for *himself.*" That put the ball back in their court.

John adds a word of explanation for this excessive caution: "These words spake his parents, because they feared the Jews: for the Jews had agreed already, that if any man did confess that he was the Christ, he should be put out of the synagogue" (9:22). Such is organized religion. With the frowns of the religious establishment in view, the parents allowed their joy at their son's healing to be swallowed up by their fear of the reprisals they could expect if they gave verbal credit to Christ. They stand in a very poor light, in company with many others who have compromised their testimonies for Christ through fear of the consequences.

The Pharisees were not through yet. They next *attacked the man's friend* (9:24-29). First comes *the demand* (9:24): "Then again called they the man that was blind, and said unto him, Give God the praise: We know that this man is a sinner."

The phrase "Give glory to God" is a solemn charge to tell the whole truth, as in Joshua 7:19. No matter what Jesus said or did, in the eyes of the dominant party he was a sinner. The word for "sinner" here is one that means to miss the mark, one who fails to keep the prescribed law. In the New Testament the word is always used in a moral sense. It is used of one who by omission or commission, in thought, word, or deed, is guilty of sin. (It is also the word used to describe the sin offering in Hebrews 10:6-8).

"We know that this man is a sinner," they said. The word for "know" is the same one used by the man's parents. "We know that this is our son" (9:20). Used by the Pharisees here, it is an arrogant claim to absolute knowledge. "It makes no difference what *you* say; *we* know that this man is a sinner."

Now comes *the declaration* (9:25-27). The blind man stands up for his friend in a bold testimony for Christ: "Whether he be a sinner or no, I know not; one thing I know, that, whereas I was blind, now I see" (9:25). He refuses to discuss the question of whether or not Jesus was a sinner. We can be quite sure he had his own views on that: no man who was not of God could have done for him what this man had done. To him the question of whether or not Jesus was a sinner was beside the point. Here was one thing he knew: "Once I was blind," he said, "now I see." That testimony has been echoed by millions down through the centuries. New Christians, not qualified to debate theological issues, can always say of their new vision of Christ as Savior: "Once I was blind, now I see." It is hard to refute a testimony like that.

So the Pharisees discovered. But the man was not through yet. There is something attractive about this man. His blindness had developed a fiercely independent strain in his character. Again they asked him: "What did he to thee? how opened he thine eyes?" They kept on needling him on this point because, to them, it was the crux of the matter. By making clay on the sabbath, Jesus had done work and broken the sabbath.

But the man was losing patience. He was not intimidated by their robes and phylacteries, by the fringes on their garments, or by the rest of their religious paraphernalia—he had never seen clothes of any kind until now. "I have told you already," he said, "and ye did not hear: wherefore would ye hear it again? will ye also be his disciples?" There is a touch of sarcasm in his words. He knew his questioners had no intention of becoming disciples of Jesus. The word *also* marks an advance in this man's understanding of Jesus. He was learning fast. He could see he had to take sides, that either loyalty or a denial was being forced on him. His gratitude precluded any possibility of denial.

Now comes *the derision* (9:28-29). "Then they reviled him, and said, Thou art his disciple; but we are Moses' disciples" (9:28). The word *reviled* means "railed at." They had passed beyond the point of rebuke. They abused him. The word is used in only three other places in the New Testament. First, when Paul called the high priest "a whited wall" because he had commanded someone to smite him on the mouth, the spectators said, "Revilest thou God's high priest?" (Acts 23:4). Paul excused himself on the ground that he did not know that his persecutor was God's high priest. There was certainly nothing about his conduct to reveal that fact. Second, the word is used by Paul to describe his own customary behavior: "Being reviled, we bless; being persecuted, we suffer it" (1 Corinthians 4:12). Third, the word is used to describe the conduct of the Lord Jesus: "Who, when he was reviled, reviled not again" (1 Peter 2:23).

To rail or revile is the answer of those who have been defeated in debate. They cannot support their position, so they resort to abuse. They reviled not only the man, they also reviled the master: "We know that God spake unto Moses: as for this fellow, we know not from whence he is" (9:29). In their estimation, Moses stood next to God. God had spoken to Moses. The oral law (the basis for their opposition to Christ, that vast and ever growing body of tradition) was supposed to have been given to Moses at Sinai along with the written law. They looked with disdain at the man before them. Their lips curled with scorn. And that was a confession of their own blindness. They were far more blind spiritually than the man standing before them had ever been physically.

Now the light began to dawn in the soul of the man who had been born blind. His enemies had given him *the clue* (9:30-34) and have *the inspired logic of the healed man* (9:30-33). It is developed in three swift steps. First there is *his astonishment* (9:30): "Why," he said, "herein is a marvelous thing, that ye know not from whence he is, and yet he hath opened mine eyes." It was what we would call today a quantum leap. There were two wonders: the wonder of the miracle and of the man who had given him his sight. Such a miracle worker could have come from only one place—heaven. The other wonder was that of the unbelief and hostility of the Jewish authorities. How could they fail to receive with open arms someone able to open blind eyes?

Then there is *his assessment* (9:31) of God's holiness and helpfulness: "Now we know," he said, "that God heareth not sinners"—that was simple logic, a universal fact—"but if any man be a worshiper of God, and doeth his will, him he heareth" (9:31). This blind man knew the Scriptures. He was quoting to these religious leaders the word of God: "The LORD is far from the wicked: but he heareth the prayer of the righteous" (Proverbs 15:29); "And when ye spread forth your hands, I will hide mine eyes from you: yea, when ye make many prayers, I will not hear: your hands are full of blood" (Isaiah 1:15); "Hear, I pray you, O heads of Jacob . . . Who hate the good, and love the evil; . . . Then shall they cry unto the LORD, but he will not hear them" (Micah 3:1-2,4); "The eyes of the LORD are upon the righteous, and his ears are open unto their cry" (Psalm 34:15); "If I regard iniquity in my heart, the LORD will not hear me" (Psalm 66:18). It was salt in the wounds of his enemies to hear this man proclaiming such truths, such sanctified common sense.

Finally we note *his assurance* (9:32-33). He cites *his solitary case* (9:32): "Since the world began was it not heard that any man opened the eyes of one that was born blind" (9:32). Their Scriptures recorded no such miracle. Memory, experience, all history, had no such miracle to display—that someone was healed of congenital blindness. His was a solitary case, a tribute to the nature of the one who had healed him.

He cites, too, *his solid conclusion* (9:33): "If this man were not of God, he could do nothing." He was now quite sure who Jesus was. As in the case of the woman at the well, we see a man growing in the knowledge of God. All the might of the Sanhedrin could not cow him. The arguments of the Pharisees could not shake him. The one who had performed this miracle was "a man that is called Jesus" (9:11). This man was a prophet (9:17). He was not a sinner as the Jewish authorities claimed. He was a man of God, a man God heard, a man who worshiped God, a man "from God."

The inspired logic of the healed man is followed by *the infuriated loathing of the Hebrew masters* (9:34). We note *what they called him* (9:34a): "They answered and said unto him, Thou wast altogether born in sins." They were enraged because they were being deflated in the argument by this unlearned man. Here was a man, singularly marked as a sinner from birth by his disability, presuming to teach them, the Pharisees. What impertinence. They were the custodians of the law, the cultured and educated elite. He was an absolute nobody. How dare he teach them!

We note also *why they cursed him* (9:34b): "Dost thou teach us?" It was bad enough that they could not get the better of him in argument. But that he should dare to answer them back and quote the Bible to them and challenge their verdict concerning Jesus! The man's words were intolerable.

We note, too, *where they cast him* (9:34c). In their rage "they cast him out." They excommunicated him from the synagogue, cut him off from the religious life of the nation, made him a pariah, a spiritual leper, to be avoided by one and all who did not want to share his fate. What that would mean to the man socially as well as spiritually can be appreciated only by those brought up in a tight religious community from earliest days, used to the comfort of religion, the compassion of the faithful, and the sense of community, of belonging, that such an association brings.

Excommunication meant that no one would employ him. His family would disown him. He could have no part in the religious services of the synagogue or in the ritual worship of the temple. Anyone caught helping him would be exposing himself to a similar fate.

But, surprised as he may have been by this turn of events, he was certainly not discouraged. He was made of tougher fiber. The all-encompassing plus that swallowed up every minus was the fact that he could see.

All this time the Lord had remained out of sight. He wanted to allow the man to "grow in grace, and in the knowledge of God." He must begin to mature as a believer and that meant trusting Christ in spite of frowning circumstances. The Lord often does that, especially at the beginning of any new venture of faith. It is God's way of developing the new spiritual senses imparted to those who put their trust in Christ. In the case of this man it was all the more imperative. He must learn that the miracle was not the important thing; it was secondary. He was to learn to walk this new life by faith, not by sight.

So far we have seen the Lord delivering the blind man; now we see him *defending the blind man* (9:35-41). Note *how Jesus exonerated his client* (9:35-38). Having found that persuasion did not work, the religious authorities resorted to persecution. When all else fails, that is the final refuge of organized religion.

The Lord knows our frame; he remembers that we are dust (Psalm 103:14). This man, resilient and mentally alert as he was, was still a man of human fears and failings. God will never allow us to be tested beyond what he in his wisdom knows to be our breaking point. And Jesus knew all about this man. We can picture him, thrilled with the novelty of being able to see, yet at the same time bewildered. He looked up and saw the blue vault of heaven and fleecy clouds in the sky; he had never seen that before. He could see the temple all agleam with gold; he had never seen that before. He could see the animals being led to the temple for sacrifice. He thinks to himself—so that's what a sheep looks like. And what an odd shape for a bullock. He could see the people; he had never seen a human face before. What a variety of faces there were!

But why did those Pharisees refuse to acknowledge this man Jesus? And who exactly was he? Where could he find him? What did Jesus look like? He would recognize him, of course, by the sound of his voice. But it was perplexing. Should he go home? Would his parents be too frightened to take him in?

He was not left to wander about the city alone for long. There was one person in town who was unafraid of the Pharisees. "Jesus heard that they had cast him out; and when he had found him, he said unto him, Dost thou believe on the Son of God?" (9:35). Some think the original text here reads, "Dost thou believe on the Son of man?" But opinions are divided. In any case, the Lord now presented himself before this man in order to give him a further revelation of himself as the one who is worthy of total allegiance.

Jesus found him, cast out by a dead religious system. He

presented himself before him as the one in whom, now and forever, he should believe. As Son of man, he was here to link himself with humanity and fulfill God's purposes on earth. As Son of God, he was coeternal, coequal, with the Father; he was worthy to be worshiped as God over all, blessed for evermore.

The man was ready for either revelation. Even if the correct reading is "Son of man," the blind man responded to him as Son of God. He first expressed his ignorance of who this one was in whom he must believe: "Who is he, Lord, that I might believe on him?" he said.

At once, Jesus revealed himself: "Thou hast both seen him, and it is he that talketh with thee" (9:37). The man's eyes were riveted to the face of Jesus. He had not seen much yet with these new eyes of his. But this he knew. If he lived to be as old as Methuselah, he would never see a more wonderful sight than the face of Jesus. And that voice—he had heard it before and he knew its authority, truth, and power. He had no hesitation. Down he went at Jesus' feet. "Lord, I believe," he said. "And he worshiped him."

Jesus accepted his worship. In truth he was the Son of God, entitled to human adoration. The blind man had begun by describing him as "a man called Jesus." He now worships him as God. The word used is *prosekunesen*, which carries the idea of prostrating oneself in homage and adoration and is used for the act of worship.

Finally we see *how Jesus exposed his critics* (9:39-41). His first statement does not seem to have been made to anyone in particular. It was more in the nature of summing up this whole incident. "And Jesus said, For judgment I am come into this world, that they which see not might see; and that they which see might be made blind." Behind those words lay the contrast between the man born blind who now could see (and not just physically) and the spiritual blindness of the Pharisees and the nation of Israel. The Lord's presence in the world was *a great divide* (9:39), separating believer from unbeliever, true from false, the seeing from the blind.

Some Pharisees standing by instantly reacted to this statement. Christ then exposed the fact that they were laboring under *a great delusion* (9:40-41): "And some of the Pharisees which were with him heard these words, and said unto him, Are we blind also? Jesus said unto them, If ye were blind, ye should have no sin: But now ye say, We see; therefore your sin remaineth."

If their eyes had been truly opened, they would have been prostrate in the dust before him, following the example of the man born blind.

The blindness of the nation of Israel toward Christ, epitomized by these Pharisees, was real. It led them to murder their messiah. It has persisted for nearly two thousand years. It led the apostle Paul, who once had been of their number, to say, "Blindness in part is happened to Israel, until the fulness of the Gentiles be come in" (Romans 11:25).

In John 9 it is not so much that organized religion excommunicated a man in touch with Jesus. Rather, Jesus excommunicated organized religion out of touch with him.

C. His Explanation of the Way of Life (10:1-42)

The apostle John has been describing the implications of the Lord's life. He has shown us his exposition of the word of God (7:1–8:1) and his exposure of the wickedness of men (8:2–9:41), ending in his statement that the Jews were not only blind but that they were sinfully blind. We now have his explanation of the way of life (10:1-42).

1. His Death in Focus (10:1-21)

In the first part of this important revelation his death is in focus (10:1-21); in the second part his deity is in focus (10:22-42). The first part of the discussion is centered around *the shepherd and the fold* (10:1-15); the remaining part of the discussion has to do with the shepherd and the flock. The monologue of this chapter follows on naturally from the fact that the blind man has left the fold of Israel for the flock of the good shepherd.

In the background of this section is the Jewish fold. The Lord begins by speaking of himself as *the door of the sheep* (10:1-7). The story revolves around three characters.

The sheep *fear the robber* (10:1): "Verily, verily, I say unto you, He that entereth not by the door into the sheepfold, but climbeth up some other way, the same is a thief and a robber" (10:1). The Lord sets the stage by depicting the false shepherds of Israel, long foretold (Ezekiel 34:1-6; Jeremiah 23:1-6; Zechariah 11:4-11), who had just demonstrated their disregard for the welfare of the sheep by casting out the blind man.

Sheepfolds in Bible lands were enclosures of stones or thornbushes, open to the sky and entered by an opening, or door. The Lord came into the fold of Israel the proper way. He had presented his credentials. He had demonstrated his love for the lost sheep of the house of Israel as he had just illustrated in his care for the man born blind.

The religious authorities by contrast were thieves (those who steal by stealth) and robbers (those who use violence to get what they want). That is what the religious leaders of Israel had become. Their pride of position and desire for power, their system of Bible interpretation which, far from feeding God's flock, stole away from them their rich heritage, their determination to oppose Christ—all marked them out as false shepherds.

That the Lord Jesus was the genuine shepherd was evident. He had entered by the door, by the legitimate means of entry. He had been born of a virgin (Isaiah 7:14; Matthew 1:21-23); he had been born in Bethlehem (Micah 5:2; Matthew 2:4-6); he had come "in the fulness of time" (Galatians 4:4); out of Egypt God had called his Son (Hosea 11:1; Matthew 2:14-15); his arrival had provoked the rage of the enemy (Jeremiah 31:15; Matthew 2:16-18). Thus he was the right person, born in the right place, arriving at the right time, summoned from the right country, and attended by the right sign.

But if sheep fear the thief and the robber, they *follow the true shepherd* (10:2-4). We are told of *his access to the fold* (10:3): "To him the porter openeth; and the sheep hear his voice; and he calleth his own sheep by name, and leadeth them out." The porter was John the baptist, the accredited forerunner of the Christ, sent to announce his coming, to validate his credentials for the nation, and to introduce him to the people.

The sheep recognized at once the voice of the true shepherd. They said of him that "he taught them as one having authority, and not as the scribes" (Matthew 7:29). Jewish teachers always appealed to tradition or to what some other teacher had to say. To this day they have an extrabiblical source of authority, the Talmud. Talmudic concepts were already flourishing and increasing in Christ's day, resulting in a vast wilderness of human opinion. Burdensome additions to the law, wearisome appeals to what this rabbi thought and what that rabbi said, were stifling the life out of God's revelation. When the common people heard Jesus, who took the people directly back to the inspired word, they recognized his voice of authority. It was the voice of God.

"He calleth his own sheep by name." They recognized him; he recognized them. He called them by name. There is a beautiful truth in that. We all like to be called by our names. The high priest carried the names of the tribes in the onyx stones on his shoulders; he carried them in the precious stones of the breastplate on his heart. He carried them in the place of strength and in the place of sympathy; he carried them into the presence of God. How wonderful to know that our high priest, that great shepherd of the sheep, knows each of his own by name, that he upholds us as individuals in strength and sympathy in the presence of God. He does not forget even the least of us.

Then, too, we have *his acceptance by the flock* (10:3b-4): "He calleth his own sheep by name, and leadeth them out. And when he putteth forth his own sheep, he goeth before them, and the sheep follow him: for they know his voice." The coloring of the parable is still that of a Palestinian shepherd in olden times. He did not round up his flock by sending a sheepdog to bark at their heels. He called his sheep by name. He did not drive them; he led them. He went before them and they followed him because they knew him and trusted him.

The Lord Jesus was now leading his sheep out of the constricting fold of Judaism. His own heard and recognized his voice of grace, truth, and power. They were following him. An immediate case in point, the case that initiated this discourse, was that of the blind man. He recognized the voice of Jesus and now was his ardent follower. The false Jewish shepherds had no use for this sheep. They hated him for wanting the true shepherd and they hated Christ for attracting the sheep to himself.

The sheep *flee from the stranger* (10:5): "And a stranger will they not follow, but will flee from him: for they know not the voice of strangers." Anyone who has walked through a field where sheep are grazing is familiar with this trait. Sheep are not drawn to strangers. They run from them. We need to be suspicious of those who seek to approach the flock of God but who are strangers. Using a different figure of speech, Paul warned the elders (shepherds) at Ephesus: "Take heed therefore unto yourselves, and to all the flock, over which the Holy Ghost hath made you overseers, . . . For I know this, that after my departing, shall grievous wolves enter in among you, not sparing the flock" (Acts 20:28-29). God's people are even more gullible than sheep. Paul told the Ephesian pastors: "Also of your own selves shall men arise, speaking perverse things, to draw away disciples after them" (10:20). After a while the stranger is no longer a stranger. He then can become a threat to the flock.

The Lord next underlines the dullness of the listeners. "This parable [proverb] spake Jesus unto them: but they understood not what things they were which he spake unto them. Then said Jesus unto them again, Verily, verily, I say unto you, I am the door of the sheep" (10:6-7). He himself had come into the fold as foretold. Now, he himself was the door. He was the way out of dead religion into life. A door divides, secures, opens, gives access. Jesus is the door.

In Bible times the shepherd was the door. At night he led his sheep into the fold where they could rest, secure from beasts of prey. He himself took up his place in the opening and thus became "the door." No prowling animal could get in so long as he was there. No restless sheep could stray off into the night. In the morning he stood aside and called his sheep out, counting and examining them, and led them in the way he wanted them to go.

Jesus now proclaimed himself to be the door. By him, and by him alone, the sheep could have access to a wide world of spiritual experience beyond the intricate confines of the fold of Judaism.

The Lord then continued his parable. He is not only the door of the sheep, he is also *the defender of the sheep* (10:8-15). In this section he discusses three kinds of shepherd.

There is *the false shepherd* (10:8-10). "All that ever came before me are thieves and robbers: but the sheep did not hear them," he said (10:8). The true shepherd could not come until God's time. Moses and the prophets were not thieves and robbers because none of them claimed to be the promised shepherd. Like John the baptist they pointed to the coming one. All others were deceivers. The rabbis substituted tradition for truth; the Talmud (then in its initial stages), for the Torah; the imagined oral law for the inspired written law. The true sheep, however, "did not hear them." As soon as they heard Jesus they recognized what it was they had been vaguely uneasy about in the ponderous and pretentious teaching of the scribes and the pious hypocrisy of the Pharisees. The Lord described himself in contrast to these false shepherds.

The true shepherd saves (10:9). "I am the door: by me if any man enter in, he shall be saved, and shall go in and out, and find pasture." It is through the Lord Jesus that we are saved and enter into new freedom and sure enjoyment of life.

The true shepherd secures (10:10a). "The thief cometh not, but for to steal, and to kill, and to destroy: I am come that they might have life." The thief is a threat to the sheep. The Lord throws the mantle of his protection around them.

The true shepherd satisfies (10:10b). "I am come that they might have life, and that they might have it more abundantly." A classic Old Testament example is found in the contrast with the descendants of Cain and the descendants of Seth (Genesis 4:1–5:32). The descendants of Cain were city builders, adventurers, people who discovered things, invented things. The arts and sciences, the refinements of a developing civilization, mechanics, music, marketing: these were concentrated in Cainite hands. No doubt the Cainites looked askance at the godly people of Seth, who took the lead in none of these things.

Yet the Holy Spirit says of each of the Sethites that "he lived." In fact, he writes it twice for each of them: "he lived." The Sethites, who in an increasingly wicked world bore quietly the torch of testimony, *lived*. The Spirit of God also records of each of the Sethites (with the exception of Enoch) that "he died." Death for them was not a terminus but a transition, a change from life on earth to life for evermore.

Jesus came that we might have life and have it more abundantly—but only on his terms. On his terms we each have life now, life on a higher plane, life in a land of fadeless day.

There is *the fearful shepherd* (10:11-13). As in the case of the false shepherd, the Lord teaches by contrast rather than by comparison. We note the mark of *the heavenly shepherd* (10:11): "I am the good shepherd: the good shepherd giveth his life for the sheep." Here, for the second time in this discourse, we have one of the Lord's I AM sayings.

The actual form of this expression is arresting: "I am the shepherd, the good." The thought carries us back to the life-types of Christ as shepherd in the Old Testament. There was Abel the righteous shepherd, Jacob the resourceful shepherd, Moses the returning shepherd, and David the royal shepherd. All these were partial types of Jesus, that great shepherd of the sheep.

The Holy Spirit underlines the predominant fact about this heavenly shepherd: he gave his life for the sheep.

The story is told of D. L. Moody and his songleader Ira Sankey as they traveled across England to a revival campaign. Sankey was perusing a magazine when he discovered a poem that caught his fancy. He clipped it out and put it in his pocket, thinking that someday he would compose music for it and turn it into a hymn. That night Moody preached on Jesus as the good shepherd. When he was through, he turned to Sankey and asked him to come and sing something. Sankey remembered the poem he had put in his pocket that very day. He set it in front of him on his little portable organ and began to sing, making up the tune as he went along.

> But all thro' the mountains, thunder-riven,
> And up from the rocky steep,
> There arose a glad cry to the gate of heaven,
> "Rejoice! I have found my sheep!"
> And the angels echoed around the throne,
> "Rejoice, for the Lord brings back His own."

That hymn, "The Ninety and Nine," became an immediate favorite.

> But none of the ransomed ever knew
> How deep were the waters crossed;
> Nor how dark was the night that the Lord passed thro',
> Ere He found His sheep that was lost.

The heavenly shepherd is contrasted by Jesus with *the hireling shepherd* (10:12-13). The hired shepherd *lacks commitment* (10:12): "But he that is an hireling, and not the shepherd, whose own the sheep are not, seeth the wolf coming, and leaveth the sheep, and fleeth: and the wolf catcheth them, and scattereth the sheep." He *lacks concern* (10:13): "The hireling fleeth, because he is an hireling, and careth not for the sheep."

The religious leaders were those hireling shepherds. They had no real investment in the sheep. Their own power and position were all they were concerned about.

The Lord then talks about the *faithful shepherd* (10:14-15). He mentions *his comprehension* (10:14-15a), first *in terms of the flock* (10:14): "I am the good shepherd, and know my sheep, and am known of mine." This is really a claim to omniscience on the part of Jesus. For many years I have traveled far and wide as an itinerant Bible teacher. Thousands of people know me. Often people come up to me or write or phone me, and remind me that they met me once, here, there, anywhere. It is easy for them to know me. But, I look out at hundreds, sometimes thousands, of people. It is impossible for me to know them. Jesus said that not only do his sheep know him, but he knows them—every one of them. He knows them by name. He knows where they live. He knows when they became his. He knows their personalities and their peculiarities. He knows all about them.

Second, he states his comprehension *in terms of the Father* (10:15a): "As the Father knoweth me, even so know I the Father." In other words, the kind of knowledge between Jesus and the flock is comparable to the knowledge that exists between the Father and the Son: complete knowledge.

The Lord continues his talk about this faithful shepherd and he speaks of *his commitment* (10:15b): "And I lay down my life for the sheep." The shadow of the cross was already on the soul of the Savior. He would be called on to lay down his life in battle with the wolves who were already in among the sheep. His confrontation with the false shepherds would lead inevitably to his death. He had no illusions about that. He knew. His Father knew. They had always known.

But God had something much wider than the nation of Israel in mind. The Lord had been talking about the shepherd and the fold. Now he considers *the shepherd and the flock* (10:16-21). The Lord enlarges the theme by speaking, first, about *his future* (10:16-18). He begins with a *great truth* (10:16): "And other sheep I have, which are not of this fold: them also I must bring, and they shall hear my voice; and there shall be one fold [flock], and one shepherd." The word *fold* at the end of this sentence is universally agreed to be incorrectly translated. It is not *aule* (used earlier in the sentence), which signifies a place, but *poimne*, the word for a flock. The word occurs only here, in Matthew 26:31, in Luke 2:8, and in 1 Corinthians 9:7. It is important that the connection be made.

There is all the difference in the world between a fold and a flock. The fold was the nation of Israel. A fold is characterized by a circumference, a wall. A flock is characterized by a center, the shepherd. The great truth announced by Jesus was that he was leading his sheep out of the fold represented by the nation of Israel. He was now gathering a flock. The "lost sheep of the house of Israel" to whom he had come had heard his call. Those who had heard and heeded were to become a new flock, the nucleus of a much larger flock, a flock in which Jews and gentiles would become one, one new flock. The "other sheep" who are "not of this fold" are the gentiles who through ensuing centuries would believe in him. What an enormous flock it has become.

The Jews are a permanent minority in this flock, but that makes no difference; now there is only one flock. There is no difference in Christ between Jew and gentile, between Greek and barbarian, between races, between sexes, between social classes. All who are his sheep belong to this flock.

As for the old fold, it still stands, a monument to unbelief. Judaism with its enmity toward Jesus still flourishes. The physical fold, the land of Israel, has fallen into disrepair and has changed hands many times during the long march of centuries. Today the Jews have been able to repossess it, and are repairing it and enlarging it.

But the shepherd they have despised and rejected is coming back to fulfill God's purposes concerning the old fold. In the meantime, in God's plans the important entity is the flock, the church. (We must never confuse the church with Israel or the flock with the fold.)

We also have a *great triumph* (10:17-18). The shepherd is still talking about himself and his future. The great triumph is centered *in his transcendent love* (10:17): "Therefore doth my Father love me, because I lay down my life, that I might take it again." There is full and eternal understanding between the Father and the Son. It was always understood that if God acted in creation he would one day have to act in redemption, and if he acted in redemption the Son would have to come to earth and die and rise again. Eternal love between the Father and the Son ordained all these things. The Lord knew that, moment by moment, situation by situation, he was bathed in his Father's love. That "everlasting love," that love without beginning or end, found its focus in the trust and obedience of the Lord Jesus.

The great triumph is centered *in his transcendent life* (10:18): "No man taketh [my life] from me, but I lay it down of myself. I have power to lay it down, and I have power to take it again. This commandment have I received of my Father." No mere man could make a claim like that. In fact, as far as his physical life was concerned, no man did take Jesus' life from him. He allowed them to arrest him after demonstrating their powerlessness to do so (18:4-12). He remained silent before his accusers, although twelve legions of angels were ready to come to his rescue (Matthew 26:53). He allowed himself to be crucified even as he demonstrated power enough to shake the earth to its foundations (Matthew 27:51-52). He waited until all the necessary prophecies were fulfilled and then majestically dismissed his spirit (Luke 23:46). So, when the soldiers came to break his legs and hasten his death, they discovered "he was dead already" (John 19:33). The Lord's death was voluntary, vicarious, and victorious. "I have power to take it again," he said. And he demonstrated that literally, gloriously, once and for all, in his resurrection.

Statements such as these were bound to elicit a response. John tells of the shepherd and *his fellows* (10:19-21). There was an immediate difference of opinion among the Jews. We note *the cause of their disunity* (10:19): "There was a division therefore again among the Jews for these sayings." Jesus' claim to have received authority from God in heaven to lay down his life and to take it again was more than some of them could take. Perhaps even those disposed to give him the benefit of the doubt felt it necessary to grope for more evidence on which to build their wavering trust.

We note *the completeness of their disunity* (10:20-21). Some defamed him and some defended him. There were many who said, "He hath a devil, and is mad; why hear ye him?" (10:20). The theory that demons could produce supernatural phenomena was a convenient one for dismissing the Lord's miracles as fraudulent. It was a terrible thing to say about the incarnate

Son of God. Others refuted the charge: "These are not the words of him that hath a devil. Can a devil open the eyes of the blind?" (10:21).

They had heard the ravings of demoniacs. The authoritative teachings of Jesus had nothing in common with demonic utterances. Nor could the more thoughtful Jews countenance the charge that the merciful, good, and well-documented miracles of Jesus had their source in the lying wonders of a demon.

2. His Deity in Focus (10:22-42)

So far, in his explanation of the way of life, the Lord has been pointing forward to his death, the key event in emptying the fold of his own sheep and in gathering the worldwide flock. Now Jesus focuses attention on his deity (10:22-42). We see *his response to their challenge* (10:22-30).

We note *the occasion* (10:22-23): "And it was at Jerusalem, the feast of the dedication, and it was winter" (10:22). In the dreadful days of Antiochus Epiphanes the Jerusalem temple had been defiled for three years (167-164 B.C.). The Syrian emperor had erected a pagan altar ("the abomination of desolation") on top of the divine altar. Jewish liberator Judas Maccabeus had reclaimed the temple site and cleansed the temple. The rededication of the temple took place on 25 Kislev (14 December) and was annually commemorated by the Jews in a joyous feast. The feast of dedication lasted for eight days. The celebration was sometimes called the feast of lights, from the Jewish custom of lighting lamps in their homes in remembrance of the occasion. If the traditional date of Christ's birth is correct, then the feast was kept at the time of his birthday. The events we have been discussing (7:1–10:21) seem to have been associated with the feast of tabernacles. Beginning at 10:22 the events are associated with the feast of dedication. Thus there is a gap in the narrative of two months—time the Lord seems to have spent in and around Jerusalem.

John reminds us it was winter. "And Jesus walked in the temple in Solomon's porch" (10:23). Solomon's porch, or colonnade, was the covered portico that ran along the east side of the outer court of Herod's temple. It was a popular spot. It is referred to in Acts 3:11 as the place where Peter healed the lame man and in Acts 5:12 as a meeting place for Christian believers. Because "it was winter" the Lord was walking in this area that provided some shelter. It was there that another challenge came.

Now comes *the occurrence* (10:24-30). We see the Jews chal-

lenging him to declare himself openly: "Then came the Jews
round about him, and said unto him, How long dost thou make
us to doubt? If thou be the Christ, tell us plainly" (10:24). So far
the Lord had told not only the Jerusalem Jews he was the
messiah, he had revealed himself as messiah to the woman at
the well. (Among the Samaritans, the title would have more
religious overtones than it would among the Jews, who vested
the title with political and martial overtones.)

Perhaps the fact that it was the feast of dedication, com-
memorating the purging of Jerusalem from Syrian oppression,
had urged the Jews on to force Jesus to declare himself. If he
was the messiah, it would be a good time for him to stop making
cryptic statements. If his claims were true, he should declare
himself and rid the country of the Romans. Solomon's porch
being a public place would enable them to force a showdown in
the open.

In his answer the Lord pointed to a twofold witness. First,
there was *the witness of his works* (10:25-29). He told them, first,
why (10:25-26) they would not believe: "Jesus answered them, I
told you, and ye believed not; the works that I do in my Father's
name, they bear witness of me. But ye believe not, because ye
are not my sheep, as I said unto you." The Lord still avoided
the politically loaded word *messiah*. But how could they doubt?
They had the evidence of his works. They had his oft-repeated
claim to a unique relationship with God as his Father and in
whose name he did everything. The Lord reminded them of his
recent claim to be the good shepherd. The idea of a king being
a shepherd was too well known to need further elaboration (for
example, David was a shepherd king). The reason they could
not recognize him was because they were, to put it bluntly, not
his sheep.

He then told them *what* (10:27-29) they would not believe.
They refused to accept *the evident sign* (10:27) of his own sheep:
"My sheep hear my voice, and I know them, and they follow
me." Those who belong to the Lord recognize his voice and
respond to his word. That is the outward proof of inward faith.
The recognition is mutual.

But there is more to it than that. There is *the eternal security*
(10:28-29) of his own sheep: "And I give unto them eternal life;
and they shall never perish, neither shall any man pluck them
out of my hand. My Father, which gave them me, is greater
than all, and no man is able to pluck them out of my Father's
hand." This statement of the eternal security of the believer is
matched only by Paul's assurances in Romans 8. We note that
our possession of eternal life is stated in the present, continuous

tense. We do not have to wait until we die to find out if we are saved. We are given present assurance.

There is something magnificent about the picture of the Lord wrapping his omnipotent hand around us, and of the Father wrapping his own almighty hand around his. Thus we are ensphered in Christ in God.

An Old Testament example is that of Noah. When the ark was finished, God shut him in. The storms of judgment fell in all their fury. The windows of heaven were opened. The fountains of the deep were broken up. But Noah was safe. He was in the ark. The waters of judgment fell on the ark, not on him. Thus our "life is hid with Christ in God" (Colossians 3:3).

Now Jesus points them to *the witness of his words* (10:30). "I and my Father are one," he said. They are one in mind, thought, heart, will, purpose, and action. True, but it goes beyond that. In the Greek the word *one* is neuter—"I and the Father are one"—not in person, but in essence. The statement springs directly from the claim, just made by Jesus, to equality of power with the Father ("my hand, my Father's hand"). Infinite power, thus claimed by Jesus, is an attribute of God.

This is the climax of the Lord's claim to oneness with the Father (10:18,25,28,29). His answer was more than they bargained for. He was not just the Christ of messianic expectation; he claimed identity of substance with God. That was his answer to their question.

Jesus' outright claim to be of the same essence as God provoked from the Jews *their response to his challenge* (10:31-42). We note *their determination* (10:31-39) to get rid of him . They made two moves against him. *The first move* (10:31-38) is in two parts. Note *what they attempted* (10:31-33). "Then the Jews took up stones again to stone him" (10:31). They had done this once before when he had announced himself as the I AM (8:58-59). The word translated "took up" here describes something borne as a heavy weight rather than something seized. Evidently they hauled their ammunition from the work site of the temple. This time they intended to make an end of him. They understood his unequivocal claims to be God, the most blatant blasphemy to their minds. But they did not hurl those stones. His time was not yet come, nor must he die in that way. A restraining hand held them back. Perhaps, too, the Lord's soft answer gave them pause, and the stones were dropped.

"Jesus answered them, Many good works have I shewed you from my Father; for which of those works do ye stone me?" Do you stone me because I gave sight to a man born blind? Do you stone me because I healed a man at the pool of Bethesda who

had been ill for thirty-eight years? Do you stone me because I
have cleansed lepers and raised the dead and cast out evil spirits
and made the dumb speak and the deaf hear and the lame walk?
Do you stone me because I fed your hungry multitudes? He
pointed to his good works, works of almighty power, as the
credentials to back his claim. He was fully accredited.

They were not the least bit interested in proof of his power.
Back they came with their angry accusation. "The Jews answered him, saying, For a good work we stone thee not; but for
blasphemy; and because that thou, being a man, makest thyself
God" (10:33). It was not simple blasphemy, they said, a man
making derogatory statements about God. He had gone far
beyond that. He, a man, had assumed prerogatives belonging to
God alone. And so he had. But he was not just a man. He was
God manifest in flesh.

We have seen what they attempted. Now John shows us *what
he attempted* (10:34-38). He came down to their level and introduced the kind of argument dear to the Pharisaic mind. Moreover he referred them back to their Scriptures. It is worth
noting the Lord's reverence for the written word of God. He
always appealed to the Scriptures as divine, inspired, authoritative, and inerrant.

"Is it not written in your law?" he said. The law is a comprehensive term here for the Hebrew Bible. In fact, the Lord
referred them to Psalm 82:6, where the civil administrators of
the theocratic nation of Israel were called "gods" *(elohim)* by the
poet under inspiration of the Holy Spirit. From what the psalmist says, it is evident that these men were unrighteous judges,
yet their office, as representatives of the heavenly righteous
judge, was such that they were actually called *elohim.* The dignity of their office was thus brought home to them by the psalmist.

The word *elohim,* then, was used in Psalm 82 of earthly
judges, to whom the word of God was entrusted by virtue of
their high office. The same word is used of Moses. "See I have
made thee a god *(elohim)* to Pharaoh" (Exodus 7:1), because
Moses stood in the place of God to that wicked king. The word
is also used of judges in general (Exodus 21:6; 22:8,9,28). It is
clear that the Holy Spirit had so clothed with dignity the office
of a judge in Israel that those who functioned as judges were
called "elohim" because they represented God in this capacity.
The word is used even of unjust judges because of the awesome
responsibility of the office itself.

This background explains what otherwise must appear a
strange defense of the Lord's claim to be God. The Jews, of

course, were familiar enough with this Old Testament use of *elohim.* The Lord reminded them of it: "Is it not written in your law, I said, Ye are gods? If he called them gods, unto whom the word of God came, and the scripture cannot be broken; Say ye of him, whom the Father hath sanctified, and sent into the world, Thou blasphemest; because I said, I am the Son of God?" (10:34-36).

We can see the point the Lord was making. If it was not blasphemy to give the title *elohim* to those, good or bad, who so distantly represented God himself (by virtue of their holy office), how was it blasphemy for him, the Son of God, sanctified and set apart by the Father and sent into the world, to say, "I am the Son of God"? Between those unworthy ancient *elohim* and himself was infinite distance. It was no blasphemy for him to tell them the truth about himself.

Once again he endorsed the sanctity of Scripture. "The scripture cannot be broken," he said. Down through the centuries many evil people have tried to break the Scriptures, but in vain. Diocletian harnessed the might of a world empire to get rid of the Bible. Voltaire held up a copy of the Scriptures and boasted he would put the Bible in the morgue. Before long he was in the morgue, and the Geneva Bible Society used his house as a Bible warehouse. The communists have done their best to reeducate generations of people and have poured scorn on the Scriptures but cannot destroy them. For centuries, the Roman church kept the Bible out of the hands of the people. Modern liberals fill the minds of millions with their God-dishonoring, rationalistic theories about the Scriptures, but in vain. "The scriptures cannot be broken."

I am reminded of an old anvil that stood in my father's workshop when I was a boy. That anvil over many years had broken many a hammer. But no hammer ever used on it ever broke it.

Again, the Lord referred the Jews back to his works—his unanswerable argument in the face of their determined unbelief: "If I do not the works of my Father, believe me not. But if I do, though ye believe not me, believe the works: that ye may know, and believe, that the Father is in me, and I in him" (10:37-38). He loved these men. If only they would believe his works, it would not be long before they would believe him. Yes, and come to see the unique relationship that existed between him and his Father.

They had made the first move against him (10:31). Now they make *the further move* (10:39) against him: "Therefore they sought again to take him: but he escaped out of their hand."

They had demanded plain speaking. He had given it. They took up stones but could not throw them. Now they were going to arrest him and arraign him before the Sanhedrin with the capital charge of blasphemy. But they could not touch him. His time was not yet come.

John now records *his departure* (10:40-42). We note *where he went* (10:40): "And went away again beyond Jordan into the place where John at first baptized; and there he abode." This was in December. He remained away until April, visiting Bethany (11:1) and spending the latter part of the time in Ephraim (11:54). The next time he came to Jerusalem the Jews would have him killed.

Jesus now went back to the place where John the baptist had first identified him as messiah. It was a silent reminder to the nation that he was what he claimed to be. Let memory speak.

We note also *why he went* (10:41-42). There were two reasons. One was *a reason centered on the baptist* (10:41): "And many resorted unto him, and said, John did no miracle: but all things that John spake of this man were true." There can be little doubt that the memory of John the baptist was still alive in that district. People remembered how John had identified Jesus.

"John," they said, "did no miracle." That was part of the greatness of John. God never places much premium on miracles. In only a few transitional periods are miracles evident in Scripture. There were miracles to get Israel out of Egypt, through the wilderness, and into Canaan; then they stopped. There were miracles in the days of Elijah and Elisha, as protest against the apostasy that would lay both Israel and Judah in the dust; then they stopped. There was a brief flurry of miracles in the days of Daniel, marking the transition of Judah from a monarchy into a dependency; then they stopped. There were miracles during the days of Christ and his apostles, to accredit both him and the church; then they stopped. There will be a brief battle of miracles after the rapture of the church, when God's two witnesses and the devil's two beasts will produce their signs; but then they will stop.

The greater part of time has been marked by lack of miracles. For, when all is said and done, miracles are a sign to unbelief. They can be explained away. We have just seen how obdurate the Jews were in refusing to believe the evidence of Christ's miracles.

"John did no miracle." People simply took him at his word. It is worth noting that after each of the above brief periods when miracles were in evidence, they were always replaced by God's written word. The miracles of Moses and Joshua gave way to the Pentateuch, the early histories, the psalms of David, the wisdom books of Solomon. The miracles of Elijah and Elisha gave way to the writing prophets: Isaiah, Jeremiah, and their colleagues. The miracles performed in Babylon were replaced by the writings of the postexilic prophets. The miracles of Jesus and the apostles were replaced by the gospels and epistles.

Let those who long for miracles today underline this statement, "John did no miracle," yet how powerful and effective was his word. How powerful and effective has been the word of Christ. God's ideal is to bring people to faith that rests not on miracles but on his word. "John did no miracle: but all things that John spake of this man were true." John, being dead, yet spoke.

So Jesus retired to the place where his public ministry had begun. There was *a reason centered on the believer* (10:42): "And many believed on him there." The word *there* is emphatic, to contrast their belief with the unbelief the Lord had encountered in Jerusalem—and also to contrast disbelief in his miracles with belief centered on the spoken word. True faith takes God at his word. It does not need miracles to bolster it.

Thus the Lord rested before his final confrontation with the Jerusalem Jews, basking in the genuine faith of those who put their trust in him because he was what he was—and not because he did what he did.

We thank God for the many marvelous miracles of Jesus. But we thank God even more for the life he lived, the truth he taught, the death he died, and the ministry he maintains at God's right hand.

We have been considering the signs of the Son of God. In the first section his deity was declared, and in the second section his deity was disputed. We have now come to the third section, where his deity is disowned. First we shall consider some examples of his rejection and then some explanations of his rejection.

Section 3. His Deity Is Disowned (11:1–12:50)

I. Some Examples of His Rejection (11:1–12:36)

We shall never get tired of the story of the raising of Lazarus. It sheds light into the realm of darkness, brings life where death reigns, and robs the tomb of its terror. It was a true miracle, but we see Christ rejected in spite of his feat of power.

A. Rejected in spite of His Feat of Power (11:1–12:11)

We have an amazing resurrection and an amazing reaction to consider.

1. An Amazing Resurrection (11:1-46)

We begin with *the summons* (11:1-16). The story opens with *the Lord and his friends* (11:1-6). The seven miracles connected with the public ministry of Jesus, and selected by John as seven of his eight "signs," begin and end with a family, one in Cana of Galilee and one in Bethany of Judea. The one was at a wedding, the other at a funeral—life's gladdest and life's saddest hours. At the one he changed water into wine. At the other he triumphed over the tomb. Both miracles were humanly impossible. The one revealed him as Lord of creation. The other revealed him as creator of life.

In the incident here we begin with *a special family* (11:1-2): "Now a certain man was sick, named Lazarus, of Bethany, the town of Mary and her sister Martha." John adds further identification by telling us that the Mary involved is "that Mary which anointed the Lord with ointment, and wiped his feet with her hair, whose brother Lazarus was sick" (11:2). There are six Marys in the New Testament, so the identification is helpful. John does not actually record the incident of the anointing until its proper place, in the next chapter.

Bethany was a village on the eastern slope of the mount of Olives, on the high road to Jericho. The family, consisting of a brother and two sisters, was close-knit. The home seems to have been one frequented by Jesus, a home away from home.

Into that peaceful Bethany home had come *a sudden fear* (11:3). It was bad enough that Lazarus was sick. The verb used ("was sick") points to great weakness and exhaustion. In the gospels it is usually translated "sick" and in Paul's epistles as "weak." It is the same word that is translated "impotent" to describe the helplessness of the man at the pool of Bethesda (5:7). What was worse, from the standpoint of the sisters, was that Jesus had gone away. They had no doubt that had he been in Jerusalem he would have hurried the two miles to Bethany and healed his friend.

Now comes what to them must have been a perplexing interlude. They sent word to Jesus: "Lord, behold, he whom thou lovest [*phileo*] is sick." His friend, the one for whom he had a brotherly love, was very ill (weakening, sinking). The situation was desperate.

The Lord at that time was at Bethabara beyond the Jordan in Perea, about twenty five miles from Jerusalem. We can picture the one sent hurrying to deliver the urgent message. We can picture, too, the anxious sisters sitting by their brother's death-bed hoping against hope that Jesus would arrive in time—or did they perhaps expect him to heal their brother from afar, as he had done for others on other occasions? And why had they waited so long to send him word? Had they perhaps counted on him knowing without having to be told? And if he knew, why had he not acted? Fear must have gripped their hearts. Lazarus was dying; perhaps they had let things go until too late.

Now comes *a seeming failure* (11:4-6). We can picture Mary sitting by the dying Lazarus, ministering to his needs. We can picture Martha, needing to be up and doing, going outside to strain her eyes for some sign that Jesus was on his way. We can picture too the astonishment when the messenger returned alone. I imagine this is how the conversation went.

"Where's Jesus?"

"He's still at Bethabara."

"Is he coming?"

"I don't think so. He said, 'This sickness is not unto death, but for the glory of God, that the Son of God might be glorified thereby' " (11:4).

We can imagine how dumbfounded the sisters were in the face of the now evident fact that Lazarus was already dead. For dead he was, and they had had his funeral and laid him to rest in the family tomb. And Jesus did not come. How could they explain this seeming failure?

We read this story as we read the story of Job, with knowl-edge of why the tragedy was allowed to happen and the happy knowledge of how it ended. But, like Job, Martha and Mary did not have this knowledge. It seemed as though Jesus had been silent when he should have spoken. It seemed he had let them down—just as it seems like that to us when we pray desperately and get no answer, or when what seems to be the wrong answer comes.

John takes us back to Jesus. He and the other disciples were also perplexed. *The Lord's logic* (11:4) was crystal clear. The end of the sickness was not to be death. Death would intervene, but death would not have the last word. This sickness was for the glory of God, and for the glory of the Son of God.

Next we have *the Lord's love* (11:5): "Now Jesus loved Martha, and her sister, and Lazarus." This time the verb for love is *agapao*. This is the highest kind of love, not just affection, like the kind of love a parent has for a child, but affection resulting from moral choice. It is a loftier love, a love not swayed by impulse.

Then comes *the Lord's leading* (11:6): "When he had heard therefore that he was sick, he abode two days still in the same place where he was." The journey to Bethany would take about a day, so Lazarus must have died soon after the messenger left Bethany. Jesus knew he was dead. There was no hurry, because every move Jesus made was in the compass of the perfect timing of God. So, while waiting for God to move, the Lord finished up the work he was doing where he was.

The focus now centers on *the Lord and his followers* (11:7-16), who must have been dumbfounded by the Lord's seeming indifference to the death of his friend and the sisters' distress. Attention is drawn first to *the decision* (11:7-10). After two days the Lord made a startling announcement, "Let us go into Judaea again." The Lord did not say, "Let us go back to Bethany," where he had friends, but to Judea, where he had enemies. At this point, of course, the disciples did not know that Lazarus was dead. They had heard the Lord say, "This sickness is not unto death." But as soon as they heard the word Judea they were filled with alarm. "Master, the Jews of late sought to stone thee; and goest thou thither again?" (11:8). It was folly, they thought, to go back there.

The Lord's eye, however, was not on the danger. That carried no weight with him. His eye was on the timing of God and the lateness of the hour. "Are there not twelve hours in the day? If any man walk in the day, he stumbleth not, because he seeth the light of this world. But if a man walk in the night, he stumbleth, because there is no light in him" (11:9-10). The Lord saw his allotted span of life on this earth as a "day," one that would be terminated by what he called "his hour." That hour had not yet come. It was still day, still time to work. All was well.

He could see quite clearly where he was going; he knew perfectly well what he was doing. He did not rush headlong, needlessly, into danger. On the other hand, he was not going to draw back just because there was danger. His times were in God's hands and he knew those times. The evening shadows might indeed be gathering. The "power of darkness" (Luke 22:53) would have its time. But not yet. Time for work was limited and the work must be finished within that time.

There is another application. We are not like him. He was the light of the world. He always walked in the light. We do not carry within us all that we require, as he did. We therefore need to be illuminated by him. We too have our allotted time. We must get on with the work while we may, making sure we are working in the light he gives.

Their objection, one that seemed to the disciples to be over-whelming—death awaited him in Judea—was overruled. The Lord was making every move in the full light of perfect day. It may be that as he gave this illustration the sun was coming up over the eastern horizon to flood the world with the light of another day.

The decision was made but the disciples were still far from satisfied. The Lord made his purpose plainer. We hear *the discussion* (11:11-15). We note, first, *what Jesus exclaimed* (11:11-13): "Our friend Lazarus sleepeth; but I go, that I may awake him out of sleep" (11:11). He thus made clear that by the word *Judea* he meant, for now at least, not Jerusalem but Bethany.

The disciples, however, exchanged one set of objections for another, because of their inability to discern when the Lord was using symbolic language. Jesus knew that Lazarus was dead. But he still called him "our friend Lazarus." There is something comforting in that.

Death is not the end of life. Death is not the extinction of being. "Our friend Lazarus" is still "our friend Lazarus." Even though dead "our friend Lazarus" is as much "our friend Lazarus" as when he was alive. Lazarus in life had been John's friend, Peter's friend, Matthew's friend, Jesus' friend. Lazarus in death was still their friend. Jesus, who could see the dead as clearly as he could see the living, knew that death had not changed anything that was essential. Death, he likened to sleep—the death of the body, that is. The soul does not sleep. The disciples promptly misunderstood the Lord's reference to death as sleep, although he had used the metaphor before (Luke 8:52). They supposed that Lazarus had now fallen into a restful, healing slumber—a good sign. The Lord must have healed Lazarus at a distance. They probably heaved a sigh of relief. Now they would not need to go to Judea and put their necks in a noose. If that is what they thought, they were soon disillusioned. "I go, that I may awake him out of sleep," Jesus added. The disciples protested at once: "Lord, if he sleep, he shall do well," they said (11:12). John adds the note that although Jesus was actually referring to the death of Lazarus, the disciples took him literally and supposed he was telling them that Lazarus was now resting comfortably.

Seeing that his disciples were unable to grasp even a simple figure of speech, the Lord spoke plainly. We note *what Jesus explained* (11:14-15): "Then said Jesus unto them plainly, Lazarus is dead. And I am glad for your sakes that I was not there, to the intent ye may believe; nevertheless, let us go unto him." Lazarus was dead. The Lord was not glad because Lazarus was dead. That would have been heartless in view of the sorrow of his sisters. He was glad because he knew the outcome. He was going to "awake him." If he had been in the immediate vicinity when his friend had been taken ill, it would have been hard not to have healed him. And the disciples, the sisters, the world, would have been robbed of an extraordinary demonstration of his power and of a remarkable illustration of the truth of resurrection. The discussion was over; the decision was made. John draws our attention for a moment back to *the disciples* (11:16).

Thomas spoke up. It was evident to him that the master was determined to go to Judea. It was also clear in his mind that there could be only one outcome. The next time the Jews would get him. We must remember that the disciples had been present on the two occasions when the Jews had shown every intention of stoning him and on other occasions when they had tried to arrest him. It was altogether too hot for comfort in Jerusalem. Still, Thomas showed of what stuff he was made: "Then said Thomas, which is called Didymus [both names mean *twin*] unto his fellow disciples, Let us also go, that we may die with him."

In those despairing words Thomas showed how little faith he really had. All he could see was the hostility of the Jews and their determination to get rid of Jesus. The other passages that mention Thomas show him true to character (14:5; 20:25).

John now tells us about *the sorrow* (11:17-37) that gripped the bereaved household, a sorrow that seems to have broken out afresh by the Lord's belated arrival. He tells us about *the sorrow of the sisters* (11:17-32), then about the sorrow of the Savior.

He begins with *Martha's reaction* (11:17-27) to *the Lord's coming* (11:17-20). Upon his arrival the Lord was told he had come too late. Lazarus was dead and buried; he had been in the grave four days (11:17). In that climate, burial was not delayed.

John, who had accompanied Jesus on this trip, mentions an incidental detail: "Now Bethany was nigh unto Jerusalem, about fifteen furlongs off." A furlong was a little over six hundred feet. Jerusalem, then, where the Lord's enemies were still smarting over his claims and continued activities, was less than two miles away.

All human hope was gone. Lazarus was rotting in his grave. The sisters' friends and neighbors could only "comfort them concerning their brother" (11:19). The word for "comfort" is *paramutheomai*, meaning "to speak tenderly, to console." They did not know it, but Jesus had delayed his coming so that he would arrive at the right moment, when all human help and hope were gone. It had been timed that way in heaven.

Into this scene of desolation came wonderful news, "Jesus is coming." Martha rushed out to meet him. Mary remained where she was in the house (11:20).

Now we have *the Lord's comment* (11:21-27). We see *Martha's faith expressed* (11:21-24). We note *her boldness* (11:21-22): "Then said Martha unto Jesus, Lord, if thou hadst been here, my brother had not died [that took in the past]. But I know, that even now, whatsoever thou wilt ask of God, God will give it thee [that took in the present]." Martha's faith was a tribute to Jesus, but it was inadequate. He had not been there on purpose; she did not discern that. He could have healed from a distance, had he so desired. Next she expressed belief that the Lord could get anything from God. She half believed that Jesus could raise her brother—after all, he had raised others. But her words outran her actual conviction, as she showed later (11:39). Often our profession of faith is far bolder than our actual faith.

We note also *her belief* (11:23-24). The Lord did not challenge this half faith of Martha's, he built on it: "Thy brother shall rise again," he said (11:23). It was a confident statement of fact. If death is the final answer to the human state, then the devil has won. God's answer to sin is death, and his answer to death is resurrection.

Martha accepted his words, understanding them as having some distant, future significance, and gave assent to the doctrine of resurrection—as we do, when confronted with the loss of a loved one. She said, "I know that he shall rise again in the resurrection at the last day" (11:24). The greatest Old Testament statement on the bodily resurrection of the believer was voiced by Job in the midst of his sufferings. He said, "Oh that my words were now written! oh that they were printed in a book! That they were graven with an iron pen and lead in the rock forever! For I know that my redeemer liveth, and that he shall stand at the latter day upon the earth: and though after my skin worms destroy this body, yet in my flesh shall I see God" (Job 19:23-26). Nor do we have a greater statement on the subject until we come to 1 Corinthians 15. Martha fully believed in the end time resurrection of believers.

The Lord, however, wanted *Martha's faith expanded* (11:25-27). Note how the truth was conveyed. "I am the resurrection and the life [that is, the Lord Jesus has the key to resurrection life, life in the body beyond death]; he that believeth in me, though he were dead, yet shall he live [that is, the Lord Jesus imparts spiritual life to those who are dead in trespasses and sins]; and whosoever liveth and believeth in me shall never die [that is, the Lord Jesus guarantees eternal life, life without end]. Believest thou this?"

No mere man could have made such a claim to have mastery over death. He prefaced that awesome claim with his emphatic I AM. He was about to prove to Martha, Mary, and the world that this was not religious rhetoric but a statement of fact.

Martha rose to the occasion: "Yea, Lord," she said, "I believe that thou art the Christ, the Son of God, which should come into the world" (11:27). She sidestepped the issue of whether she believed in the Lord's claim to have mastery over death, to be *the* resurrection. But she did confess her heartfelt belief in Jesus as messiah of Israel and Son of God. She used an emphatic pronoun: "I, even I, have believed. This belief is personal, my very own."

Now comes *Mary's reaction* (11:28-32). Martha lost no time in running back to the house with the good news that Jesus was on his way. Mary, taken up with grief, was not aware that Jesus was near. With real tact, Martha sought out her sister alone and told her the good news: "The Master is come, and calleth for thee" (11:28).

Then Mary rushed out of the house. Her entourage of com-forters, supposing she was going to the tomb to weep there, hurried after her. But Mary did not go to the sepulcher; instead she ran to the Savior.

When Mary reached Jesus she fell at his feet. Using the same words as her sister, she confessed her thoughts: "Lord, if thou hadst been here, my brother had not died" (11:32). No doubt the two sisters had said that to each other many times during the past few days. Jesus said nothing. His heart was over-whelmed at the anguish he saw in her. Certainly he took no notice of the hint of reproach in her words.

We have seen the sorrow of the sisters; now we see *the sorrow of the Savior* (11:33-35). John now shows us *a weeping Christ* (11:33-35).

We note, first, *what he saw* (11:33a): "When Jesus therefore saw her weeping, and the Jews also weeping which came with her . . . " The word for "weeping" means "to wail." All around him Jesus could see these almost passionate expressions of grief. He had come from a land where there is no sin and therefore no sorrow, where there are no tombs and no tears. His home was far away, a land of eternal bliss, a land of "joy unspeakable and full of glory." He had been on earth for thirty-three years. He had seen many tears, helped heal many broken hearts.

But these were his special friends. Their home had been his home. Many a time he had relaxed there with Lazarus and his sisters—Martha busy and bustling about preparing this, offer-ing that, ministering to his comfort; Mary thoughtful, earnest, and eager to learn. Now Lazarus was dead and the sisters desolate. Instead of the happy buzz of conversation and occasional bursts of laughter, there were tears.

We note *what he suffered* (11:33b): "He groaned in the spirit and was troubled." The word for "groaned" is *embrimaomai,* meaning "to be deeply agitated." The word literally means "to snort," as a horse does from fear or anger. It is used in the New Testament to indicate displeasure or indignation. It is used, for instance, to describe the indignation some persons felt at what they considered the waste of a rare and costly ointment poured over Jesus' head in the house of Simon the leper at Bethany (Mark 14:4). The Lord felt indignation and outrage at what death had done.

He was "troubled." That is, he literally shook with emotion. He was so moved it caused his body to tremble with indignation and grief.

We note *what he said* (11:34): "Where have ye laid him?" "They said unto him, Lord, come and see." He asked to be taken to the tomb, not because he wanted to see a grave, but because he wanted to gather everyone now to the place where his mightiest miracle would be wrought. (And will be again when he descends from heaven with a shout!)

Nowhere in the Bible is the deity of Christ more in evidence than in this story. Nowhere is his humanity more in evidence. He was going to a tomb. So was everyone else. Not just to the tomb of Lazarus. All were on their way to their own tomb. Sooner or later the tomb would claim them all. They were all on the way to the tomb because of their sins. He was on the way to the tomb for the same reason—their sins. He had no sin, so the tomb had no claim upon him. But he was on the way to the tomb just the same—to open its grim portals forever, for himself and for all who believe in him.

So he allowed himself to be led by Martha and Mary to where Lazarus was buried.

We note *what he showed* (11:35): "Jesus wept," John said. The word is *dakruo.* It occurs only here, although the noun is found elsewhere. He burst into tears. It is not the same word used of the weeping of Mary (11:31) and the Jews (11:33). Here was no wail of despair. Here was that "strong crying and tears" (Hebrews 5:7) of the Son of God.

He wept because he was a man of sorrows and acquainted with grief. He wept out of sorrow for Martha and Mary and for Lazarus's friends. He wept because his heart was broken at the sadness of death and by sorrows that knew no solace.

He wept because he was God. He could see what they could

not see. He could see Lazarus in paradise, surrounded by the
saints of God. The angelic hosts were standing by. He had
entered into rest beyond the reach of earthly woes. He was with
Abraham, Isaac, and Jacob, the spirits of just men made perfect. He was in a land where time stands still, where all were
eagerly waiting the earth-shaking tread of the triumphant Son
of God.

Why, Lazarus had barely been introduced. Eager questioners
had perhaps only begun to ask him what he knew about Jesus.
And Jesus was going to call him back to a world of sin, anguish,
and pain. Jesus wept out of sorrow for Lazarus.

We also see *a wondering crowd* (11:36-37). They wondered at
his strong display of feeling (11:36): "Then said the Jews, Behold
how he loved him!" That was true. They did not realize it, but
he loved them too, just as much as he loved Lazarus—each and
every one of them. He loved Caiaphas and Annas and the wicked plotters in the temple as much as he loved Lazarus. He loved
crafty Herod and weak Pilate. He loved the man who would
punch him in the face and the men who would nail him to the
tree. And he loves you and me as much as he loved his "friend
Lazarus."

They wondered, too, at *his seeming display of failure* (11:37):
"And some of them said, Could not this man, which opened the
eyes of the blind, have caused that even this man should not
have died?" There it is, out in the open at last, the question the
atheist, the agnostic, the unbeliever, always asks in the end:
"Why does an omnipotent God, if he is a good God, allow
suffering, sorrow, injustice, pain, and death? If he is all-power-
ful, then he is not good; if he is good, then he is not all-
powerful. Otherwise he would intervene." That is more or less
the position adopted by these Jews who, it seems, had hurried to
join this expedition to the dead man's tomb. "Surely he could
have prevented this death, so why didn't he?" they asked.

Now we are invited to look at *the sepulcher* (11:38-44). Jesus is
about to do something unique in the annals of history. We see
the grave confronted (11:38-40).

First, however, we have *a comment* (11:38) by John. He tells us
of *the feelings of the Savior* (11:38a): "Jesus therefore again groan-
ing in himself cometh to the grave." Probably the unbelief of
the Jews added to the Lord's distress at this time. There is a
strong possibility that the words of the Jews about his not healing Lazarus were said with a sneer. They were questioning his
power.

John tells of *the finality of the sepulcher* (11:38b): "It was a cave,
and a stone lay upon it." Caves, sealed by stone doors, were

frequently used as tombs. Often the door was in the shape of a millstone and was fitted into a groove along which it was rolled either to seal or open the tomb. The sealed tomb, shut tight and secured by just such a boulder, had about it an unmistakable air of finality. Lazarus was dead, buried, sealed in his grave.

Next we have *a command* (11:39-40). Jesus said, "Take ye away the stone" (11:39a). That was the first order of business. It is worth noting that God will not do for us what we can do for ourselves. Jesus, armed with omnipotent power, could have blasted that stone into oblivion. He could have commanded that stone to roll away. He did no such thing. He had not come to perform cheap wonders, nor would he do what they could do.

People were stunned by this command, the first intimation that Jesus intended to do something out of the ordinary. Martha, especially, was shocked. "Lord," she said, "by this time he stinketh: for he hath been dead four days" (11:30b). She misunderstood his purpose, his words about being the resurrection and the life. She thought he wanted to view the body of his friend. Such a thing was no longer possible. It was unthinkable. Decay had set in.

Jesus simply reinforced his command. "Said I not unto thee, that, if thou wouldest believe, thou shouldest see the glory of God?" (11:40). There is something sad about his words. "Didn't I tell you, Martha?" Think of those words. Put the emphasis first on one word, then on another: "Didn't I *tell* you, Martha?" Could she have forgotten so soon? Less than half an hour ago he had told her that he was the resurrection and the life and had challenged her to believe it. "Didn't *I* tell you, Martha?" Had she already forgotten her declaration of faith that placed him first on the throne of David and then on the throne of the universe: "Thou art the Christ, the Son of God!" "Didn't I tell *you*, Martha?" There may be some excuse for others objecting to the tomb being opened, but you, Martha? How our chronic unbelief must grieve him.

We now see *the grave conquered* (11:41-44). First, there was *the daring move* (11:41a): "Then they took away the stone from the place where the dead was laid." The Lord's command prevailed. Martha's objection was overruled. Mary voiced no protest at what under any other circumstance must have been a horror to the loved ones, the exhumation of a corpse. Perhaps Mary, with her spiritual insight, already had an inkling of what her beloved Lord was about to do.

Then *the divine mediator* (11:41b-42) is seen. We note *his trust godward* (11:41b): "And Jesus lifted up his eyes, and said, Father, I thank thee that thou hast heard me," and *his testimony manward* (11:42): "And I know that thou hearest me always: but because of the people which stand by I said it, that they may believe that thou hast sent me."

Have you ever attended a prayer meeting where you sensed that the person praying was preaching, directing his words at someone in the meeting as much as to God? It is never a courteous or commendable thing for one poor sinner to do to another. It strikes us as being cowardly and hypocritical. But when the incarnate Christ did it, it was done deliberately, openly, without pretense, and for a very good reason.

The Lord had already done his private praying over the death and proposed resurrection of Lazarus. He already had his Father's mind on this matter and was assured of his approval. That was one thing.

This public prayer was for the sake of those now gathered around the open tomb. This was an occasion for public thanksgiving; an occasion to declare his oneness with his Father at all times and in all situations; an opportunity to declare, as a man, his dependence on his Father. As God, this was an occasion to convince people that he was all he claimed to be; an occasion to demonstrate the power and effectiveness of prayer, an occasion to make a solemn appeal to his foes.

Finally we come to *the dramatic miracle* (11:43-44): "And when he thus had spoken, he cried with a loud voice, Lazarus, come forth. And he that was dead came forth, bound hand and foot with graveclothes: and his face was bound about with a napkin." He spoke with that word of power which, in the dawn of time, commanded "Light," and light was. It was that word which said to heaving waves and howling winds, "Be still," and immediately there was a great calm; that word which said to the leper, "I will, be clean," and immediately his leprosy vanished; that word which commanded a legion of angels to be gone from a tormented demoniac's soul, and at once they fled.

Now that word again rang out. Of course Lazarus came forth. What else could he do? At the sound of that voice, corruption put on incorruption. What was sown in weakness was raised in power. Death was swallowed up in victory. It was a foreshadowing of things to come (1 Corinthians 15:35-57).

Many years ago an infidel was lecturing to a capacity crowd on the subject of his unbelief. In the course of his lecture he ridiculed the story of the raising of Lazarus. Throwing out his arm he cried rhetorically: "Why did Jesus say, 'Lazarus, come forth'?" An old believer at the back of the hall rose to the occasion. "That is very simple, sir," he said. "Because, if Jesus had not said 'Lazarus, come forth,' every dead person in the world would have come forth." And so they would. As so, one day, they will.

There was a double miracle here. The word for graveclothes is *keiriai*, used only here in the New Testament. The grave-clothes were winding sheets wrapped tightly around the embalmed body of the dead man. The word for napkin is *soudarion*, a word borrowed from the Latin that literally means "sweat cloth." Because this was wrapped around the dead man's head, Lazarus could not see. Yet forth he came into the broad light of day.

"Loose him, and let him go," said Jesus. Again, he did not do what they could do. It needed no special miracle to unwind the wrappings. And there, at last, Lazarus stood before them, alive from the dead.

John has finished with the sepulcher. He draws our attention to *the sign* (11:45-46). Face to face with this astonishing miracle, people were forced to make up their minds once and for all about Jesus. There were *those who believed* (11:45) him: "Then many of the Jews which came to Mary, and had seen the things which Jesus did, believed on him." It was the only sensible thing to do.

This was the climax of these "signs" so characteristic of John's story of Christ's public ministry. Before this evidence of almighty power it was impossible to remain neutral. Many believed. That word *many* records a supreme tragedy: that John could not write *all*.

But it was not to be. Some refuse to believe, no matter what the evidence. So John tells of *those who betrayed* (11:46) Jesus: "But some of them went their ways to the Pharisees, and told them what things Jesus had done." The word *but* shows that they did so with the meanest of motives. Hostile from the start, off they went to curry favor with the authorities.

What they had to say tipped the scales. The Sanhedrin was now more determined than ever to get rid of Jesus.

2. An Amazing Reaction (11:47–12:11)

The official reaction to the raising of Lazarus is incredible. Instead of the whole Sanhedrin hurrying out to Bethany to investigate the miracle on the spot and then candidly hailing Jesus as messiah and God, the opposite happened. John records two interludes, *an interlude of plots* (11:47-57) and one of peace (12:1-11). The first scene centers around *the Jewish priest* (11:47-54) and *his companions* (11:47-48). They made up the Sanhedrin, the supreme governing body of the Jews. It consisted of seventy-one members, including the chief priests (the high priest himself, the captain of the temple, and members of the leading families of priests). The majority in the Sanhedrin were Sadducees but the Pharisees wielded considerable influence. Their meeting place was the "stone chamber" located within the temple precincts.

This influential body, of which even the Roman governors had to take account, was deeply agitated by news of this latest miracle of Jesus: "What do we?" they said one to another, "for this man doeth many miracles" (11:47). They could not deny that all Jerusalem was agog with excitement. They recognized that things were now coming to a head. A crisis was at hand. They reproached themselves for their inaction. They had long since decided they wanted no part of a messiah who showed so little respect for the ruling religious establishment. They could well envision that if this radical, reforming, miracle working messiah once established himself in power they were likely to be swept out of office.

On the other hand, there was danger from the Romans. The Romans had given the Sanhedrin considerable leeway in handling domestic, and especially religious, issues in the country. The Romans were bound to be suspicious of a messiah who claimed to be "King of the Jews."

So the religious leaders were on the horns of a dilemma. If they made a move against Christ they faced the possibility of a popular national uprising, especially in view of this astounding miracle. Besides, who knew what other powers this miracle worker possessed? All the way through, we see the timidity of the Sanhedrin. They never grasped the fact that Christ's mission was essentially spiritual, and that until his spiritual kingdom was established he had no intention of setting up a material one.

But if they did nothing to put a stop to this unwanted messiah's activities, the Roman army might intervene: "If we let him thus alone, all men will believe on him: and the Romans shall come and take away both our place and nation" (11:48). They were afraid of losing their place and power.

The key word is *our*, which is emphatic. They claimed as *theirs* what belonged to God. By *place* they doubtless meant the temple, which was the center of their influence. The emphatic *our* relates to the nation as well, which they controlled as though it were their own. The presence of Christ was a threat.

The high priest listened to this discussion. Now comes *his counsel* (11:49-52). We note, first, *his person* (11:49a): "And one of them named Caiaphas, being high priest that same year . . ." Caiaphas was appointed high priest in A.D. 18 by the Roman prefect Valerius Gratus and he continued in office until A.D. 36. He was son-in-law to Annas, who had been high priest from A.D. 6 to A.D. 15, but continued to exert much power over what went on in the nation. John's statement about Caiaphas means that he was steering the affairs of the nation when Christ was crucified. Like most members of the chief priest segment of the Sanhedrin, Caiaphas was a Sadducee. Since the Sadducees denied the possibility of resurrection, this miracle struck a particularly sour note.

We note also *his pride* (11:49b). Caiaphas rudely cut into the discussion being carried on by his colleagues. "Ye know nothing at all," he said. He used a double negative for emphasis. In effect he told his fellow rulers that they did not know what they were talking about.

Now comes *his policy* (11:50): "Nor consider that it is expedient that one man should die for the people, and that the whole nation perish not." Caiaphas was not concerned about the law or the rights and wrongs of this situation—just in what was expedient. Far better, in his view, to get rid of an unwanted messiah than subject himself to deposition and the nation to Roman martial law, along with possible cancellation of domestic autonomy, and Roman interference in the temple economy. It just made sense to throw Jesus to the wolves. They would achieve two objectives: they would save the nation from more rigid Roman rule and they would get rid of a man they hated.

We note, too, *his prophecy* (11:51-52): "And thus spake he not of himself: but being high priest that year, he prophesied that Jesus should die for that nation" (11:51). His words had a double meaning of which he himself was not aware. He was just being a politician; God used him, in spite of himself, as a prophet—as he had once used Balaam (Numbers 22:38).

This prophecy went far beyond the nation of Israel: "And not for that nation only, but that also he should gather together in one the children of God that were scattered abroad" (11:52). The high priest spoke what was in his evil heart. But, by a mysterious intervention of divine inspiration, he pronounced the national and global benefits of Christ's death.

Before leaving the high priest, John added a note about *his crime* (11:53-54). His colleagues were impressed. He carried all before him. His callous opportunism was to their liking. *The motion was passed* (11:53): "Then from that day forth they took counsel together for to put him to death." Acting on the criminal counsel of Caiaphas, the Sanhedrin condemned Jesus to death, and that without a hearing. They thereby guaranteed that the evils of a fresh insurgence of Roman arms, which Caiaphas wanted to avoid, would eventually be visited on the nation by God.

The motion was passed, but *the murder was postponed* (11:54) because Jesus withdrew temporarily from the vicinity: "Jesus therefore walked no more openly among the Jews; but went thence unto a country near to the wilderness, into a city called Ephraim, and there continued with his disciples." Opinions differ as to where this place of retirement was. Some place it at Tayibeh and thus locate it on a cone shaped hill about sixteen miles northeast of Jerusalem and five miles east of Bethel. It was on the edge of the wilderness, commanding an extensive view of the Jordan. Jesus secluded himself at this spot until just before going back to Jerusalem for his last Passover.

In concluding this section of his gospel, John brings the focus from the Jewish priest to *the Jewish Passover* (11:55-57). He mentions *the pilgrimage* (11:55): "And the Jews' passover was nigh at hand: and many went out of the country up to Jerusalem, before the passover to purify themselves." No one had any idea, except Jesus, how eventful this particular Passover was going to be.

The Jews were strict about making sure they were purified from ritual uncleanness before the feast. They were under law to be ceremonially clean before any important event (Exodus 19:10-11; 2 Chronicles 30:13-20). Those ceremonially unclean could not partake of the feast (John 18:28). The necessity of being ceremonially clean before keeping the Passover is made clear in Numbers 9:6-14.

This Passover in A.D. 30 is the third one mentioned by John. It was the last Passover to have any real significance; the true Passover lamb was about to be slain for the sin of the world.

John mentions *the people* (11:56): "Then sought they for Jesus, and spake among themselves, as they stood in the temple, What think ye, that he will not come to the feast?" Jesus was the general topic of conversation. The Galilean Jews had not seen him for some time. The Jerusalem Jews had heard nothing of him since the raising of Lazarus. We can envision the knots of people gathering here and there in the temple wondering if Jesus would appear. His miracles, his messages, had provided food for many a conversation in the past. "Would he come?" That was the burning question.

No power on earth or in hell could keep him away. They did not know that. The hour for which he had come into the world was fast approaching. And that hour coincided with the killing of the Passover lamb. For that hour he had to be in Jerusalem.

John mentions *the priests* (11:57): "Now both the chief priests and the Pharisees had given commandment, that, if any man knew where he were, he should shew it, that they might take him."

The decree of the Sanhedrin was now common knowledge—hence the debates as to whether Jesus would dare show his face in the capital. All Jews were conversant with the official position. The rulers had rejected Christ's claims and were anxious to lay hands on him. The multitudes had a general knowledge of the evil intentions of the Sanhedrin toward Jesus. When they later cried, "Let him be crucified," it was not because the rulers had sprung this on them. They were accessories to the official rejection of Christ, of which they were well aware.

An interlude of peace (12:1-11) in the happy home at Bethany was the calm before the storm. We see Jesus enjoying the company of friends before going out to encounter the cruelty of his foes.

John gives us *the date of the Lord's visit to Bethany* (12:1): "Then Jesus six days before the passover came to Bethany, where Lazarus was which had been dead, whom he raised from the dead."

The chronology of the Lord's last week on earth is not simple, and various views have been taken. Some think the Lord was crucified on Friday, others that he was crucified on Wednesday of the Passover week. Part of the confusion arises over the fact that our day begins with sunrise, whereas the Jewish day begins at sunset. Part of the confusion arises over the various kinds of sabbaths involved. Part of the discussion centers around how long the Lord was in the tomb, which in turn hinges on whether we count part of a day as a whole day or whether we take the view that Jesus was a full three days and three nights in the grave.

It will be helpful at this point to summarize the main sequence of events.

A. The Sixth Day before the Passover
   The 9th day of Nisan
   Our Thursday Sunset to Friday Sunset
   • The Lord approaches Jerusalem from Jericho (Luke 19:1-10)
   • He spends Thursday night with Zaccheus (Luke 19:11-27)
   • He enters Jerusalem and cleanses the temple (Matthew 21:1-16)
   • He goes to Bethany (John 12:1)

B. The Fifth Day before the Passover
   The 10th day of Nisan

Our Friday Sunset to Saturday Sunset
- The Lord spends the sabbath at Bethany. After sunset the first of three suppers was given, probably at the house of Lazarus (John 12:2)
- Mary of Bethany anointed Jesus (John 12:3-11)

C. The Fourth Day before the Passover
   The 11th day of Nisan
   Our Saturday Sunset to Sunday Sunset
   - The triumphal entry into Jerusalem (Mark 11:1-7; Luke 19:29-35; John 12:12)
   - He returns to Bethany (Mark 11:11)

D. The Third Day before the Passover
   The 12th day of Nisan
   Our Sunday Sunset to Monday Sunset
   - The Lord returns to Jerusalem and curses the fig tree (Matthew 21:18-22)
   - The coming of the Greeks (John 12:20-50)
   - Opposition from the rulers (Mark 11:12-18)
   - The Lord leaves Jerusalem, probably for Bethany (Luke 11:19)

E. The Second Day before the Passover
   The 13th day of Nisan
   Our Monday Sunset to Tuesday Sunset
   - The Lord returns to Jerusalem (Matthew 21:23–23:39; Mark 11:20–12:44; Luke 20:1–21:38)
   - The Lord gives his Olivet discourse (Matthew 24:1–25:46)
   - The time note: "After two days is the Passover" (Matthew 26:1-5; Mark 14:1-2)
   - The Lord returns to Bethany. The second supper, in the house of Simon the leper. The second anointing (Matthew 26:6-13; Luke 14:3-9)

F. The Day before the Passover
   The 14th day of Nisan
   Our Tuesday Sunset to Wednesday Sunset
   The Day of the Crucifixion
   - The plot of Judas (Matthew 26:14-16)
   - The "preparation" for the last supper (Matthew 26:17-19). The words in Mark 14:12 and Luke 22:7 refer to "the first day of unleavened bread" (the 14th day of Nisan, "the preparation day")

- In the evening the Lord goes to the upper room and washes the disciples' feet (Matthew 26:21-25; John 13:1-20)
- The Lord reveals the traitor (John 13:21-30)
- The Lord eats the Passover and makes the New Covenant (Matthew 26:26-29)
- The Lord foretells Peter's denials (John 13:31-38)
- The Lord talks to his disciples and prays for them (John 14:1–17:26)
- They go to Gethsemane (Matthew 26:30-35; John 18:1)
- The Lord is arrested (Matthew 26:47-56; John 18:2-11)
- The trials (Matthew 26:57–27:31; John 18:12–19:13)
- The crucifixion (the "third hour"–9 a.m. Wednesday) (Mark 15:25-26)
- The Lord's mother commended to John's care (John 19:25-27)
- The Lord dies at "the ninth hour" (3 p.m. Wednesday) (John 19:31-37)
- The Lord's hasty burial (John 19:38-42)

Thus the Lord was already in the tomb on the first day of the feast, the 15th day of Nisan (Wednesday sunset to Thursday sunset). This day was called "the high day" or "the high sabbath." He remained in the tomb through the second and third days of the feast (Thursday sunset through Saturday sunset). Saturday was the regular Jewish sabbath, the 17th day of Nisan. He rose from the dead on "the first day of the week," the 18th day of Nisan: "Very early in the morning," the "third day" as foretold by Jesus (Matthew 16:21).

Now John gives us *the details of the Lord's visit to Bethany* (12:2-11). The lovely story here recorded revolves around Martha, Mary, and Lazarus. The whole scene is a cameo of the local church: when "two or three are gathered together" in his name, he is "in the midst of them."

Every local church needs a Martha. Martha was *a worker* (12:2): "There they made him a supper; and Martha served." (This supper does not seem to be the same as the one recorded in Matthew 26:6-13 and Mark 14:1-9, nor does the anointing appear to be the same as in Matthew 26:7-13 and Mark 14:3-9.) John adds the note that "Lazarus was one of them that sat at the table with him." The wonder about Lazarus had by no means died down. Nowadays, of course, Lazarus would be a guest on a TV talk show or signed up by some enterprising publicist to write a book and travel the continent giving his testimony and boosting sales. Here we see Lazarus quietly and inconspicuously taking his seat at the table with Jesus.

Martha was a worker. But there was no criticizing or complaining now, as there had been once before (Luke 10:38-42).

Mary was *a worshiper* (12:3-8). Every local church needs those who put themselves at Jesus' feet. How frequently we find Mary of Bethany at Jesus' feet (Luke 10:39; John 11:32; 12:3).

We note how *her worship was expressed* (12:3): "Then took Mary a pound of ointment of spikenard, very costly, and anointed the feet of Jesus, and wiped his feet with her hair: and the house was filled with the odor of the ointment." Nard was a liquid perfume, extremely expensive. The word *spikenard* may refer to the fact that the perfume was genuine or pure, the best that money could buy. She poured it out in a lavish gesture, unexpected, generous, spontaneous, and wiped his feet with her hair. Genuine worship never counts the cost. It is not intimidated by the stares or sneers of carnal minds. It has thought only for Christ. It leaves behind a fragrance none can mistake or avoid. A little of that fragrance is carried away by everyone.

Her worship was examined (12:4-6). We note the sour comment of Judas: "Then saith one of his disciples, Judas Iscariot, Simon's Son, which should betray him, Why was not this ointment sold for three hundred pence, and given to the poor?" To be so extravagant in giving to Jesus was in Judas's opinion a waste. It is so in the minds of many people to this day. Many think that money given to the Lord's work would be better spent on social services. They think that a life poured out in trying to reach some remote tribe with the gospel is a life wasted.

Judas put an immediate price tag on Mary's act of love. "Three hundred pence" was his calculation of the market value of the spikenard. Since in Bible times a man would work all day for a penny, the price of that spikenard was the better part of a working man's annual wage. The size of the sum was not lost on Judas.

Nor was the avarice lost on John: "This he said," John comments, "not that he cared for the poor; but because he was a thief, and had the bag, and bare what was put therein" (12:6). John is looking back to these things after many years. Although now old, he had not lost his horror at the duplicity of Judas. "The man was a thief," he said. The word is *kleptes*, from which we get our word *kleptomaniac*. Judas had been able to pull the wool over the eyes of his colleagues right up to the end. But once he was unmasked by his treachery, many other things were explained. All along the other unsuspecting disciples had assumed that Judas had been giving money to the poor. Now it was obvious where it had been going: to line the pockets of a thief. Judas was furious that so large a sum should not have been put in the bag so that he could take what he considered to be his share.

The caustic remark of Judas must have cut Mary like a lash, but the Lord leaped to her defense: "Then said Jesus, Let her alone: against the day of my burying hath she kept this. For the poor always ye have with you; but me ye have not always" (12:78).

This is the key. We need to try to put ourselves in Mary's place. She had listened to Jesus, had sat at his feet, had learned from him. She had heard him talk about his death and burial. She had thought it through and realized that he was to die.

At some point she, in preparation for that death, bought this rare and costly nard and hid it away. Then Lazarus had died suddenly and unexpectedly, and spices were needed for his burial. Had Mary been tempted to lavish her treasure on her brother's remains? No, she had not bought this for Lazarus; she had bought it for Jesus. It was not for Lazarus's burial; it was for Jesus' burial. Jesus knew she had it, and why.

Then one day there was a resurrection! Jesus came to Bethany and raised her brother from the dead. We can imagine that many a time around the supper table Martha would tell her brother and sister what Jesus had said: "I am the resurrection and the life." Mary hid this saying in her heart.

Then one day the light went on in her soul. Jesus said he was going to be crucified, he was going to be buried, and he was going to rise again. There was to be a resurrection like that of Lazarus. That had to be it. He was the resurrection. Death would not be able to hold him. He had said he would rise on the third day. As for his body, it would need no spices. David had prophesied: "Thou wilt not . . . suffer thine Holy One to see corruption" (Psalm 16:10). Jesus would not need the spikenard when he was buried after all.

So, she said to herself, I'll give it to him the next time he's here. It was a marvelous demonstration of her faith. She had kept that ointment for his burial, but she gave it to him a week before—because she now believed in his resurrection. No wonder the house was filled with the fragrance!

Mary of Bethany seems to have been the only one who believed the truth of resurrection. You won't find her at the cross or at the tomb. Nor was it cowardice or despair that kept her away. You'll find Mary, the Lord's mother, at the cross. You'll find Mary Magdalene at the tomb. You'll find Mary the mother of James and Joses at the cross and at the tomb. But not Mary of Bethany. She had not the slightest need to be at either place.

She was already standing on resurrection ground.

Every local church needs Marthas to get things done. Every church needs Marys to help others enter into the deep things of God. Every local church needs men like Lazarus, *a witness* (12:9-11) in a special sense.

John underlines for us *the tremendous reality* (12:9) of Lazarus's witness: "Much people of the Jews therefore knew that he [Jesus] was there: and they came not for Jesus' sake only, but that they might see Lazarus also, whom he had raised from the dead."

We have no idea how long Lazarus had lived at Bethany, possibly all his life. As far as we know, he had always been a decent, moral, law abiding, synagogue attending man. Now he had become a believer in Christ. His home had become a center where the Lord Jesus was loved, welcomed, honored. He knew Jesus personally. He made his people welcome. But nobody had ever made the two mile trip out from Jerusalem to see him because he was a believer in Christ. Nobody ever crossed the Kedron and climbed Olivet to see an ordinary believer.

What made the difference? Now he was a man living a resurrected life. He was a man living day by day, situation by situation, in the power of resurrection. Until that point, Lazarus had been a genuine believer, even a committed believer. But he had not been a particularly outstanding witness for Christ. Now, by virtue of the life he was living, he was a witness. He did not say: "Today I am going to do house-to-house visitation and try to win people for Jesus." He did not take a course in soulwinning or memorize a string of key Bible verses. He simply lived a resurrection life. And people believed the witness of Lazarus. And people came from all over to see the miracle of that resurrection life. They came to see the man who had died and now lived.

Suppose we were to have asked him: "Lazarus, how do you do it? What is the secret of this dynamic new life of yours?" He might have said something like this: "I wasn't always this way. For some years I was a nominal believer in Jesus. I loved him; I wanted to please him. He was the most important person in my life. I loved my sisters; I loved his people. I did all the right things, said all the right things. And I was perfectly sincere. Then one day I died. I died to everybody, died to everything. I even died to my own testimony for Jesus. The old Lazarus was very dead indeed. And everybody knew it. You don't expect anything of a dead man, do you? I died. And I was buried. I came to an utter end of myself. Then Jesus came and he gave me a new life—his life, resurrection life. I found myself on resurrection ground. So you see I am not the old Lazarus you used to know . . ."

There is something attractive about the life of a person who has died to the old life and is now living a resurrection life in Christ. God's Son brings life to people who are dead in sins. He speaks and calls all spiritually dead people to life.

John goes on to show *the terrible reaction* (12:10-11). "But the chief priests consulted that they might put Lazarus to death; because that by reason of him many of the Jews went away, and believed on Jesus." The witness of Lazarus's new life was enormously effective. People came, saw, went away, and believed in Jesus. The religious authorities were powerless to stop it. They could not deny it.

So the reaction of the authorities was to plot the murder of Lazarus. Jesus had confronted a dead man and made him live. These leaders confronted a resurrected man and sought his death. They were filled with venom against Christ, and against the man living in the power of Christ.

B. Rejected in spite of His Fulfillment of Prophecy (12:12-19)

Things were now rapidly coming to a head. The Lord had been rejected in spite of his feat of power. Now he was to be rejected in spite of his fulfillment of prophecy (12:12-19). He was about to ride into Jerusalem as foretold, and officially present himself to Israel as the nation's rightful king.

1. The Pilgrims (12:12-13a)

The first thing that impressed John about the Lord's triumphant entry into Jerusalem were *the pilgrims* (12:12-13a). We note *the importance of the day* (12:12): "On the next day much people that were come to the feast, when they heard that Jesus was coming to Jerusalem, . . . " The day was the fourth day before Passover, what we call Palm Sunday.

Although John does not say so, this was an important date. Scripturally literate Jews ought to have had this date circled on their calendars. The Sanhedrin should have been counting down to this date. They should have known its special significance from all the other days and dates, times and seasons, in the religious calendar. This was a day and a date foretold 483 years before by Daniel the prophet, who had marked off for Israel a period of seventy sevens of years. After sixty nine of those seven-year periods, something was going to happen. Daniel gave the date from which they were to keep track of the passing years:

Seventy weeks are determined upon thy people and upon thy holy city, to finish the transgression, and to make an end of sins, and to make reconciliation for iniquity, and to bring in everlasting righteousness, and to seal up the vision and prophecy, and to anoint the most Holy. Know therefore and understand, that from the going forth of the commandment to restore and to build Jerusalem unto the Messiah the Prince shall be seven weeks, and three-score and two weeks: the street shall be built again, and the wall, even in troublous times. And after threescore and two weeks shall Messiah be cut off, but not for himself: and the people of the prince that shall come shall destroy the city and the sanctuary; and the end thereof shall be with a flood, and unto the end of the war desolations are determined. And he shall confirm the covenant with many for one week: and in the midst of the week he shall cause the sacrifice and the oblation to cease, and for the overspreading of abominations he shall make it desolate even until the consummation, and that determined shall be poured upon the desolate (Daniel 9:24-27).

This prophecy was divided into three periods. The first (7x7) took the Jews to the end of the Old Testament period, through the rebuilding of the city in troublesome times—starting with the date 445 B.C. when, in the twentieth year of his reign, Artaxerxes issued his decree permitting Nehemiah to return to Jerusalem and build it (Nehemiah 2:1-8).

Then would follow the second period (62x7) which took the Jews down through the so-called "silent centuries," the intertestamental period, to the time when messiah would come and be "cut off, but not for himself." According to Sir Robert Anderson, this period ended on the very day of Christ's triumphant entry into Jerusalem. Within the week he was indeed "cut off, but not for himself" by the leaders of the Jews who should have known the prophetic significance of this day.

The third period (1x7) swayed in the balance. Suppose the Jews *had* accepted Jesus as messiah, and the authorities as well as the crowds had hailed him as king. Doubtless the events connected with the final week would have followed at once. The Romans would have crucified Christ. They would have signed a seven year treaty with the Jews, broken it as foretold, inaugurated the great tribulation, and been swept away by the return of Christ to set up his kingdom. The forebodings and foretellings of Caiaphas would have had an immediate fulfill-

ment, but God would have made "short work" of things and
hastened the second coming of Christ.

As it was, the Jews brought about the fulfillment of the
prophecy that messiah would be cut off. Nor did they repent
even in the face of Christ's resurrection and the coming of the
Holy Spirit at Pentecost. As a result the final week of Daniel's
prophecy was indefinitely postponed. God inserted the church
age in between the sixty-ninth and seventieth week. As for the
fears of Caiaphas that the Romans would come and destroy
Jerusalem, the Jews brought that fate on themselves within a
generation.

Such was the day, surely the most critical day in the history of
the Jewish people—in the history of the world, perhaps, since
the alternative of an immediate or a long-delayed millennial
reign swung in its balance.

That was the day when the common people, still agog with
excitement because of the raising of Lazarus, "heard that Jesus
was coming to Jerusalem."

We note, with that, *the implications of the deed* (12:13a): "They
took branches of palm trees, and went forth to meet him." The
crowd was likely made up mostly of the thousands of pilgrims
from all over the country who had come to Jerusalem to keep
the feast.

Ever since the days of the Maccabees, palm branches had
been used by the Jews as symbols of victory. When the Jews
celebrated the rededication of their temple in 164 B.C. the
rejoicing people in the procession waved palm branches. When
the Jews gained full independence under Simon in 141 B.C.,
they waved palm leaves. In the war against the Romans in A.D.
66-70 and again under Bar Kochba in A.D. 132-135 the Jews
stamped palm leaves as symbols on their coins. Thus here, the
pilgrims waved palm leaves as they cheered. The messiah was
coming. Victory was at hand. It was finally the end of Roman
rule.

2. The Praise (12:13b)

John could remember the praise: ". . . and cried, Hosanna: Blessed is the King of Israel that cometh in the name of
the Lord." This was a quotation from Psalm 118:25-26. The
word *hosanna* meant "Save now!" or "Give the victory now!"
There can be no doubt that they were enthused by the political
and military implications of the coming of the king. They had
never grasped the fact that the millennial kingdom could be
manifested only on the foundation of a spiritual kingdom.

3. The Procession (12:14a)

We note the procession: "And Jesus, when he had found a young ass, sat thereon." The chanting crowds, pouring out toward the mount of Olives from Jerusalem, met Jesus and his disciples coming down the slopes toward Jerusalem. The Lord was riding a donkey. Had he wanted to encourage the martial aspirations of the Jews, he would have ridden into Jerusalem on a war horse. No doubt the fact that this "messiah" was riding in triumph on a donkey would have helped disarm Roman suspicions. We can be sure that this populist movement was being closely watched by the Romans. But a king riding on a donkey would pose no threat. They would see that as amusing, even something to ridicule.

4. The Prophecy (12:14b-16)

But it was not amusing to those who knew their Bible. There was the prophecy: "Fear not, daughter of Sion: behold thy King cometh, sitting on an ass's colt." The prophet Zechariah had foretold this event (Zechariah 9:9) in an unmistakably millennial context (Zechariah 9:10). The disciples themselves had forgotten this prophecy: "These things understood not his disciples at the first: but when Jesus was glorified, then remembered they that these things were written of him, and that they had done these things unto him" (12:16). Evidently the disciples themselves, at the time, were not conscious of fulfilling prophecy. There may have been some more astute minds in the Sanhedrin, however, who remembered this prophecy and saw, in Christ's fulfillment of it, ominous implications—from their point of view.

5. The People (12:17-18)

Our attention is drawn back to the people: "The people, therefore that was with him when he called Lazarus out of his grave, and raised him from the dead, bare record. For this cause the people also met him, for that they heard that he had done this miracle." The two crowds converged. There was the company coming into Jerusalem from Bethany, filled with enthusiasm because of the recent miracle. The story of the raising of Lazarus was evidently well known in the city. The pilgrims from the city marching out to meet the coming king were fired up too by word of that miracle. A man who could raise the dead could deal with Romans.

6. The Perception (12:19)

John concludes this incident with the perception of the Lord's enemies. It did not take a great deal of perceptivity to see that this opposition, even organized and official opposition, backed by the power of the priesthood and by the authority of the Sanhedrin, was getting nowhere. "The Pharisees therefore said among themselves, Perceive ye how ye prevail nothing? Behold, the world is gone after him" (12:19). The Sadducees, their purpose stiffened by the determined high priest, Caiaphas, did not give way to this pessimism. They were making their plans and biding their time. Yet the Pharisees were more right than they knew. The world was going after him. John takes this comment of the Pharisees as an opportune moment to illustrate this.

C. Rejected in spite of His Fervor in Prayer (12:20-36)

Next we see Christ rejected in spite of his fervor in prayer.

1. The Visit of the Greeks (12:20-26)

John now tells us of the visit of the Greeks, a matter of considerable interest in light of the world mission of Christ. The incident begins with *a plea* (12:20-24). These Greeks were Greek speaking gentiles *(Hellenes)*, not just Greek speaking Jews. They were representatives of the gentile world beyond Palestine. They might well have been God fearing gentiles, those who were attracted to the Jewish religion but who would not take the irrevocable step of becoming full proselytes. These gentiles would occasionally go to Jerusalem on festive occasions. They were allowed to go into the court of the gentiles in the temple. Some of these approached Philip the disciple with *a spontaneous request* (12:20-22). Evidently they had been impressed by the fervor in the city about this miracle working Jesus. They were in Jerusalem "to worship at the feast."

Several days possibly elapsed between the Lord's triumphant entry and the visit of these gentiles. (The Lord's life on earth began with a visit of gentiles from the east and drew to a close with a visit of gentiles from the west.) In the meantime the Lord had cleansed the moneychangers from the court of the gentiles (Mark 11:15-17). Perhaps these gentiles had read in that act a goodwill gesture of this messiah toward themselves. In any case, they approached Philip (a Jew with a gentile name) with a request: "The same came therefore to Philip, which was of

Bethsaida of Galilee, and desired him, saying, Sir, we would see Jesus" (12:20-22). It may be that Philip spoke Greek, or perhaps these Greeks were from Galilee. Philip referred the request to Andrew, and then the two of them went and told Jesus.

Philip and Andrew received *a specific reply* (12:23-24). Before looking at that reply we should note that so far as we can tell from the passage, the request of the Greeks was not granted. There are two possible reasons for this. One reason is that a Christ, on earth, in the flesh, the king of the Jews, sent to "the lost sheep of the house of Israel," was not the appropriate object for the faith of the gentiles. The Jews should have believed in him in this capacity. For gentiles, Christ first had to die, be buried, and be raised again. He was to be offered to the gentiles as seed of Abraham (Genesis 12:1-3), not the seed of David (Ephesians 2:11-13).

Another reason is based on the raising of Lazarus. We must not lose sight of the whole background of this incident. There really was no reason why these gentiles should see Jesus. The Lord might well have said to them: "You don't need to see me. Go and see Lazarus. He is now living the same kind of life that I am living. As the resurrection and the life, my life is now his life. When you see the life Lazarus is living you see the life I am living. So, when you see Lazarus, you see me."

That is what Jesus has been saying to his people for two thousand years. The life that Lazarus was living was an impossible life, made possible because it was an imparted life. Paul put the Christian life this way: "I live: yet not I, but Christ liveth in me: and the life which I now live in the flesh I live by the faith of the Son of God, who loved me and gave himself for me" (Galatians 2:20). God expects that Christ's life shall so be expressed in our lives that, even though people cannot see him in the flesh, they will be able to see him in us. This is the truth that Jesus now goes on to expound.

The Lord's reply was to Andrew and Philip. It was in three parts. We are to see *the Lord glorified* (12:23): "And Jesus answered them, saying, The hour is come, that the Son of man should be glorified." Persistently and blindly the Jews rejected him. In contrast, these gentiles had come seeking him. In these gentiles Jesus saw the first few of that vast flock of "other sheep" which were not of the Jewish fold. He could see his name being exalted and glorified in the gentile world, churches being established for his worship in all parts of the earth. These Greeks were the vanguard of an enormous multitude that no one can number, called out of gentile lands, ransomed and restored, their names written in his book, their voices raised in his praise.

We are to see *the Lord crucified* (12:24a): "Verily, verily, I say unto you, Except a corn of wheat fall into the ground and die, it abideth alone . . . " The "corn of wheat is *kokkos*, signifying the seed corn of the wheat. All gardening and farming are founded on the principle that a seed has to be sown into the ground, that its germ of life can reproduce only when the seed is sown and dies. A grain of corn can never fulfill the "law of its being" apart from the process of death, burial, and reproduction in resurrection.

Thus the Lord picked up the crude and wicked philosophy of Caiaphas and transformed it. He had to die and be buried or else he would abide alone.

We are to see *the Lord multiplied* (12:24b): ". . . but if it die, it bringeth forth much fruit." The visit of these Greeks enabled the Lord to see the harvest. It is perhaps significant that in the book of Acts the church's first major missionary enterprise was begun by a work in Antioch among the Greeks of the city (Acts 11:20). This, in turn, sparked Paul's missionary journeys in which he concentrated on work in the Greek cities of the Roman empire. "Much fruit." The Lord could see himself multiplied in the ages to come as a result of his being obedient unto death.

Next we have *a paradox* (12:25): "He that loveth his life shall lose it; and he that hateth his life in this world shall keep it unto life eternal." The paradox is that death is the way to life. We must be so committed to Christ that there is no self-centeredness, no concern for self.

Next comes *a principle* (12:26). There is first a word about *the Lord's followers* (12:26a,b): "If any man serve me, let him follow me; and where I am, there also shall my servant be." The paradox is part of a principle: every person has to determine which world he or she intends to live for. We can live for Jesus and the world to come, and be with him for all eternity. Or we can live for this world and be the losers in eternity, as the next clause shows.

For, there is also a word about *the Lord's Father* (12:26c): "If any man serve me, him will my Father honor." It is possible to have a saved soul and a lost life. Millions have been saved but have never served. At the judgment seat of Christ, those who have served will be honored. The honored will be those who have died martyrs' deaths, those who have forsaken houses and lands, loved ones and friends, home and business, to serve him in far off places of the world, living with godless tribes, translating the Bible into strange tongues, healing the sick, preaching the gospel, blazing new trails, winning souls, planting churches, building hospitals. The honored will be those who have gone forth weeping, bearing precious seed. They will be honored by the Father.

2. The Voice of God (12:27-36)

All this stemmed from the visit of the Greeks. It was followed by the voice of God. We observe now *the Lord's distress* (12:27): "Now is my soul troubled; and what shall I say? Father, save me from this hour: but for this cause came I unto this hour." The Lord's thoughts go to Calvary. The way to the cross would be no easy road for him to travel. It would be a deadly reality for him: the agony in the garden, the mocking trials, the physical abuse, the scourging, the crown of thorns, the heavy cross, the agony of crucifixion, the anguish of being made sin for us, the horror of the darkness, the bitter taste of death. These things made up that "lone, mysterious hour" toward which he had been wending his way from a past eternity.

That hour had come much closer the hour he was born. It had come closer still the hour he was baptized by John, and identified with the race he had come to redeem. It had come closer when he descended from the mount after meeting with Moses and Elijah to talk of his decease. It had come closer when he had performed those miracles in Jerusalem on the sabbath to challenge the shibboleths of the rabbis. It had come closer when he had declared himself to be God. It had come closer when he had ridden into Jerusalem in triumph to proclaim himself messiah in spite of the opposition of the Sanhedrin. It had come closer now that he resolutely refused to pray that his Father in heaven would keep him from that hour.

We note *the Lord's desire* (12:28-30). The Lord burst suddenly into prayer—not a prayer that he might be kept from the hour, but that his Father might be glorified. "Father, glorify thy name. Then came a voice from heaven, saying, I have both glorified it, and will glorify it again. The people therefore, that stood by, and heard it, said that it thundered: others said, An angel spake to him. Jesus answered and said, This voice came not because of me, but for your sakes."

This is the third time God had now spoken audibly from heaven. The first time was at his baptism, at the commencement of his ministry (Matthew 3:17); the second time was on the mount of transfiguration, at the climax of his ministry (Matthew 17:5); the third time is here, at the crisis of his ministry. The first time was when he went down into the waters of Jordan; the second time was when he was about to come down from the mount; the third time was when he prepared himself to go down into death.

The people standing around heard something loud but they were mystified as to how to explain it. Some thought it was a natural phenomenon, a thunderclap. Others thought it was a supernatural phenomenon, the voice of an angel. Neither group was able to discern what was said. The Lord instantly recognized his Father's voice. He explained to the crowds that it was indeed a voice. But he himself did not need audible confirmation that he was in the Father's will.

Evidently the disciples themselves either understood what was said to Jesus in this pronouncement, or else he told them. In it, God declared that he had already glorified his name in the ministry of Jesus and he would glorify it again. From the context we deduce that the Father's name had been glorified in the wilderness by the Lord's victory over Satan and would be glorified again by the victory over Satan at Calvary and in the apocalypse. Satan is the one great moral blot in the universe. His character, career, and crimes constitute an abiding insult to the holiness and goodness of God. The Lord's victories over Satan bring glory to God.

We note, too, *the Lord's declaration* (12:31): "Now is the judgment of this world: now shall the prince of this world be cast out." The prince of this world is Satan. The word used for "prince" is *archon*. The title is applied to Satan three times (here, in 14:30, and 16:11). He is the prince of demons (Matthew 12:24) and the prince of the power of the air (Ephesians 2:2).

The Bible has a great deal to say about this archenemy of God and of the human race. As the prince of this world Satan exercises that power over the world which God originally entrusted to Adam and Eve (Genesis 1:26-28). In the fall that influence was surrendered to Satan. When Satan tempted Jesus in the wilderness he offered the kingdoms of this world as a bribe to entice Jesus to worship him (Matthew 4:8-10). We learn from the book of Daniel that Satan sets his own princes over the nations in the unseen world. These princes are fallen angels of great power (Daniel 10:11-21). Paul tells us we wrestle against them when we pray (Ephesians 6:12). He also tells us that Jesus triumphed over them on the cross (Colossians 2:15).

Here the Lord proclaimed that this world's judgment day had come. He had presented himself as Israel's messiah. The unstable crowd had been momentarily excited but the rulers had remained opposed to him.

The die was cast. The world, as represented by the Jews,

God's especially chosen people, and as represented by their leaders, had passed judgment on Jesus. He was a demoniac, a blasphemer, a national danger. Their verdict was to get rid of him. Behind their opposition was the prince of this world. From the moment of Christ's birth, Satan himself, and no mere subordinate angelic prince, led the opposition to Jesus.

In the Bible we can discern a pattern: the Spirit is opposed by the flesh, the Father is opposed by the world, the Son is opposed by the devil. With the advent of Christ, Satan's kingdom on earth was put under siege. From the beginning Satan had fought back in desperation, the opening move being the massacre of the baby boys in Bethlehem. Now he had lined up the Sanhedrin to further his plan to terminate Christ's life on a Roman gibbet.

But he had made a grave error. The cross of Christ was God's chosen instrument to sound the eternal death knell of Satan, his kingdom, and his power. By instigating the Jews to pass sentence on Christ, he set in motion the flow of events that would guarantee his own destruction.

So Jesus could say, "Now is the judgment of this world: Now shall the prince of this world be cast out." The same word for expulsion is used in connection with the Sanhedrin, when they took the blind man whom Jesus had healed and cast him out of the synagogue (9:34-35). The word was used by Jesus in his parable of the vineyard: "When the husbandmen saw the son, they said among themselves, This is the heir; come, let us kill him, and let us seize on his inheritance. And they caught him, and cast him out of the vineyard, and slew him" (Matthew 21:38-39). It was used by Luke in describing the stoning of Stephen: "Then they . . . ran upon him with one accord, and cast him out of the city, and stoned him" (Acts 7:57-58). Satan organized all this opposition to Christ and to those committed to him. The Lord, seeing the true significance of the cross, says, "Now shall the prince of this world be cast out."

The Lord's death (12:32-34) is God's means of tearing down Satan's world system. That death is *described* (12:32-33): "And I, if I be lifted up from the earth, will draw all men unto me. This he said, signifying what death he should die." The cross is the great divide of humanity. On the one side of the cross we see a dying thief, a man who died blaspheming and went out into a lost eternity. On the other side of the cross we see a dying thief, a man who died believing and went out to be with Christ in paradise. The cross thus divides the world. Everyone is drawn to the cross. Everyone has to decide on which side of the cross to stand—Jew and gentile, rich and poor, good and bad, religious and irreligious, Greeks and barbarians.

This was the Lord's answer to the Greeks. In his death, Jesus would deal decisively with the prince of this world; he would set the stage for the judgment of this world; he would act in judgment on the people of the world and provide salvation for all, regardless of country, culture, or creed.

Then we have his death *discussed* (12:34): "The people answered him, We have heard out of the law that Christ abideth for ever: and how sayest thou, The Son of man must be lifted up? who is this Son of man?" Thus the judgment process began to work at once. The Jews interrupted Jesus. They had heard more than enough. They had their ideas about the messiah. Jesus had proclaimed himself to be the messiah in his triumphant entry. Now he was talking about being "lifted up" (the expression occurs twenty times and in John's gospel always has reference to the cross). They remembered previous occasions when he had spoken of himself as the Son of man, and of the Son of man being lifted up (3:14; 8:28).

They referred Jesus to "the law." Psalm 89:29 and Psalm 92, read on the sabbath since the days of Ezra, might have been in their minds. If Christ was to abide forever, what was all this talk about being "lifted up"? Who was this Son of man anyway? There seems to have been a note of contempt in their question. Thus, victims of their preconceived ideas about the kind of messiah to expect, and mystified by the Lord's way of doing things and by his sayings, they asked their question. It came halfway between their hosannas and their howls for his crucifixion.

Now comes *the Lord's discernment* (12:35-36a): "Then Jesus said unto them, Yet a little while is the light with you. Walk while ye have the light, lest darkness come upon you: for he that walketh in darkness knoweth not whither he goeth. While ye have light, believe in the light, that ye may be the children of light. These things spake Jesus, and departed, and did hide himself from them." That was his answer to their unbelief. Although he was the light, they refused to see it. He knew where he was going, and how, and why.

His earthly ministry was nearly over. How urgent was their need to take advantage of the light while it still shone on their nation. There was still a chance to walk in the light, even to become children of light, to become partakers of his nature. But the light would soon be withdrawn. Then they would walk in darkness, stumbling along, not knowing where they went.

The subsequent history of the Jewish people has been one long commentary on this. They rejected the Savior; they rejected the Spirit. They stumbled into the disaster of war with Rome. They went on to the even worse disaster of the Bar Kochba rebellion. They saw no light in Christ. They plunged into the ever expanding darkness of the Talmud. They have persisted in unbelief to this day, and will go on doing so until they stumble into the arms of the antichrist.

Foreshadowing this, the Lord withdrew from their presence and went and hid himself. This seems to have been his last public appeal to the Jewish people. He went away, in all probability, to Bethany, and they saw no more of him until they saw him in the hands of his foes and responded to the incitement of the Sanhedrin to shout for his death. So the segment ends with *the Lord's departure* (12:36b).

John has given us some examples of the Lord's deity being disowned by rejection. He has a few more things to say by way of explanation.

II. Some Explanations of His Rejection (12:37-50)

A. An Ancient Prophecy (12:37-43)

1. Solid Disbelief (12:37-41)

John advances two major causes for the stubborn unbelief of the Jewish people. One has to do with an ancient prophecy, the other with an abiding principle. John begins by underlining the solid disbelief of the Jews (12:37-41).

This disbelief was no accident. It was *deliberately fostered* (12:37): "But though he had done so many miracles before them, yet they believed not on him." They deliberately, persistently, stubbornly tore up his credentials.

Only thirty-six miracles of Jesus are recorded in the gospels. But the evangelists also include summary statements showing that Jesus performed many more miracles than those specifically documented. Here John mentions "so many miracles." The Lord's public ministry was extraordinary. He performed miracle after miracle, day after day. He demonstrated his deity in countless ways, showing his lordship over the processes and forces of nature, over all kinds of sickness and disability, over hordes of evil spirits, and over death itself. Unbelief, in the face of such proof, had to be deliberately fostered.

It was also *divinely foretold* (12:38-41). John alludes to two Old Testament prophecies, both from the prophet Isaiah, to demonstrate this. The first was from Isaiah 53, the prophecy of the messiah's sufferings: "That the saying of Esaias the prophet might be fulfilled, which he spake, Lord, who hath believed our report? and to whom hath the arm of the Lord been revealed?" (12:38). The Old Testament spoke of the Lord's fingers, the Lord's hand, and the Lord's arm. The psalmist declared that the heavens were the work of God's fingers (Psalm 8:3). The exodus from Egypt, for instance, is said to have been wrought by God's mighty hand (Exodus 32:11). The Holy Spirit dismisses the creation of all the suns and stars of space as a very small thing with God, the work of his fingers. The miracles of Jesus, by contrast, are said to be a demonstration of the power of God's arm. Yet the Jews had written off such displays of power.

John quotes a further prophecy: "Therefore they could not believe, because that Esaias said again, He hath blinded their eyes, and hardened their heart; that they should not see with their eyes, nor understand with their heart, and be converted, and I should heal them" (12:39-40). Unbelief is self-propagating. A sobering Old Testament illustration is that of pharaoh, who continued to harden his heart until there came a time when God hardened it for him. The Jews were now guilty of similar behavior. A time comes in the lives of those who will not repent when at last they cannot repent. Israel's persistent unbelief was clearly foretold by Isaiah. He had experienced it in his own lifetime and in response to his ministry.

John adds, "These things said Esaias, when he saw his glory, and spake of him" (12:41). The Lord, whose glory he saw, was Jesus. The reference is to the call of Isaiah, to the time when he saw the Lord "high and lifted up," surrounded by the seraphim (the "burning ones"), celestial beings whose voices proclaimed the holiness of God (Isaiah 6). The same day he was called to his ministry, Isaiah was forewarned, in the words now quoted by John, of the obdurate unbelief of Israel.

2. Secret Disciples (12:42-43)

John now adds that there were believers in the Lord Jesus, but they were secret disciples. He speaks of *their convictions* (12:42a), *their cowardice* (12:42b), and *their compromise* (12:43): "Nevertheless among the chief rulers also many believed on him; but because of the Pharisees they did not confess him, lest they should be put out of the synagogue: For they loved the praise of men more than the praise of God." Numbered among these were Nicodemus and Joseph of Arimathaea, both of whom cast off their compromise when they saw what the Sanhedrin had done to Jesus.

Their compromise was costly. True, they would have been

excommunicated, because of the antagonism to Jesus of the more vocal Pharisees, but they might instead have been included in the inner circle of the Lord's own and have shared in his upper room ministry—had they dared to have the courage of their convictions. They were the losers. We wonder who the others were, whom John numbers among the many chief rulers who believed. No doubt, after Pentecost, they found their way into the church. The resurrection of Christ changed a lot of things.

B. An Abiding Principle (12:44-50)

Having shown the ancient prophecy and its bearing on Jewish unbelief, John turns his attention to an abiding principle.

1. A Great Fact (12:44-46)

There is, first of all, a great fact. The Lord had something to say *about deity* (12:44-45): "Jesus cried and said, He that believeth on me, believeth not on me, but on him that sent me. And he that seeth me seeth him that sent me." Jesus could say that, because of his unique relationship with his Father. The Lord Jesus was willing to come down here to our planet to become a man and to behave as man, dependent on his Father, moment by moment, situation by situation, so that the invisible God might be made visible in him. Though he was God, and never once repudiated or renounced his identity as God, or his equality with God, he deliberately made himself of no reputation and acted solely in dependence on his Father. He made himself wholly available to his Father in heaven, and his Father made himself wholly available to his Son on earth. Because this was so, people who believed in Jesus believed not in him but in the one who sent him. Those who saw him with the eyes of faith, saw the one who sent him.

The Lord had something to say too *about darkness* (12:46): "I am come a light into the world, that whosoever believeth on me should not abide in darkness." He kept on bringing them back to light and darkness. At the end of life's journey it is either one or the other: to go out into a light beyond the brightness of the noonday sun and to bask in that light forever, eternally entering into more and more of God's wisdom, power, and love, in ever-expanding horizons and dimensions of bliss, or to go out into the horror of great darkness, the blackness of eternal doom.

2. A Grave Future (12:47-50)

There is a grave future to be considered. First, *judgment is decreed* (12:47-48): "And if any man hear my words, and believe not, I judge him not: for I came not to judge the world, but to save the world. He that rejecteth me, and receiveth not my words, hath one that judgeth him: the word that I have spoken, the same shall judge him in the last day." The word for "rejecteth" is *atheteo*. It literally means "to count as nothing." It is a terrible offense to treat the words of the Lord Jesus in this way.

The Lord refers to "the last day," the day of judgment. People will be held accountable for what they have done with his words. Ignorance will be no excuse, especially for those living in lands long enlightened by the gospel.

Recently I was in the Bahamas, where people drive on the left side of the road. Suppose I were to hire a car in Nassau and start driving down the righthand side of the road. I am pulled over by a policeman and taken before the judge and found guilty. The judge asks, "Do you have anything to say?" I reply, "In the United States and Canada everyone drives on the righthand side of the road." The judge says: "You are not being judged by the laws of the United States and Canada. You should have acquainted yourself with the laws by which you would be judged. Your ignorance and negligence are no excuse."

God has sent his Son into this world. The "Word was made flesh." God has in these last days spoken to us by his Son. He has no more to say until he speaks again in judgment. He holds men and women accountable to acquaint themselves with that word by which they will be judged.

Judgment is deserved (12:49-50) for two reasons. The first is *the source* (12:49) of the Lord's words: "For I have not spoken of myself; but the Father which sent me, he gave me a commandment what I should say, and what I should speak." The words of anyone else are the words of human beings. They are no more than faulty formulations of human wisdom, even of fallen man's religious thinking. They may influence millions but they have no divine authority. The essence of man's religious thinking is "the way of Cain," dressed up in other garb. It all boils down to doing the best we can and offering God the fruits of our own efforts. The words of Jesus are the words of God: That was the Lord's unvarying claim (14:24; 17:8). He was God's final, authoritative, and perfect vehicle of expression. It is folly of the highest consequence to ignore his words, to say to God in effect,

"I am not interested in what you have to say."

A second reason why judgment is deserved has to do with *the substance* (12:50) of the Lord's words: "And I know that his commandment is life everlasting: whatsoever I speak therefore, even as the Father said unto me, so I speak." That was the Lord's last word to the Jews in John's gospel. Eternal life is to be found in what the Father had given him to say. It is to be found nowhere else. To turn away from those words is to turn away from all hope of eternal life.

From now on, the Lord turns to his disciples to instruct them personally and privately in deeper truths. John ignores the Lord's Olivet discourse, the approach of the Passover, the nefarious dealings of Judas with the Sanhedrin. He takes us instead straight to the upper room.

PART THREE

The Secrets of the
Son of God

John 13:1–17:26

J ohn has set before us the signs of the Son of God. Now he sets before us the secrets of the Son of God. The first major section of this gospel is public, the second is private; the first part is full of controversy, the second is full of confidences; in the first part the Lord reveals his person, in the second he reveals his passion.

Section 1. The Talk in the Upper Room (13:1–14:31)

I. BACKGROUND OF THE TALK (13:1-30)

Here we consider the talk in the upper room and the walk on the Gethsemane road. The Lord is unburdening his heart and comforting his friends throughout. The talk in the upper room has a background and a burden. We begin with the background. Three things come immediately to view: the table, the towel, and the traitor.

A. The Table (13:1-3)

1. His Facts (13:1a)

We observe how, as always, the Lord had all his facts well in hand: "Now before the feast of the passover, when Jesus knew that his hour was come that he should depart out of this world unto the Father . . . " The hour was come. The day was the preparation day, the fourteenth day of Nisan (our Tuesday sunset to Wednesday sunset), the day of the crucifixion. A lot of discussion has centered on whether Jesus ate the Passover at the proper time or before. John makes it clear it was before. All the gospels agree that the Lord was laid in the tomb on the preparation day (Matthew 27:62; Mark 15:42; Luke 23:54; John 19:31, 42).

What the Lord Jesus refers to as "his hour" had been present in his thoughts from the beginning. He had said to his mother, at the outset of his public ministry, "Mine hour is not yet come" (2:4). When the Jews tried to arrest him on previous occasions they could not, because his hour was not yet come (7:30; 8:20). The coming of the Greeks precipitated a prayer by Jesus: "Now is my soul troubled; and what shall I say? Father, save me from this hour: but for this cause came I unto this hour" (12:27).

The dreadful hour had now come. But instead of thinking of himself, Jesus thought of others, especially of his disciples. We can see them grouped about him, puzzled, full of forebodings, twelve men who, except for one, had come to love him with all their hearts.

He was going away, going home. His departure was to be in two stages: first Calvary, then Olivet. The trauma of the next few days might well shake his disciples' faith. He must prepare them, forewarn them, that they might be forearmed.

2. His Feelings (13:1b)

We learn, too, of his feelings: "When Jesus knew . . . that he should depart out of this world unto the Father, having loved his own which were in the world, he loved them unto the end" (13:1b). The word for "depart" is used only here in this connection; it speaks of a transfer from one sphere to another. Death was not going to interrupt his being; it would only change its mode. He was going to depart out of this world, but his loved ones were still to be in the world. That fact brought a flood of feeling to his heart. This world was about to be unmasked, about to show its true face at last.

He loved them with holy love, everlasting God-like love, *agapao* love. He loved them to the end *(eis telos)*, to the furthest extent, to the uttermost, not in terms of time but in terms of readiness to save them and serve them.

3. His Foe (13:2)

At this point John inserts a note about his foe: "And supper being ended, the devil having now put into the heart of Judas Iscariot, Simon's Son, to betray him . . ." (13:2). All was now ready for the meal, with the table laid and everyone in place. One of the twelve had already made a pact with the priests (Matthew 26:14-16), and behind that plot was an even darker one. Judas's treachery played into the devil's hands. His contract with the priests was "an agreement with hell" (Isaiah 28:15,18), to borrow the prophet's descriptive phrase of Israel's coming treaty with the antichrist. It was an additional burden for Jesus

to bear, to have the traitor at the table with him and the others,
pretending to be a loyal disciple, when all along Jesus knew his
heart.

4. His Future (13:3)

The Lord was also aware of his future: "Jesus knowing that
the Father had given all things into his hands, and that he was
come from God, and went to God . . ." (13:3). These statements
about the origin and destiny of the Lord Jesus enhance the
astonishing condescension of the service to which the Lord now
humbled himself. The ministry he was about to perform was
that of a slave. Not one of the disciples was prepared to render
this service even to the master, let alone to the other disciples.

The Lord was fully cognizant of who he was. He knew that
lordship over the universe was his. The sinless sons of light, the
shining seraphim, angels and archangels, bowed before him. He
knew too where he was going: up to the gates of glory, up to the
throne of God. Yet he "made himself of no reputation" and
stooped to the work of a household slave.

B. The Towel (13:4-17)

1. Demonstration of Humility (13:4-11)

John now points us to Jesus' demonstration of true humility
and declaration about true humility. First the example, then the
exhortation; first the deed, then the discourse; deeds first,
words later—once the deed has silenced protest and subdued
pride.

We begin with *an imperial renunciation* (13:4-5): "He riseth
from supper, and laid aside his garments; and took a towel, and
girded himself. After that he poureth water into a basin, and
began to wash the disciples' feet, and to wipe them with the
towel wherewith he was girded."

They had all taken their places around the table. It would
seem that the customary service of washing the feet of the
guests had been omitted when they arrived in the upper room.
There was no slave there to perform this usual function.

There was great deliberateness about the Lord's action. He
took off his outer garment, usually taken off for working and
generally used as a cover when sleeping. He girded himself with
a towel, took a basin and filled it with water, and approached
the first of the disciples to wash his feet and remove the sand
and soil of the day.

We can imagine the sudden hush, the embarrassed looks, the sense of shame. What a contrast to their own recent self-seeking and ambition (Luke 22:24-27). What condescension for the incarnate Son of God to take the feet of Judas into his holy hands and wash them. But not all the washing in the world could wash away the stains on those feet, which had already stolen away to the priests on one nefarious errand and soon would be hurrying away through the night on another (and then on to a place from which they would launch him into a christless eternity). We see the feet of Judas, feet washed by the Savior—and, a few chapters later, the feet of Jesus, feet wounded by the sinner.

We have next *an impulsive reaction* (13:6-9). At last Jesus came to Peter and we have *Peter's question* (13:6-7): "Peter saith unto him, Lord, dost thou wash my feet? Jesus answered and said unto him, What I do thou knowest not now; but thou shalt know hereafter." The emphasis is on the pronouns *thou* and *my*. Peter was aghast that the one he had confessed as Son of God should wash his feet. It was unthinkable. No doubt Peter had expressed what the others were thinking.

The same emphasis can be discerned in the Lord's reply: "What I do thou knowest not now." There was evidently a deeper lesson in this than mere foot washing. The significance was in the realm of the spiritual, not in the realm of the ritual. Peter would have to await the advent of the Holy Spirit before he would understand that.

Then we have *Peter's quibble* (13:8-9). Instead of bowing to the Lord's will, Peter argued, going from one extreme to the other. "Thou shalt never wash my feet," he declared. "Not while the world lasts," he said. That is the force of his vehement protest. The Lord was equally emphatic: "If I wash thee not, thou hast no part with me." Peter gave in at once at the thought that his rebellious spirit could cause a breakdown of fellowship with his beloved Lord. Impulsively as before, he said, "Lord, not my feet only, but also my hands and my head." Before, he wished to tell the Lord what he could and could not do. Now he wanted to tell the Lord how things should be done.

Next comes *an important revelation* (13:10-11). We note *what the Lord cautioned* (13:10). There was first a word for *the twelve* (13:10a,b): "Jesus saith to him, He that is washed needeth not save to wash his feet, but is clean every whit." This explains the significance of the Lord's previous statement, "You shall know later on."

It was Calvary that brought the light of day to shine on this. The blood of Christ provides us with a once-for-all, *radical cleansing* (13:10a) from sin—a complete bath, so to speak. But in our daily walk through this world we become defiled. So our feet, which come in contact with the world, need to be cleansed. We need, in other words, *recurrent cleansing* (13:10b) from sin. At this stage of their spiritual pilgrimage, Peter and the others were not able to grasp these truths. Indeed, they continually misunderstood the Lord's spiritual, symbolic, pictorial teaching, interpreting his words (as many have continued to do down the ages) with wooden literalism, failing to comprehend his use of parables, types, and figures of speech.

There was also a word for *the traitor* (13:10c): "And ye are clean, but not all." There was one there for whom the blood of Christ would be shed in vain. A "fountain for uncleanness" was soon to be opened in Jerusalem but this man would never plunge beneath its crimson flood. The Lord could see the others cleansed, beneficiaries of that radical cleansing for sin he was to provide at such cost. But one man had become an apostate, had turned his back on the Savior of sinners, was now ensnared by the evil one, and would never repent, never be cleansed. Jesus had a veiled word for him. The others probably did not know what the Lord was talking about, but Judas did.

John adds his own word of explanation. He tells *what the Lord concealed* (13:11): "For he knew who should betray him; therefore said he, Ye are not all clean." Doubtless his words were yet another warning to Judas. Perhaps, even though he had gone so far, he was not yet gone beyond recall. If so, he must grasp at once the lifeline being thrown out to him; already he was in the grip of a terrible tide carrying him swiftly to destruction. The Lord knew who the traitor was, but in love for Judas, he concealed that knowledge a little longer.

2. Declaration about Humility (13:12-17)

Having given his disciples this demonstration of humility, the Lord now gave them a declaration about humility. First, we see him *approaching the issue* (13:12): "So after he washed their feet, and had taken his garment, and was set down again, he said unto them, Know ye what I have done to you?" He was going to help Peter and the others understand the meaning of his actions. We can almost feel the silence in the room as Jesus took off the towel, put on his outer garment, and reassumed his place at the table. Except for Judas, all would be filled with a sense of shame. Was Judas perhaps filled with contempt at such a spectacle of abasement, mingled with alarm generated by the Lord's words, "Ye are clean, but not all"? Suppose he were to be exposed. Judas could not deny the God-like power of Jesus. We can imagine that he eyed Jesus with fear newly generated. He had no cause to worry. Jesus was willing to save him from sin, self, and Satan even in that late hour.

Now comes the task of *apprehending the issue* (13:13-16). The Lord began by reviewing the contrast between the lofty titles he bore and the lowly task he had undertaken. "Ye call me Master and Lord: and ye say well; for so I am." The word for "Master" is *didaskalos*, teacher. The Lord was addressed this way thirty-one times; he referred to himself this way eight times. In the Lord's day the word was the equivalent of "Rabbi," the common title of dignity conferred by students on their teachers. The Greek word for "Lord" is *kurios* (literally "owner"), a word that expresses authority and lordship.

At this point a brief digression might be in order. Many people today refer to the Lord in public prayer as "Jesus," "dear Jesus," and similar expressions of endearment. It is worth noting that in the gospel record no one addressed him that way except evil spirits, and those he silenced. The sole exception is Bartimeus, and he added the title, "thou Son of David" (Mark 10:47; Luke 18:38).

"You call me Master and Lord: and you do well; for so I am." With that preliminary statement before us we note three swift lessons. There is *an exposition* (13:14) of practical humility: "If I then, your Lord and Master, have washed your feet; ye also ought to wash one another's feet." Here we have a figure of speech known as *synecdoche*, the exchange of one idea for an associated idea. The act of foot-washing stands for all kinds of acts of self-denying love. Some groups have elevated this to a church ordinance, but it is not introduced in the epistles as such (as are the two ordinances of the Lord's supper and baptism) nor does it seem to have been practiced as such until some four hundred years after Christ. The reference in 1 Timothy 5:10 is simply to the custom of washing a guest's feet when being welcomed into an eastern home. "You ought to wash one another's feet," Jesus said. It is a call to loving care for others that regards no task as too menial, no service too great. Nothing should stand in our way of ministering humbly to all.

There is *an example* (13:15) of practical humility: "For I have given you an example, that ye should do as I have done to you." Jesus laid aside his dignity. He took the lowest place, the place of a slave. He performed a menial task that none of the others was willing to accept. He did it out of love. Can we afford to minister lovingly to others, even at the expense of our cherished dignity?

There is *an expectation* (13:16) of practical humility: "Verily, verily, I say unto you, The servant is not greater than his lord;

neither he that is sent greater than he that sent him."

Many years later Peter wrote a letter to God's beleaguered people in those terrible days when Nero was on the rampage, when savage and terrible things were being done to God's own, not only at Rome, but far and wide across the empire. Peter had many helpful words for those facing this fiery trial.

To younger members of the fellowship, he wrote: "Submit yourselves unto the elder . . . and be clothed with humility" (1 Peter 5:5). The word he used for "be clothed," *egkomboomai*, means "gird yourselves with humility." The word comes from a root signifying "knotted," or "to be clothed in a knotted garment." The noun referred to the garment of a slave. Peter may have had in his mind's eye the unforgettable sight of the Lord Jesus, just before he went out to face the cross, girding himself with a knotted towel, coming to him, and saying, "Now then, Peter, let me wash your feet." He saw his Lord "clothed with humility," as we are to be also.

The Lord ends by *applying the issue* (13:17): "If ye know these things, happy are ye if ye do them." The world cannot see any happiness in taking such a humble place. But who was the happiest person in the upper room just then? Certainly not Peter, who perhaps was taking himself to task in his heart for not having rushed upstairs before all the others in order to be first at the basin. Nor Judas, with his ill-gotten gains in hand and filled with alarm lest his next move should be exposed. Surely Jesus was the happiest of them all.

Happiness does not consist in knowing, but in doing. It is then that blessing begins to flow and this beatitude comes into its own.

C. The Traitor (13:18-30)

We are still concerned with the background of the upper room talk. John now focuses on the traitor. Writing from the perspective of sixty or seventy years after the event, John was still moved to indignation against Judas. When he thinks and writes about Judas it is with loathing. In his gospel, perhaps more than in the others, we see Judas held up to view for the pitiable hypocrite, liar, thief, and traitor John now knew him to have been.

1. The Traitor Was Expected by Him (13:18-22)

In the first place, the traitor was expected by Christ. The Lord drew attention to *what the Scripture said* (13:18): "I speak not of you all: I know whom I have chosen: but that the scripture may be fulfilled, He that eateth bread with me hath lifted up his heel against me." That was an allusion to Psalm 41:9. David had his Ahithophel; Jesus had his Judas. In David's case some excuse could be found for Ahithophel, David's cleverest counselor, who betrayed him and became both the power behind Absalom's rebellion and Absalom's counselor in evil. Ahithophel was Bathsheba's grandfather, and one does not have to be a great student of human nature to understand his feelings at David's seduction of his granddaughter and his murder of her husband.

But Judas had no such excuse. He was chosen by Christ to be a disciple. He had become a disciple of his own free will. It was by his own choice he became a traitor. His own frustrated ambition, greed, and dishonesty drove him further and further from Christ. John has already recorded earlier veiled and not so veiled warnings of Jesus about the traitor (6:71; 12:4; 13:2). Already, in the upper room, the Lord revealed his knowledge of Judas's uncleanness—to no avail. Although his warnings became more explicit, they fell on deaf ears.

The fact that the treachery of Judas was foreknown and foretold does not in any way take away from the fact that Judas acted of his own free will in this matter. Judas was a traitor by his own choice and behavior. Our knowledge is afterknowledge. We look back to the fact and know it for the simple reason that the fact exists. God's knowledge is foreknowledge. He could look ahead to the fact, but Judas established that fact himself. This sequence is basic to all biblical prophetic statements. God's foreknowledge is based on facts that he foresees will be established when the time comes. He knows what is going to happen because he is not trammeled by having to live out events a day at a time.

The Lord's quotation of Psalm 41:9 was forceful. The original Hebrew is literally "hath made his heel great against me," the idea being of bringing about a great fall or of taking terrible advantage of someone. One wonders what Judas's thoughts were when he heard this familiar psalm quoted, knowing he was indeed taking cruel advantage of his position in the inner circle to bring about the master's fall.

John now tells us *what the Savior said* (13:19-22). The context is the great crime of Judas. The Lord has something to say about *receiving him* (13:19-20): "Now I tell you before it come, that, when it is come to pass, ye may believe that I am he." We can omit the word *he*. Again Jesus asserted his deity: "Ye may believe that I am." His foreknowledge was another proof of it. Perhaps, looking Judas in the eye, Jesus calmly claimed for himself the ineffable name. In the New English Bible it is rendered "I am what I am."

Some good would come out of the despicable treachery of Judas. The Lord's evident omniscience, as the disciples would come to look back on it and reflect on it, would be evidence of his deity.

The uniqueness of his person is matched by the uniqueness of our position: "Verily, verily, I say unto you, He that receiveth whomsoever I send receiveth me; and he that receiveth me, receiveth him that sent me" (13:20). Thus the Lord joins himself, his Father, and his followers in one union. The Lord was anticipating the coming commissioning of the apostles (20:21).

The greatness of an envoy is in direct ratio to the greatness of the one he or she represents. Christ's ambassadors in this world, the ones he sends, represent no petty princedom. Our calling is the most glorious one in the universe. We are ambassadors of the king of kings. Those who welcome us receive not only us but Christ, and not only Christ but his Father.

The traitor in their midst could no more halt the onward march of Christ and his kingdom than he could reverse the spin of the globe on its axis in space.

The Lord has something pointed to say, too, about *rejecting him* (13:21-22): "When Jesus had thus said, he was troubled in spirit, and testified, and said, Verily, verily [Indeed and in truth, as it has been phrased] I say unto you, that one of you shall betray me. Then the disciples looked one on another doubting of whom he spake."

He has troubled in spirit. We have the same word used about him as he was on his way to the tomb of Lazarus (11:33) and again when the Greeks came to him (12:27). Approaching the grave of Lazarus "he was troubled" and then wept. That was in the realm of the physical. When the Greeks came and the Lord spoke of the coming hour and was troubled, it was mental suffering; it was in the realm of the soul. Now, with Judas at the table with him, Jesus was troubled in spirit.

He had given Judas every opportunity to repent. He could postpone the inevitable no longer. He had things to say to his own, things that could not be said so long as Judas and the evil and treachery he stood for were present in the room. The Lord now took deliberate steps to expose him. It is interesting to observe how greatly this final, irrevocable, and terrible action troubled the friend of sinners.

But not only Jesus, the Lord's disciples were troubled. They were speechless with horror as, at last, the truth dawned on them. They knew their own faults and failings well enough, but to be a traitor, to betray their beloved Lord to his foes, this seemed incredible. They searched their own hearts and each other's faces. They looked around in bewilderment.

2. The Traitor Was Exposed by Him (13:23-26)

We are shown how the traitor was exposed by Christ. Three people are brought into the picture. First, we see *John in focus* (13:23-24).

"Now there was leaning on Jesus' bosom one of his disciples, whom Jesus loved. Simon Peter therefore beckoned to him, that he should ask who it should be of whom he spake." At this special meal the disciples reclined, as was the custom, on their left side, leaving their right arms free. The beloved disciple, whom we identify as John, the author of this gospel, occupied the position of honor, reclining next to Jesus on the right. Peter seems to have been some distance away. Judas must have been on Jesus' left. The suspense of not knowing who the traitor was, was more than Peter could bear. Finally he caught John's eye and gave him a nod to indicate he should ask Jesus to be more specific.

Next we see *Jesus in focus* (13:25-26a). "He then lying on Jesus' breast saith unto him, Lord who is it? Jesus answered, He it is, to whom I shall give a sop, when I have dipped it." John put the question to Jesus. Nowadays we would give an honored guest a different mark of recognition. It would be more customary in our culture to propose a toast or to lift a glass in acknowledgment. In Jesus' day a choice morsel was dipped in the sauce by the host and presented to the special one. Jesus indicated to John that he would mark out the traitor in this way. It is doubtful whether any of the other disciples heard the exchange, since even after the sop was passed they still seem not to have suspected Judas. Indeed, for Jesus thus to single Judas out for this special honor would eliminate him from their minds.

Last we see *Judas in focus* (13:26b). "And when he had dipped the sop, he gave it to Judas Iscariot, the son of Simon." The Lord had appealed to the conscience of Judas; now he made one last appeal, to his heart. Eternity swung in the balance for this man. It was his last opportunity before the dreadful deed was done. Judas evidently misinterpreted the Lord's friendly gesture. The alarms ringing in his soul, that his secret had been discovered and he was about to be exposed and judged, died down. He was being treated as the honored guest. Far from being overwhelmed by the mark of honor, perhaps it simply confirmed him in his opinion that Christ was no messiah for him. He would cash in on the situation and decamp while the going was good.

3. The Traitor Was Expelled by Him (13:27-30)

We are shown how the traitor was expelled by Christ. Three graphic pictures are painted for us by the artistry of the Holy Spirit. We see *Judas and the devil* (13:27). "And after the sop Satan entered into him. Then said Jesus unto him, That thou doest, do quickly." The literal rendering of this would be: "And after the sop then Satan entered into him." The exact moment is marked when Judas crossed the final frontier from which there was no return, the moment when his doom was sealed.

The rejection of the Lord's final appeal, marking him out for a gesture of special friendship and honor, so hardened the heart of Judas against Christ that it was now possible for Satan to move in and take full possession of the man. Up to this moment Judas had been possessed by an evil intention. Now he was possessed by the evil one.

The Lord knew what had happened. The devil himself now leered at Jesus through the eyes of Judas. Abruptly Jesus dismissed Judas from the fellowship of his people. He bade him be about his terrible business and to hurry up with it. That is the first picture.

The second picture shows *Judas and the disciples* (13:28-29). "Now no man at the table knew for what intent he spake this unto him. For some of them thought, because Judas had the bag, that Jesus had said unto him, Buy those things that we have need of against the feast; or, that he should give something to the poor." So great was Judas's reputation, so well had he acted the part of a genuine disciple, that he deceived the others right to the end. Even when those fatal words of excommunication were spoken, they thought that the Lord was sending Judas out on an errand or to perform a work of charity. Whoever they might or might not have suspected of being the traitor, they do not seem to have suspected Judas. The Lord's words of dismissal were interpreted by them in the light of their own mistaken conceptions of Judas's character. Little did they know that the errand on which he was now embarked would pay off its dreadful dividends before the next day was out, in the murder of their master and the suicide of Judas.

The third picture is that of *Judas and the darkness* (13:30). "He then having received the sop went immediately out: and it was night." The words of Psalm 41, from which Jesus had quoted in beginning this final struggle for the soul of Judas, now had their fulfillment: "His heart gathereth iniquity to itself; when he goeth abroad, he telleth . . . " That is just what Judas did.

"And it was night." For Judas there was now reserved what the Holy Spirit elsewhere calls "the blackness of darkness for ever" (Jude 13). We see Judas leave the light of the upper room, the fellowship of the saints of God, and the presence of the Lord Jesus in the midst of his own. We see him close the door. The darkness wraps him around. He makes his way down the stairs. He pauses to get his bearings and then goes his accursed way to the place where the enemies of Christ were awaiting him. He was now walking in the counsel of the ungodly, standing in the way of sinners, sitting in the seat of the scornful. Henceforth his name would be a universal synonym for treachery. He would never know again, in this life or eternity, another moment of happiness. It was night.

Such was the background of the long heart to heart talk the Lord now had with his disciples in the upper room. Now we consider the burden of the talk.

II. Burden of the Talk (13:31–14:31)

A. Another Commandment (13:31-35)

Four themes dominate the upper room discourse: another commandment, another coming, another commission, and another comforter. We begin with the first of these.

1. The Lord of Life (13:31-33)

The Lord's teaching about a new commandment can be divided into two parts. He sets before us, first, the Lord of life, the one Judas was on his way to betray, the one who, undismayed, saw beyond death to resurrection, to life for evermore.

In this connection the Lord had something to say about *his glory* (13:31-32). "Therefore, when he was gone out, Jesus said, Now is the Son of man glorified, and God is glorified in him. If God be glorified in him, God shall also glorify him in himself, and shall straightway glorify him."

One can almost hear the Lord Jesus heave a sigh of relief when Judas finally closed the door behind him. We need to note the expression "he was gone out"; it underlines the voluntary act of Judas. It is true that Jesus excommunicated Judas but it is equally true that Judas excommunicated himself. In the last analysis God does not send people to hell; they send themselves. God endorses the decisions they themselves make.

The atmosphere of the upper room was now purged. The evil one had gone, taking his human agent with him, hurrying him through the night and on into the dark. The Lord turned to his disciples. "Now," he said, "Now!" The departure of Judas marked a crisis and a turning point. His departure was the first step in the last lap of the journey toward the passion and all that lay beyond.

The Lord saw beyond the dark valley to the glory crowned peaks beyond. He saw the rainbow high on the storm clouds. Golgotha was not the end; glory was the goal. "Now is the Son of man glorified," he said. The first man, Adam, forfeited his dominion through the fall. The second man, Christ, arrived on earth to regain what had been lost through that fall.

John uses the title *Son of man* twelve times. The first time was in conversing with Nathanael. Now John uses it for the last time. Did Nathanael look up as he heard Jesus again use that name? He would remember Jesus saying to him, "Ye shall see . . . the angels of God ascending and descending upon the Son of man."

The departure of Judas heralded the departure of Jesus. He was on his way home. The road was dark and steep. The cross stood astride the way, but death and the tomb were to be conquered. Sin and Satan were vanquished. Already the Son of man was glorified, and God was glorified by the sinless humanity of Jesus.

Jesus was now on his way back to that glory he had with the Father before the worlds began, the glory he had laid aside when he came to earth. God was glorified in the Son of man; the Son of man was to be glorified as he trod that path of obedience by way of Gethsemane, Gabbatha, Golgotha, and the grave right back to glory, there to be seated on the throne of God.

The Lord has something to say about *his goal* (13:33). "Little children, yet a little while I am with you. Ye shall seek me: and as I said unto the Jews, Whither I go, ye cannot come." The coming crises were going to affect not only him, they were going to affect his disciples. He could picture their despair as the events of the next few hours closed in. Moreover, the full realization of his heavenly glory necessitated his withdrawal from earth. His heart went out to them.

He called them "little children." The words not only convey the thought of relationship, but in the diminutive they carry the idea of deep affection and care for those not yet mature. The Lord's heart went out to Peter, James, John, Matthew, Thomas, Philip, Andrew, Nathanael, and the rest. He could see the stunned looks on their faces as the words began to sink in: "Ye shall seek me . . . Whither I go, ye cannot come." So far as we know he had never addressed them as "little children" before. They were the words his mother had used to him when, having lost him, she found him in the temple (Luke 2:48).

The Lord reminded them that he had already told the Jews that they would seek him. But he had added two things in his statement to the Jews (7:34) that he omits here: they would die in their sins, and they would not find him. To his disciples he simply affirmed that the path now opening up before him he must tread alone.

2. The Law of Love (13:34-35)

He comes now to the law of love and to the new commandment. Here is *its impulse* (13:34): "A new commandment I give unto you, That ye love one another; as I have loved you, that ye also love one another." Peter and John, I know you are so different in temperament—but love one another. Simon Zelotes and Matthew, I know you came to me from opposite backgrounds—but love one another. Daring Andrew and doubting Thomas, love one another. "As I have loved you." With that love which suffers long and is kind, with that love which many waters cannot quench, with that love which is stronger than death. I am going, but you will still be here. You will need each other, so love one another. Sink all your differences in love's wide sea.

Love is the new law. And what is the impulse of that love? It is his love.

Here is *its impact* (13:35): "By this shall all men know that ye are my disciples, if ye have love one to another." The badge of true discipleship is not in the doctrinal statements to which we subscribe, not in the types of hymns and music we prefer, not in the rituals we observe or the ordinances we cherish, not in our soulwinning zeal, our faithfulness to the churches of our choice—but in our love for all those who love the Lord. When people see that, they will recognize Christ in his disciples and recognize that love as truly his own.

Peter had been taking all this in. He had given the nod to John to find out who the traitor was, but had been too far away to hear what Jesus had answered. He had seen Jesus dip the sop and give it to Judas, and perhaps that action had stilled any suspicions he might have had of him. After all, Judas was a Judean and all the rest of them were Galileans, so maybe the Lord was honoring Judas as the only Judean in the company. He

had seen Judas rise from the table and may have heard the
Lord's word to him to hurry. Nothing was extraordinary in all
that to Peter's mind.

B. Another Coming (13:36–14:6)

1. The Human Heart Revealed (13:36-38)

But this talk of Jesus about going away. Suddenly Peter sat up
and paid special heed. He had something to say, so he said it. In
his words we see the human heart revealed. We note, at once,
Peter's bewilderment (13:36-37a): "Simon Peter said unto him,
Lord, whither goest thou? Jesus answered him, Whither I go,
thou canst not follow me now; but thou shalt follow me after-
wards. Peter said unto him, Lord why cannot I follow thee
now?"

The Lord had been telling them for the past six months that
he was going away, that he was going to die, and that he was
going to be raised again. It was now dawning on them that he
actually was going to die. Beyond that they were unable to go as
yet, even in thought.

The Old Testament revelation of the afterlife was by no
means so bright as the hope we now have from the New Testament. The resurrection of Christ and the coming of the Holy
Spirit have made a significant difference. Paul reminds us that
the Lord Jesus has "abolished death, and hath brought life and
immortality to light through the gospel" (2 Timothy 1:10). Peter, grappling with the dawning realization that Jesus was soon
going to die, wants to know what that means. What lies beyond
death? "Where are you going?" he asks. "Where will you be?
And why can't I come with you now?" The Lord's heart must
have warmed again to his friend Peter, whose warmth and love
were as different as night from day to the cold hate of Judas.

We note, too, *Peter's boastfulness* (13:37b): "I will lay down my
life for thy sake," Peter said. If the Lord was going to die—and
Peter seems to have come to grips now with that fact—well, he
was willing to die for him.

But the Lord knew Peter better than Peter knew himself:
"Jesus answered him, Wilt thou lay down thy life for my sake?
Verily, verily, I say unto thee, The cock shall not crow, till thou
hast denied me thrice" (13:38). The word the Lord used for
"denied" is *aparneomai* meaning "to deny utterly." Cockcrow
was the third of the four Roman night watches, midway between midnight and dawn. That night, for all his bold words,
Peter would plumb the depths of cowardice. There is no blame

in the Lord's words. He had nothing but appreciation for Peter's good intent, but he knew better than to count on it. As he had warned Judas, now he warned Peter. Peter seems to have been overwhelmed at this prediction; he lasped into silence. Indeed he has no more to say during the discourses that follow.

2. The Heavenly House Revealed (14:1-3)

Times without number, God's bereaved people in all ages have turned to these three verses for comfort when death invades the home—and rightly so. Here we have one of the highlights of this gospel. We would be immeasurably impoverished if John had not penned these wonderful words.

He begins with *a new peace* (14:1): "Let not your heart be troubled: ye believe in God, believe also in me." There is some controversy over whether or not the verb *believe*, twice repeated in this verse, should be in the indicative ("ye believe") or imperative ("believe!"). There is added force if we read them both in the imperative: "Believe in God, believe in me!"

The Lord points to himself as the proper object of the same religious trust as God. "Trust God!" he says, "and trust me!"

Trust goes much deeper than belief. Belief can be cold and intellectual; trust is warm and personal. He challenges us to render to him the same response we give to God. This is even more forceful in the Greek text, which has the words in the second clause inverted. It reads, "Trust in God; in me also trust." This puts God and Christ as close together as possible and puts the two identical responses at the beginning and the end. Whatever we render to God we are to render to Jesus. There is not one particle of difference between the two. Jesus is God as God is God. Both can and must be equally trusted. Other religions put the heart of the matter in fear, good works, self-immolation, rites, rituals, creeds. Christianity alone puts it in trust. The bond between us and God is trust. We can trust him.

Often, well-meaning people, when faced with some actual or impending tragedy, will console the threatened or bereaved neighbor, friend, or loved one with the words, "Everything's going to be all right." That kind of optimism is based on wishful thinking. It is no use saying to anyone, "Let not your heart be troubled," unless we finish the statement, "Believe in God; believe also in Jesus." That links the sentiment to omnipotence.

So a new peace is introduced on earth. "When sorrows like sea billows roll" we have a place to which to flee, "a shelter in the time of storm." The disciples were about to face the darkest three days in the history of this planet. Every prop and anchor, every familiar landmark and guiding star, were to be swept away. Jesus would lie still and cold in death, his body riddled with wounds, his voice silent, his presence gone, his personality removed somewhere on the other side of the grave, beyond their reach. Jesus prepared them. He offered them a new peace: "Believe."

He talked about *a new place* (14:2). As has been noted, the Old Testament has little to say about heaven. "Paradise" and "Abraham's bosom" conveyed some such ideas, but such light as there was at best was dim. Jesus says, "In my Father's house are many mansions: If it were not so, I would have told you. I go to prepare a place for you."

Only one other occasion is recorded in which the Lord used the expression "my Father's house" and that was when he first cleansed the temple. He said, "Make not my Father's house an house of merchandise." With its courts and chambers, its pillars and porticos, its wide spaces for the throngs of worshipers, the temple was a shadow, in a sense, of that even more spacious home on high.

How wonderful that Jesus should describe heaven in the homey way he does: "My Father's house." Death can be a terror to our souls, chilling our thoughts. Often the doorway by which human beings make their exit from this life is terrible enough. Our total lack of acquaintance with what lies beyond the portal adds to our fears. Nobody comes back. There is a stillness, a silence, a distance, a great gulf fixed, which strikes our hearts with dread. Even those who have the assurance that all is well with their souls draw back at death. We have an instinctive horror of the grave. But the words "my Father's house" give us a gleam in the gloom.

Most of us can remember our childhood days, when our parents' house was home, a place where we were loved, cared for, and protected, where we could be ourselves, where we enjoyed warmth and fellowship and stored up a thousand precious memories. His Father's house is like that. It is home.

If heaven were a strange and unfamiliar place, he would have told us. It is not like some bizarre locale, full of the weird and grotesque, as might be imagined by a science fiction writer. "I would have told you," Jesus assures us. We shall instinctively feel at home there. It is a real place. When Paul was "caught up" there, he knew he could never describe it to us, yet at the same time, he really did not know whether he was in or out of the body. It was tangible, so much so, indeed, he might have been "in the body." Yet it was other dimensional, spiritual, extraterrestrial too, so much so he could have been "out of the body." But it was not frightening; rather, it was so wonderfully attractive and satisfying and thrilling that ever afterward he had a desire to depart and be with Christ which, he said, is "far better."

What we gather from this is that heaven is localized. It is somewhere and it is substantial, because Jesus is living there now. There are many mansions, or "abiding places," there, Jesus said. That militates against smallness and narrowness.

We would like to know more. John gives us a glimpse of more in his description of the celestial city in the apocalypse. All we know about it now can be summed up in the precious truth that Jesus is there now, and when we get there he will still be there.

He talked too about *a new pledge* (14:3): "And if I go and prepare a place for you, I will come again, and receive you unto myself; that where I am, there ye may be also." The message was confirmed after the resurrection, as the disciples stood on the mount of Olives and watched him ascend the skyway to glory. The angels announced, "This same Jesus . . . shall so come in like manner as ye have seen him go into heaven." It is what Paul calls "the blessed hope" of the church: Jesus is coming again. Around those words, "I will come again," the Holy Spirit has built an entire eschatology in the New Testament epistles.

Benjamin Disraeli was a member of the British House of Commons in the days of empire. When he was elected to Parliament he stood out from his fellows. His dress was foppish, his manner eccentric. And he was Jewish. When he rose to make his first speech he was mocked by his fellow Members of Parliament. The uproar was so loud he had to abandon his attempt to speak. He raised his voice in defiance. "I will sit down now," he said, "but you will hear from me again." He went on to lead Britain to greatness.

This is the day of the Lord's rejection. Judas betrayed him, Peter denied him, the Jews mocked him, the Romans crucified him. To this day the world at large has no use for him. He has gone back home now. He is saying, "I will sit down now, but you will hear from me again."

He is coming back to earth. The good news was first announced to his own in the upper room. It is the next item on God's prophetic program. The actual day and hour are the best-kept secrets in the universe. Right now he is putting the finishing touches on that wondrous place he has gone to prepare. So we have his pledge, "I will come again." The Bible ends with the same strong voice ringing down the ages, "Surely I come quickly," and the glad response of the church, "Even so, come, Lord Jesus."

3. The Highway Home Revealed (14:4-6)

First, there is *the assertion* (14:4): "And whither I go ye know, and the way ye know." The disciples were not so sure. He had been telling them where he was going: home. As for the way—well, he would make that clear too in a moment—he was himself the way. They were looking right at it.

A pioneer missionary in Africa tells how he was taking the gospel to a new tribe, far to the north. With his bearers, he arrived at a village, a point beyond which his porters refused to go. The missionary appealed to the local chief. Was there someone in his village who could act as his guide to the distant northern tribe? The chief summoned a man, tall, battle scarred, carrying a large axe. A bargain was made and the next morning the missionary set off through the bush, following his new guide. The way became increasingly rough and the path had all but disappeared. There was an occasional mark blazed on a tree, occasionally a narrow path. Finally the missionary called a halt. He asked the guide if he was sure he knew the way. The man pulled himself up to his full height. "White man," he said, "you see this axe in my hand? You see these scars on my body? With this axe I blazed the trail to the tribal village to which we go. I came from there. These scars I received when I made the way. You ask me if I know the way? Before I came, there was no way. I am the way."

The Lord Jesus came from glory. Now he was on his way back to glory, by way of the cross. Before he came, there was no way. The scars of Calvary on his body attest to the price he paid to blaze that trail for us back to God. He points to his scars and says, "I am the way." The disciples would understand it better later on. But the fact was true. They knew where he was going because he had told them. They knew the way because they knew him and he was the way.

Then there is *the assessment* (14:5): "Thomas saith unto him, Lord, we know not whither thou goest; and how can we know the way?" Thomas was not a man to pretend he had a faith he did not have. We can thank Thomas for his question. It gave the Lord an opportunity to make one of his great I AM statements, a concise but definitive summary of "God's way to heaven."

So comes *the assurance* (14:6): "Jesus saith unto him, I am the way, the truth, and the life: no man cometh unto the Father, but by me." In that magnificent statement Jesus answered the three greatest questions of the human heart.

He answered the question, *"How can I be saved?"* (14:6a). "He said, "I am the way."

When I was a boy an aunt and uncle took me to Hampton

Court on the outskirts of London, a famous palace built by
Cardinal Wolsey and confiscated by Henry VIII. On the
grounds there is a maze of hedges and for a small fee one can go
in, wander around, and possibly get lost. The hedges are high,
the lanes are narrow and constantly intersected by other lanes
wandering off in all directions. In the middle of the maze is an
open space with some seats where, thoroughly lost, a person can
sit down and rest. Well, it didn't take us long to get lost. After
arriving back in the middle of the maze a number of times I
began to think there was no way out. At last a park attendant
appeared. "You people lost?" he asked. Indeed we were. "Follow
me!" he said. We did. He took a turn this way and a turn that
way, a turn that way and a turn this way, and there we were,
outside. What made the difference? Giving up our own efforts,
admitting we were lost, trusting and following the one who
knew the way.

How can I be saved? I must admit I am lost, cease from my
own efforts, receive into my life the one who said, "I am the
way." When I know him, I know the way. He is the way, and
there is no other way. Jesus said, "No man cometh unto the
Father, but by me." There are many ways to come to Christ but
only one way to get to heaven: by him.

He answered the question, "*How can I be sure?*" (14:6b). He
said, "I am the truth." He sums up all that is eternal and absolute in himself.

Buddha, the Greek philosophers, the Indian mystics, had
come and gone. The world had had five thousand years to
discover the limitations and bankruptcy of religion and philosophy when Jesus came. He spoke with authority. We need only
to read the sermon on the mount, the parables and discourses of
Jesus, the Olivet discourse, the truths now being set before the
disciples, to discover that the Lord Jesus is in a class by himself.
He did not merely teach the truth; he was the truth.

He was dogmatic. "I am the truth," he said. Every religious
dogma, every philosophical concept, every scientific theory, every political, economic, social, or psychological proposition that
does not ultimately find its center, sum, and substance in him is
bound, in the end, to prove itself wrong. Part of the bold dog-
matism of Jesus is asserted in that all exclusive statement of his,
appended to this great claim to be the truth: "No man cometh
unto the Father, but by me."

No matter how rich, successful, religious moral and upright,
popular or powerful you are, you come to God through Jesus or
you don't come at all. That statement is not arrogant—just
true.

Truth is always exclusive, always dogmatic, always intolerant of non-truth. Otherwise it would not be truth, eternal and absolute. It makes no difference whether the truth is a mathematical truth, a scientific truth, or, as here, a spiritual truth. Truth is always in some sense narrow. It is error that is broad and accommodating.

Here, for instance is a mathematical truth: "Two multiplied by two equals four." That is a narrow, dogmatic, intolerant statement. Error says, "Two multiplied by two is three." Truth cannot accept that kind of "tolerance." Since Jesus is the truth, he excludes all error, no matter how popular, widespread, ancient, or convincing it may be. "No man cometh unto the Father, but by me," he says. That rules out all the world's false religions; it demands that all persons everywhere repent of their wrong ideas and come to him.

He answered the question, *"How can I be satisfied?"* (14:6c). He said, "I am the life." The word is *zoe*, life in all its forms from the life of God on down to the life of the simplest microorgansim. His is the opposite of death; it is resurrection life and eternal life. *Life* is one of the words that especially captivated John; he used it and its cognates some fifty-six times. The word was first used by the Lord when speaking of the two gates, the two ways, and the two destinies: "Strait is the gate, and narrow is the way, which leadeth unto life, and few there be that find it" (Matthew 7:14). The Lord used the word when assuring Martha that her brother would live again. "I am the resurrection," he said, "and the life" (11:25).

We can be satisfied with nothing less than life—a full-orbed, vibrant, happy life down here, and then life eternal over there. That was Solomon's great quest, as recorded in the book of Ecclesiastes. The problem with Solomon, however, was that he thought he could find the answer "under the sun," in this world of time and sense.

One of the many sad laments of Solomon was: "He hath made every thing beautiful in his time [its proper season]: also he hath set the world [eternity] in their heart" (Ecclesiastes 3:11). Solomon was haunted by the thought of death. What he wanted was life—life more abundant, life for evermore. He discovered that this world can offer many pleasures and pursuits but it cannot satisfy and it cannot offer life.

Life is God's monopoly. If we want to live life to the full down here and then enjoy life in a new and more thrilling dimension, with "joy unspeakable and full of glory" over there, we must come to Christ.

The way. The truth. The life. The offer corresponds with the three entrances of the tabernacle. The sinner came first to the gate, the wide open gate with its invitation to the people to come in. That way led directly to the altar and to the laver, to cleansing from sin and to peace with God. Then came the door, half as wide and twice as high as the gate. Not so many ever passed this portal, but those who could and did entered into the holy place and stood in the presence of truth—the lampstand promising illumination, the shewbread on the table offering communion, the golden altar indicating intercession—all higher truths than are grasped by those who never progress beyond a bare salvation. Beyond all this was the veil, leading into the holy of holies, where few could penetrate. There was the mystery of life: the cherubim overshadowing the mercy seat, ever occupied with the blood sprinkled there; the ark with pot of manna, the unbroken law, the rod of Aaron with its buds, blossoms, and almonds, all speaking of the deep things of Christ; and over all the shekinah glory cloud in which God himself dwelled.

C. Another Commission (14:7-15)

Jesus has spoken of another commandment and of another coming. Now he speaks of another commission, responding to Philip. Although these disciples of Jesus, faced with his imminent departure, were struggling to grasp the meaning of his words, for the most part they failed to do so. How like us they were.

1. The Request (14:7-8)

The Lord had just said, "If ye had known me, ye should have known my Father also: and from henceforth ye know him, and have seen him" (14:7). In other words, the disciples would have had no need to ask the Lord about where he was going or how he was to get there if they had really known him. He himself was the full revelation of the Father.

Many times the Lord had spoken to his disciples about his Father. He delighted to use this novel name for God. Throughout the Old Testament, God is seldom spoken of as a Father. This lovely name for God was, really, the Lord's revelation, and a wonderfully comforting one it is. God is not merely *Elohim*, the awesome God of creation, omniscient in his purpose, omnipotent in his power, omnipresent in his person; he is not just *Jehovah*, the God of covenant, wise and loving, but strict in his requirements; nor is he merely *Adonai*, God of command, sovereign Lord, and owner of the universe, who must be obeyed. He is a *Father*, a God of comfort, a God of compassion, one who has a home and a family. The Lord used this name for God over and over again. How well John remembered it! In his gospel the expression "the Father" or its kindred expression "my Father" occurs 156 times.

Jesus had shown his Father to them, he said. That was too much for Philip. He said, "Lord, shew us the Father, and it sufficeth us" (14:7). He did not perceive that Jesus had already shown them the Father.

Thomas was not satisfied with a purely spiritual approach to God—he wanted something more substantial than a path he could not see. Philip was not satisfied with a purely spiritual apprehension of God—he wanted something more substantial than a person he could not see.

This craving for something tangible and visible is behind all ritual religion. To go on a pilgrimage to Mecca, to wash in the Ganges, to crawl up Pilate's staircase in Rome on bare knees—these are tangible; to have an image to which to pray, or a statue of the virgin Mary, or a crucifix, or some candles to light, or some elaborate ceremony to watch—these are visible. That was the essence of Old Testament religion, now abolished in Christ. All such cravings are wrong. God indulged some of them in the ritual religion of the Old Testament, in the "picture book stage" of divine revelation. Others he condemned, especially idolatry, which he roundly condemned as an expression of demon religion. The Lord instantly rebuked Philip for demanding some further revelation of the Father.

2. The Reply (14:9-11)

We have *the truth stated* (14:9): "Jesus saith unto him, Have I been so long time with you, and yet hast thou not known me, Philip? He that hath seen me hath seen the Father; and how sayest thou then, Shew us the Father?" In other words, Jesus told Philip that there was no difference between himself and God. He was God manifest in flesh.

The only concept we have of God is to take the lines of our own personality and extend them into infinity. We take, for instance, our own ability to think, extend that into infinity, and conceive of God as omniscient, all knowing, all wise. We take our own ability to feel and love, extend that into infinity, and think of God as one who is all loving. We take our ability to will and to do, extend that into infinity, and think of God as omnipotent, all powerful, able to enforce his absolute will. We think of our own moral nature and think of God as absolutely holy. The problem with this process, of course, lies in the fact that all of us are fallen creatures. Therefore, when we extend the lines of fallen human personality into infinity, the concept we get of God can be as bent and twisted as we are.

When Jesus came, God gave to the world a perfect human being. We can take the lines of his personality, extend them into infinity, and that is what God is like. He is like Jesus. Jesus was God in focus, so to speak. "Have I been so long with you, Philip, and you have not grasped that?"

The truth was not only stated, *the truth* was *supported* (14:10-11): "Believest thou not that I am in the Father, and the Father in me? the words that I speak unto you I speak not of myself: but the Father that dwelleth in me, he doeth the works. Believe me that I am in the Father, and the Father in me; or else believe me for the very works' sake." Jesus said to Philip that what he said was just what the Father said, no more, no less; what he did was just what the Father did, no more, no less; what he was was just what the Father was. In other words, through his sinless, perfect humanity the disciples could see deity. They could see the Father in action in the Son. They could know what the Father was like because they knew what Jesus was like. They could hear the Father in everything Jesus said. They could see the Father in everything Jesus did. They could know the Father because they knew the Son. What Jesus was, God was. He was in the Father; the Father was in him. If they had trouble with the concept, let them be satisfied with his conduct and believe him for his works' sake. His works were the daily moment by moment, situation by situation demonstration of the fact.

3. The Result (14:12-15)

The Lord was not content to leave all this in the realm of himself and his Father. He translates it into the realm of himself and us. The Lord Jesus as God wants to be to me as man what he as man had let the Father as God be to him. That is the truth behind these next few verses.

He explains this first *in terms of Christian life* (14:12-14). The new life we have in him will be seen in *our effective practice* (14:12): "Verily, verily, I say unto you, He that believeth on me, the works that I do shall he do also; and greater works than these shall he do; because I go unto my Father." The apostles proved these words true on the day of Pentecost, when three thousand were converted. The Lord rarely went beyond the borders of Palestine, but they went everywhere preaching the word (Acts 8:4). Paul could say of the church at Rome, "Your faith is spoken of throughout the whole world" (Romans 1:8).

Moreover, the "greater works" were spiritual in nature. It is a miracle to open a blind man's eyes; it is a greater miracle to open the eyes of his sin-blinded soul so that he can see beauty in Jesus. It is a miracle to cleanse a man of leprosy; it is a greater miracle to change a sinner so that he becomes pure in heart and life. It is a miracle to make a deaf man hear; it is a greater miracle to speak so that a person, deaf to the gospel, hears and heeds the message. It is a miracle to raise someone from the dead; it is a greater miracle to bring eternal life to someone dead in trespasses and sins.

This new life we have in Christ will also be seen in *our efficacious prayer* (14:13-14): "And whatsoever ye shall ask in my name, that will I do, that the Father may be glorified in the Son. If ye shall ask anything in my name, I will do it." The conditioning phrase is, of course, "in my name." We cannot ask things incompatible with his name, with what his name represents, and expect him to honor such requests. Prayer in the name of Jesus must be in accord with the Lord's changeless purpose of bringing glory to the Father. That, and not our own comfort and convenience, must be the object of prayer offered in his name. It is useless to offer a prayer full of self-will, add the formula "in Christ's name," and expect the Lord to respond affirmatively to that. Study the gospels. See the things Jesus prayed for. Explore the reasons why he prayed for such things. Then we will have a better understanding of praying in his name.

This new commission is also stated *in terms of Christian love* (14:15): "If ye love me, keep my commandments." Love is always the first and the last, the beginning and the ending, in the teaching of Jesus. If we love him, we will do what he says. We will want to please him. His slightest wish will be our law. That is the essence of love. Henry Drummond wrote a famous little book called *The Greatest Thing in the World* in which he sets forth what love does. Love drives out lesser things and reigns supreme in the heart in which it dwells.

The object of such love is *Jesus.* "If ye love me, keep my commandments." Christianity is not a creed, it is a living Christ; it is not a matter of obeying precepts and principles, it is a matter of obeying a person; it is not law, it is love for the kindest, most generous, most powerful, most loving person in the universe. Christianity is not a theological proposition, it is choosing to love Jesus. All the rest follows as a matter of course. Observe a man in love, a woman in love. Everything centers in the beloved: how to please the beloved, how to know the beloved better, how to tell others about the beloved, how to be with the beloved.

D. Another Comforter (14:16-31)

The Lord now turns to another of the great realities of New Testament Christianity, the truth of another comforter, the Holy Spirit. The Holy Spirit is the subject of considerable Old Testament revelation, beginning with the second verse in the Bible. Mention is made of the Holy Spirit too in connection with the Lord and his people earlier in this gospel (1:32; 3:5-8; 4:23; 6:63; 7:39). But the fullest revelation of the Holy Spirit, his person and his work, is given in these final discourses of the Lord with his disciples (14:15-17,25-26; 15:26-27; 16:4-11,13-15). The background is the Lord's devastating announcement that he is going away. The disciples are not to be alarmed. Another comforter is coming.

1. The Promise of the Comforter (14:16)

We note, first, *the Savior's promised prayer* (14:16a): "And I will pray the Father, and he shall give you another Comforter"— which of course he did. He ascended on high, sat down at God's right hand in heaven, and ten days later, on the day of Pentecost, on the day foreordained by Old Testament prophetic type, the Holy Spirit came in a new and unique way. He came to do something he had never done before. He came to baptize believers into the church, the mystical body of Christ. He came to inaugurate a new day, a new beginning, a new age, one that will run from Pentecost to the rapture, one characterized by this unprecedented baptizing work of the Holy Spirit of God.

We note next *the Spirit's promised presence* (14:16b): "Another Comforter, that he may abide with you for ever." The Greek word for "comforter" *(parakleton)* is rendered "advocate" in 1 John 2:1. The word means "one called alongside" for protection or counsel. The word is one of John's words, found only here, in 14:26, 15:26, 16:7, and 1 John 2:1. We note also the word *another (allon,* meaning "another of the same kind"). Jesus was one comforter. The Holy Spirit was another comforter, another of the same kind.

Earthly fellowship with the Lord Jesus was about to be terminated. The Holy Spirit ("the Lord's other self," as he has been described) would come to abide with us forever. The word for "abide" is *meno,* a word already used by the Lord to describe his own relationship with the Father ("the Father that dwelleth in me, he doeth the works," 14:10). In his capacity as helper, the Holy Spirit takes up permanent residence with us. The Holy Spirit, in the person of Christ, had been abiding with his disciples; now they were to be conscious of his abiding presence in their own lives.

2. The Person of the Comforter (14:17-31)

All this was preliminary instruction. The Lord goes on now to describe in greater detail what he means. First he describes *the reality* (14:17) of the abiding presence of the third person of the godhead.

There is *a great impossibility* (14:17a): "Even the Spirit of truth; whom the world cannot receive, because it seeth him not, neither knoweth him." The philosophy of the world is "seeing is believing." This materialist philosophy makes it impossible for unregenerate individuals either to know or to receive the Spirit of God. He is real, but he is invisible.

The Holy Spirit's function to the world is considered elsewhere. He has a reproving ministry (16:8-9), a regenerating ministry (3:5-6), and a restraining ministry (2 Thessalonians 2:6-7) toward lost people. But for the most part the world is ignorant of him. The world cannot receive him.

There is also *a great implantation* (14:17b,c): "But ye know him; for he dwelleth with you, and shall be in you." At Pentecost, the Holy Spirit began not only a baptizing work in relation to those who believed, which puts believers in Christ and makes them members of Christ's body, but he began an indwelling work, by which he puts Christ in the believers. The Holy Spirit comes to take up permanent residence in a believer's heart and life. Thus the body of the believer becomes the temple of the Holy Spirit, a truth of immense importance. It is only our doctrinal familiarity with it that prevents us from appreciating its immensity. To think that a member of the triune godhead has condescended to take up residence in our hearts! We have the Lord's word for it that these things are integral to our faith. They are realities, more enduring than the stars.

Now come *the reasons* (14:18-31) for the abiding presence of the Holy Spirit. Two are basic: to make good to us the Lord's presence and to make good to us the Lord's promise (14:25-31).

We need *the Lord's abiding presence* (14:18-24) for the simple but sublime reason that Christianity is Christ. The only one who can live the Christian life is Christ. All the Lord expects from us is failure. For thirty-three and a half years the Lord Jesus lived a supernatural life on earth. Incarnated, he allowed his Father as

God to live his life in him through the indwelling Holy Spirit. Now we as regenerated men and women, boys and girls, are to allow him as God to live his life in us through the indwelling Holy Spirit. The Holy Spirit is the one through whom God makes himself available to us. All that Jesus is as God is put, by the Holy Spirit, at the disposal of the individual who will put, by the Holy Spirit, all that he or she is at the disposal of Jesus as God. That is the essence of the Christian life.

The Christian life is a supernatural life. It is the life of Christ lived out in every believer by means of the indwelling Holy Spirit.

In other words, *his life is to be ours* (14:18-20). This is stated in three ways. First, there is *a word of comfort* (14:18): "I will not leave you comfortless: I will come to you." The word for "comfortless" is *orphanous*, from which we derive our word *orphan*. The only other place where the word occurs is in James 1:27, where it refers to literal orphans. The news that the Lord was going away devastated the disciples. They felt orphaned. They felt helpless and hopeless, bewildered, frightened, lost. "I will not leave you orphans," Jesus said. "I will come to you." Here is "a promise of his coming which is contemporaneous with his absence." True, he was departing from them physically but he would be with them spiritually in a new way.

There is *a word of commitment* (14:19): "Yet a little while, and the world seeth me no more; but ye see me: because I live, ye shall live also." The world saw the last of him when it crucified him and sealed his tomb. Since then it has seen him no more. The disciples saw him again in his various resurrection appearances. But that does not exhaust the Lord's commitment to his own: "Ye see me." The use of the present tense indicates a continuing vision; it therefore means more than the resurrection appearances, which came to an end with his ascension. Those who believe in him will go on seeing him with the eye of faith until, at last, as John puts it elsewhere, when life's temporal journey is over we shall "see his face" (Revelation 22:4).

He added, "Because I live, ye shall live also." With death staring him in the face, with sublime indifference to its outward threatening, Jesus boldly stated, "I live." He used the dateless, timeless present tense, indicating undying life. Death could not rob him of that. He lived even when he died. No man could take his life from him. He was in complete control of the entire process. He had an orderly exodus from this world and came back in resurrection power with the keys of death in his hand when his business in hades was complete.

Although he stood within a stone's throw of the cross, in

divine self-confidence he assured his own that they were about to partake of the very life that he lived. We live because he lives. We shall live as long as he lives. We live the life that he lives. All this commitment is made good to us by the Holy Spirit.

There is also *a word of comprehension* (14:20): "At that day ye shall know that I am in my Father, and ye in me, and I in you." This mystical relationship was made good on the day of Pentecost. The disciples were unable to comprehend the dimensions of all this, when the words were spoken in the upper room. The reality burst on them at Pentecost; later the apostle Paul began to unfold its mysteries in his epistles, notably Ephesians.

The Lord Jesus is in his Father; we are in him; he is in us. This marvelous interlock of persons and personalities absolutely guarantees the eternal security of the believer, as well as the transformation of our lives in him by the transmission of his life through us.

His life is to be ours. Further, *his love is to be ours* (14:21): "He that hath my commandments, and keepeth them, he it is that loveth me: and he that loveth me shall be loved of my Father, and I will love him, and will manifest myself to him." The art of the romantic novelist is to create tension, and this is often done by a device known as "the eternal triangle." The novelist has one hero and two women who want him, or one heroine and two men who want her. The Lord introduces us to a true eternal triangle, one in which there is no tension, only glorious oneness. There is our love for Jesus, the Father's love for us, and the love of Jesus for us. All three loves are mutually interdependent and all work together in harmony.

Love is quick to find out what pleases the beloved. The Lord says that our practical obedience to his commands is love's sure test. This is more than mere sentiment, more than singing "My Jesus, I love thee, I know Thou art mine." This love is evidenced in character and conduct. It embraces the highest heights: "If a man loves me," Jesus said, "my Father will love him." God's heart goes out in a special way to those who love his beloved Son. "And I will love him, and will manifest myself to him," Jesus says. The word for "manifest" is *emphaniso*, which carries the idea of presenting something in a clear and conspicuous form, the idea of disclosing a hidden presence. The word is first used of the resurrected saints who came out of their graves after Christ's resurrection and who went into Jerusalem and appeared *(emphaniso)* unto many (Matthew 27:53). The Lord promises that he will reward this love that is his love by a special manifestation of himself to the spiritual gaze of his own. As Bernard of Clairvaux put it:

But what to those who find? Ah, this
   Nor tongue nor pen can show:
The love of Jesus, what it is
   None by His loved ones know.

Then, too, *his loyalty is to be ours* (14:22-24). This was heady stuff—and, at this stage of their spiritual development, it was over the heads of the Lord's bewildered disciples. They were struggling to grasp these epochal truths. John could remember how Judas asked a question (14:22). He is careful to add a qualifier, "not Iscariot." Was this Judas a low man on the apostolic totem pole? He is always mentioned in the last of the four groups. Alexander MacLaren thinks they were listed according to their spiritual nearness to the master. (Peter, James, John, and Andrew always appear in the first group. Judas Iscariot always appears in the last group and is always listed last of all). It must have been a source of chagrin to this Judas that he had the same name as the traitor.

"How is it that thou wilt manifest thyself unto us, and not unto the world?" he asked. He understood the Lord's words about his manifestation. He rightly concluded that he and the others loved the Lord sufficiently to be the subjects of the promise. He understood too what the Lord said about there being no public display of himself, and that seemed to bother him. It was only a few days since the Lord's triumphant entry, something that may have led the apostles to feel that at last things were beginning to move in the right direction. Now his question was, as it can be rendered, "What has happened to bring about this change, this going back to secrecy?"

These questions, by Thomas, Philip, and now Judas, must have been like cold water on the Lord's soul. This was his last night with them. Tomorrow he would be dead. They had grasped so little. All they wanted was some shekinah brightness, some display of messianic glory that would dazzle the wavering multitudes and bring the Sanhedrin to its senses.

The Lord was patient. He answered the question of Judas, but not directly. He knew that Pentecost must come before further enlightenment could take place. But here he could lay the foundation for post-Pentecost revelation.

In resolving the problem thus raised, the Lord first set before the disciples *an important concept* (14:23): "Jesus answered and said unto him, If a man love me, he will keep my words: and my Father will love him, and we will come unto him, and make our abode with him." This is another passage of Scripture in which it helps to put the emphasis in turn on every word or clause (italics have been added to the following Scripture quotes).

Jesus says, "*We* will come unto him, and make our abode with him." The Father will. The Son will. Think for a moment what that means. Living alongside us, living with us, living where we live, are the two most powerful, loving, wise, and wonderful persons in the universe. They control all the factors of matter, time, and space. They are the objects of ceaseless angelic adoration, tribute, service, and song. Yet *they* have chosen to make their abode with us.

Jesus says, "We *will* come unto him, and make our abode with him." There is no room for doubt. This is the determined decision of the Father and the Son, part of a plan worked out before time began—as much a decision within the godhead as the decision to create an angelic hierarchy or to create a hundred million galaxies or to stoop down and fashion Adam's clay. We *will* come. And when the Father and the Son say "We will," they say what they mean and they mean what they say. No power in heaven, earth, or hell can prevent them from doing what they have determined to do.

Jesus says, "We will *come unto* him and make our abode with him." That implies a move of some kind. Granted, God is omnipresent, yet at the same time God accommodates himself to our space-matter-time way of living and from time to time localizes himself in a special place without in any way altering his omnipresence. He did that in the Old Testament when he met Moses at the burning bush. He went before the Israelites in the shekinah glory cloud. He took up residence on the mercy seat between the cherubim in the holy of holies. Now, Jesus says, he and his Father will come and take up residence with us. Imagine living every moment of every day in the company of Jesus and his Father.

Jesus says, "We will come unto *him,* and make our abode with *him.*" With whom? With the person who loves Jesus. God is not impressed by the high and mighty of this world, by princes and presidents, by the rich and famous, the learned and great. He is, however, drawn irresistibly to the man, woman, boy, or girl who loves him. Of all the people on this planet with whom God could take up his abode, if he so desired, he takes up his abode with those who love Jesus. By so doing, he makes them the aristocracy of the universe.

Jesus says, "We will come unto him, and make our *abode* with him." The word for "abode" is the same word translated "mansions" in verse 2. God gladly vacates them all, those glorious mansions in the sky, those ivory palaces beyond the reach of time and space, to take up our dwellings as his dwelling, to convert our cottages into his place of residence and thus turn our places into his palace, centers from which he rules the universe. Needless to say, the fact that God the Father and God the Son have now made their abode there ought to convert that human life into one with the fragrance of heaven.

There is not only an important concept at the heart of the Lord's answer to Judas, but also an *important contrast* (14:24), the contrast between a God-rejecting world and a God-revealing word: "He that loveth me not keepeth not my sayings: and the word which ye hear is not mine, but the Father's which sent me." This gives the reverse side of the coin. No love, no obedience. Love is the only power that can draw a person to keep the Lord's commands; they are too foreign to fallen human nature for it to be otherwise. Further, disobedience to the Lord Jesus is rebellion against God. Jesus said, "The word which ye hear is not mine but the Father's." Therefore, not to do what Jesus says is not to do what the Father says. That rules out all the world's Christ-rejecting religions as false. They may be rich, powerful, ancient, philosophically attractive, numerically vast. But if they do not love our Lord Jesus, whose voice was the voice of God, they are a deception and a lie.

These, then, are the reasons for the Lord's abiding presence: his life is to be ours, his love is to be ours, his loyalty is to be ours. The Lord goes on to show the results of *the Lord's abundant promise* (14:25-31). First, he will *quicken faith* (14:25-26): "These things have I spoken unto you, being yet present with you" (14:25). The Lord had revealed many remarkable things to these men. But it was evident, from the nature of the questions they were asking, how little they had grasped. How purposeless it would be, at this stage, to tell them more. And soon he was going away.

The answer was the Holy Spirit. When he came, he would complete the revelation and would confirm what had already been revealed: "But the Comforter, which is the Holy Ghost, whom the Father will send in my name, he shall teach you all things, and bring all things to your remembrance, whatsoever I have said unto you" (14:26). The Lord Jesus, during his earthly ministry, frequently put his divine imprimatur on the Old Testament, which he treated as the word of God. He quoted frequently from all parts of the Old Testament, which he regarded as the plenary, verbally inspired word of God. Now he gave his authoritative endorsement to the (as yet unwritten) books of the New Testament.

Here we have the first of three references to the New Testament which, Jesus said, would be given to the apostles by direct inspiration of the Holy Spirit. In this reference, the Lord endorsed what we now have in the gospels ("he shall . . . bring all things to your remembrance, whatsoever I have said unto you"). The gospel of John, with its long intricate discourses, written by a very old man many years later, is an illustration of this. The Holy Spirit not only quickened John's memory but enabled him to write down accurately the story and sayings of Jesus.

In this reference also, the Lord endorsed what we now have in the epistles ("he shall teach you all things"). The Holy Spirit not only interpreted to these disciples the things that Jesus had said (which at the time were very much over their heads), but he revealed to them new aspects of truth, much found only in germ form in the Lord's teaching.

So then, the Holy Spirit was coming to quicken faith and to write a book that would be the objective and infallible depository of New Testament truth for God's people for all the rest of time. Moreover, he was coming to *quell fear* (14:27-31). In the closing verses of this chapter we have, first, a vision of *the Lord and his disciples* (14:27-29). He bequeathed four things to them. He gave them *his peace* (14:27a): "Peace I leave with you, my peace I give unto you: not as the world giveth, give I unto you." This word *peace (eirenen)* occurs six times in John's gospel and is always used by Jesus.

Their world was about to fall apart. Soon there would be the tramp of marching men; the incredible would happen: Christ would be crucified. They would be overwhelmed. Already Judas Iscariot was out there somewhere in the dark paving the way. The Lord said to these apprehensive men, upset because of his continuing insistence on the changes now imminent, "Peace! Peace, even my peace, I give to you." They had seen that peace in action on the stormy sea when he walked on the wild billows of the raging deep and stilled wind and wave. His peace. That was unruffled calm no matter how great the demand made on him, no matter how many or malicious or mighty his foes.

"Not as the world giveth, give I unto you." The world talks about peace—and prepares for war. The world has its disarmament conferences—and invents new and more fearsome weapons of doom. The world promises a peace it cannot give.

Jesus said, "Peace be unto you." *Shalom* is the eastern word for "hello" and "goodbye." But his *goodbye* would be the comforter's *hello.* He was going. His peace would remain. It was his bequest.

Second, he gave them *his pledge* (14:27b-28a): "Let not your heart be troubled, neither let it be afraid. Ye have heard how I said unto you, I go away, and come again unto you." The storms will come. Natural fears will clamor to be seated on the throne of panic in our hearts. Our task is to allow Christ's peace to drive out the insolent usurper and to reign within, come what may. He pledges his peace, reinforced by his presence.

Third, he gave them *his perspective* (14:28b): "If ye loved me, ye would rejoice, because I said, I go unto the Father: for my Father is greater than I."

There is order within the godhead. There are three persons—Father, Son, and Holy Spirit—but one God. All three persons are equally and eternally God. We speak of the Father as the first person, the Son as the second person, and the Holy Spirit as the third person. There is order but no rivalry; position but no superiority or inferiority. When Jesus said, "My Father is greater than I," he was stating a fact having to do with relationship within the godhead. Finite beings cannot comprehend the infinite so we should not be surprised if we have trouble grasping this.

When Jesus came to earth he was "sent" by the Father (John 13:16). Everything he did was according to a prearranged plan whereby the second, uncreated, self-existing person of the godhead voluntarily became human. He assumed a human body. He lived life on human terms. In a unique way he subordinated himself to his Father. He never ceased to be anything less than God.

He could say, "My Father is greater than I," not because the Father was any more God than he was but because, as man, he had assumed a position of dependence on the Father. Jesus had come to earth not to behave as God, though he was God, but to behave as man, because he was man.

Jesus was not just God; he was man. He was not just man; he was God. He was not half God and half man. He was God manifest in flesh, a mysterious and perfect blending in one person of the human and the divine.

When he spoke these words in the upper room, he was preparing to go back to his Father, by way of crucifixion, resurrection, and ascension. He was about to take back to heaven a battle scarred, glorified resurrection body.

Jesus was looking at things from this perspective. He told his disciples they should rejoice, if they loved him, because he was going home. He seldom spoke like this. It is a rare glimpse of the Lord's passion as it related to himself. His homegoing was something he anticipated with joy. His exaltation and joy should be a source of joy for those who love him. We can almost hear him say to his disciples, as he looked into their glum faces, "If you would only look at it from my perspective for a moment, you would be glad because I am going home."

They could not know it yet. It was one of those truths the Holy Spirit would reveal to them later. But there was something in it for them too. Once he was ascended and seated on his Father's throne, he would be their great high priest, their advocate with the Father. They should have been glad for him, and glad for themselves.

Fourth, he gave them *his prediction* (14:29): "And now I have told you before it come to pass, that, when it come to pass, ye might believe." He knew what a catastrophic upheaval was coming—was already under way. He was doing everything he could to bolster their faith—so that, even if it should falter, afterward it would be all the stronger as they recalled this incident. We can be sure that John, for one, had reflected on these predictions of Jesus with great spiritual profit in his long career as an apostle. His loving "I told you so" must have been reassuring to John in the severe testings that later came his way.

John tells something, next, of *the Lord and the devil* (14:30): "Hereafter I will not talk much with you: for the prince of this world cometh, and hath nothing in me." "Prince of this world" is one of Satan's titles. The kingdoms of this world became his province when Adam sinned. In the temptation he offered them to Jesus, at a price. Satan did not know it, but his own downfall and doom were in the cross he was so busily preparing for the Lord.

The coming of Satan, riding the now demented soul of Judas Iscariot, would interrupt the earthly teaching of Jesus, never to be resumed except in a few fragments.

Satan was on the way. All the Lord's other enemies were dupes and tools of this great enemy. He wields enormous power in this world. He had his men lined up: Judas and the mob, the Sanhedrin and the priests, the Pharisees and the scribes, Herod and his men of war, Pilate and his cohorts. He evidently thought he was going to triumph.

He was wrong. "He has nothing in me," Jesus said. He used a double negative for emphasis *(ouk ouden)*. No sin in his life would give the enemy anything upon which to seize. In all others there is sin. Satan enforces death as his due. Jesus was a voluntary sacrifice. Indeed he was "not of this world" over which Satan was the usurper prince.

After the Lord's temptation in the wilderness, about which John is silent, Satan "departed from him for a season." In Gethsemane, about which John is also silent, he came back with an even fiercer temptation: to induce Jesus to seek some way other than the cross. Satan was doomed to failure. The Lord's sole rule of life was "Father, not my will, but thine, be done." Satan had no weapon to penetrate armor like that.

Next, John directs our attention to *the Lord and his duty* (14:31): "But that the world may know that I love the Father; and as the Father gave me commandment, even so I do." His duty was two fold. First, by going to the cross, he would bear *testimony to the world* (14:31a). The world would know how great was that love he had for his Father, which caused him to become "obedient unto death, even the death of the cross." Our view of Christ's death, the subject of so many of our hymns, is centered on his love for us. "He loved me and gave himself for me" was Paul's way of putting it. The Lord's view of the cross is centered in his love for the Father: "That the world may know that I love the Father." We look at Calvary and see the sin offering: what the cross has wrought for us. Jesus looked at the cross and saw the burnt offering: what the cross wrought for the Father.

By going to the cross, the Lord would bear *tribute to the word* (14:31b): "As the Father gave me commandment, even so I do." His was unqualified, unquestioning obedience. A moment or two before, Jesus had said, "If a man love me, he will keep my words" (14:23). Now he says, in effect, "I practice what I preach." He knew "those things that pleased the Father" and he did them.

This segment ends with *the Lord and his departure* (14:31c): "Arise, let us go hence," he said, abruptly ending the talk in the upper room. The words imply haste. Evidently as he spoke he rose to his feet, even as the disciples still lounged around the table. The time for action had come. The Lord had decided to go out now and meet the foe head-on. He was resolved to carry out the purpose of his Father for the redemption of the human race. The rest of the words in this private discourse were spoken somewhere between the house where he had kept the feast and the crossing of the brook of Kidron on the edge of Gethsemane.

Section 2. The Walk on the Gethsemane Road (15:1-17:26)

I. THE LORD TALKS TO HIS FOLLOWERS (15:1-16:33)

With the solitude of the upper room now over and the agony ahead, Jesus talked as he walked, first to his followers, then to his Father. His talk with his followers gave them revelations about God the Son, and God the Spirit, and God the Father.

A. Revelations about God the Son (15:1-25)

1. The Lord—His Followers and Their Fruit (15:1-17)

The Lord's followers are to be fruitful, and fruitfulness results when we learn *the secret of abiding* (15:1-5) in him. This first
segment is built around the Lord's famous analogy of the vine.

We must look first at *the vine and its background* (15:1): "I am
the true vine, and my Father is the husbandman." Some Bible
students have thought that this discourse was suggested by vine-
yards on the hillsides and especially by the fires of vine prunings
in the Kidron Valley. Others have thought that the discourse
was prompted by the golden vine that embellished the gates in
the temple court. On the other hand, the Lord's discourse may
have been prompted by something more profound.

The vine was one of three trees that symbolized the nation of
Israel. It is referred to as such in Psalm 80:8-19, for instance,
and in Isaiah's famous song of the vineyard (Isaiah 5:1-7). The
day before, the Lord had told his provocative parable of the
vineyard and the evil husbandmen who were now plotting the
murder of the divine owner's Son (Matthew 21:33-46). The
Lord applied this parable to the nation of Israel and especially
to its leaders: "Therefore say I unto you, The kingdom of God
shall be taken away from you, and given to a nation bringing
forth the fruits thereof" (Matthew 21:43). We read: "When the
chief priests and Pharisees had heard his parables, they perceived that he spake of them. But when they sought to lay hands
on him, they feared the multitude, because they took him for a
prophet" (Matthew 21:45-46).

It is against this background that we must interpret this I AM
saying of Jesus. Israel was God's vine. He had taken the nation
from Egypt, carried it across the sands of Sinai, planted it in the
promised land, hedged it around, and entrusted it to a series of
divinely appointed leaders, husbandmen. Time and again he
had sent his servants, looking for a return on his investment in
the nation. But the nation's leaders had ill-treated some of those
servants, and murdered others. Last of all he had sent his Son
and they were now preparing to murder him.

There could be only one result: a visitation of wrath on the
leaders of the nation in particular and on the nation of Israel in
general. Since the nation, the custodian of God's purpose on
earth, was so devoid of fruit, the kingdom of God would be
taken away and invested elsewhere. In short, with the light of
completed New Testament revelation in our hands, we can see

that the Lord was referring to the church. For this present age,
God's purposes are centered in the church; the nation of Israel
is in divine disfavor. During this present age Israel is the fig tree
(Matthew 24:32-33). After the rapture, God will again take up
his dealings with the nation of Israel, which during the millennium will be the olive tree.

We must interpret these verses in John 15 with the greatest
care when we apply them to the individual Christian; otherwise
we shall have difficulty with the erroneous "falling away" doctrine which espouses the idea that believers can lose their salvation. In the Old Testament, the vine symbolized Israel corporately as a nation. The true vine and its branches, in the New
Testament, view the church corporately. Israel having failed in
its mission, the Lord now turned to his disciples and said that
from now on he was the true vine (15:1a). In place of the evil
husbandmen, his Father was the vinedresser *(georgos)*, the divine
farmer (15:1b).

This is the background. God has a new instrument, a new
"nation," for carrying on his purposes during this age: Christ
and his church. Those who wish to come into the good of the
kingdom of God in this age must be incorporated into the
mystical church, here viewed as a fruitful vine.

In some ways this concept of the church is similar to Paul's
analogy of the church as a body. In that case, however, the
individual believers are members of the body and Christ is the
head. The picture of Christ as the true vine and the church as
the branches views the believer both individually and corporately, inasmuch as the church in its local and universal aspects is
made up of individuals. Any local gathering of God's people is
the aggregate of its members; its corporate spiritual life is a
reflection of the spirituality or carnality of its members, and
especially of its leaders. This was true also of the nation of Israel
when it was God's vine. The corporate life of the nation reflected the strengths or weaknesses, godliness or wickedness, of its
leaders and citizens.

Now we must look at *the vine and its branches* (15:2-4). The
Lord speaks, first, of *the purging of the branches* (15:2-3). We note
what he has to say about *the cleansing work* (15:2) of God. "Every
branch in me that beareth not fruit he taketh away: and every
branch that beareth fruit, he purgeth it, that it may bring forth
more fruit."

The disciples were the embryonic church. They were related
to Christ as a branch is related to the vine. The Father, as
husbandman, tends to the branches, both the true ones and
those that had no place in the vine. We see him at work with the

pruning saw, cutting off dead, useless, and unproductive branches.

As far as the Lord's immediate disciples were concerned, a vivid illustration of that was before them in the case of the apostate Judas. He had been cut off. There are many who have a false profession of faith. The evidence lies in whether or not these professing branches bear fruit. We know what is the fruit of the Spirit: "Love, joy, peace, longsuffering, gentleness, goodness, faith, meekness, temperance" (Galatians 5:22-23), the very character of Christ. Viewed corporately, the church at Ephesus illustrates the dire plight of a church which, while active, doing all the right things, saying all the right things, was in peril of being cut off. "I have somewhat against thee, because thou has left thy first love" (Revelation 2:4). The Lord referred to this church as "fallen" and demanded repentance. "Repent, . . . or else I will come unto thee quickly, and will remove thy candlestick out of his place, except thou repent" (Revelation 2:5).

The Lord had no use for a church that did not love him any more. Despite its activity and zeal, it had become a fruitless branch. The lack of love for Christ in this church was a reflection of the worldliness and carnality of the Christians who comprised it. Possibly many of its members were not even saved at all, although vigorous and vocal in its affairs.

When the Father sees a branch of the vine that is bearing fruit, he purges it that it might bring forth more fruit. The word used is *kathairo*, which literally means "to cleanse." Everything is removed from the branch that would tend to divert vital power from producing fruit; without constant pruning away of saplings the vine would run to leaves. The great husbandman alone knows how and where to bring the knife to bear both in the life of an individual and in the corporate life of a local church.

Again, corporately, this is illustrated in the church at Smyrna. Persecution was allowed to raise its head in that church. There were those in the church at Smyrna whom the Lord called blasphemers; they considered themselves Jews but they were nothing of the kind. They were Judaizers, legalists within the church. They are called "the synagogue of Satan" (Revelation 2:9). It was to purge out these false members, to cleanse the church of this evil, that the Lord allowed tribulation to come. Historically we know that the apostolic age (as represented by the church at Ephesus) ended in the emergence of all kinds of heretical cults and apostasies. The persecuting Caesars were a pruning knife in the hands of the divine husbandman to cut away these unfruitful growths.

Next we are told something about *the cleansing word* (15:3) of
Christ: "Now are ye clean through the word which I have spok-
en unto you." The great husbandman, in dealing with the
church and its members, does not always have to resort to the
pruning knife. A gentler method is the cleansing power of the
word of Christ. The disciples and the local church who keep
Christ's word are kept clean by its effective power. It is a source
of continual cleansing to the soul. It keeps us from evil. It drives
away pretenders. Hearing, believing, and obeying the word of
Christ are the springs of vital spiritual life in the vine. Think,
for instance, of the sermon on the mount and these last moment
discourses of the Lord. If these are applied in the life of an
individual there is no room for anything dead or false. Similarly,
in the corporate life of a local church, people will not stay where
his principles, precepts, and practices are the rule of life unless
they know and love the Lord.

Having spoken of the purging of the branches the Lord spoke
next of *the place of the branches* (15:4): "Abide in me, and I in
you. As the branch cannot bear fruit of itself, except it abide in
the vine; no more can ye, except ye abide in me." The place of
the branch is in the vine. It has no life and no fruit of its own.
All life and fruit are derived from its organic connection with
the vine. The fibers of the vine run from the root to the farthest
branch. It is this connection that gives vitality to each branch.
Sever a branch from the parent stem and it will die. A vine
branch is lifeless, useless, and fruitless unless it abides in the
vine, remaining vitally attached to the vine. The lifegiving sap
rises up from the roots and enables the branches to bear green
foliage and produce clusters of grapes. Thus the branch is an
organic part of the vine, and the vine expresses its life through
the branches.

This illustration depicts the need for the believer individually
and for the local church to be linked with Christ, and for Christ
to express his life through them. The Lord uses the word *abide*
to convey the idea of remaining close to one another, in intimate
connection. The believer takes up his abode in Christ; Christ
takes up his abode in the believer. The life of Christ becomes
the life of the believer, supplying grace and power for living the
"Christ life" on earth. The life of the believer becomes the life
through which the Lord expresses his life today in a world of
time and sense.

Apart from him there can be no spiritual life, no spiritual
fruit. No man or woman, boy or girl, has what it takes to live
the Christian life, because it is a supernatural life. The only
person who can live it is Christ. Anyone who has tried to live the

Christ life apart from Christ knows how impossible it is to do so. There must be a moment by moment, situation by situation resting in Christ so that his life might flow through and be seen in the green freshness and abundant fruitfulness that character-ized his life on earth. This teaching is an expansion of the Lord's earlier teaching about his abiding in his Father (14:10) and of his and the Holy Spirit's abiding in us.

The same, of course, is true of a local church. It has no life of its own. It can flourish and bear fruit only by maintaining its connection with Christ. There are imitation churches. There are dead churches. There are churches like the church of Sardis of which the Lord said, "Thou hast a name that thou livest, and art dead" (Revelation 3:1). But there are also churches living in union with Christ like the church at Philadelphia (Revelation 3:7-8).

Having looked at the vine and its background and at the vine and its branches, we must now look at *the vine and its bounty* (15:5): "I am the vine, ye are the branches: He that abideth in me, and I in him, the same bringeth forth much fruit: for without me ye can do nothing."

In Hampton Court in London is a large greenhouse contain-ing an old and magnificent vine. Its branches run everywhere. Its foliage is beautiful, its fruit colorful and abundant. Even the remotest tiny tendril, seeking a corner to which it can cling, is vitally connected with the parent stem. That vast vine is an organic whole. One branch does not try to dominate or direct another branch. Each branch runs back to the source. The branches are independent yet dependent. Each reaches out to its corner of the greenhouse. Each adds its contribution to the splendor of the whole. Each is busy producing its own foliage, flowers, and fruit.

Such is the Christian life, whether expressed individually in the life of each believer or corporately as local churches, branches, reaching out with the life of Christ to the far corners of the world.

"Without me ye can do nothing," Jesus added, re-enforcing the lesson. There is no such thing as a freelance Christian. To be a Christian in the biblical sense of the word involves an organic spiritual relationship with Christ. In the Bible there is no such thing as a denominational church being ruled from some headquarters, or an independent church ignoring all oth-er gatherings of believers. All are united to Christ and through him to one another, in a many branched whole. Christ is the head of the church. Christ is the vine. Severed from him there is no life at all, individual or corporate, and what passes for life is a wretched imitation, lifeless and sowing death. Denominational-ism, tradition, programs, or money might keep a dead church going through the motions for a time. But all it produces is wordliness, carnality, legalism, death.

The abiding life is to become the abounding life, a life that brings glory to the Father by being a reflection of the life of Christ. How does a branch abide? How does it keep its place in the vine? What does it have to do? Nothing. It just abides. It remains where it finds itself, a part of the vine, placed there by God, content to fulfill the law of its being by receiving in fair weather and foul the life of the vine flowing up from the root.

The branch is not responsible for pruning itself. That is the husbandman's duty. A branch is not responsible for other branches, to censure them or to prune them. The husbandman takes care of that. All a branch does is abide and abound.

The secret of abounding (15:6-17) in Christ relates to *the fruitful ness of Christ* (15:6-8). His life is ours. His fruit is ours, which brings us to *the tragedy of being severed* (15:6): "If a man abide not in me, he is cast forth as a branch, and is withered; and men gather them, and cast them into the fire, and they are burned." A vine branch no longer attached to the vine is useless. Vine wood cannot be used for making furniture, for building, or for making a kitchen utensil. It will not even serve as a peg on which to hang a hat. A vine branch that does not bear grapes is worthless.

The Lord now depicts the fate of a branch severed from the vine. It withers. It is cast into the fire. It is burned. There is a notable change here, however, in the Lord's pronouns. Up to now he has been using what grammarians call first and second person pronouns, "I, me, ye." He now uses third person pro-nouns, "He, them, they." There is a difference. The *ye* referred to the disciples and those who are truly his. The *he, them,* and *they* refer to a different group. The same distinction can be seen in 1 Thessalonians 4:13–5:11 and in Hebrews 5:12–6:20. In both of those often misunderstood passages, the key to interpre-tation lies in the pronoun use.

Here the severed branches are carefully distinguished from the real ones. Judas was a severed branch. He had an attach-ment to the cause but not to the Christ. When the cause col-lapsed, as he thought, he sold Christ and died an apostate's death. He is representative of those who attach themselves to the church but who are alien to Christ. What is true of such people individually is also true of churches collectively. They are symbolized by the church at Laodicea, to which Christ gave the solemn warning, "I will spue thee out of my mouth" (Revelation 3:16).

The Lord's warning here is equally adamant: "Men gather them," he says, "and cast them into the fire, and they are burned." No clue is given as to who the "men" are or as to what or where the "fire" is. The Lord leaves it thus, so that the mysteriousness and horror of it can do its own work of penetrating the conscience. Surely Judas, his imminent deed, and his impending doom were in the Lord's mind.

In contrast with the tragedy of being severed is the *triumph of being spiritual* (15:7-8). The abiding life is the abounding life. This is shown in our approach to God: "If ye abide in me, and my words abide in you, ye shall ask what ye will, and it shall be done unto you" (15:7). This is not an unconditional guarantee that any child of God can make any demand and have instantly from God whatever he wants. God is too loving and too wise to put the key to his treasury into the hands of carnal, worldly minded, selfish believers.

The key to obtaining is abiding. This tremendous guarantee is entirely conditional. Still, it is an astonishing pledge ("ask what ye will" can be rendered "demand as your due"). The key to God's inexhaustible riches is given to those who abide in Christ and who have his words abiding in them.

The key to getting what we want is wanting what he wants. To have Christ's words "abiding" in us means more than merely memorizing them. It means meditating on them until our conscious natures are impregnated with them, until they become a vital part of us, so that they enlighten our understanding, enthuse our emotions, energize our wills. When our innermost beings are influenced by the indwelling, pervading words of the Lord Jesus, then we can demand as our due and it shall be done—for the simple reason that there will be nothing out of harmony between what we want and what he wants.

The abiding life is the abounding life. This is further shown in God's approval of us: "Herein is my Father glorified, that ye bear much fruit; so shall ye be my disciples" (15:8). The Father was certainly not glorified in the behavior of these disciples within the hour: Peter, James, and John sound asleep in Gethsemane; Peter slashing about him with a sword and then cursing, swearing, and denying Christ; and the rest of them taking to their heels and running away.

Why did they do such things? His word was not abiding in them. Why do we do such things? His word is not abiding in us. When his word does abide in us we bring forth fruit and his Father is glorified.

The Lord's discussion now moves away from the analogy of the vine. The secret of abounding is now shown to be connected with *the fellowship of Christ* (15:9-12). We begin with *the wonder of his heart* (15:9a): "As the Father hath loved me, so have I loved you." Some of these statements of the Lord Jesus are so familiar to us we lose all sense of the wonder of them. How much does the Lord love us? As much as the Father loves him. How much does the Father love him? With measureless love, without beginning or end.

There stood Simon Peter, about to deny him, and Thomas, so full of doubts, and Philip, wanting to see things eternal, immortal, and invisible when all the time they were plainly set before his face. There were James and John, the "sons of thunder," and Matthew, not long ago a common publican, and Simon Zelotes, not far removed from nationalistic fanaticism. Jesus looked at them. He said, I love you men. I love you very much. I love you as much as my Father loves me. I love you with an everlasting love, with love that is stronger than death, with love that many waters cannot quench, neither can floods drown. His heart went out to them in a surge of emotion as they crowded around him, making their way to the brook of Kidron, the slopes of Olivet and Gethsemane.

We think of *the way to his heart* (15:9b-10). This is summed up in *an exclamation* (15:9b), *an exhortation* (15:10a), and *an example* (15:10b): "Continue ye in my love. If ye keep my commandments, ye shall abide in my love; even as I have kept my Father's commandments, and abide in his love." The Lord claimed for himself complete and unbroken conformity to the Father's law and consequently complete and unbroken communion in the Father's love. It was the claim of one who knew no sin.

Had there but once, for the briefest possible instant, been the slightest deviation from that good and acceptable and perfect will of God, the briefest flash of resentment or rebellion, then that communion would have been broken. His holiness as God and his innocence as man would have been breached. Such a thing never happened—as a baby or as a boy, as a youth or as a man, in that Nazareth home, in school or synagogue, at the carpenter's bench, tramping the highways and byways of the promised land, when alone or when in the company of his disciples. When jostled by the multitudes or heckled by foes, moment by moment, day by day, year by year, between him on earth and his Father in heaven, law and love walked hand in hand. Jesus did always those things that pleased his Father.

Now then, he said to his disciples, that's how I have lived, and that's how you are to live. Between you as men on earth and me

as God in heaven there is to exist the same love-law relationship
that has existed between me as man on earth and my Father as
God in heaven. Love rules at the center; law rules at the circumference.

Next comes *the word from his heart* (15:11): "These things have
I spoken unto you, that my joy might remain in you, and that
your joy might be full." Joy is manufactured in heaven. It is
God's monopoly. It is not like happiness, which depends very
largely on what happens. The Lord's heart was full of joy even
with Gethsemane a few hundred yards ahead. It was for the joy
that was set before him that he endured the cross, despising the
shame.

Joy is one of the fruits of the Spirit, second only to love. This
joy he offers to us, joy resulting from obedience, flanked on one
side by love and on the other side by peace. Joy is like a rainbow
shining above our tears.

There is also *the will of his heart* (15:12): "This is my commandment, That ye love one another, as I have loved you." He
keeps coming back to that. His sacrificial love is to be the norm.
The disciples are to love one another as fervently and genuinely
as Christ loved them. There on the way to Gethsemane he
wrapped each and every one of them in his limitless love. While
still glowing in its warm embrace they heard him say, Love each
other just like this.

The secret of abounding is also found in *the friendship of Christ*
(15:13-17) and in how he *demonstrated* (15:13) it: "Greater love
hath no man than this, that a man lay down his life for his
friends." The Lord is not speaking here of his death as an
atoning sacrifice in which he laid down his life for the sins of
humankind, for our redemption. He is speaking of his death as
a voluntary surrender for the good and wellbeing of those he
loves. The greatest love anyone can show for a friend is to die
for him.

Then too the friendship of Jesus was *declared* (15:14-15). "Ye
are my friends, if ye do whatsoever I command you." That is *the
condition* (15:14). Anyone can be Jesus' friend. All that is necessary to love him is to do what he says.

"Henceforth I call you not servants; for the servant knoweth
not what his lord doeth: but I have called you friends; for all
things that I have heard of my Father I have made known unto
you." That is *the concept* (15:15). The Lord seems to linger
lovingly over that new word he has just dropped into his talk:
friends. His friends do things for him. Friends put themselves
out for each other. We do things for him—we do whatsoever he
commands us. He does things for us—he makes known to us

the things he has heard from his Father. He shares confidences with us. That is what friends do.

The Lord does not tell us what he wants done because we are his servants (*douloi*, "slaves"). A slave does what he is told to do but, even at the moment of action when he is obeying his lord's command, there is probably no bond of love, no intimacy by which the lord's mind and heart and purpose are communicated. The slave is merely the instrument of the master's will, to do what he is told, promptly and without question. The Lord tells us his will because we are his friends. He takes us into his confidence, shares with us what is in his mind and on his heart. That is what the Lord had been doing throughout this long discourse.

Next, we have the friendship of Jesus *determined* (15:16). "Ye have not chosen me, but I have chosen you," Jesus said. That was *the divine initiative* (15:16a). The Lord wanted them to understand that he was the one who made the first move. He was the one who sought out the disciples. He knew all about each of them, as one by one they were attracted into the orbit of his life. He did not choose them because they were rich or famous, clever or influential, educated or of high social standing. Normally students chose their own rabbis. Not in this case. He chose them. He engineered the background events of their lives so that they were brought within the sphere of his influence. Then with purpose and aforethought he chose them. And, amazing truth, he chose them to be his friends.

He could have chosen anyone he liked from the roll call of this world's millions. He chose them. And he has chosen us, all of us who have responded to the call of his love.

"I have chosen you, and ordained you, that ye should go and bring forth fruit, and that your fruit should remain." That is *the divine intention* (15:16b). The word for "ordained" is *etheka*, which means to be placed, sent, or appointed. Here the word describes their assignment as apostles to the special position that was being given to them in that church about to burst on the world at Pentecost. Not only does the shadow of Golgotha lie across this discourse, so does the shining light of Pentecost. These eleven men were specially chosen and ordained by Jesus to occupy a unique, once-for-all role in the church. Some would become famous, others would remain obscure. All were appointed. Similarly, down through the ages the Lord ordains his servants for the place, great or small, that he has chosen for them in his church.

Their fruit would remain. Satan cannot uproot God's vine. He cannot destroy its fruit. The apostles were to "go" and bring forth fruit. On the day of Pentecost, Peter went to reach three thousand. A few years later he went to Caesarea to reach a gentile and fling wide the door of the church to the world. True fruit remains because it is produced by the Holy Spirit, not by human beings, however gifted or prominent or influential.

"I have chosen you, . . . that whatsoever ye shall ask of the Father in my name, he may give it you." That is *the divine invitation* (15:16c) to storm heaven's heights, to come into the presence of God, to present our petitions with the blessed assurance that prayers offered in the name of Jesus have top priority with the Father. Of course, we cannot attach that name to selfish petitions, to pleas that would be contrary to his nature, person, and personality.

There is one more secret of abounding and it is key. We have the friendship of Jesus *duplicated* (15:17). "These things I command you, that ye love one another." Friends of a friend should be friends. An analogy that comes to mind is that of the spokes of a wheel. As those spokes draw closer to the hub they draw closer to one another. If we find ourselves at some distance from another of Jesus' friends, let us move closer to Jesus. The closer we get to him, the closer we will get to one another.

2. The Lord—His Followers and Their Foes (15:18-25)

We begin with *the hatred of the world for his friends* (15:18-22). The opposite of love is hate. The Lord has been commanding his disciples to love one another. One reason why such love is imperative is because of the hatred of the world for the Lord and his own. The Lord therefore introduces this discordant note into the harmony he has been setting before his people. They can expect the world's hatred.

He begins with *reasons for that hate* (15:18-21). There are two; the first is *intolerance* (15:18-20). The world's intolerance toward the Lord's people is irrational. The world hates God's people because *they are different* (15:18-19). "If the world hates you, ye know that it hated me before it hated you. If ye were of the world, the world would love its own: but because ye are not of the world, but I have chosen you out of the world, therefore the world hateth you."

The Lord Jesus was different from other men. He was sinless. He made no mistakes. He never failed. He spoke the truth without fear or favor, though always in love. He refused to compromise with moral evil, doctrinal error, personal hypocrisy. He exposed the corruption and decay of the establishment. He taught in a memorable and pungent fashion exposing the incompetence and fatuous fallacies of the authorized doctors of the law—so they hated him. They will hate us too, if we are different as he was different.

"Ye are not of the world," Jesus said. We are in the world but not of the world. Our citizenship is in another world, not this one. We are aliens here, pilgrims and strangers. The Lord's disciples came to be hated. All of them, with the possible exception of John, were martyred, and John himself endured persecution. For three hundred years, from Nero to Diocletian, the church was the object of constant and at times overwhelming tribulation. The history of the church down through the centuries has been one of hostility from the world because God's people are different. They separate themselves from the world. They are a people chosen out of the world.

The world hates God's people because *they are disciples* (15:20). "Remember the word that I said unto you, The servant is not greater than his lord. If they have persecuted me, they will also persecute you; if they have kept my saying, they will keep yours also." The Lord's people can expect hostile treatment; people's attitudes toward the Lord will determine their attitudes toward his people. They had no use for him, and often they will have no use for us.

There is in vogue today a so-called "prosperity gospel." This false gospel promises that God's people will be rich, happy, powerful, successful, and healthy in this world, if they meet certain conditions. We are told to espouse "prosperity thinking" and to embrace "the power of positive thinking." This kind of "gospel" is far removed from the Lord's teaching. When God seeks to attract someone to Christ, he does not hand out slick brochures offering houses and land, wealth and health, success and security in this world. He tells things as they are. The world hated Jesus and it will hate his people.

The second fundamental reason for the world's hate is *ignorance* (15:21): "But all these things will they do unto you for my name's sake, because they know not him that sent me" (15:21). Let us remember that the persecution of Christ and his church came chiefly from religious people. That has been true in almost all the ages of the Christian era. Just because people are religious, or sincere in their beliefs, or active in their faith does not prove that they know God. Behind all Christ-rejecting religion is Satan, who masquerades as an angel of light, who is the father of lies and a deceiver from the beginning.

The world's first false religion was founded by Cain. It was a religion of self-effort, good words, and Satan inspired sacrifice. No blood, no cross, no lamb, no Christ, and no truth were in that religion. When Cain discovered that his brand of religion was rejected by God, whereas his brother Abel's was accepted, Cain was furious. He baptized his false religion in his brother's blood. Such is the religion of this world.

"They have not known him that sent me," Jesus said. Out of that ignorance of God the tides of persecution arise.

Results of that hate (15:22) are soon evident: "If I had not come and spoken unto them, they had not had sin: but now they have no cloak for their sin." The Lord's presence and preaching exposed all false religion. It did then; it does now.

This world stands guilty of the greatest crime in the annals of time and eternity: the crime of turning its back on the incarnate Son of God, of nailing him to a cross, and of endorsing that crime generation after generation by ignoring God's word and persecuting his people. The result of this persistent hate is that the world stands exposed before God in all its sin.

The Lord reveals not only the hatred of the world for his friends, but also *the hatred of the world for his Father* (15:23-25). We note how *this hatred is focused* (15:23-24): "He that hateth me hateth my Father also. If I had not done among them the works which none other man did, they had not had sin: but now have they both seen and hated both me and my Father."

It was not only that Christ had borne witness in his words, he had borne witness also in his works. And what works they were, "works which none other man did." Who else has walked on the heaving wave and stilled the tempestuous storm? Who else has changed water into wine or multiplied loaves and fishes to provide a feast for a multitude? Who else has cleansed the leper, given sight to the blind, or raised a man rotting in his grave? Who else has performed miracle after miracle beyond count? Who else has risen from the dead after being three full days and nights in the tomb? This is the record of Jesus alone. Those who constitute themselves his enemies, and consequently the enemies of his Father, are without excuse.

Such an indictment is true generally of all who have been brought under the sound of the gospel. It is true in particular of the Jews of Jesus' day. We must remember that even as the Lord was speaking thus to his disciples he was walking resolutely toward Gethsemane and the imminent encounter with Judas and the mob, the Sanhedrin and the Roman authorities, all of whom would join hands in hastening him to the cross. No greater privilege could have been given to a generation than to have heard Jesus teach, to have watched him perform his miracles, and to have seen his face alight with the love and luster of another world. To repay him with a cross was the crime of crimes. The only explanation of such behavior was to be found in this world's hatred of God.

This hatred was foretold (15:25): "But this cometh to pass, that the word might be fulfilled that is written in their law, They hated me without a cause." The quotation is from Psalm 35:19 or Psalm 69:4, which added to the culpability of the Jews especially. It was written in "their law," the sacred Scriptures they acknowledged. The Bible that the Sanhedrin and the synagogues claimed as their own, professed to believe, and sought to protect and teach, foretold their wickedness. Possession of the Scriptures adds to the guilt of those who reject Christ.

B. Revelations about God the Spirit (15:26–16:15)

Much of what we know about the ministry of the Holy Spirit in this age we learn from these words of Jesus. He has a threefold ministry, as recorded here.

1. His Reminding Ministry (15:26-27)

The Holy Spirit is here to remind people about Christ. John 14:26 has its fulfillment in the writing of the gospels. John 15:26-27 has its fulfillment in the events and writing of the book of Acts. There we see the Holy Spirit at work through the disciples, empowering and endorsing their witness. The general title of the book of Acts suggests that in that book we have the "acts of the apostles." A more appropriate title would be the "acts of the Holy Spirit." He is mentioned over and over again in the book's first twenty chapters. Always his witness is to Christ.

We note, here, *the mystery of the Holy Spirit* (15:26a-c). Jesus told the disciples *why he would come* (15:26a,b): "But when the Comforter is come, . . . even the Spirit of truth . . ." He comes to bear witness of the truth in a world of lies. The "father of lies" (8:44), who is active in this world, is far too clever for us. But he is no match for the Holy Spirit. The lies and deceptions of Satan, by means of which he reigns in the hearts and lives of deluded men and women, boys and girls, are exposed by the Spirit of truth who has come to remind people that the truth (John 14:6) is to be found in Christ and in him alone. The Lord Jesus is the truth; the Holy Spirit is the truth. As Jesus prepared to leave, the Holy Spirit prepared to come.

So Jesus told the disciples *whence he would come* (15:26c): "When the Comforter is come, whom I will send unto you from the Father, even the Spirit of truth, which proceedeth from the

Father, . . ." In John 14:26 it is the Father who sends the Holy Spirit; here (John 15:26) it is the Son who sends him. So the Spirit proceeds from both the Father and the Son, a clear incidental proof of the deity of Christ.

Students of church history will recognize this as one of the verses that have been the subject of much controversy. The Nicene Creed refers to the Holy Spirit as "the One who proceedeth from the Father and the Son," an article of faith substantiated by John 14:26 and 15:26. The truth is thus confessed that the Holy Spirit is truly God and of the same power and nature as the Father and the Son. In both passages the word *he* (referring to the Holy Spirit) is *ekeinos,* remarkable because a masculine pronoun is made to refer to a neuter noun, thus emphasizing the personality of the Holy Spirit.

The clause "and the Son" (called by theologians "the *Filioque* clause") was added to the Nicene Creed at the Council of Toledo in Spain in A.D. 589. The "Double Procession of the Holy Ghost," as it is called, led to the controversy that separated the Greek church from the western church.

The real squabble, however, was not so much over the doctrinal issue as over the way the clause was added. The Council of Ephesus (sixth session, July 22, A.D. 431) had decided that the Nicene formula should not be altered, and that none other should be used. The objection, therefore, was not so much as to whether the *Filioque* clause should be added to the creed as it was over the arbitrary way the alteration in the wording of an ecumenical creed was made by one segment of the church without reference to the rest of the church.

By many the phrase "proceedeth from the Father and the Son" is taken to mean that he goes forth eternally. The significance of this lies in its making the Holy Spirit the medium of intercourse of the Father and Son and thus, in a trinity, completing a unity. Were the "Procession" from the Father only, the idea of disseverance would be more marked—and injury done to the completed doctrine of the trinity. (See T. C. Hammond, *The One Hundred Texts,* pp. 269-270.)

The word *comforter,* used here to describe the Holy Spirit, is too restricted. He is the one "called alongside" to keep us, the one who supplies all our needs.

The word *from,* used in both clauses in our text, is not the ordinary word *ek* ("out of") which indicates the source, but *para* ("from the side of") which expresses position.

The word *proceedeth (ekporeuomai)* may in itself describe either proceeding from a source or proceeding on a mission. The argument has been advanced that in the former sense the prep-

osition *ek* would be required to define that source; in the latter
sense the preposition *para* would be appropriate. This preposition is habitually used with the verb "to come forth" to express
the mission of the Son (16:27; 17:8). The use of this preposition
here suggests strongly that the reference to the "proceeding" of
the Holy Spirit has to do with his temporal mission and not to
the eternal procession.

Probably, the Lord's words here in John 15:26 do not refer
primarily to "the eternal depths of the divine nature" nor to the
mysterious relationship that exists between the three persons of
the godhead. It is probable that the Lord here is simply referring to the historical coming forth of the Holy Spirit to his
mission on earth. Probably the word *proceeds* is used here in
contrast with the word *send* (14:26) to demonstrate the Holy
Spirit's voluntary, independent action as one, not only sent by
the Father but who "proceeds" of his own volition to his work
on earth.

The Lord mentions *the motivation of the Holy Spirit* (15:26d-
27). *His supreme ministry is to exalt the Son of God* (15:26d): "He
shall testify of me," Jesus said. His work on earth is to remind
people about Jesus, to win men and women, boys and girls, to
Jesus.

His supplementary ministry is to energize the saints of God (15:27):
"And ye also shall bear witness, because ye have been with me
from the beginning." How the apostles did that is recorded
partially in the book of Acts. They did it through the baptizing,
filling, and anointing of the Holy Spirit. Without him they
would have accomplished nothing. With him they turned the
world upside down.

Here then are the facts. A divine person, whose dwelling
place from all eternity has been at the Father's side, has been
sent by Christ to earth to bear witness to him, to be his representative, to be, as it were, his other self. This almighty one, the
personal Holy Spirit, armed with the truth as it is in Christ
Jesus, has invaded this planet to exalt Jesus, hinder the working
of Satan, rescue souls from hell, energize believers, and stand
alongside them as their comforter, counselor, and companion,
empowering them, leading them, and using them.

No wonder these men—powerless, afraid, and ineffective—
suddenly became brave, convincing, and successful. Once the
Holy Spirit came, there was no stopping them.

2. His Reproving Ministry (16:1-11)

The second great work of the Holy Spirit, as taught by Jesus
on the way to Gethsemane, is to reprove this wicked world for

its rejection of Christ. There are three main subjects in this section. First, *the appalling dislike of the synagogue* (16:1-4a). The synagogue was the local center of Jewish religious life in Palestine and throughout the Diaspora. Wherever Jews were to be found in a given community, if there were ten men present, they formed a synagogue for worship and religious instruction. John practically ignores the synagogue in his gospel. By the time he wrote his gospel, however, it had become an institutionalized center of enmity to the gospel. The Lord had tasted its hostility. Now he warns the disciples against it.

First, he urged the disciples not to be *stumbled* (16:1-3) by the hostility of the synagogue: "These things have I spoken unto you, that ye should not be offended. They shall put you out of the synagogues: yea, the time cometh, that whosoever killeth you will think that he doeth God a service. And these things will they do unto you, because they have not known the Father, nor me." The verb for "offended" is *skandalizo* (literally, "to scandalize" or "to cause to stumble"). John used it in describing the people of Capernaum who were offended by the substance of the Lord's teaching in their synagogue (6:61). In actual fact the disciples were "offended" (scandalized) by the Lord's meek submission to his arrest in Gethsemane just a short while later (Mark 14:27). The man born blind, healed by Jesus, was excommunicated from the synagogue for his bold testimony to Christ (John 9:22,34). The threat of expulsion from the synagogue for supporting Christ was already being held over the people, with considerable success (12:42).

Hostility would continue. The synagogues in city after city turned against Paul once the full implication of his message was grasped. By John's day a special curse on the Nazarenes had been incorporated into the synagogue prayers to make sure that none of the Lord's followers would participate in the service. The curse, approved by the Sanhedrin, declaimed: "Let Nazarenes and heretics perish as in a moment; let them be blotted out of the book of life and not be enrolled with the righteous."

The Lord's warning went even further. The day would come when killing Christians would be considered service to God, a meritorious act. The day came very soon, as illustrated in the martyrdom of Stephen. Paul himself confessed that before he came to know Christ he considered the killing and persecuting of Christians to be a true expression of religious zeal (Philippians 3:6).

The Lord warned his disciples that they were not to be *startled* (16:4a) by these things: "But these things have I told you, that when the time shall come, ye may remember that I told you of them." The disciples were few; their foes would be many.

The disciples were ignorant and unlearned men, despised Galileans indeed; their foes would be the learned and the powerful. The disciples would be weak; their foes would be strong, able to harness the religious, political, economic, and military forces of the nation against them. And so it has been down through the ages. All this has been foreknown in the councils of God and counterbalanced by God's inscrutable purpose.

We watch an eclipse of the sun and take it in our stride. It has happened before; it will happen again. The eclipse will pass; the darkness is only temporary. All is under control. There, beyond the hatred and persecution of this world, is that world. High and lifted up and seated in the glory at God's right hand sits one who wears the scars of Calvary. Here on earth, within us and all about us, is the Holy Spirit. Persecution will come. Given the character of Christianity, the wickedness of this world, and the hatred of its evil prince, it is inevitable that persecutions great and small will arise. But Satan cannot win. It has all been worked out in the eternal counsels of God. The blood of the martyrs becomes the seed of the church. In time, God's people emerge, purified and more powerful than ever.

We are not to be startled by the hatred of this world. It is to be expected. But there's all eternity to come after that! That is what poor old Uncle Tom said to the cruel Simon Legree when his wicked owner threatened to roast him in a slow fire. "Eternity!" exclaimed Harriet Beecher Stowe. The word brought joy to the soul of the Christian slave. It ran like a spasm of horror through Simon Legree's soul.

The opposition of the synagogue was bad enough. But from the perspective of these silent disciples woe was added to woe. There was also *the approaching departure of the Savior* (16:4b-6). The Lord reintroduced this topic to explain *his past concealment of these things* (16:4b): "And these things I said not unto you at the beginning, because I was with you." He was there to bear the brunt of the world's hate. They were in no danger. He stood between them and the foe. Why dishearten them unnecessarily? Why fill their hearts with foreboding before it was necessary to speak more plainly about the inevitable hatred of the world? He wanted to give them time to know him better, time to get a firmer grasp on his deity, on the spiritual side of things.

When God called Israel out of Egypt, he did not tell them about the giants, the cities "walled up to heaven," and the sons of the Anakim. They would find out about those in due time. But by then they would have seen God's power unleashed against Egypt, they would have experienced the crossing of the Red Sea and miracle after miracle in the wilderness. They

would have drunk water from the riven rock and experienced
war with Amalek and the sweet taste of victory. They would
have spent a year at Sinai and learned the principles of a life of
obedience. By then the giants of Canaan should have been
pygmies to their faith. Thus too the Lord postponed talking
about the sterner realities of the Christian life until now.

He reintroduced the topic of his approaching departure,
moreover, to explain *his present candor about these things* (16:5):
"But now I go my way to him that sent me; and none of you
asketh me, Whither goest thou?" Of course, Peter and Thomas
had asked the Lord questions about his departure; the Lord
obviously had not forgotten that. But they had not asked him
where he was going in the sense meant here. They had been
concerned with their own immediate loss and with the desperation that had filled their souls. They were concerned with how
his departure would affect them; they had not asked how it
would affect him. All they could think of was the empty place at
the table. They had no thought of the glorious place to which
he was going.

Surely they could have asked him that: "What will this departure mean to *you?*" In their selfishness all they could think of was
their sorrow. In their love they might have talked about the
happiness his departure would mean to him. If they had been a
little less selfish and a little more loving, thoughts of his departure would have been tinctured with thoughts of the glory and
joy that were soon to be his. Further, if they had occupied their
thoughts with an ascended Christ, seated on their behalf at the
right hand of the "Majesty on high," such thoughts would have
filled them with joy too. To think that they would have a friend
at God's right hand, a great high priest, touched with the feelings of their infirmities, an advocate with the Father, one able to
intercede for them in sovereign power.

Instead, they were filled with natural but unspiritual sorrow:
"But because I have said these things unto you, sorrow hath
filled your heart" (16:6) How tender this great shepherd of the
sheep was. He submerged his own feelings in order to deal with
theirs, even as every step brought him closer to Gethsemane.
No greater commentary can be found than this on Paul's words
about true love: "Charity suffereth long, and is kind . . . vaun-
teth not itself . . . seeketh not her own . . . love never faileth" (1
Corinthians 13:4-8). Our Lord just went on loving them, talking
to them, pouring the balm of his boundless sympathy and limitless concern onto their broken hearts and frightened souls.

All this was leading up to something else: *the appointed descent
of the Spirit* (16:7-11). Jesus had already told them much about

this other comforter. Now he tells them more. John's mind and memory, quickened by that Spirit, goes back over his words, noting *what was expedient for them* (16:7): "Nevertheless I tell you the truth; It is expedient for you that I go away: for if I go not away, the Comforter will not come unto you; but if I depart, I will send him unto you."

In their hearts they might well have thought they would much rather have the Lord's physical presence than have his invisible Holy Spirit. They were not yet able to grasp the significance of the replacement of a limited bodily presence with an unlimited universal presence. They did not know the Holy Spirit yet; certainly they did not know him as Jesus knew him.

Suppose that after his resurrection Jesus had announced to his disciples that, instead of going home to heaven and instead of sending the Holy Spirit, he had decided to stay himself. Suppose he had said, "And now Peter, I intend to set up my headquarters here in Jerusalem. This upper room will do for the time being. I intend to stay for a very long time. You can be in charge of appointments. People will want to see me. No interview can last more than fifteen minutes. From time to time I will arrange a tour of other lands, but Jerusalem is to be my place of permanent residence. Audience with myself will be in strict order of application. There is to be no favoritism, no concession to rank or privilege. Each person will be allowed a private audience and will be allowed to speak to me and request of me whatever is on their heart or mind."

We can imagine the result. Before long the waiting list would be endless. People would wait a lifetime for one brief interview. Many would never make it. Altogether, it would be an unsatisfactory arrangement. Instead, Jesus is accessible to one and all who call his name. The Holy Spirit is here to make good in our hearts all those great and exceeding precious promises that are part of the gospel of God's grace. No wonder Jesus said, "It is expedient for you that I go away."

John also notes *what was expounded to them* (16:8-11) about the descent of the Holy Spirit. First the Holy Spirit's reproving ministry was declared (16:8). This important work tells us of another ministry of the Holy Spirit in the world. In John 3 we learn of his regenerating ministry. In Thessalonians 2 we learn of his restraining ministry. Here we learn more fully about his reproving ministry: "And when he is come, he will reprove the world of sin, and of righteousness, and of judgment" (16:8). We see first *the Spirit's reproving ministry declared* (16:8).

This reproving ministry of the Spirit of God is done in the soul. The first work of the Holy Spirit in an individual's soul is that of conviction. A person has to see himself as God sees him, become alive to his own lostness and desperate need.

Thus the Holy Spirit "reproves" of *the nature of sin* (16:8a). The word for "reprove" is *elegxei,* meaning "to convict," to bring in a verdict of guilty. No person is in a condition to be saved who has not first come under this conviction of the Holy Spirit that he or she is lost.

The Holy Spirit reproves, also, of *the need for righteousness* (16:8b), the need to be made right with God. A way has to be found to clothe the sinner in the righteousness of Christ. The book of Romans begins with a demonstration of the Holy Spirit's siege of the human conscience along these lines.

Then, too, the Holy Spirit warns of *the nearness of judgment* (16:8c). The word used for "judgment" is *krisis* which gives us the English cognate. A word used of judicial proceedings, it is variously translated as "damnation," "condemnation," "accusation," and "judgment." Romans begins with a warning that "the wrath of God is revealed from heaven against all ungodliness and unrighteousness of men" (Romans 1:18). The letter goes on to explain how ungodliness and unrighteousness manifest themselves in unregenerate human behavior.

Next we see *the Spirit's reproving ministry detailed* (16:9-11). We are told something of *the jurisdiction of sin* (16:9): "Of sin, because they believe not on me." That is the sin which damns, the finally unforgivable sin. God will forgive us of all our sins except the sin of refusing to believe in Jesus. The word for "sin" in both these verses is the general word for sin in the New Testament (*hamartia*), a word meaning "to miss the mark" and always used in a moral sense in the Bible to describe sins of both omission and commission. It is also the word used to describe the sin offering (Hebrews 10:6,8; 13:11), the Old Testament offering dealing with the principle (as differentiated from the practice of sin)—with what I am (a sinner) as differentiated from what I do.

The greatest sin a person can commit is not to believe in God's beloved Son. That is the sin of sins, the ultimate sin, the damning sin. It is like a man who has a deadly but curable disease. He goes to the doctor who prescribes a remedy but the man refuses to take it. He dies of his disease, not because he had the disease but because he spurned the remedy. All of us have this fatal sin virus in our souls. But God has provided an infallible remedy in his Son, a remedy that he offers us on the simple basis of belief (John 3:16). Those who will not believe in the Son go to a lost eternity—not because they are sinners but because they have refused God's remedy. The jurisdiction of sin is over when Jesus comes into one's heart. Its jurisdiction is eternally confirmed in the damned souls of those who turn their backs on God's Son.

To reject Christ deliberately or foolishly neglect him is an insult that God will not forgive. Indeed, he cannot. That is why Jesus here defines sin as not believing in him.

We are told something of *the justification of saints* (16:10): "Of righteousness, because I go to my Father." The Jews, in common with most people, regarded only moral offenses, transgressions of the ceremonial law, and deflections from religious traditions as sin (Matthew 15:2). The Lord Jesus was the only truly righteous one ever to live in this world. His standard of behavior was to do the will of God (8:29; Hebrews 10:7), a will that he obeyed perfectly every moment of every day. Now it is possible for all people to be made righteous by accepting him as Savior. God sees all such persons as "in him," the one "who is made unto us righteousness" (1 Corinthians 1:30; 2 Corinthians 3:9; 5:21). This is one of the major themes of the book of Romans, where the key word is *righteous.*

But the work of Christ continues on behalf of his own. We have "an advocate with the Father, Jesus Christ the righteous" (1 John 2:1) He is there to minister on behalf of his blood bought people until at last he brings us all safely home.

We are told something of *the judgment of sinners* (16:11): "Of judgment, because the prince of this world is judged." Satan, the lord of all those who live in their sins, has already been judged (12:31) and sentenced. The Lord Jesus has now triumphed over him and all his "principalities and powers" (Colossians 2:15). The cross is Satan's doom. As that old serpent fastened his evil fangs on the Savior's heel at Calvary, he felt that foot begin to crush his head (Genesis 3:14-15). He seems to have suddenly awakened to his folly for again we hear that satanic "If thou be the Son of God" suddenly ring out. The voice was the voice of wicked men, but the cry was the mortal cry of the evil one: "If thou be the Son of God, come down from the cross" (Matthew 27:40,42). Satan's ultimate doom is to be cast into the lake of fire (Revelation 20:10). All sinners are judged along with him and will share his terrible abode (Revelation 20:11-15).

3. His Revealing Ministry (16:12-15)

Having spoken of the Holy Spirit's reminding and reproving ministries, the Lord now speaks of his revealing ministry. He reveals two quite different kinds of truth. First is what we can call *the ecclesiastical truth* (16:12-13b), the kind of truth we have in the epistles. The Lord had mentioned the coming of his church on previous occasions (Matthew 16:18; 18:17) but did not reveal much about it. The reason lay in the disciples themselves. There was *a dispositional barrier* (16:12): "I have yet many things to say unto you, but ye cannot bear them now." The word for "bear" is *bastazo*. The word is used of the Lord himself: "And he bearing his cross went forth" (19:17). The Lord used it in denouncing the Jewish religious leaders: "Woe unto you also, ye lawyers! For ye lade men with burdens grievous to be borne, and ye yourselves touch not the burdens with one of your fingers" (Luke 11:46). The word here does not mean "bear" in the sense of endure or tolerate, but in the sense of carrying something. The withheld teaching was more than the disciples were constitutionally able to bear, spiritually speaking, at this stage of their development. The picture is that of a weight laid on a man unable to carry it. The weight might be pure gold, but if he cannot bear it, it will be too much for him. "Ye cannot bear them now" Jesus said—at this point in your spiritual growth. God never lays on us more than we are able to bear.

There was a sense, of course, in which the Lord had already told them everything. He had just finished telling them: "All things that I have heard of my Father I have made known unto you" (15:15). In the Lord's teaching, as recorded in the gospels, we find the embryo of all that is found later in the epistles. The great truths of his atoning death, of being "in Christ," of the universal and local church, of endtime events, and so on are all latent in the Lord's teaching. "As lies the rainbow in the rain, as in the bud the flower," so the germ of all church and New Testament truth can be found in Christ's teachings. The point was that there was a dispositional barrier to their full unfolding at this point in the disciples' spiritual development. They were already floundering with the truths he was giving them. He was too wise to load them to the point of drowning altogether. Besides, there was no hurry. The Holy Spirit would unfold the rest of it in due time.

The Spirit would break through *the dispensational barrier* (16:13a,b) as well. The day of Pentecost would usher in a change of dispensations. Israel as a nation would be replaced for this age by the church. The Holy Spirit would do something never done before in all his dealings with humankind. He would baptize people into the church, the mystical body of Christ (Acts 1:5; 1 Corinthians 12:13). Their spiritual faculties would be enlarged. Then they would be able to grasp divine truths only dimly comprehended in the mystical teaching of Christ.

In explaining this, the Lord spoke of *a revealing process*

(16:13a): "Howbeit when he, the Spirit of truth, is come, he will guide you into all truth." The word for "guide" is *hodegeo,* meaning "to lead the way." That suggests a pilgrimage and a process, a moving forward. The Ethiopian eunuch used this word when challenged by Philip as to whether he could understand Isaiah 53. "How can I," confessed the puzzled man, "except some man should guide me? . . . Philip opened his mouth, and began at the same scripture, and preached unto him Jesus" (Acts 8:31,35). The same word is used of the countless multitude saved after the rapture and martyred by the beast. The Holy Spirit highlights their eternal reward: "Therefore are they before the throne of God, and . . . the Lamb which is in the midst of the throne shall . . . lead them unto living fountains of waters" (Revelation 7:15-17).

Step by step, the Holy Spirit unfolded the truths that make up the epistles of the New Testament and comprise what we call "church truth." It took considerable time and the saving, enlightening, and quickening of the apostle Paul before some of the profounder truths could be verbalized. The Spirit of truth took incarnate truth (14:6), and enshrined it in written truths.

The Lord spoke also of *a revealing principle* (16:13b): "For he shall not speak of himself; but whatsoever he shall hear, that shall he speak." In other words, the Holy Spirit followed the same principle of divine revelation as the one that governed the Lord Jesus. The Lord had previously told his disciples, "He that sent me is true; and I speak to the world those things which I have heard of him" (8:26). In this discourse the Lord repeated the same principle: "All things that I have heard of my Father I have made known unto you" (15:15). The teaching of the Son and the Spirit comes from the same infallible source of truth. The Holy Spirit would have no message beyond what was already implicit in the incarnate word; he would make it explicit in the inspired word.

This coming Holy Spirit would also reveal *the eschatological truth* (16:13c-15), the kind of truth we have in the prophetic sections of the New Testament, and particularly in the apocalypse.

We can now pause for a moment to see how the Lord Jesus, who so authoritatively put his divine imprimatur on the Old Testament—in the way he consistently appealed to it, in all its parts, as being the verbally inspired and inerrant word of God—has also put his divine imprimatur on the New Testament. The same infallible Holy Spirit who inspired the writing of the Old Testament, which bears all the hallmarks of plenary and verbal inspiration, inspired the writing of the New Testament, which also bears all the hallmarks of plenary and verbal inspiration:

• *The Gospels:* "But the Comforter, which is the Holy Ghost, whom the Father will send in my name, he shall teach you all things, and bring all things to your remembrance, whatsoever I have said unto you" (14:26).

• *The Book of Acts:* "But when the Comforter is come, whom I will send unto you from the Father, even the Spirit of truth, which proceedeth from the Father, he shall testify of me: And ye also shall bear witness, because ye have been with me from the beginning" (15:26-27; cf. Acts 1:8).

• *The Epistles:* "I have yet many things to say unto you, but ye cannot bear them now. Howbeit when he, the Spirit of truth, is come, he will guide you into all truth: for he shall not speak of himself; but whatsoever he shall hear, that shall he speak" (16:12-13).

• *The Apocalypse:* "And he will shew you things to come. He shall glorify me: for he shall receive of mine, and shall shew it unto you" (16:13-14).

Returning to the Lord's words about the revealing of eschatological truth, we note that the Holy Spirit would unveil *the things to come* (16:15c): "And he will shew you things to come." "He will show" (literally, "he will declare") is repeated like a litany at the end of verses 13, 14, and 15 by way of solemn emphasis. Truth concerning things to come is found in various places in the New Testament: in the Lord's parabolic teaching, in his Olivet discourse, in Paul's writing (notably to the Thessalonian church and to Timothy), in Peter's second epistle, in Jude, and in the book of Revelation.

The Spirit's revelation would pre-eminently embrace *the things of Christ* (16:14-15); as has been said, the Holy Spirit's major work is to exalt *the person of Christ* (16:14a): "He shall glorify me," Jesus said. Soon men would spit in his face, they would blindfold him and punch him, they would array him in mocking purple and crown him with thorns. They would scourge him, crucify him, and mock him as he died. The Lord saw beyond all that to the glory that would follow. The Holy Spirit would reveal that glory in many a glowing New Testament passage, but especially in the apocalypse, "the revelation [unveiling] of Jesus Christ" (Revelation 1:1).

The Holy Spirit's work is also that of exalting *the pre-eminence of Christ* (16:14b-15): "For he shall receive of mine, and shall shew it unto you. All things that the Father hath are mine: therefore said I, that he shall take of mine, and shall shew it unto you." The Lord Jesus had been a living exegesis of the

Father; now the Spirit was to be a living exegesis of the Son. All
that the Father was had been interpreted by the Son; all that the
Son was would be interpreted by the Spirit. The Lord Jesus
taught his disciples to think great thoughts about the Father;
the Holy Spirit is here to teach us great thoughts about the Son.
If anything calling itself Christian teaching makes its approach
to us and does not exalt and glorify Christ, it is not of the Holy
Spirit.

C. Revelations about God the Father (16:16-33)

Thus ends the Lord's extensive teaching about the Holy Spirit. He was still walking through the night toward Gethsemane.
In closing this long and intricate discourse, he now talks to his
disciples one more time about his Father. He loved his Father.
He cannot talk to them too much about him. His Father was
everything to him, and he wanted him to be everything to us.

1. Wonderful Words of Life (16:16-28)

We can summarize the wonderful words of life around four
points: *a little while* (16:16-19), a little weeping, a little word, and
a little wait.

Beginning with the first of these we note *what Jesus declared*
(16:16-18). He had a mysterious statement to make. That statement was *uttered to the disciples* (16:16): "A little while, and ye
shall not see me: and again, a little while, and ye shall see me,
because I go to the Father." The last clause "because I go to the
Father" is omitted on textual grounds by many. It is not included by the Lord when he repeated the statement (16:19). It is
something the disciples added in their bewilderment (16:17). So
it seems likely that the clause in verse 16 is a copyist's error,
transposed from verse 17.

The statement has puzzled more than the Lord's immediate
disciples, and various explanations have been offered. "A little
while, and ye shall not see me," he said. The word for "see" is
theoreo (literally, "to be a spectator"; it is the word from which
we get our word *theater*). The idea is that of contemplating him,
seeing him face to face, looking at him in the way the disciples
were at that moment. He was going to pass out of their sight.
The "little while" was a very little while indeed. He was already
on his way to the grave.

"Again, a little while." That possibly refers to the transition
periods between his resurrection and ascension, that mysterious
forty days when he appeared and disappeared, when they saw

him only to have him vanish before their eyes. This was a strange time when they neither had the closeness to him that they had enjoyed in the days of his flesh nor yet had the spiritual oneness with him that was theirs after Pentecost.

"Ye shall see me," he concluded. The word for "see" is not the same word as the one just used. They were going to see him in a new way, see him as they had never seen him before. It is this clause that is the problem. What did Jesus mean when he said "Ye shall see me"? The word here is *orao,* which means "to comprehend." They had been observing him for three and a half years and little by little they had begun to see something of his glory and divine personality. In a little while they were going to seize intuitively upon all that Christ was. Pentecost would make the difference. Thus this statement of the Lord is not an abrupt changing of the subject. The Holy Spirit would effect the change. The beginning of this new vision was at the resurrection. The enlargement of that new vision was suddenly theirs at Pentecost. The final manifestation of it awaits the rapture when we shall see him "face to face" (1 Corinthians 13:12). Today we see him with the eye of faith.

This statement was *undeciphered by the disciples* (16:17-18): "Then said some of his disciples among themselves, What is this that he saith unto us, A little while, and ye shall not see me: and again, a little while, and ye shall see me: and, Because I go to the Father?" (This is a clause they seem to have inserted from his previous statement in verse 10—"I go to my Father, and ye see me no more.") "They said therefore, What is this that he saith, A little while? We cannot tell what he saith."

They had been listening to him all this while, trying hard to follow him. They were depressed by his repeated insistence that he was going away. More than once they had felt they were out of their depth. Now they felt they were being totally submerged. We can sense the note of irritation and despair in their voices as they finally express their bewilderment—not to him, but to each other. We can appreciate that. Even with the full light of New Testament revelation in our hands, and with the Holy Spirit here to guide us, and with scores of commentaries on our shelves, we still fail to touch bottom in this upper room-Gethsemane road discourse.

The disciples were not so different from the rest of us. They threw up their hands in impatience. They were still in their spiritual infancy, still in need of milk. Yet this was strong meat that the Lord was setting before them. They were about ready to jettison it all. But in six weeks' time, most of their confusion would be blown away by the mighty rushing pentecostal wind.

Note *what Jesus discerned* (16:19): "Now Jesus knew that they were desirous to ask him, and said unto them, Do ye inquire among yourselves of that I said, A little while, and ye shall not see me: and again, a little while, and ye shall see me?" He saw them talking to one another, shaking their heads in perplexity. They were like children in school when the teacher has just introduced a new mathematical concept, one beyond their present stages of learning. None of them can grasp it. They are afraid to ask the teacher for more instruction, so they ask one another, "Do you get it? I don't. What does he mean?"

The Lord broke into their discussion. Why pool their ignorance? Why not ask him to explain?

If the disciples were impatient with the Lord, he was certainly not impatient with them. Tenderly he went on to explain more. "A little while!" They did not understand that? Then maybe they would understand *a little weeping* (16:20-22). First he gave them *a word of information* (16:20) or explanation: "Verily, verily, I say unto you, That ye shall weep and lament, but the world shall rejoice: and ye shall be sorrowful, but your sorrow shall be turned into joy." Lamentation? Yes, but soon to be swallowed up in laughter.

Nothing more terribly reveals this world for what it is than this statement of the Lord, "The world shall rejoice." Peter would go out and weep bitterly. All of them would shed tears over the murder of their beloved master. But the world would rejoice. Stripped of its mask, the world's hatred for God and his Son is revealed. Worse, it was the religious authorities who took the lead in mocking Christ. Let any believer who is tempted to make friends with this world remember how it responded to the cross.

The Lord gave his disciples *a word of illustration* (16:21-22): "A woman when she is in travail hath sorrow, because her hour is come: but as soon as she is delivered of the child, she remembereth no more the anguish, for the joy that a man is born into the world. And ye now therefore have sorrow: but I will see you again, and your heart shall rejoice, and your joy no man taketh from you." This was an illustration anyone could understand. The birth of a child swallows up the pain of the delivery. By his appearances after his resurrection, the Lord Jesus turned the disciples' sorrow into joy. They forgot the dark three days and three nights of their anguish. Nor could the world, for all its malice and hate and organized spite, take away that joy.

Now comes *a little word* (16:23-24): *ask*. Note *whom we are to ask* (16:23): "And in that day ye shall ask me nothing. Verily,

verily, I say unto you, Whatsoever ye shall ask the Father in my name, he will give it you."

Some have seen in this verse a reference to the nation of Israel in the future. They link it with the woman in travail of the Lord's illustration (16:21) and link that woman with the woman of Revelation 12. The woman of Revelation 12 is undoubtedly the nation of Israel and the chapter itself a foreview of the coming great tribulation through which Israel is to pass. This prophetic view of these verses in John 16:21,23 is strengthened by the use of the definite article in verse 21 ("the woman" rather than "a woman") and by the Hebraism "in that day." This latter expression is a well-known prophetic formula. The formula first appears in Isaiah 2:11 where it is linked with "the day of the Lord" (Isaiah 2:12), another important prophetic phrase, also occurring for the first time there. If this prophetic view of the Lord's word "in that day" here is followed through, then we have here a glimpse of Israel, after the rapture of the church, appealing directly to Jehovah for help and not, as yet, using the name *Jesus* as the basis of appeal.

Whatever merits there may be in this view, and it is an interesting one, it hardly seems to be the primary meaning of the verse. "In that day ye shall ask me nothing." Our English word *ask* bears a double meaning. It can mean to make a request and it can mean to ask a question. The word is used in this latter sense in this statement. The word for "ask" here is *erotao* as in verses 5 and 19. In both those verses it is used of asking a question. The disciples had been asking one question after another, mostly questions betraying their lack of spiritual comprehension.

Peter had asked the Lord where he was going. Thomas had contradicted the Lord, saying they did not know where he was going and asking how then could they know the way. Philip had not asked a question but had wanted to be shown the Father. Jude wanted to know why the Lord was revealing himself to them, rather than to the world. Now they were asking one another what he meant by these sayings.

"In that day," he said, pointing to a not too distant day, "you will ask me nothing." The day was soon to come when the disciples would stop asking the Lord such questions. Although he would be gone, that other comforter, of whom he had been telling them, would be present. Pentecost would have effected a marvelous change. They would have the answers then, in that day.

At this point the Lord introduced a formula of his own, one

we have met frequently in the gospel of John: "Verily, verily" ("Indeed and in truth!"). According to the uniform employment of this formula, it introduces a new thought. The Lord continued: "Verily, verily, I say unto you, Whatsoever ye shall ask the Father in my name, he will give it you." The word for "ask" here is *aiteo,* the word for asking for something to be given, a word commonly used by an inferior addressing a superior. In the future, the Lord's people will be able to make their petitions directly to the Father. The fact that the Lord was going back to the Father effected this change. The return of Christ to the Father restored completely the connection broken by the sin of Adam. With perfect fellowship restored we can be sure that the Father will give us anything we ask in the name of his beloved Son, our Lord Jesus Christ. Needless to say, that rules out all petitions incongruent with Jesus' character.

We note also *why we are to ask* (16:24): "Hitherto have ye asked nothing in my name: ask, and ye shall receive, that your joy may be full." The Lord had already taught them this revolutionary concept of coming to God and appealing to him as "our Father which art in heaven" (Matthew 6:9; 7:7-11). But up to now they had not appealed to him in Jesus' name.

Coming to the Father in the name of Jesus would fill their souls with joy. Every time they did so, it would remind them of him and where he now was, and of what a friend they had in him.

There is also *a little wait* (16:25-28). We see the Lord now *speaking distinctly about the Father* (16:25): "These things have I spoken unto you in proverbs: but the time cometh, when I shall no more speak unto you in proverbs, but I will shew you plainly of the Father." From here to the end of the chapter we have an epilogue to the discourse, a kind of summing up without "proverbs" *(paroimiais,* "allegories" or "wayside sayings"). In this discourse he had used figures like the vine and the woman in travail. Much of his teaching in the past had been in parables and in figures of speech. Many of the Lord's discourses in John, centering around his I AM sayings, carried a deeper meaning than lay upon the surface. These mines of truth contained treasures the disciples themselves had not grasped.

In the closing summary of his discourse the Lord dispenses with all such devices, partly because of the attitude of the multitudes and partly because of the dullness of the disciples. The words, however, seem to go beyond that. Within twenty-four hours he was to be dead, but the grave would not silence him. He would rise from the dead, he would ascend on high, the Holy Spirit would come, light would dawn, the epistles would

shed new light on the gospels. The Holy Spirit would complete
the New Testament canon of Scripture. He would continue
throughout all the centuries of the Christian era to bring God's
redeemed people face to face with the storehouse of divine
truth its pages contain. Thus Christ would speak plainly; his
teaching would be unfolded, its innermost meanings made
clear.

There is also a word about our *speaking directly to the Father*
(16:26-28). No mediator, no intervening priest, will be needed,
for two reasons. First, because *the Son's Father loves the Son's
followers* (16:26-27a): "At that day ye shall ask in my name: and I
say not unto you, that I will pray the Father for you: For the
Father himself loveth you." The Lord does not promise to
petition the Father on their behalf. That might suggest distance, coldness, between the Father and them. They must never
get the idea that the Father somehow had to be persuaded to
answer their prayers. He loved them. He was eager to hear
them and answer them.

That does not rule out the Lord's high priestly ministry or his
advocacy of our needs. When Satan comes as the accuser, the
Lord is there. When any question is raised about our human
frailty and shortcomings, our sins and falls and failures, the
Lord is there to raise his pierced hands as token that his precious blood has not lost anything of its power. What the Lord is
teaching here is that the Father loves us as much as the Son
loves us, and reaches out to us as much as he, Jesus, reaches out
to us.

No mediator is needed for a second reason, *the Son's followers
love the Son's Father* (16:27b-28): "The Father himself loveth
you, because ye have loved me, and have believed that I came
out from God. I came forth from the Father, and am come into
the world: again, I leave the world, and go to the Father." So
completely does the Father identify with the Son and the Son
identify with the Father, that for us to love Christ is to love the
Father.

The Lord sums up his life on earth in four majestic statements: "I came forth from the Father" [his incarnation]. "I am
come into the world" [his mission]. "I leave the world" [his
passion]. "I go to the Father" [his ascension]. "For God so loved
the world, that he gave his only begotten Son, that whosoever
believeth in him should not perish, but have everlasting life"
(3:16).

It is love from beginning to end. Love conceived the plan of
our redemption. Love set it in motion and carried it through.
Love flowing ever and eternally between Father, Son, and Holy

Spirit; love embracing us, saving us, changing us, filling us, flowing back from us in Christ through the Spirit to the Father. Love is the stuff of which eternity is made.

2. Warning Words of Love (16:29-33)

The disciples were swept off their feet by the Lord's fourfold summary of his coming and going. Immediately they reacted. But in their reaction *their overconfidence was revealed* (16:29-30). Note first what they said about *his proverbs* (16:29): "His disciples said unto him, Lo, now speakest thou plainly, and speakest no proverb." The Lord's last statement was like a laser beam, concentrating into one powerful ray all the brightness of focused light. It penetrated into each of their hearts and for a moment they saw. They saw the master, the mission, the marvel, the mystery, and the ultimate majesty of it all. They burst out enthusiastically, "Lo, now speakest thou plainly!"

Note also what they said about *his person* (16:30): "Now are we sure that thou knowest all things, and needest not that any man should ask thee: by this we believe that thou camest forth from God." "Now we know!" they said. "Now we believe!" They were sincere. Christ had answered their unspoken questions. What more convincing proof could they have of his omniscience?

Again, the disciples had misinterpreted Christ's words, and as for the manner by which he was about to leave the world, the horror of that had not even begun to penetrate their minds.

"In that day ye shall ask me nothing," Jesus had said (16:23). Because the Lord had answered their questions, without their even putting them into words, the disciples interpreted his word at face value: "You will not need to ask me because in my omniscience I shall know and anticipate your every want." But what the Lord meant was quite different: "You will ask me nothing because you will have the Holy Spirit to illuminate and lead you." That was a different thing altogether.

"We believe that thou camest forth from God," the disciples added. As a group they barely surpassed Nicodemus who had said, "We know that thou art a teacher come from God" (3:1), and who had been surpassed by John the baptist who had said, "Behold the Lamb of God, which taketh away the sin of the world" (1:29). Their confession was a sad mix of dullness and discernment. The Lord did not reject their flawed confession of faith out of hand, but he clearly saw its inadequacy. Their enthusiasm was about to receive some very rude shocks, as well he knew.

So we see how *their overconfidence was rebuked* (16:31-33).

Their faith was *to be tested* (16:31-32): "Jesus answered them, Do ye now believe? Behold, the hour cometh, yea, is now come, that ye shall be scattered, every man to his own, and ye shall leave me alone: and yet I am not alone, because the Father is with me."

"Now we are sure!" the disciples said. "Do ye now believe?" Jesus replied. The Lord's *now* is not the same as theirs. He did not cast doubt on their newfound faith and joy. But he knew it would not last. "Do ye now believe?" he said. The Greek word suggests a crisis. And what that crisis was, he knew full well. Marching feet were beating out their tattoo on the cloistered courts of the temple. The voice of the mob was sounding in the streets. Judas was coming. The disciples could not hear these ominous sounds and were still complacent about Judas. But Jesus knew that the storm would break within the hour.

"Ye shall be scattered," he warned, "every man to his own." The word is *ta idia*, "to his own home" (19:27). The bond that held them together was about to be severed. Each one, thinking only of his personal safety, would run off into the night, making for his own home as fast as he could. How much they needed to beware of the fleeting emotion of the moment.

"Do ye now believe?" Jesus asked. Take the question and put the emphasis on each word in turn. See what it yields in terms of self-examination. Let us put the acid to the professed gold of our own profession of faith and make sure that what we have is real.

Was the Lord looking disconsolately at these men as he said, "Ye . . . shall leave me alone"? They all would abandon him, though later John would recover and Peter would come back and follow afar off until his denials drove him in self-horror to his own Gethsemane.

Surely part of the Lord's anguish was the loneliness of it all. "Yet I am not alone," he added, "because the Father is with me." It was a good thing the Lord was not counting on their support in the terrible hours ahead (Zechariah 13:7). His Father would still be there. Peter, James, and John would fall asleep, even after he tried three times to awaken them, but his Father would still be there. Judas and the mob would come and the disciples would all flee, but his Father would be there. Caiaphas, Herod, and Pilate would browbeat and bully him, but his Father would still be there. Peter would curse, swear, and then run away in tears, but his Father would still be there. He would be bruised and beaten, scoffed at and scourged, but his Father would still be there. He would stumble beneath his cross, he would be nailed in anguish to the tree, the rabbis and the rabble would mock him, but his Father would still be there. Right down to that terrible moment when even God would forsake him.

But that dread time would pass and his Father would still be there. "I am not alone; the Father is with me." It was our Lord's sole comfort as he looked into the faces of these men, so suddenly confident in their flaming but fleeting faith.

Their faith would be tested, would fail, but that would not be the end of it. Their faith was *to be triumphant* (16:33) at last. They would have *peace through his word* (16:33a): "These things I have spoken unto you, that in me ye might have peace." We must note the first and most important sphere in which the believer lives. "In me," Jesus said, "you will have peace."

Every believer in Christ has taken up abode in Christ. The best illustration of the Lord's words are found in the Old Testament. The storms of God's wrath were about to sweep across the antediluvian hills and plains. The cities of that civilization were to be swept away. The scouring waters of the flood were to search out the mountaintops. There was only one way of salvation, only one place of safety: in the ark. What it meant for Noah to be in the ark is what it means for us to be in Christ. In that ark, Noah could rest in peace. In Christ, come what may, the believer has peace. The Lord has pledged his word to that.

Despite the disciples' failure—and it was total—and despite their remorse—and it was real—in the end their faith would triumph. They would have *power in this world* (16:33b): "In the world ye shall have tribulation: but be of good cheer, I have overcome the world." That is the believer's other address. Each of us is "in Christ" and we are also "in the world." And as long as we are in the world that hated God and his Christ, we can expect tribulation. The word is *thlipsis,* the same word used by Jesus to describe the anguish of the woman in travail (16:21). We must be careful not to confuse the agelong, worldwide persecution of God's people in this age with the great tribulation that awaits the Jewish people in particular and the world in general after the rapture of the church (Matthew 24:21,29). That period of torment is to last a prescribed three and a half years and is called "the time of Jacob's trouble" (Jeremiah 30:7). It is also a time when God will be pouring out his undiluted wrath on this world.

Did the Lord allow his eye to run down the long centuries of the Christian era? Was he seeing all the terrible persecutions that Christians would be forced to face? He warns the disciples what to expect. He bequeaths to them good cheer, good courage. He himself was to die on a Roman cross the next day. His own unwavering courage he left his people as their legacy. "I have overcome the world," he said. With that he showed his disciples (and us) how it is done: he began to pray.

II. The Lord Talks to His Father (17:1-26)

The Lord is still walking along the Gethsemane road. We have been listening to him talk to his followers. We continue listening as he talks to his Father. Like Moses at the burning bush, we would do well to remove the shoes from our feet. The place whereon we now stand is holy ground.

This remarkable model prayer contains none of the things that take up so much room in our prayers. All its items of petition and praise are of a spiritual nature.

We can picture the Lord Jesus pausing now, in his walk toward Gethsemane. The disciples are clustered around him in a tight little group.

"Their way led them through one of the city gates," says Archbishop French,

probably that which then corresponded to the present gate of St. Stephen, down the steep sides of the ravine, across the wady of the Kidron, which lay a hundred feet below, and up to the green and quiet slope beyond it. To one who has visited the scene at that season of the year and at that hour of the night, who has felt the solemn hush of the silence even at this short distance from the city wall, who has seen the deep shadows flung by the great boles of the ancient olive trees, and the chequering of light that falls on the sward through their moon-silvered leaves, it is more easy to realise the awe which crept over those few Galileans, as in almost unbroken silence, with something perhaps of secrecy, and with a weight of mysterious dread brooding over their spirits, they followed him, who with bowed head and sorrowing heart, walked before them to his willing doom (Frederick W. Farrar, *The Life of Christ, Vol. 2.*, London: Cassell, Petter and Galpin, n.d., pp. 305-306).

A. The World from Which He Had Come (17:1-10)

1. His Supreme Goals (17:1-4)

The first part of this prayer is occupied with the fact that he himself was from another world than this sin cursed earth. We note what he had to say about four things. First, we see his supreme goals. His foremost goal was to manifest down here *the person of his Father* (17:1): "These words spake Jesus, and lifted up his eyes to heaven, and said, Father, the hour is come; glorify thy Son, that thy Son also may glorify thee."

Between him as Son and God as Father was an indissoluble relationship. For the Father to glorify the Son was for the Son to glorify the Father. The prayer that the Father might glorify the Son was a prayer that there might be a fuller display of the Son's true, divine nature.

So much had been veiled when the word became flesh. As has been noted, the Lord had not laid aside his deity when he was incarnated in human flesh. Rather, he had put aside his glory. He had restricted himself to be and behave as man—man as God always intended man to be. Except for rare glimpses given to his inner circle of disciples, what people saw when they saw Jesus was an extraordinary man, a uniquely gifted man; an attractive, kind, and loving man; an astonishingly good, perfect, and sinless man—but a man.

Now "the hour is come," Jesus said. It was toward this focal point in time that his way had led, ever since in a past eternity God the Father, God the Son, and God the Holy Spirit had decided to act in creation and consequently in redemption.

We never have reference to the sufferings of Christ without corresponding references to the glory that was to follow. So, as the hour was upon him when he must be betrayed and beaten, accused by men and accursed of God, cursed and crucified, mocked and murdered, the Lord prayed that, even as men heaped on him every indignity and God heaped on him the burden of all human sin and guilt, even so he might be glorified. And indeed he was. The cross—that Roman gallows, an object of suffering and shame—was about to become the symbol of hope to millions of people in all ages and from all lands.

The cross reigns supreme at the center of all true faith. It has become the theme of a thousand hymns. "God forbid," cried Paul, "that I should glory, save in the cross of our Lord Jesus Christ" (Galatians 6:14).

Jesus also wanted to manifest down here *the power of his Father* (17:2). "As thou hast given him power over all flesh, that he should give eternal life to as many as thou hast given him." We note *the everlasting lordship* (17:2a) invested in the Son. He has been given "power over all flesh." He had power over the fish of the sea—whether in schools of fish or as individuals they flung themselves into nets or brought coins in their mouths at his command. He had power over the beasts of the earth. Mark tells us that in his temptation, he was with wild animals in the wilderness (Mark 1:13). When he rode into Jerusalem in triumph, he did so astride an unbroken colt. He had power over the fowl of the air. The cock crowed not a fraction of a second too soon or a moment too late, just at that critical moment to awaken Peter's conscience and recover his faith.

"Power over all flesh," however, doubtless refers primarily to all human flesh, over humankind in all its weakness, sinfulness, and transitoriness. It was God's plan that the first man Adam should have enormous power and authority invested in him and that he should rule over this planet and, for all we know, eventually over the galaxy. "Have dominion," was God's divine decree to humankind, to the first couple (Genesis 1:26-28). Even today, with our primeval powers impaired and limited by the fall, humankind still retains extraordinary abilities and skills. We are able to put people on the moon, split the atom, tinker with the genetic code. We perform prodigious feats of engineering; our technology is to be seen on every hand. What we might have accomplished in the universe, had we never fallen into sin, we cannot tell. We have some glimpses in the miracles of Christ of the kind of sovereignty over material things God evidently intended human beings to exercise.

Sadly, the human race instead bears the marks of the fall. Our history on this planet has been one of enmity and war. God had invested all authority in Jesus (Hebrews 2), the second man. The world awaits his return. Romans 8 tells us that the world of created things is "standing on tiptoe" (as J. B. Phillips renders it) waiting to see the sons of God coming into their own. When Jesus returns and reigns and exercises that "power over all flesh" about which he here talked to his Father, we shall see indeed what human beings might have done with this wonderful planet on which we live.

The power of the Lord Jesus is evidenced also in terms of *the everlasting life* (17:2b): "That he should give eternal life to as many as thou hast given him." Here we touch the fringe of that robe of God's sovereignty in redemption. Such statements must never be isolated from the whole body of revelation. That God has given certain members of Adam's race to Christ, and that Christ has given to those chosen ones eternal life, is perfectly clear. But statements such as this must always be balanced by those equally inspired statements of Scripture that attribute to us power of choice, moral accountability, and responsibility to believe. In this prayer, for instance, verse 3 is clearly modified by verse 12. The fact remains that God has chosen us in Christ and Christ has given us life without end.

The hallmark of saving faith follows quickly: "And this is life eternal, that they might know thee the only true God, and Jesus Christ, whom thou hast sent" (17:3). Millions of people claim to know God but do not know Christ. They are the victims of false religion. To claim to know God but to deny the deity of Christ is a fatal error. What we have here, however, is not so much a definition of eternal life as a statement of the reason why Christ imparts that life—so that we may know his Father, the only true God, as Christ knows him.

The Lord's goals not only include manifesting the person and power of his Father, but also manifesting *the purposes of his Father* (17:4): "I have glorified thee on the earth: I have finished the work which thou gavest me to do." Thus the Lord summed up the divine purpose in his coming to this planet. From the incarnation to the ascension, the Lord Jesus glorified his Father. He finished the work entrusted to him. Although the crucial part of that work still lay ahead, the Lord put it all in the past tense. There would be no wavering, no turning back, no failure. He was wholly committed to the work of the cross, as he and his Father both knew. The agony in the garden would not shake this resolve. The indignities and injustices of Gabbatha, the horror of Golgotha, and the silence of the grave were stepping stones on the predetermined way. That the Lord would carry the divine purpose out to fulfillment was never in question. His obedience would stand the test. It was as good as done.

2. His Special Glory (17:5)

"And now, O Father, glorify thou me with thine own self with the glory which I had with thee before the world was" (17:5). To paraphrase those words: "So far this world has seen me only as the incarnate Son; now let the world see me as the infinite one."

There is a glory beyond the brightness of the noonday sun, a glory more splendid than the rainbow in the sky, a glory not of this world, inherent in the godhead, before which the shining ones shrink (Isaiah 6:2), which blinded Saul of Tarsus (Acts 9:3), which laid the apostle John prostrate (Revelation 1:17). This was the glory that Jesus put aside when he came to earth. The sight of it would have dazzled one and all. The glory the disciples saw on the mount of transfiguration was not the glory of his deity but the glory of his sinless humanity. The Lord is asking that, once again, though now garbed in human clay, his pristine glory, the glory he shared with his Father before he spoke the world into being, might be his again. It is his now. It will be displayed for all to see at his coming again.

3. His Spiritual Gifts (17:6-8)

The gifts that were *given to him* (17:6-7) were of two kinds. The Lord was given *certain people* (17:6): "I have manifested thy name unto the men which thou gavest me out of the world: thine they were, and thou gavest them me; and they have kept thy word." We were God's before we were Christ's. All people belong to God by virtue of the fact that he is creator. Some belong to Christ by virtue of the fact that he is redeemer and they have believed in him. They have accepted the truth about the Father that his Son came to reveal. The world had failed to recognize Jesus as the one who revealed the Father, but these men and women *(anthropoi)*, this select group, had been given to Christ as the Father's spiritual gift to his Son.

One wonders what the disciples made of all this. Did their eyes open in wonder at such amazing truths? Once they had said to him, "Teach us to pray." Were they all ears now, hanging on every word, treasuring up each precious phrase? John evidently was. But what about the others? Were they already yawning and fighting their boneweary tiredness after this long and strenuous day?

We speak of a gift fit for a king. We wonder what we can give to the person who has everything. What about a gift for God—for one who has only to speak and angels appear by the myriad, bright and shining, fair as the morning, swift and strong and gifted and eager to serve? What about a gift for one whose word can create a hundred million galaxies full of astounding wonders that stretch to the breaking point our human powers even to count, to say nothing of comprehend? What about a gift for God? What would God give his Son? *Us!* Wonder of wonders! Mystery of mysteries!

The Lord was also given *certain prerogatives* (17:7): "Now they have known that all things whatsoever thou hast given me are of thee." Not only certain people, but certain things. These men had entered into these things. He had shown many of these things to an unbelieving world. Already they had trampled them underfoot and were turning again to rend him. But these men who were now with him had believed. They had recognized that the things given to him had been given to him by the Father: his power to cleanse lepers, set demoniacs free, give sight to the blind, raise the dead, and speak "wonderful words of life" such as no one ever spoke before.

The response of these men did not seem like very much. But for them to see the source of these things was a spiritual miracle more wonderful than the miracle of a man born physically blind being enabled, for the first time, to see the wonder of a tree, the glory of a sunset, the mobile mystery of a human face.

The Lord spoke to his Father also of the gifts *given by him* (17:8): "For I have given unto them the words which thou gavest me; and they have received them, and have known surely that I came out from thee, and they have believed that thou didst send me." Did Pilate believe that? Or Caiaphas? Or Herod Antipas? Not for a moment. Did the learned rabbis believe that? Gamaliel, for instance, the revered disciple of Hillel and the teacher of young Saul of Tarsus? Did Caesar on his throne believe that? Or Philo, the renowned teacher of Alexandria? Did the scholars on Mars Hill in Athens believe it? Not for a moment. But it was true.

Peter, James, John, and the others believed it. In the vast desert of this world's barren unbelief, the belief of these men in his words, as coming directly from God, and in his ultimate origin as coming out from the Father, was a glorious oasis where the thirsty soul of the Savior could rejoice and stoop and drink. He had given the most precious gift in the universe to them: the knowledge of what he was, the channel through which the Father's lifegiving words could flow out to humankind; and the knowledge of who he was, the one who, eternally coequal and coexistent with the Father, had come out from the Father to assume human form and sojourn on earth for a while.

4. His Sovereign Grace (17:9-10)

He talks to the Father about *those excluded from his prayer* (17:9a): "I pray for them: I pray not for the world." That is not to say of course that the Lord did not care about the lost. He cared for each and every person with a compassion that was even at that moment taking him step by step to the cross. But these were the men who were to take the news to the world and right now it was more important that he pray for them than that he should pray for the world. Nothing now could change the course of the world. Within hours it would have done its worst.

He talks of *those exalted in his prayer* (17:9b-10): "I pray . . . for them which thou hast given me; for they are thine. And all mine are thine, and thine are mine; and I am glorified in them." What an astonishing thing for him to say about these men. The foul oaths and curses with which he would deny his Lord were already in Peter's heart. The swift feet by means of which these men would flee headlong through the night, leaving him abandoned to his foes, were already shod. Their fear was but sleeping for the moment. "I am glorified in them," Jesus said. "They are thine . . . and mine!"—as though he were talking about the crown jewels of heaven. Which he was.

Jesus did not see these men as they were just then, huddled around him, half listening, minds wandering, full of questions and interruptions. He saw them as "complete in him." He saw, not just the rough stone, but the cut and shining diamond. He saw these men as we too shall see them in a coming day when at last they (and we) shall be like him "for we shall see him as he is."

Thus the Lord talked to his Father about the world from which he had come. He had just told the disciples he was going back home. The opening verses of this great prayer are full of his thoughts of home. The terrors of the way between are swallowed up by the glory that awaits him on the other side.

Heaven to Jesus was a real place. His heart was full to over-flowing with thoughts of that eternal home. Now his prayer turned to deal with the hostile world in which he still was.

B. The World in Which He Was Now (17:11-23)

Once this world had been a kind of suburb of the world from which he had come. But that was before "by one man sin entered into the world, and death by sin; and so death passed upon all men, for that all have sinned" (Romans 5:12). This world had now become an alient outpost in the universe, a plague spot in the galaxy. This world was preparing to murder him. The wood for the cross was already cut. The nails for his hands and feet were already forged. The spear with which to pierce his hands and feet was already made. The place for the dark and dreadful deed was already marked out, a skull shaped hill outside a city wall. The legal machinery of kangaroo courts, lying witnesses, malicious prosecutors, howling mobs, bullying soldiers, cowardly judge, and illegal sentence was already fueled, oiled, and ready to go.

Jesus knew this. What did he pray about, just an hour or so before? He prayed for others; he prayed that his Father might be praised in this world; he prayed that his followers might be protected in this world.

1. His Detachment from This World (17:11-13)

The second theme of this prayer is in two parts. We note first *his separation* (17:11a): "And now I am no more in the world." His own detachment from the world was complete. He was finished with the world, as far as his physical presence was concerned. Heart and soul he regarded himself as with his Father. By three o'clock of the coming afternoon he would be dead, and the world would be finished with him. Thereafter, until his coming again in glory, heaven's dealings with this world would be in the hands of the Holy Spirit. Once his physical protection was removed, the disciples (and his bloodbought people down the ages) would need the special protection of the Father.

Second, we have *his solicitation* (17:11b-12). First comes *a request* (17:11b): "But these are in the world, and I come to thee. Holy Father, keep through thine own name those whom thou hast given me." When speaking of himself the Lord says "Father"; when speaking of his disciples he says "Holy Father"; when speaking of the world he says "righteous Father."

Between himself and his Father there was a simple relationship, a Father-Son relationship. No qualifying adjective was needed. The relationship was one of complete harmony, unspoiled by any clash of wills.

Between the disciples and the Father there was a sanctifying relationship. They were to remember that although he was their Father, he was a holy Father. Let them beware of the inherent sinfulness of their old natures, of sin, carnality, and worldliness. Let there be none of that familiarity with holy things that breeds flippancy.

Between the world and the Father there was a solemn relationship. He is the righteous Father. Between him and the world stands the cross, on which the world murdered his Son—and also some terrible unfinished business held in abeyance for the time being only because where sin abounds there does grace much more abound.

The world that had turned on the Savior would turn on the saints. "I come to thee," Jesus said and no doubt his heart leaped at the thought. He was going home. "But these are in the world." His heart went out to them. Soon the world's rage and ridicule would be turned on these men and their converts down the ages. The world would not change. He had not come to change the world but to call out of the world a people for his name. In the end the world would have to be destroyed. So there was a request: "Keep through thine own name those whom thou hast given me." God's own good name is pledged on their behalf.

Then comes *a review* (17:12). First, the Lord reviews his *testimony* (17:12a): "While I was with them in the world, I kept them in thy name: those that thou gavest me I have kept." He always stood between them and the world. He came to their rescue when the world demanded of the disciples why John's disciples fasted, but they didn't (Matthew 9:14-15). He came to their rescue at the foot of the mount of transfiguration, when the powerless disciples were confronted by a distressed Father, a demoniac boy, and a deriding world (Matthew 17:14-21). He came to their rescue when an official investigated their tax status (Matthew 17:24-27). He would come to their rescue that very night, when Judas arrived with the mob (John 18:7-9).

Then the Lord reviewed a *tragedy* (17:12b): "And none of them is lost, but the son of perdition; that the scripture might be fulfilled." One such Scripture was Psalm 41:9, already quoted by Jesus (John 13:18). The word the Lord used here for "lost" is *apollumi* (it occurs twelve times in John), a word used of the doom of the sinner, and one of the strongest words in the Greek language for stating final and hopeless destruction.

The title "son of perdition" is used elsewhere in Scripture in only one place, and there it is a title of the lawless one, the man of sin, the devil's messiah (2 Thessalonians 2:3). In both cases the definite article is used, *the* son of perdition. Some have taken this to be a positive identification of Judas with the antichrist and believe that the antichrist will be Judas raised from the dead. That is unlikely since the man of sin is to be a gentile, not a Jew. He comes up out of the sea (Revelation 13) and is "the little horn" of Daniel 7:8, a coming gentile world ruler. The word for "perdition" is *apoleia,* a cognate word to *apollumi*—"not one perished but the son of perishing," the solemn repetition of kindred words adding to the force of the statement. Judas, at that very moment, at the head of his armed mob, was marching straight to perdition. He would be dead and damned before Jesus dismissed his own spirit and marched down to the nether region to proclaim the triumph of his cross.

Then we have *his satisfaction* (17:13): "And now come I to thee; and these things I speak in the world, that they might have my joy fulfilled in themselves." The Lord keeps on talking about it. It was for "the joy that was set before him" that he "endured the cross, despising the shame" (Hebrews 12:2). He had said it only a moment before (17:11), and he says it again: "I come to thee." Beyond was glory!

The joy that filled his soul was to spill over into the souls of his saints. His joy could not be full if their cup was not full too. So he prayed that "they might have my joy fulfilled in themselves."

2. His Disciples in This World (17:14-23)

Our Lord had a fivefold request for his disciples. First, he prayed for *their protection* (17:14a) in this world: "I have given them thy word; and the world hath hated them." It is the

Father's word that determines the world's attitude toward those who cherish that word. The world will not accept it. That word disproves the world's religions, denies its philosophies, disregards its wisdom. The world hates God's word and also those who proclaim it.

It is interesting to observe how often in this prayer the world is seen as the special antagonist of God the Father. This is uniformly true throughout Scripture. "If any man love the world, the love of the Father is not in him" (1 John 2:15). "For all that is in the world, the lust of the flesh, and the lust of the eyes, and the pride of life, is not of the Father, but of the world" (1 John 2:16).

In like manner, the devil is the particular adversary of God the Son. Thus we see Satan as "a great red dragon" standing "before the woman which was ready to be delivered, for to devour her child as soon as it was born" (Revelation 12:4, something fulfilled in history by Herod at Christ's birth, Matthew 2:7-18). "For this purpose the Son of God was manifested, that he might destroy the works of the devil" (1 John 3:8).

Similarly the flesh and the Holy Spirit are set one against the other: "My spirit shall not always strive with man, for that he also is flesh" (Genesis 6:3). "That which is born of the flesh is flesh; and that which is born of the Spirit is spirit" (John 3:6). "For the flesh lusteth against the Spirit, and the Spirit against the flesh: and these are contrary the one to the other" (Galatians 5:17).

The determined enmity of the world toward God's people centers around the fact that God's people have a book the world hates. The Lord urges this as another reason why his Father should take them under his own wing.

The Lord prayed also about *their prospects* (17:14b,c) in this world: "And the world hath hated them, because they are not of the world even as I am not of the world." The world likes to reduce everything to its own mediocrity. It demands conformity. It likes to reduce everything to room temperature. We are not to be too hot or too cold. We are not to rock the boat. If we do, the world will turn nasty.

Jesus rocked the boat; he refused to conform. The world could not pour him into its mold. He was too good, too clever, too brave, too honest, too different. So the world murdered him. Now it reaches out its bloodstained hand to us. We are expected to shake hands with the world over the blood of Jesus. But we are not of the world, just as he was not of the world. We are in the world, but we are not of the world. Sooner or later the world will treat us as it treated him, and for the same reasons. Thus the world killed the apostles and has persecuted the saints. So Jesus prayed about the prospects of his people in a world held captive by the devil.

The Lord prayed, too, about *their purity* (17:15-17) in this world. Despite its fair façade, this world is a foul place. The Lord prayed about *their security* (17:15-16) in a world where every path, every offer, every thing is potentially defiling. As his people in this world, our security is twofold. We are to keep in mind *his almighty strength* (17:15): "I pray not that thou shouldest take them out of the world, but that thou shouldest keep them from the evil." The prayer is not just that we might be kept from evil, but that we be kept from the evil one, the prince of this world, the god of this world (cf. the parallel phrase in 1 John 5:18-19). Jesus prayed that his people might be protected from a personal and real devil. This world is his lair. As the believer is ensphered in Christ, so the unbeliever is ensphered in the evil one. Our citizenship is in heaven; the unbeliever's citizenship is on earth. "The whole world lieth in wickedness" (1 John 5:19).

The Lord did not pray that his people be at once removed from the scene of danger; this world is also the scene of duty. We are left here as his ambassadors. The Lord prayed rather that the Father would make bare his almighty arm and keep us from the evil one. His strength is available to us in the hour of temptation. The evil one is no match for the holy one.

We are to keep in mind also *our alien status* (17:16): "They are not of the world, even as I am not of the world." We belong to another world. We have been "translated into the kingdom of [God's] dear Son," as Paul puts it (Colossians 1:13). This vision of citizenship in another world gripped Abraham and made him a stranger and sojourner down here (Hebrews 11:9-10; Genesis 23:3-4). When we are tempted to sin we should claim our citizenship. We should say: "No, I cannot do that. I am the child of a king. God is my Father; his Son is my Savior; his Spirit is my comforter and guide. I would not think of thus bringing dishonor on my family or my country."

The Lord talked to his Father about his disciples and *their sanctification* (17:17) in this world: "Sanctify them through thy truth: thy word is truth." God's truth is the separating force. Let us get it into our hearts that what God has to say about everything is true—absolutely and not relatively, completely and not partially, vitally and not incidentally. The end of God's truth is not wisdom—the goal of the Greeks, the philosophers, and the learned of this world—but holiness. The word of God has a transforming virtue about it.

Next the Lord prays about the disciples and *their program* (17:18-21) in this world. They were to be in this world as *his sent ones* (17:18): "As thou hast sent me into the world, even so have I also sent them into the world." The expression "as . . . even so" denotes an exact parallel. Jesus said to Nicodemus, "As Moses lifted up the serpent in the wilderness, even so must the Son of man be lifted up" (John 3:14). Paul wrote, "As Christ was raised up from the dead by the glory of the Father, even so we also should walk in newness of life" (Romans 6:4).

The Lord Jesus came into this world to make himself wholly available to God through the indwelling, ungrieved Holy Spirit; for the Holy Spirit is the one through whom human beings make themselves available to God. The Holy Spirit is the one through whom God makes himself available to us.

All that Jesus is as God is available to all that we are as human beings, through the indwelling Holy Spirit, as we make all that we are as human beings available to all that Jesus is as God. The Holy Spirit is the one through whom we make ourselves available to Christ and the one through whom Christ makes himself available to us. Thus, as the Lord Jesus lived on earth to represent the Father, so we now live on earth to represent Christ. He prolongs his days (Isaiah 53:10) through us and carries on his work on earth through us.

The disciples were his "sent" ones. The word is *apostello,* the same as that used by the Lord of himself. The Lord said he was the sent one six times in this prayer and (together with the use of the word *pempo)* no less than forty-three times in John's gospel. The word *apostello* gives us our English word *apostle.*

The disciples were to be in this world as *his sanctified ones* (17:19): "And for their sakes I sanctify myself, that they also might be sanctified through the truth." The word for "sanctified" as used here carries the idea of consecration or dedication. The idea is not so much that of making holy in terms of moral character as that of being set apart for God, as for instance the Old Testament animals, destined for the altar, were set apart for God. John does not show us the Lord's agony in Gethsemane and his determined consecration to his Father's purpose: "Not my will, but thine, be done." Here he shows us the Lord's resolute determination to be "obedient unto death, even the death of the cross."

The Lord's consecration was to be not just the disciples' example, but also the expression of the disciples' own consecration. "For their sakes I sanctify myself, that they also might be sanctified." The Lord was set apart for God in life (Hebrews 10:5-8) and now he is set apart for God in death (Hebrews 10:9-

10). Thus the writer of Hebrews says, "We are sanctified through the offering of the body of Jesus Christ once for all." The death of Christ automatically sets the believer aside from the world that perpetrated that murder and sets the believer apart for God. "That they also might be sanctified through the truth," Jesus added, or "in truth," as some have rendered it— truly, really, not just in name or empty profession. Once let the truth of Calvary grip our souls and the cross will slay any lingering appeal the world may have for us. Thus Paul speaks of the cross: "God forbid that I should glory, save in the cross of our Lord Jesus Christ, by whom the world is crucified unto me, and I unto the world" (Galatians 6:14). Let us but catch a glimpse of what the world did to our Lord and that will be enough to transform our attitudes toward both the world and him. The world becomes at once both a battlefield and a missionfield.

Then too the disciples were to be in this world as *his successful ones* (17:20-21). The Lord's vision and prayer are now broadened to embrace the apostolic mission in the world. The church is now *envisioned by Christ* (17:20): "Neither pray I for these alone, but for them also which shall believe on me through their word." The church is not mentioned by name in John's gospel. By the time he wrote this gospel, however, it was already a force to be reckoned with in the world. The apostles left Jerusalem to evangelize the world. Indeed, by the time John wrote, the Romans had made an end of Jerusalem, the temple, and whatever myth there might have been about a "mother church."

The Lord here prays for the church. The apostolic mission in the world was not to bring in the millennial kingdom, not to reform and revitalize Judaism, but to be the Holy Spirit's instruments to bring into being a new, divine entity called the church, to win souls, build up believers, pass on Christ's teachings, and write the New Testament.

The Lord's all seeing eye ran down the centuries. He saw all those who would believe as a result of what these first Christians did in the power of the Holy Spirit. He prayed for them. He saw us. He prayed for us.

The Lord continued with this new thought. We see the church now *ensphered in Christ* (17:21): "That they all may be one; as thou, Father, art in me, and I in thee, that they also may be one in us: that the world may believe that thou hast sent me." Here are both a mystical oneness and a manifest oneness.

What we have in the world today is a church divided against itself, torn into factions large and small. There is the Roman Catholic Church, the Greek Orthodox Church, the Coptic Church. There are state churches. There are various nonconformist denominational churches. There are cults, quasi-Christian cancers on the body of the church. Unsaved people look at "the church" and see Baptists and Brethren, Methodists and Mormons, Presbyterians and Pentecostals, Catholics and Congregationalists. They are both skeptical and confused.

Many of these churches started in times of revival, but with the passing of years have become moribund, dead. Some started as a protest against liberalism, legalism, or false doctrine. Some followed forceful leaders, determined to have their own way over this, that, or the other. Some have been spawned by the father of lies himself. Many, even in churches that hold to vital truth, are divided over particular issues. Baptism, eternal security, the second coming of Christ, the nature and validity of gifts, the person of Christ, the sovereignty of God, church government—there is hardly an area of doctrine over which one church does not disagree with another church.

How then can we be one? What agreement can there be between the amillennialist and the dispensationalist, between the Arminian and the Calvinist, between the fundamentalist and the liberal, between those who hold to infant baptism and those who hold to baptism of believers? The answer of the liberal is compromise—an ecumenical church in which doctrinal differences are waived in favor of a vast, organized world church council. That kind of conglomerate is certainly not what Christ had in mind when he prayed for the unity of the church.

As we come back to the Lord's prayer for the unity of believers we must recognize his omniscience. He knew the divisions, many of them necessary divisions, that would develop during ensuing centuries and would produce what, for want of a better word, we can call Christendom. In what way, then, can we understand the Lord's prayer?

In the first place, he prayed for a mystical oneness, and that prayer has been answered to the full. The mystical church of Christ is one, wholly, completely, indivisibly one. This is the unique work of the Holy Spirit on the day of Pentecost and throughout this present age. He is baptizing individual believers into the mystical body of Christ (1 Corinthians 12:12-27). There is no schism in the mystical body of Christ. He is the head; we are the members. Each member is washed in his blood, energized by his Holy Spirit, united to Christ, perfect and complete in him. This is the church in its universal aspect, the church as seen in Ephesians, a glorious church without spot or wrinkle or any such thing, untarnished, untouched by time, spread out through all time and space, rooted in eternity, the bride of Christ.

In the second place, the Lord prayed for a manifest oneness. This is not the universal church, which no one has yet seen; this refers to the local church—be it a Baptist church or a Presbyterian church, or a Lutheran church or some other kind of church—to any local body of believers who love the Lord Jesus, who are saved by his grace, who are seeking to walk in the light of God's word, who are drawn together for worship and fellowship and Christian service, holding fast to the truth as it is in Christ. Here the Lord is praying for unity and peace within these local congregations of his people. Then as the ungodly look on, or are introduced to the church, they are convinced that this is of God. They believe in Christ for themselves because they have seen and sensed Christ in the midst of his people.

The Lord continues in his prayer for his disciples and prays for *their perfection* (17:22-23) in this world. He included two things in this particular request. He prayed that *his glory might be imparted to them* (17:22a): "And the glory which thou gavest me I have given them." This is not the glory of his deity—he laid aside that glory at his incarnation (Philippians 2:6-8) for the duration of his earthly sojourn. This is the glory of his perfect and sinless humanity: "God manifest in flesh," God seen, known, heard, and touched in the glorious person of the Lord Jesus.

The Lord has now handed on the torch to us. As he made himself available to his Father, we are to make ourselves available to Christ. The measure in which we through the indwelling Holy Spirit make ourselves available to Christ is the measure in which Christ makes himself available to us. The more we are available to him, the more of his glory will be seen in us. We have all known saints of God who radiate the loveliness of Jesus.

He prayed that *his goals might be implemented by them* (17:22b-23), that there might be *a character transformation* (17:22b-23a) in them: "That they may be one, even as we are one: I in them, and thou in me, that they may be made perfect in one." God's ultimate goal for his people is that they may be brought into perfect oneness with him, and that involves a transformation of character. They have to be perfected. The word is *teleioo*, the same word previously translated "finish"—"I have finished the work which thou gavest me to do" (17:4).

From the standpoint of our standing, that has already been accomplished in Christ. God sees us perfect and complete in Christ. That is our position. From the standpoint of our state, the work is still going on. The indwelling Holy Spirit continues the perfecting process. We are not perfect yet, in the everyday practice of the Christian life. That is our condition. At the rapture "we shall all be changed, In a moment, in the twinkling of an eye, at the last trump" (1 Corinthians 15:51-52). "We shall be like him; for we shall see him as he is" (1 John 3:2). Our state will be brought up to our standing instantly and eternally.

He prays too that there might be a *convincing testimony* (17:23b): "And that the world may know that thou hast sent me, and hast loved them, as thou hast loved me." That is what the world is waiting to see: divine love in action. The most distinctive thing about Jesus was his love for his Father, family, friends, followers, foes. He loved Judas as much as he loved John; he loved Annas as much as he loved Andrew; he loved Pilate as much as he loved Peter. He loved the two dying thieves. He loved the Roman soldier whose spear pierced his side. He loved the man who punched him in the face, the man who wrenched the beard from his cheeks, the man who crowned him with thorns, the man who scourged him to the bone, the man who spat in his face.

The Lord Jesus lived his life on earth bathed in his Father's love. We are to live our lives on earth bathed in his. Then the world will "know," Jesus said. The centurion and the soldiers did. "This was the Son of God," they said. The word for "know" is *ginosko*. It means to know by experience, to know by becoming acquainted, to learn, to perceive; it is the knowledge of grateful recognition.

C. The World and Who He Was (17:24-26)

The Lord, then, prayed about the world in which he was. He comes now to the closing sentences. These sentences are taken up primarily with the Lord's person—with who he was and how the knowledge of that should affect his own.

1. His Pre-existence in That World (17:24)

We note *his desire* (17:24a): "Father, I will that they also, whom thou hast given me, be with me where I am." He wants us. He wants us to be where he is. Heaven would be incomplete for us without him. Of that we are quite sure. It is not the house that makes the home. It is the loved ones we find there. But the opposite is also equally true, and it is amazing that it should be so. Heaven is incomplete for him without us.

There in the darkness on the road to Gethsemane, he was surrounded by a group of men at whom this world's great would not have looked twice. "Unlearned and ignorant men" was their contemptuous estimate of them (Acts 4:13). They were not polished or cultured members of the social elite. They were not successful financiers controlling commercial empires. They were not the intellectuals of the day. They were not scions of noble descent. They were not powerful members of the ruling establishment. They wore homespun peasant clothes. They were fishermen folk from the north, speaking the native Aramaic with a thick country accent. They were a motley group, typical of the majority of those down through the ages who have given their hearts to Christ. They barely understood much of what he had said. They would run away at the first sign of serious trouble. They could not be compared for a moment with the shining ones who surrounded his throne on high. In the original order of creation they were lower than the angels. Gabriel the messenger angel or Michael the martial angel were far greater and more gifted than any member of Adam's race, let alone this particular group. Yet Jesus prayed, "Father, I will that they... be with me where I am." And not only they, but us. That was his desire, his last "I will" in this prayer.

We note also *his deity* (17:24b): "That they may behold my glory, which thou hast given me: for thou lovest me before the foundation of the world." He wanted them all to see the glory of his deity, the glory that was his long before time began. He longed for these men who loved and trusted him, however imperfectly, to see him as he really was. He longed to bring them, themselves glorified, into that realm where they could bear to gaze on "the brightness of his glory" (Hebrews 1:3).

2. His Presence in This World (17:25-26)

Again his thoughts go out to this world's *blind majority* (17:25a): "O righteous Father, the world hath not known thee." That is his final, sad lament. He had come to make the Father known. He had so lived, taught, and behaved that the Father had been made known. The demonstration had gone on for over thirty-three years, the last three of them on the public stage before the eyes of all. What an indictment of this world—and the world still does not know him.

His thoughts conclude with this world's *believing minority* (17:25b-26). *His light is their light* (17:25b-26a): "But I have known thee, and these have known that thou hast sent me. And I have declared unto them thy name, and will declare it." Nobody knows God the Father better than God the Son. Nobody has known him longer. Before the rustle of an angel's wing stirred the silence of eternity, God the Father, God the Son, and God the Holy Spirit existed in a mystery of being beyond anything we can imagine or think. They lived together in mutual love, joy, and harmony, in sweet fellowship and communion one with another, in depths and dimensions of being that were fully satisfying and absorbing.

The Lord Jesus, concluding his prayer as a man on earth, as God now manifest in flesh, could say, "The world hath not known thee: but I have known thee." Then, sweeping up these bewildered disciples into the warm embrace of his love, he added, "And these have known that thou hast sent me." That was the final revelation of the nature of God. The God of the universe was a God who had an only begotten and well beloved Son, a Son he was willing to send to a world that did not want to know him, and would crown its other crimes and conceits by crucifying him. He would send that Son in order that a way of salvation might be provided for lost humanity.

"And I have declared unto them thy name, and will declare it," he added. The Lord Jesus gave us the final revelation of the name of God. He had revealed himself in Old Testament times by means of his primary names—Elohim, Jehovah, Adonai—and by a galaxy of composite names: Jehovah Jireh, Jehovah Tsidkenu, Jehovah Shalom, El Elyon, El Shaddai, and so on. But it was Jesus who brought to earth that greatest of all names for God: Father. Jesus had revealed these things to his disciples, so that now his light was their light.

Finally, *his love is their love* (17:26b): "That the love wherewith thou hast loved me may be in them, and I in them." The great word of the gospel is *love*. It is one of John's favorite words. He uses the noun *agape* seven times and the corresponding verb thirty-seven times. He uses the word *phileo* thirteen times, so that some fifty-seven times he talks about love. Love is what it is all about, whether in time or in eternity, whether on earth or in heaven.

Jesus concluded his prayer on this note of love. Let the disciples forget all else.

> Could we with ink the oceans fill,
> Were every stalk on earth a quill,
> Were the whole heaven of parchment made,
> And every man a scribe by trade,
> To write the love, of God above
> Would drain the ocean dry
> Nor could the scroll contain the whole
> Tho' stretched from sky to sky.

The wealth of love that God the Father invested in the person of his Son, he has now invested in us. That is the nature of love. It reaches out. It gives. The more it is given away, the more there is that remains. It is inexhaustible. It is "the love where-with thou hast loved me . . . in them."

But that is not quite the last word. Just in case someone may still think of love in the abstract, or love as an emotion or a feeling, Jesus added, "And I in them." Love, the essence of God's being, was embodied in Jesus. Jesus walked this earth as a living, moving, breathing, three dimensional, stereophonic, visual, full color incarnation of love. Love shone in all he was and said and did.

"Now, Father," Jesus said in closing this prayer, "these people of ours must love like that. My love is to be their love. But I know these people. They mean well, but they don't have what it takes. So, I'll be in them, and then my love will be their love." The prayer was over. The passion was upon him.

PART FOUR

The Sorrows of the Son of God
John 18:1–20:31

J ohn now draws on his memory of the greatest crime in all of history, the murder of the Son of God by the sons of men. He covers the scene in three movements: the condemnation, the crucifixion, and the conqueror.

Section 1. He Is Falsely Condemned (18:1–19:15)

I. JESUS WAS ARRESTED (18:1-12)

A. His Departure (18:1)

"When Jesus had spoken these words, he went forth with his disciples over the brook Cedron, where was a garden, into the which he entered, and his disciples." The Kidron valley is a prominent feature of the topography of Jerusalem. It follows a winding course down to the Dead Sea. In a coming day a river will flow down this valley from a secret source in the millennial temple (Ezekiel 47:1; Zechariah 14:8). In Jesus' day the floor of the valley, as it ran by the temple, was two hundred feet below the pavement of the outer court. The mount of Olives rises to the east of the valley and on its lower slopes was the garden of Gethsemane.

John is silent about the Lord's agony in the garden. He is silent about a great deal. He does not tell of the Lord's claim to have power to summon heaven's hosts to his aid. He is silent about the traitor's kiss, about the Lord's desertion by all the disciples, about the false witnesses, the adjuration, the great confession, about the examination before Herod, about Pilate's wife's message, about Pilate's handwashing, about the self-imposed curse of the Jews, about the impressment of Simon to carry the cross, about the mockery at Calvary, about the darkness, about the terrible orphan cry, about the earthquake, the rending of the veil, the confession of the centurion, about the repentance of one of the thieves.

Although John could have written books about those things (20:30; 21:25), he passed over them. Matthew, Mark, and Luke had already said all that was necessary about them. John never intended his gospel to be just a historical supplement to the other gospels. His concern was to emphasize the person of Christ and especially the signs that underscored his deity.

B. His Deity (18:2-9)

1. The Coming of Judas (18:2-3)

"And Judas also, which betrayed him, knew the place; for Jesus ofttimes resorted thither with his disciples" (18:2). The Lord loved that quiet garden where all about him were reminders of the creative genius he had displayed long years before in planting the garden of Eden. Jesus had often met with his disciples in this spot, and Judas knew it well.

Now that his intercessory prayer was over, Jesus made no attempt to hide from his foes. On the contrary he deliberately went to a place where Judas could expect to find him. Although all four gospel writers record the treachery of Judas, John particularly dwells on its wickedness and horror.

Judas did not come to the garden alone: "Judas then, having received a band of men and officers from the chief priests and Pharisees, cometh thither with lanterns and torches and weapons." The transition in John from the holy of holies to this wasp's nest of rogues is startling. Even though Jesus had talked and prayed about what would soon come to pass, it still seemed remote and far away. Now suddenly, with this mention of Judas and the chief priests and the Pharisees, the world of evil has intruded.

Judas made sure he had sufficient men to carry out his dark design. He had "a band of men," literally, a cohort, which in the Roman army numbered a thousand men, both infantry and cavalry. Judas had with him a detachment of Roman soldiers from the nearby garrison (the Antonia fortress) along with the commanding officer of the whole garrison (18:12). He also had some temple police provided by the Sanhedrin. So Jews and gentiles joined in this nefarious expedition led by Judas.

Evidently the authorities were not at all sure how Jesus and his disciples would react. Perhaps he would resist arrest, and force would be required. Besides, the Jewish authorities stood in considerable awe of Christ's miracle working power. Jesus, however, had no intention of resisting arrest.

2. The Comprehension of Jesus (18:4-9)

Jesus knew perfectly well what was going on; his insight was *supernatural* (18:4-6). He heard the measured tramp of the soldiers, the upraised voices of the officers. The bobbing lanterns and lights and the glint of weapons had long been expected. John underlines *his omniscience* (18:4): "Jesus therefore, knowing all things that should come upon him, went forth, and said unto them, Whom seek ye?" He did that to protect his disciples. He put himself between them and danger, directing the attention of the intruders to himself. He spoke with quiet authority that was unmistakable.

John underlines *his omnipotence* (18:5-6). We note, first, *how Jesus confronted his foes* (18:5): "They answered him, Jesus of Nazareth. Jesus saith unto them, I am he. And Judas also, which betrayed him, stood with them. Their answer reflected a measure of contempt: "Jesus of Nazareth." In Judean eyes it was bad enough to be a Galilean, but to be from Nazareth! To call him a Nazarene was intended as an insult.

Jesus again answered with an I AM. The Greek is *ego eimi.* The term is used nine times in John (4:26; 6:20; 8:24,28,58; 13:19; 18:5,6,8). The Lord clearly laid full claim to the divine, ineffable name. They said, "We seek Jesus the Nazarene." In other words, Jesus said, "I am—that is, I am Jehovah."

John adds the note, "And Judas also, which betrayed him, stood with them." He was numbered with the wrong people. He was with them, fitting company for a traitor. He had made his choice. Now he stood aligned with the enemies of the great I AM.

John tells us immediately *how Jesus confounded his foes* (18:6): "As soon then as he said unto them, I am he, they went backward, and fell to the ground." He was in complete control of the situation. It was not without grounds that authorities were unsure whether they could arrest him. In vain was their Roman cohort. Had Caesar summoned all his legions from the remotest outposts of his empire and hurled them in iron ranks against that "Nazarene," the result would have been the same. They would have gone backward and fallen to the ground. The Lord had already declared, "No man taketh [my life] from me, but I lay it down of myself" (10:18). He now demonstrated that claim to be true. Had he so desired, he could have walked away from them as at other times before. Twelve legions of angels were poised on the battlements of heaven ready to come to his aid. But what need had he of aid? As it was, he simply wished to

show them how helpless they were—swords and staves and
spears and soldiers and all.

John tells us also of the *scriptural* (18:7-9). As always, the
Lord was guided in what he did by the directives of God. By
now his enemies were back on their feet. They appear to have
been dazed. Before them they saw an unarmed man. They
stood there hesitating. Again he put the question, only this time
it was stronger. He demanded of them *(eperotao)*, "Whom seek
ye?" It was as though they still hung back in awe of him and he
was recalling them to their duty. They gave the same answer,
"Jesus of Nazareth." Were they now not so sure that this was the
man they sought? They had come looking for a Galilean peasant
masquerading as the Jewish messiah. They found a man who
claimed to be God and whose words were enough to send them
staggering backward to fall flat on the ground.

By now the Lord's disciples had gathered around him. Somehow they had plucked up a measure of courage. Nonetheless,
the Lord intended to prevent a showdown that would have been
disastrous for them. He again answered his foes, drawing attention to himself: "I have told you that I am [he]: if therefore ye
seek me, let these go their way" (18:8). He had come into the
garden to be arrested, but he did not want the disciples arrested. There was a Scripture to be fulfilled, as he had reminded
them (17:12). "That the saying [*logos*] might be fulfilled, which
he spake, Of them which thou gavest me have I lost none"
(18:9).

C. His Defender (18:10-12)

1. Peter's Fervor (18:10)

Peter had a sudden flow of adrenalin. His impetuous nature
flared up. He was carrying a sword and now made a clumsy
attempt to defend the Lord. Slashing around inexpertly with it,
he cut off the right ear of a man named Malchus, bondservant
of the high priest. All the evangelists tell of the incident, but
only John names Peter and Malchus. By the time John wrote,
Peter was dead, Malchus had faded into oblivion, Jerusalem was
no more. It now made no difference if everyone knew the
names of those concerned. It would seem from the use of the
definite article *(the* high priest's servant) by all four gospel writers that Malchus pushed to the fore to arrest the Lord. His
prominent action apparently marked him out for Peter's attack.

2. Peter's Failure (18:11-12)

But Peter's action now put himself and the other disciples in peril. The Lord stepped forward, told Peter to put up his sword, and explained: "The cup which my Father hath given me, shall I not drink it?" (18:11). If Peter had stayed awake in Gethsemane he would have known that (Matthew 26:38-45). Luke tells us that Jesus healed Malchus (Luke 22:50-51), an act that no doubt helped to defuse the situation.

Peter's show of force brought the Roman soldiers into action: "Then the band and the captain and officers of the Jews took Jesus, and bound him" (18:12). The heavenly hosts must have drawn their swords at that. But the word for which they waited never came. "As a sheep before her shearers is dumb, so he opened not his mouth" (Isaiah 53:7).

II. Jesus Was Arraigned (18:13-19:15)

A. Before the Priests (18:13-27)

In his account, John ignored the appearance before Herod and concentrated on the two trials. The trial before the Jewish Sanhedrin was illegal. According to the Mishnah:

• Capital offenses could be tried by a quorum of twenty-three. A case concerning a false prophet, however, had to be brought before the entire Sanhedrin of seventy-one members. The judges were to sit in a semicircle with the president in the middle, so that the faces of each judge might be seen by each of the others.

• The witnesses were to be strictly separated and examined individually. If the testimony of two agreed, it was taken as valid. When the case involved the death penalty, the witnesses were cautioned as to the consequences of their testimony. They were not allowed to inject their own conjectures or hearsay into the proceedings.

• In capital cases everything was done to give the accused the benefit of the doubt. Votes for acquittal were to be taken first.

• Although civil cases could be tried at night, decisions had to be returned during the day. Capital cases could be tried by day only. An acquittal could be pronounced on the day it was reached, but a sentence of condemnation leading to the death sentence could not be given until the next day, allowing time for a change of mind. Capital cases could not be tried on the eve of a sabbath or a feast.

• In cases of alleged blasphemy the witnesses were rigorously cross-examined to ascertain the exact words used by the accused. If blasphemy was established, the judges stood and rent their clothes.

• On the way to execution, further efforts were made to establish the prisoner's innocence. Four or five times opportunity was provided for the condemned to bring fresh pleas that might exonerate him. A herald went ahead of the procession proclaiming the name of the prisoner, the name of his father, the nature of his offense, and the names of the witnesses on whose testimony he was condemned. The herald urged anyone who could prove his innocence to step forward.

• The blasphemer was to be stoned. The witnesses, on whose testimony he had been condemned, were to cast the first stones. After stoning, the blasphemer's corpse was to be hung on a gibbet, taken down that same night, and buried in a common grave.

1. The Tribunal (18:13-14)

John first draws attention to the trial before the priests. "And led him away to Annas first; for he was father in law to Caiaphas, which was the high priest that same year. Now Caiaphas was he, which gave counsel to the Jews, that it was expedient that one man should die for the people" (18:13-14). We need to look at these two evil men on whose shoulders rests full responsibility for the farce of the Jewish trial. Together they put such pressure on Pilate that he caved in to their demands.

Annas had been appointed to the office of high priest by Quirinius, governor of Syria, in A.D. 6, about the time Judea was incorporated into the Roman empire as a minor province. Annas was deposed in A.D. 15 by Valerius Gratus, prefect of Judea. A skillful manipulator, he then exercised power through members of his family and it was he who really ran the high priesthood as head of the Sadducean party. Five sons, a grandson, and a son-in-law (Caiaphas) held that office. He is said to have been about sixty years old at this time. The Lord was taken to him first because his experience in the law would enable him to formulate a better charge against him.

His son-in-law, Joseph Caiaphas, was the current high priest, having been appointed to that office by Valerius Gratus in A.D. 18. Caiaphas was high priest for eighteen years, longer than anyone else in New Testament times. When Gratus was replaced by Pontius Pilate, Caiaphas was allowed to continue in office. It is likely that Caiaphas made it worth his while not to remove him, either through a bribe or by coming to some other understanding. To govern Judea was no easy task for any Roman. Some under-the-table deal with Caiaphas that would work to their mutual benefit would have appealed to Pilate. They were both deposed in A.D. 36 by Lucius Vitellius, governor of Syria.

John reminds us that it was Caiaphas who had made the cynical remark about Jesus that it would be better for one man to die for the people than that the whole nation perish (11:51). John restates this to remind his readers that Jesus was about to be tried by those who had already decided on his death.

2. The Trial (18:15-27)

We look first at *the disciples* (18:15-18). Here, two identification problems have been the subject of frequent discussion. Who is the high priest mentioned in these verses, and who is the disciple whose influence was sufficient to secure Peter's entry into the precincts of the official residence?

It would seem that after the initial panic and flight some of the disciples took courage (Matthew 26:56,58) and came back, notably John and Peter. Trailing the procession now marching Jesus through the night we can see Peter. He finds himself at last outside the high priest's palace, presumably that of Caiaphas, although it is likely that Annas had rooms there too. Coming to the gate, Peter was stopped. "Another disciple," John says, also "followed Jesus" through the darkness (18:15).

This other disciple had some sort of influence both with the high priest and with members of his staff. The text says that he "was known" to the high priest. The word used is *gnostos*, suggesting more than a nodding acquaintance. Some commentators have decided that it was someone of considerable influence, like Nicodemus or Joseph of Arimathaea, both of whom were members of the Sanhedrin. On the other hand, we should not be too quick to dismiss John. Textual scholar B. F. Westcott remarks, "The reader cannot fail to identify the disciple with St. John." Although we do not know what connections John's family had in Jerusalem, certainly he writes almost as an eyewitness of what follows. But whoever the other disciple was, he was able to enter unchallenged and, perhaps, seeing Peter standing forlornly at the gate, he went back out, had a word with the servant girl in charge of the gate, and secured Peter's admission.

John tells us about *Peter's false profession* (18:17): "Then saith the damsel that kept the door unto Peter, Art not thou also one of this man's disciples? He saith, I am not." The way the question was put to him, in the negative, expressed surprise that he would show up there. There was also a note of contempt: "You are not one of this fellow's disciples, are you?" Feeling suddenly vulnerable, Peter caved in at once. "I am not," he said.

We are now shown *Peter's false position* (18:18): "And the servants and officers stood there, who had made a fire of coals; for it was cold: and they warmed themselves: and Peter stood with them, and warmed himself." "Peter stood with them." We have met those words before. Right after telling us how Jesus boldly proclaimed himself as the I AM to the arresting officers and their men, John says, "And Judas . . . stood with them" (18:5). Now we read: "Peter stood with them." It was a dishonorable position for a disciple. It is always dangerous for the Lord's people to put themselves in compromising positions, always dangerous to stand and warm one's hands at the world's fire.

Mention of that charcoal fire suggests that here we have the story of an eyewitness to the sad incident. Who more likely than John? That charcoal fire was only incidental but it evidently made an impression on someone. The Roman soldiers seem to have gone back to their barracks. Peter was surrounded by the most hostile people of all: the servants and officers of the high priest. There Jesus leaves him for a while, warming his hands, in dire spiritual peril, protected by the words of the Lord he had already denied: "I have prayed for thee."

Now comes *the defense* (18:19-24). The question was *asked* (18:19): "The high priest then asked Jesus of his disciples, and of his doctrine." Opinions are divided as to whether the question was asked by Annas or by Caiaphas. If we connect it with verse 24, it was Annas. Probably this was a private, unofficial interrogation during which Caiaphas was present but Annas took the lead. Annas was looking for something on which to build a case. The entire proceeding was illegal.

The first part of the question had to do with the Lord's disciples. What did the high priest want to know about them? How many were there? What kind of threat did they pose? The Lord ignored the question, determined to shield them. They were no threat to the establishment. They were, for the most part, totally disorganized and demoralized. One of them would repeatedly deny him right outside in the courtyard. The high priest already had Judas in his pocket. There was no conspiracy.

As for Jesus' doctrine, there was no secret about that. He said (using emphatic pronouns): "I spake openly to the world; I even taught in the synagogue and in the temple, whither the Jews always resort; and in secret have I said nothing. Why askest

thou me? ask them which heard me, what I have said unto
them: behold, they know what I said." Thus the question was
answered (18:20-24), and *the rebuttal* (18:20-21) was bold and to
the point. The Lord's teaching had been open. During the past
week he had been teaching in the temple. His teaching in the
synagogues throughout the country was well known. The open-
ness of his teaching contrasted with the secretive plots of Annas,
Caiaphas, and the rest of them. As for the Lord's private instruction to his disciples in the upper room, there was no need
to tell the authorities about that. What he had said there was
not subversive, it had violated no law, and, even if he had repeated it to the priests, they would neither have understood it
nor had the patience to listen to it.

The reaction (18:22) was swift: "And when he had thus spoken,
one of the officers which stood by struck Jesus with the palm of
his hand, saying, Answerest thou the high priest so?" The man
who did that was a Jew, one of the temple police. He did not
know it, but he had smitten his maker. If he never afterward
repented, one day, at the great white throne, he will stand,
before this very one, vainly trying to hide that deed. Or if after
the resurrection and Pentecost, he finally found his way in
repentance to Jesus, then one day Jesus will welcome him home.
But for as long as he lived, he would carry with him a hand that
had once been violently laid across the cheek of God incarnate.

John records *the response* (18:23-24): "Jesus answered him, If I
have spoken evil, bear witness of the evil: but if well, why
smitest thou me? Now Annas had sent him bound unto Caiaphas the high priest." Jesus turned to the man who had so
abused him, challenging him to bring charges in a legal manner
and thus bear proper witness against him, rather than resort to
brute force. The word for "smitest" is *dero,* which occurs fifteen
times, and elsewhere is always rendered "beat."

It says something too about the high priest, that he did not
rebuke the officer. The blow ended this part of the proceeding.
This private interrogation at which Caiaphas was present yield-
ed nothing, so Annas had Jesus rebound and went through the
formality of transferring the proceeding officially to Caiaphas,
the legal high priest.

John does not describe the trial before Caiaphas. Instead he
takes us back to Peter, still in the courtyard and in the company
of a hostile group of people.

We have now *the denial* (18:25-27). We again note *where Peter
stood* (18:25a): "And Simon Peter stood and warmed himself."
He should have remembered the first psalm in the Hebrew
hymn book: "Blessed is the man that . . . standeth [not] in the

way of sinners." He should have remembered Psalm 2 as he thought of his Lord in there, surrounded by his foes: "The kings of the earth set themselves, and the rulers take counsel together, against the Lord, and against his anointed" (Psalm 2:2). Then he should have either stood up boldly for his Lord, or excused himself and gone home.

But few of us have not badly compromised our testimonies at some time or another, as Peter did, and for similar reasons. The world's fire seemed to offer Peter some comfort, but he was about to be badly burned.

We note *what Peter said* (18:25b): "They said therefore unto him, Art not thou also one of his disciples? He denied it, and said, I am not." These members of the household staff and some of the temple police echoed the words of the woman doorkeeper. By now, Peter was thoroughly intimidated. Again he flatly denied being one of the Lord's disciples.

We note *whom Peter saw* (18:26): "One of the servants of the high priest, being his kinsman whose ear Peter cut off [a kinsman of the man whose ear Peter had cut off], saith, Did not I see thee in the garden with him?" Peter now saw a man looking at him with particular attention, and John adds a detail that shows specific knowledge of the household staff. The man was a relative of Malchus, the man whose ear Peter had cut off a short while before. He had been putting two and two together, and now the light dawned. "I know *you,*" he thought. "You're the man who had the sword. You cut off the ear of my kinsman Malchus." He made his thrust: "Didn't I see you in the garden?" he demanded. "You were with him, weren't you?"

That was *when Peter sinned* (18:27): "Peter then denied again: and immediately the cock crew." It was the knell of doom. The familiar sound of a rooster crowing smote Peter's soul with grief and despair.

B. Before the Procurator (18:28–19:15)

John devotes a comparatively large amount of space to the Lord's trial before Pilate, Roman procurator of Judea. We can divide this important section into four parts.

1. The Accusation (18:28-32)

In detailing the accusation, John tells us first of *the scruples of the priests* (18:28). We note *their spiritual bondage* (18:28a): "Then led they Jesus from Caiaphas unto the hall of judgment: and it was early; and they themselves went not into the judg-

ment hall, lest they should be defiled." John omits the formal
trial before the Sanhedrin recorded in Matthew (26:58–27:2)
and parallel passages.

The place chosen for this gentile trial is called "the judgment
hall," the praetorium. Normally the Roman governor of Judea
held court at the Roman city of Caesarea, where the palace that
Herod the Great had built for himself was used as the headquarters. When the pressure of events brought the governor to
Jerusalem, wherever he took up residence became his temporary praetorium. At this time it seems to have been the fortress
of Antonia, located on the northwest end of the temple area. It
had been rebuilt by Herod the Great on the site of an earlier
Hasmonean fortress and was named for Herod's friend Mark
Antony.

Having already condemned Jesus to death, the Jewish authorities now led him to Pilate so that the Roman governor
might examine him and ratify their sentence. It was Passover
time. The Jews had their sacrificial lambs ready. They had rid
their houses of leaven. They had performed the rituals so that
they were ceremonially clean. They would be required to kill
their Passover lambs that very afternoon and keep the feast
immediately after sunset. They had no intention of risking ceremonial defilement by entering a gentile place of residence
where there would be leaven.

Further, a praetorium would be under the protection of Roman tutelary gods and, although it is unlikely that Pilate would
risk displaying them openly in Jerusalem, the priests were not
taking any chances. They had no intention of contracting ritual
defilement. Their religion demanded its ritual dues and the
priests were scrupulous to observe these, even while plotting
cold blooded murder. We can sense John's touch of sarcasm in
the way he records these things.

He mentions not only their bondage to the forms and ceremonies of a dead religion but also *their spiritual blindness*
(18:28b). They were scrupulous about the rituals, "that they
might eat the passover," he says. Little did they know that
Christ was the true Passover lamb, and that they were about to
kill him in that capacity.

John now tells us about *the sarcasm of the priests* (18:29-30).
"Pilate then went out unto them." The governor had learned by
bitter experience how fiercely the Jews opposed any semblance
of violation of their religious scruples. So, in order to accommo-
date their taboos, he went out to where they were. Pilate was
not about to squabble with them over that, at least not on this
occasion.

Throughout John's account of this Roman trial we see Pilate going in and out repeatedly. We see him:

- *Outside* (18:28-32) to hear the Jews demand the ratification of their death sentence
- *Inside* (18:33-38a) to hear Christ's own testimony to his kingship
- *Outside* (18:38b-40) to make his first declaration of Christ's innocence and to offer them the choice between Jesus and Barabbas
- *Inside* (19:1-3) for the scourging and mockery of Jesus
- *Outside* (19:4-7) for his second declaration of Christ's innocence: "Behold the man!"
- *Inside* (19:8-11) to examine Jesus about the frightening accusation of the Jews that this one claimed to be the Son of God
- *Outside* (19:12-16) for the final capitulation before the Jews and the shameful miscarriage of justice

So, for the first of a series of trips back and forth, Pilate then "went out unto them, and said: What accusation bring ye against this man?" Their answer reeked of sarcasm: "If he were not a malefactor, we would not have delivered him up unto thee." A malefactor. What a name for the Son of God. The word is *kakopoios*, an evildoer, a criminal. It carries the idea of one actively engaged in evil. Peter later said, "[He] went about doing good" (Acts 10:38). The slander was terrible. Jesus had healed the sick, given sight to the blind, cast out evil spirits, fed hungry multitudes, raised the dead. He had taught the truth about God in memorable ways. They had searched his life looking for flaws and had found none. They had been forced in the end to hire false witnesses against him.

When Pilate asked for their charge against Jesus they seem to have been taken by surprise. They evidently thought Pilate would take their word for it that this prisoner was worthy of death. Pilate's hesitation irked them and we hear irritation in their reply.

Next we note *the scheme of the priests* (18:31-32). They wanted this man put to death and they wanted him put to death by crucifixion. They wanted this one who claimed to be God to die under the curse of God (Galatians 3:13). Pilate said, "Take ye him, and judge him according to your law." He knew they were bringing a capital case to him, but he played dumb and referred the case back to their court. "If he is just a criminal, then you take care of the case," he said. That forced their hand. "It is not lawful for us to put any man to death," they said. They would cite Roman law when it suited their purpose. The right to exercise capital punishment was the most jealously guarded of all a Roman governor's prerogatives.

The Jews had forgotten an important prophecy which they were now helping to bring to pass: "That the saying of Jesus might be fulfilled, which he spake, signifying what death he should die" (18:32). They were proving him to be a true prophet (12:33). If the Jews had executed Jesus, they would have done so by stoning, not by crucifixion. The whole incident was sovereignly overruled by God. The Lord's prophecy of the manner of his death was corroborated by the Old Testament prophets (Psalm 22:16; Zechariah 12:10).

2. The Examination (18:33-40)

The formal examination of Jesus by Pilate revolves around five questions. As we study John's account of this terrible business we get the feeling that Pilate was on trial rather than Jesus. Certainly he had never met anyone in his life like Jesus and, before he was through, he was frightened of him.

First comes *the salient question* (18:33-34), the key question to begin with as far as Pilate was concerned: "Then Pilate entered into the judgment hall again, and called Jesus, and said unto him, Art thou the King of the Jews? Jesus answered him, Sayest thou this thing of thyself, or did others tell it thee of me?" Pilate went back into the praetorium and had Jesus brought in before him. By now the Lord's malicious enemies had thought up a charge that no Roman governor could afford to ignore. Jesus had claimed to be a king—the king of the Jews, no less. In all four gospels the first words of Pilate to Jesus are the same: "Are you the king of the Jews?" The question contained an element of astonishment. Nothing about Jesus suggested royalty. He was obviously poor. He had been up all night and had endured not only the agony in the garden but he had been bullied by the Sanhedrin and beaten by the temple police. Nor did Jesus exhibit any of the fierce traits or fanatical patriotism the Romans were accustomed to meet in other Jewish liberators and insurrectionists. If this man was a king, a king of the Jews, he was certainly a different kind of king than Pilate would have expected. The Lord's reply reinforced that.

Jesus said, in effect, "Who told you that? Is that something you have deduced for yourself? Or has someone else put the thought in your mind?" The Lord wanted Pilate to ponder the implications of the charge.

It can be taken for granted that Pilate was well informed on Jesus' recent activities. His ride into Jerusalem amid the hosannahs of the people would, if nothing else, call for prompt investigation at the highest government level. But the reports had evidently been mild enough, if not downright amusing—this new "messiah" had ridden into Jerusalem on a donkey cheered by peasants! The Jewish officials, the scribes and Pharisees, the Sanhedrin, had frowned on the whole affair.

Doubtless that incident had provoked a wider investigation into the speeches and activities of this "messiah." Again there was nothing there. Anything that could be gleaned from diligent questioning was harmless. He seemed to be a new religious teacher particularly apt at putting Jewish religious concepts in a new light, with a reputation for doing good.

So Jesus put the question to him. Who told you that? If I am a king, what kind of a king am I? You are a Roman—do I pose any threat to Rome? Do you really understand what is meant by this title "king of the Jews"? Have you any desire to know its deeper, spiritual significance, or are you content to accept the surface meaning of the words? To be satisfied with a vague accusation?

All of a sudden the tables were turned. With one question Jesus put Pilate in the dock. Pilate didn't like it. He countered with *the scornful question* (18:35a): "Pilate answered, Am I a Jew? Thine own nation and the chief priests have delivered thee unto me." Pilate's question reflected the Roman bias against Jews, their scorn of Jewish ethnic and religious ideas. It was the answer of a proud Roman, son-in-law of a Caesar, commander of cohorts, legal representative of an empire that held the world in thrall.

"Your own nation has turned you in." To Pilate, something was implausible about that. Normally the Jews, in their bitter and undisguised hatred of Rome, were ready to encourage anyone, however wild his claims, who would foster and promote their cravings for national independence.

Pilate sensed he was being used by the crafty Caiaphas. He was not sure what the Jewish leaders were up to, and he was suspicious of them. But at the same time he was puzzled by something else: why were they so full of malice against this man? He put the question to Jesus: "What hast thou done?"

Why are your own people so bitterly opposed to you? That was *the serious question* (18:35b-36). The Lord Jesus answered it at once. That was the whole point. He was not the kind of king the Jews either expected or wanted: "Jesus answered, My kingdom is not of this world: if my kingdom were of this world, then would my servants fight, that I should not be delivered unto the

Jews: but now is my kingdom not from hence" (18:36).

The Lord's teaching concerning the kingdom is more the subject of Matthew's gospel than John's. The Lord did not enlarge on the spiritual or millennial aspects of his kingdom to Pilate. Pilate had no concern or interest in the kingdom except as that kingdom might enlist some kind of military action against Rome. Nevertheless Jesus let Pilate know that he was not nearly so helpless as he looked. He had his servants—twelve legions of them in heaven, any one member of which could have annihilated the whole Roman army.

Perhaps Pilate had already received the report of the military tribune (18:12) who had been in charge of the arrest of Jesus. If so, he may have heard of the extraordinary overthrow of the arresting cohort by a single word from this man, who nevertheless had thereafter meekly surrendered to the authorities. It is not likely that the tribune would have suppressed this incident in his report—too many people knew about it. If Pilate had received this report, it is no wonder he handled Jesus with kid gloves at this stage of the trial.

Jesus made no attempt to hide from Pilate the fact that he was a king, but his kingdom was a spiritual kingdom. He had not come to establish it by force. It drew its power from another world. It did not depend on the support of earthly forces, nor could it be overthrown by military might. As for the Jews, he had voluntarily put himself in their hands. The Jews were looking for a militant messiah, one who would lead them to victory over Rome and over the world, one who would make Jerusalem the capital of a new empire. They were scornful of him because he was a meek messiah. They had long since rejected him and his claims.

Then came *the sobering question* (18:37): "Pilate therefore said unto him, Art thou a king then? Jesus answered, Thou sayest that I am a king. To this end was I born, and for this cause came I into the world, that I should bear witness unto the truth. Every one that is of the truth heareth my voice." Pilate seized on the word *king*. That was a word he could understand. A man obviously poor, a man bound, and a prisoner—a king?

Jesus gave him back his word: "Thou sayest that I am a king." Pilate was the one who was toying with this word. Jesus put matters on another footing. "My realm is truth," he said in effect. "I was born to be king. For this cause I came into the world." We note the double emphasis: "I was born; I came." As Son of man he was born king of the Jews (Matthew 2:1-6). As Son of God he came from another world, from another form of existence.

He came, he told Pilate, to "bear witness unto the truth." He was claiming to be the incarnate word (John 1:14), the one who personally embodied truth. All who loved truth recognized him for what he was and crowned him king.

But things were now getting too close for comfort. Pilate had no wish to face the personal implications of all this. He countered with *the speculative question* (18:38a): "Pilate saith unto him, What is truth?" It was a flippant question in the sense that Pilate did not wait for an answer. The world's religions and philosophies have debated that question for centuries. Nowadays the idea is current that truth is relative. Jesus stood before Pilate as the answer to that question. He was the truth (14:6), absolute, perfect, clothed for all to see in flesh and blood. Then and there Pilate could have slain his doubts, put his fears to rest, embraced Christ, and entered into the truth. But he was not serious. With a touch of cynicism he shrugged off the magic moment. It never came again, as far as we know. He simply dismissed the Lord's statement. He was not going to discuss the nature of truth with this Galilean peasant. He abruptly left the praetorium.

Now comes *the scandalous question* (18:38b-40). For the moment, Pilate had made up his vacillating mind. He was impressed by this prisoner. Whatever else this Jesus of Nazareth had said or done, whatever it was he claimed to be, he was clearly no threat to Rome. He had committed no offense against Roman law, as Pilate understood that law. He said so: "And when he had said this, he went out again unto the Jews, and saith unto them, I find in him no fault at all" (18:38b). He should have acquitted him and set him free. It would have been a feather in the cap of Roman justice. Pilate would have gone down in history as the ideal judge.

But Pilate did not stop there. He went on—to his undoing. He wanted to avoid a confrontation with the Jews just as much as he wanted to avoid a confrontation with Jesus. Because their frowns and angry murmurs were already threatening a very nasty storm, he asked a scandalous question: "But ye have a custom, that I should release unto you one at the passover: will ye therefore that I release unto you the King of the Jews?" (18:39).

All four gospels tell this sad story. It was a wholly unprincipled act on Pilate's part to offer to release Jesus based on this custom rather than on the established basis of his innocence. Moreover, whatever Pilate hoped to gain by this move—and doubtless he hoped the Jews would accept Jesus, a good man, over Barabbas, a violent man—he did not further his end in the way he worded the offer. He could not resist the temptation of goading the Jews. He only annoyed them further by referring to Jesus as "the King of the Jews," a title the Jewish authorities violently opposed.

Nor did he have long to wait for their response to this crass political maneuver: "Then cried they all again, saying, Not this man, but Barabbas. Now Barabbas was a robber" (18:40). He was a bandit, a highway robber. There is a note of terrible pathos in that brief comment by John. The Jews chose a bandit—and down through their history, from that day to this, they have been robbed and plundered.

Pilate still had Jesus on his hands. Moreover, the Jewish authorities now knew that Pilate was putty in theirs.

3. The Persecution (19:1-3)

This brief section adds to Pilate's shame. He went back into the praetorium, still undecided. He had gambled and lost. Next he resorted to a typical Roman expedient when questioning a helpless man not protected by powerful friends or by Roman citizenship. We are told now about *the scourging* (19:1): "Then Pilate therefore took Jesus, and scourged him." Perhaps under the lash this frustrating prioner would say something that could be used against him.

Trial by scourging was a terrible ordeal. The victim was fastened to a post. A soldier took the many-thonged whip into which were woven pieces of metal or bone. He brought that whip down with all the force of his arm across the victim's back. The first blow knocked all the breath out of the body. The second lay open the skin. As the punishment proceeded, flesh was ripped from bone. Sometimes vital organs were exposed. People died beneath the scourge. Often those who survived were maimed for life. Pilate callously handed over to this systematic torture a man he had just pronounced innocent.

It says something about the magnificent physique of the Lord Jesus that he survived that ordeal. But that was by no means all. Not a word of complaint passed his lips, not a word of any kind that the callous Roman, brought up on the sights and sounds of the arena, could use as a pretext for changing the verdict. So he handed the battered and bleeding man over to the soldiers. Maybe under their rough horseplay he could be provoked into some hostile remark, perhaps some curse against Rome.

So comes *the scoffing* (19:2-3). We note *how Jesus was attired* (19:2): "And the soldiers platted a crown of thorns, and put it on his head, and they put on him a purple robe." There was something very comical to these soldiers about Jesus being a

king, especially the king of the Jews. The average Roman had
little love for the average Jew. That the Jews should have a king
and that this meek man should be he! That was almost too
funny for words.

One wag, with a more inventive mind than his fellows, remembered a thorn bush outside. It is thought that the thorns
came from a date palm. They were formidable in themselves
but, when twisted into a crown and rammed on his head, would
have caused sharp pain. Thorns are a symbol of the curse (Genesis 3:18).

The sight of Jesus standing there, crowned with thorns, inspired another idea. Someone fetched a military cloak and
flung it over his shoulders. There! Now he looked more like a
real king. They mocked him. "Hail, King of the Jews!" they said.
We can imagine the ribald laughter, the coarse jests, the foul
language.

Seeing they evoked no response, some of them resorted to
further violence and "smote him with their hands." It is the
word used in 18:22. So we see *how Jesus was attacked* (19:3).
They beat him. Still he stood there, turning the other cheek,
and let them so pound his face that the Old Testament prophet
could proclaim: "His visage was so marred more than any man"
(Isaiah 52:14).

4. The Condemnation (19:4-15)

The final condemnation of Jesus by Pilate, as recorded by
John, was in three stages. First he was rejected *as the Son of man*
(19:4-6), then as the Son of God, and finally as the Son of
David. We see Pilate fighting a losing battle with the Jews,
forced back step by step, until at last he gave in—the victim of
his own cowardly compromise.

When the soldiers had finished with their verbal and violent
mockery of the prisoner and had drawn nothing out of him, he
was once again taken in charge by Pilate. He had him brought
out of the praetorium and *Christ was exhibited* (19:4-5). By now
he was hardly recognizable. It is a wonder he could still stand
on his feet. Perhaps Pilate hoped to arouse some pity in the
implacable priests.

Pilate began with *a declaration of complete innocence* (19:4):
"Pilate therefore went forth again, and said unto them, Behold,
I bring him forth to you, that ye may know that I find no fault
in him." This appeal to their sense of justice fell on deaf ears.
They were not interested in justice, but rather in a conviction
and speedy death sentence.

Pilate apparently had preceded Jesus out of the praetorium. Now he appeared and Pilate set before them *a demonstration of cowardly injustice* (19:5): "Then came Jesus forth, wearing the crown of thorns, and the purple robe." If Pilate expected the sight of a man scourged and beaten to appeal to their sense of humanity he was mistaken. Although he had proclaimed him innocent, he had scourged him. He had allowed him to be brutalized by the soldiers. He paraded before them evidence of his own cowardice. He hoped, it seems, that his fresh affirmation of the prisoner's innocence, coupled with his already terrible suffering, would move them to settle for that.

He was mistaken. The sight of that crown of thorns and that purple robe moved them to even greater fury. To think that this Jesus of Nazareth could have brought such scorn and ridicule on their messianic aspirations and their claims to national, sovereign independence from Rome! Their rage knew no bounds.

At this point Pilate made a statement that has become famous. It has echoed down the centuries: *Ecce homo!* "Behold the man!" He was man as God intended man to be: man inhabited by God.

And see what fallen man did to that sinless one. Here sin in all its ugliness met holiness in all its beauty.

"Behold the man!" cried Pilate with a gesture that pointed out his handiwork. The chief priests looked at him, Caiaphas and his crowd. The temple officers looked at him. And from the lips of these religious men, too scrupulous to enter into Pilate's judgment hall, there burst forth a hellish cry: "Crucify him! Crucify him!"

All of us face this timeless challenge and respond one way or another. We cry either "Crucify him" or "Crown him." There is no middle ground, as Pilate soon found out.

So we see that *Christ was execrated* (19:6). Now the rage of the priests gave way to the response of the procurator: "Pilate saith unto them, Take ye him, and crucify him: for I find no fault in him." It was the third time he declared the prisoner's innocence. "You take him and crucify him," he said—as though he could shift responsibility from his shoulders to theirs.

Nobody can do that. When it comes to Jesus, each of us makes his own decision and is responsible for his own reaction.

Now a new dimension was introduced. He had tried Jesus as a man and that did not satisfy the Jews. It was not so much what he was as the Son of man that infuriated them. It was what he claimed to be *as the Son of God* (19:7-12).

Once more, we must look at this sudden upping of the stakes through the eyes of the unhappy Roman governor. We note how *fear was instilled in Pilate* (19:7-9). He made a sudden *discovery* (19:7): "The Jews answered him, We have a law, and by our law he ought to die, because he made himself the Son of God." He did no such thing! He did not make himself the Son of God. He truly was the Son of God. The law to which the Jews alluded was in Leviticus 24:16. Their appeal to that law was fraudulent because Jesus not only was the Son of God, as he claimed, but he had proved over and over that to be so.

The Jews had no doubt that Jesus claimed to be God's Son in an absolute and total sense. They now unloaded this piece of information on Pilate, who was instantly overwhelmed by *dread* (19:8-9). If the Jews thought that the charge of blasphemy was going to secure the instant death sentence they sought, they were wrong. Pilate was not so much interested in their religious reasons for wanting to be rid of Jesus as he was horrified at the possibility that what they said about him might be true. Pilate was already half afraid of his unusual prisoner. Never before had a man looked at him with such clear and honest eyes. Never before had a man been so calm, reserved, silent, unafraid. Never before had a man endured scourging and scoffing with such dignity. It was not just stoicism. It was absolute victory. And most amazing of all—what he read in this man's face, what shone out of his wonderful face, was love. Love that transcended hate.

He hurried back into the praetorium to sort out his thoughts and to have another talk with this disconcerting prisoner. He must find out more about this claim of his to be the Son of God. What if it was true? Pilate, hardened as he was, was not without his superstitions—and these had been heightened by an urgent message he had just received from his wife (Matthew 27:9).

"When Pilate therefore heard that saying, he was the more afraid; And went again into the judgment hall, and saith unto Jesus, Whence art thou? But Jesus gave him no answer" (19:9).

A dreadful presentiment was taking root in Pilate's heart. He would perhaps recall accounts he had heard from his spies about the miracles this man had performed, too numerous and varied to be ignored. But he had ignored them—until now. Now he tried to hide his uneasiness with bluster: "Where do you come from anyway?" he demanded. Jesus met the question with a total silence that unnerved Pilate more than any answer could have done.

What answer could Jesus have given? Pilate's notions about an incarnate deity would have been colored by pagan concepts of Mount Olympus and Roman idolatry. How could Jesus have conveyed to this man, who had proved himself to be a trifler with truth, any concept of his Father as God in heaven and himself as Son on earth? What would Pilate have done with this truth? He had already shown what he was prepared to do with the truth of Christ's innocence. Let him act on that truth; then he would be able to receive more truth—truth at present beyond his comprehension. To have revealed to Pilate, at this stage, absolute truth about his being God manifest in flesh would only have added to Pilate's guilt and condemnation.

The question before Pilate was one of justice, of a prisoner's innocence, and of rights that had already been terribly violated.

We note how *fear was intensified in Pilate* (19:10-12), first, by *the dignity of the man* (19:10-11). Note *his bullying claim* (19:10): "Then saith Pilate unto him, Speakest thou not unto me? knowest thou not that I have power to crucify thee, and have power to release thee?" It was an empty claim at best. He had already attested to the prisoner's innocence three times, yet he still had not released him. He was himself a prisoner, a captive of his own fear of the Jews and their ability to make trouble for him with Rome. There was not an official in the Roman empire who did not know that the fanatical and unpredictable Jews had to be handled with kid gloves.

The silence of Jesus smote Pilate's conscience as nothing else could. This time we see *his bluff called* (19:11): "Jesus answered, Thou couldest have no power at all against me, except it were given thee from above." Throughout the Bible the fact is established that human government is God ordained and that those in positions of authority, whether they recognize it or not, are ultimately responsible to God for the way they conduct themselves in office (Proverbs 8:15; Romans 13:1-7). Pilate's authority *(exousia)* was derived from Caesar; both Pilate's and Caesar's authority were derived from God. Pilate was going to act as he pleased. Jesus reminded him that his arbitrary, unjust, and illegal abuse of his authority would not go unrecorded. He had received his authority "from above" *(anothen,* a word that denotes from heaven as in John 3:3,7,31) and he would be accountable for what he did. This warning was urgently needed by Pilate, who had already allowed one miscarriage of justice in scourging a man he knew to be innocent and was about to permit a worse one.

But the Lord was not through. He did not mitigate Pilate's sin—and it is a remarkable instance of the Lord's honesty and courage that he should talk to his judge about his personal sin—but there was one who was an even greater sinner than Pilate: "He that delivered me unto thee hath the greater sin," Jesus added. The Greek indicates one person, undoubtedly the wicked high priest Caiaphas. The verb for "delivered" here is *paradidomi*. It occurs fifteen times in John's gospel. Nine times it is translated "betray" in connection with the sin of Judas in handing Jesus over to the Sanhedrin. John has already used the word twice in describing the action of the Sanhedrin in handing Jesus over to Pilate. Here the Lord used the word specifically of the high priest.

The office held by Caiaphas, in the sight of God, was an office far higher than that of a mere emperor of Rome. The office of high priest carried with it the highest and holiest functions. That office had been disgraced by a succession of politically active, spiritually insensitive, worldly minded, self-seeking opportunists. Caiaphas, a godless and unprincipled man, was the present high priest. If Pilate's abuse of his office was great and would one day be called to account by God, how much worse was the abuse of his holy office by Caiaphas?

It is significant that the Holy Spirit uses the same word to describe the action of Caiaphas that he used to describe the action of Judas. Judas had betrayed Jesus to Caiaphas and Caiaphas had betrayed Jesus to Pilate. Pilate's sin in his unprincipled handling of his prisoner was great. That of Caiaphas was greater still. All this made a deep impression on Pilate, who accepted without challenge this remarkable statement on the ethics and divine dynamics of the exercise of human authority.

But if Pilate had a sudden surge of resolve to do the right thing by his prisoner it was soon stilled. His fear, intensified by the dignity of Jesus, was even more intensified by *the demand of the mob* (19:12): "And from thenceforth Pilate sought to release him: but the Jews cried out, saying, If thou let this man go, thou art not Caesar's friend: whosoever maketh himself a king speaketh against Caesar."

The Jews had now changed their tactics. They had the measure of their man. They pressed a political charge instead of a religious charge. The Caesars would not tolerate sedition or even the suspicion of sedition. Woe betide any provincial governor who was lenient with insurrectionists. As for anyone claiming to be a king, the Caesars expected swift judgment to be meted out to him.

Pilate had already acquitted Jesus of being a serious rival to Caesar. But by now the Jewish leaders had organized the mob. The multitude "cried out," John says. They "raised a shout." The thought behind the expression is that of one loud, unified cry rather than a discordant noise. It was a loud, decisive, and determined demand, as in 19:6,15 and 18:40. Pilate was far more afraid of Caesar than he was of Jesus, more concerned with being "Caesar's friend" than in being a friend to this stranger whose destiny, so he thought, lay in his hands. Judas sold Christ for money. Caiaphas sold him out of religious prejudice. Pilate sold him in order to hang onto his job. People still sell him for material gain, for wrong religion, for godless friendship—for a handful of tinsel or a round of applause.

Jesus has been rejected as the Son of man and as the Son of God. Now we see him rejected *as the Son of David* (19:13-15).

We come now to *the climax of the trial* (19:13): "When Pilate therefore heard that saying, he brought Jesus forth, and sat down in the judgment seat in a place that is called the Pavement, but in the Hebrew, Gabbatha." The procurator could delay no longer. The time had come to make up his mind once and for all one way or another. Accordingly he seated himself on the judgment seat *(bema)*. This was a raised platform with a seat in the open court in front of the praetorium. It was called "the pavement" *(lithostrotos)*; the word literally means "strewn with stone" and suggests some kind of mosaic. In the vernacular of the Jews, in Hebrew (Aramaic), it was called Gabbatha ("the ridge"). The place is generally identified with the magnificent Roman pavement that has been excavated beneath the Ecce Homo arch. It measured about three thousand square yards and is thought to be the actual courtyard of the Antonia fortress. John gives this detail because of the solemnity of both place and occasion. He who is one day to sit on his own *bema* (Romans 14:10; 2 Corinthians 5:10) and who one day is to judge all the wicked dead (Revelation 20:11-15) was about to have sentence passed on him by Jew and gentile alike.

Now came *the crux of the trial* (19:14-15). The Jews would now reject Jesus formally and fatally as the Son of David, rightful heir to the throne of Israel, mighty lion of the tribe of Judah.

We see first *the king presented to Israel* (19:14-15a) and we note Pilate's *unintentional quotation* (19:14): "And it was the preparation of the passover, and about the sixth hour: and he saith unto the Jews, Behold your King!"

Again we note John's deliberate and painstaking accuracy in citing both place and time. It was "the sixth hour." If this was Hebrew time, it was midnight. If John used Roman time, it was six o'clock in the morning. It was "the preparation of the passover," Preparation Day (all four gospels attest that the Lord's burial took place on this day), the day the Jews killed their Passover lamb.

Pilate seated himself. He had made up his mind to cast Jesus to the wolves, but his soul was filled with bitterness toward the Jews who had outmaneuvered him. He would do all he could to make their victory as unpalatable as possible. He had Jesus brought forward. There he stood, his face beaten, his head crowned with thorns, his bleeding back covered by a purple robe. He had been up all night. He had agonized in the garden. He had been bullied by the Sanhedrin and abused by their police. He had been marched here, there, and everywhere across the city. He was exhausted and racked with pain. Pilate pointed to him. He looked at Caiaphas and his motley crew of self-righteous hypocrites. "Behold your King!" he said.

Although he did not know it, he had touched on one of the great messianic prophecies. In foretelling Christ's triumphant entry into Jerusalem, one of the last of the prophets had used those very words. With what rage the Jews heard them now! Who among them could have escaped making the ironic connection: "Rejoice greatly, O daughter of Zion; shout, O daughter of Jerusalem: behold, thy King cometh unto thee: he is just, and having salvation; lowly, and riding upon an ass, and upon a colt the foal of an ass" (Zechariah 9:9).

He was the last rightful claimant to the throne of David— descended directly from David along two lines, as the temple records clearly showed. There he stood—their king. The Jews looked from the king they rejected to the sneering Roman they detested and back again to that pitiful figure standing silently there, clothed in a majesty all his own.

But Pilate was not quite through. His unintentional quotation was followed by an *unequivocal question* (19:15a): "Shall I crucify your King?" he asked. Did he hope that even in this final moment the Jews would relent? If so, he was quickly disillusioned. Not even Pilate, cynical as he was, could fail to be surprised at the answer he received: "The chief priests answered, We have no king but Caesar." Caesar was *the king preferred by Israel* (19:15b).

The Jews hated Rome, hated its occupying army, hated its governor, hated its institutions, hated Caesar. In less than forty years they would fight one of the fiercest wars in history to rid themselves of Caesar. Sixty years after that, they would fight another one. To hear them say "we have no king but Caesar" must have been an all time first.

Note who said it: the chief priests. Not the rabble, not the rabbis, but the nation's rulers, the official custodians of the Jewish faith. They publicly proclaimed they would rather have Caesar as king than Jesus as king; they would rather have Roman rule and gentile dominion than any kingdom with Jesus as monarch. They would rather have no messiah, no millennium, than have to have these things with Jesus. It was a terrible abandonment of the faith by which the nation had lived.

It was the formal abdication of the nation's messianic hope, and God has taken them at their word. For the greater part of the Christian era the Jews have been aliens in gentile lands. They have known no king but Caesar. They have been made to drink to the dregs the bitter cup they raised to heaven that day. They have now begun a return to their ancestral home. But there is to arise yet a Caesar to be their king, a Roman antichrist who will wring even more dregs than could ever be imagined for them out of this cup (Revelation 13) until at long last they "look on him whom they pierced" and own him king indeed.

Section 2. He Is Finally Crucified (19:16-42)

The long trial was over. The die was cast. The stage was set for the final acts of this terrible drama. As we move reverently to Calvary we see four main acts.

I. An Act of Government (19:16-24)

A. The Sentence (19:16-18)

The first of these acts is in three parts. Our attention is directed to the sentence. Pilate had washed his hands (or so he thought) of this matter (Matthew 27:24). He now handed Jesus over to the chief priests, doubtless along with the signed death sentence and a detachment of Roman soldiers to carry out the actual execution. As far as Pilate was concerned, he was through with the whole affair. It was now a matter for the Jews. "Then delivered he him therefore unto them [the chief priests] to be crucified" (19:16a).

"And he bearing his cross went forth into a place called the place of a skull, which is called in the Hebrew Golgotha" (19:7). John does not tell us how Simon of Cyrene was compelled to carry the cross for Christ at least part of the way to Calvary (Mark 15:21). It would seem that at last even the Lord's strong physique broke down.

"The place of a skull"—what an ugly thing a skull is, with its empty eye sockets and protruding teeth. What a mockery of life. What an appropriate symbol of death. What a parody of a human head, with its flowing locks and dancing eyes and mobile lips and changing expressions and marvelous brain.

They led the Lord of life to the place of death, "Where they crucified him, and two other with him, on either side one, and Jesus in the midst" (19:18). He was hung up between two crimi-

nals. John follows the other gospel writers in drawing the veil
over the terrible details of the actual crucifixion. No crueler
death has ever been devised by men. There was nothing un-
common in Roman times about a crucifixion. The callous Romans crucified people by the thousand. Everything about crucifixion was horrible. The excruciating pain, the unnatural position, the prolonged agony, sometimes dragging on for days, the
heat, the thirst, the flies, the nakedness, the shame. And men
did this to their maker.

Yet, even in death he took his proper place, "in the midst." He
began his conscious journey to the cross by being "in the midst
of the doctors" (Luke 2:46). Here he is "in the midst" of the
malefactors. Later we see him "in the midst" of the disciples in
the upper room on the resurrection side of the grave (John
20:19). Later still he takes up his place "in the midst" of the
seven golden lampstands (Revelation 1:13). We see him "in the
midst of the throne" in glory (Revelation 4:6). Today wherever
his blood-bought people gather in his name, there he is "in the
midst" (Matthew 18:20).

B. The Superscription (19:19-22)

Next John draws our attention to the superscription. There
could be no doubt about *what it proclaimed* (19:19-20): "And
Pilate wrote a title, and put it on the cross. And the writing was
JESUS OF NAZARETH THE KING OF THE JEWS. This title then read
many of the Jews: for the place where Jesus was crucified was
nigh to the city: and it was written in Hebrew, and Greek, and
Latin." If Pilate wanted to annoy the Jewish leaders he could
hardly have chosen a more effective way. The crucifixion was in a
place where large numbers of people came and went, near one of
the most famous cities in the world. The title was written in the
three official languages of the country. What it proclaimed was
the plain, unvarnished truth—a truth the Jewish religious establishment vehemently denied. We can imagine the triumphant
smile on Pilate's face as he authorized the title. It was probably
the only satisfaction he derived from the whole business.

John considers the title and *whom it provoked* (19:21-22):
"Then said the chief priests of the Jews to Pilate, Write not, The
King of the Jews; but that he said, I am King of the Jews"
(19:21). Pilate knew when he was in the driver's seat. His answer has become famous: "Pilate answered, What I have written I have written" (19:22). Thus two of the Lord's enemies
proclaimed the truth about him in spite of themselves. Caiaphas
the high priest proclaimed him to be the Savior (John 11:49-52)
and Pilate the gentile procurator proclaimed him to be the

sovereign. Neither man knew what he was doing. Thus God made the "wrath of man" to praise him (Psalm 76:10).

C. The Soldiers (19:23-24)

"Then the soldiers, when they had crucified Jesus, took his garments, and made four parts, to every soldier a part; and also his coat: now the coat was without seam, woven from the top throughout" (19:23). The soldiers had done their dreadful deed. Now they had time to turn to their own interests. They were far more interested in the spoils than in the Savior.

There seem to have been four of them. Their rightful spoil was the dying man's clothes. There were two principal garments: the cloak or outer garment and the tunic or inner garment. They made short work of the cloak, simply tearing it into four parts along the seams. Each would thus have a serviceable piece of cloth to be adapted to other uses.

But the tunic was different. It was a seamless robe, evidently a garment of some value, perhaps woven for the master by one of his disciples or by his mother or sisters. In its seamless perfection it was like the robe of the high priest; and it was like the inner life of the Lord—flawless, perfect. It was fitting that Israel's wicked high priest should rend his robe (Matthew 26:65). He was an evil man and he disgraced his office. Although he did not know it, he graphically enacted the rending of the office he bore, which through Calvary was rendered obsolete. God endorsed the action by rending the temple veil (Matthew 27:51), thereby proclaiming Judaism null and void. But no such thing was permitted to the inner tunic worn by the sinless Savior of the world.

Motivated by a mean purpose, desire for maximum worldly gain, and resorting to the casting of lots, the soldiers fulfilled an ancient prophecy. John was there and saw the whole thing. His account is an eyewitness account. He had thought about it often. John wrote it all down: "They said therefore among themselves, Let us not rend it, but cast lots for it, whose it shall be: that the scripture might be fulfilled, which saith, They parted my raiment among them, and for my vesture they did cast lots. These things therefore the soldiers did" (19:24). John had no doubt that the behavior of the Roman soldiers on this occasion was an accurate fulfillment of Psalm 22:18.

II. An Act of Grace (19:25-27)

John now turns from a sordid scene to a sad scene, away from the Lord's foes to his friends, away from a scene of greed to a scene of grief, away from the soldiers to the sufferers. For there were others who had come to Calvary. "Now there stood by the cross of Jesus his mother, and his mother's sister, Mary the wife of Cleophas, and Mary Magdalene" (19:25).

A. Those Who Were Standing by the Cross (19:25)

It is uncertain whether John mentions three women or four. If we compare the various accounts it would seem that the following is the case. Reference is made to the women at the cross here, in Matthew 27:56, and in Mark 15:40. Comparing the accounts we see that:

• John alone mentions Mary the mother of Jesus
• All three mention Mary Magdalene
• Matthew and Mark mention Mary the mother of James and Joses, a woman John describes as the wife of Cleophas. Mark adds the information that her son James was known as James the Less (to distinguish him from James the son of Zebedee)
• Matthew mentions "the mother of the sons of Zebedee," Mark mentions Salome, and John mentions "the sisters of Jesus' mother." Evidently they are all referring to the same woman (thus Salome was Mary's sister, the aunt of the Lord Jesus, and her sons James and John were his cousins)

Apart from John, the only loved ones of Jesus who came to the cross were women.

It is impossible to describe the anguish and suffering of these four women. His mother had a million memories of him, all of them precious. Mary Magdalene had been delivered by him from a terrible form of demon possession and would have gone through fire and flood for him. The sons of Mary, the wife of Cleophas, and Salome were among his followers. It is generally accepted that Joseph, the husband of Mary the Lord's mother, was dead and that she was now a widow. Her other children were not yet believers.

The Lord looked down from his cross and saw this forlorn little group, especially his mother. This was no place for her. He acted in love and grace. He would not send her back to her natural home where she might have to listen to words from her unbelieving family which would only add to her grief. He would send her home with John. "When Jesus therefore saw his mother, and the disciple standing by, whom he loved, he saith unto his mother, Woman, behold thy son! Then saith he to the disciple, Behold thy mother! And from that hour that disciple took her unto his own home" (19:26-27).

B. Those Who Were Sent from the Cross (19:26-27)

It was an act of tender compassion on the part of the suffering Savior thus to make this loving provision for his mother. But there was more to it than that. Again we note how Jesus addressed her: "Woman," he said, "behold thy son!" (cf. 2:4). He did not address her as "mother." Earthly relationships were ending. The parental title was replaced by a more general title of respect.

We understand from subsequent history how far-seeing this was. The Roman church has elevated Mary to the point of idolatry. Some years ago I was in Vichy, France, and went to the church of Mary the Healer. In the dome of the church can be seen a mural of Mary and Jesus, with Mary predominating. Around the base of the dome are two messages, one exalting Jesus, the other exalting Mary. The one message is a quotation from John 3:16, "For God so loved the world, he gave his only begotten Son." The other quotation is from St. Bernard: "It is God's will that we should receive all things through Mary." The first quotation is true; the second is false.

In Rome there is a church devoted to the worship of Mary. It is one of the major churches in the city, the church of Mary Maggiore. It is the heart of the worship of Mary in the Roman Catholic church. In the courtyard of this church is a tall crucifix. On one side of this cross, high and lifted up, is a figure of Christ. On the other side of this cross, back to back with him, nailed to the cross with him, is a figure of the virgin Mary. Nor is this simply the expression of some artist's exaggerated enthusiasm for Mary. Official Roman Catholic dogma teaches not only the immaculate conception of "the blessed virgin Mary" and her bodily (corporeal) presence in heaven, not only that people should bow before her images, light candles to her, and pray to her, but they call her "co-redemptrix." By that the church of Rome means that Mary is just as much our redeemer as Christ. No wonder Jesus sent her away from the cross!

III. AN ACT OF GREATNESS (19:28-30)

John passes over in silence the three hours of darkness that lasted from noon until three o'clock in the afternoon. Instead he draws our attention to the greatness of the Lord, even as he hung on the cross.

A. The Lord Deliberately Received the Sponge (19:28-29)

"After this, Jesus knowing that all things were now accomplished, that the scripture might be fulfilled, saith, I thirst" The word for "fulfilled" here is *teleioo* ("consummated"). The Lord had been observing one after the other the fulfillment of the Scriptures that foretold various aspects of his suffering. He had been crucified, and his hands and feet pierced (Psalm 22:16). His enemies had mocked him, using the very words of the psalmist (Psalm 22:8). The soldiers had gambled for his garment (Psalm 22:18). He had been abandoned by God and had cried out (Psalm 22:1).

1. The Request (19:28)

But one Scripture had not yet been fulfilled, the prediction of Psalm 69:21. Then the whole prophetic picture concerning his death would be finished. So he said, "I thirst."

2. The Response (19:29)

Instantly those who were standing around consummated the prophetic word: "Now there was set a vessel full of vinegar: and they filled a spunge with vinegar, and put it upon hyssop, and put it to his mouth." Presumably it was the soldiers, awestruck by the scene, who rendered this last service for Jesus. The vinegar soaked sponge was fixed to the hyssop (perhaps the caper plant, which has long stems) and reached up to Jesus' parched lips.

B. The Lord Deliberately Released His Spirit (19:30)

"When Jesus therefore had received the vinegar, he said, It is finished: and he bowed his head, and gave up the ghost." He was in complete control. *Tetelestai*. Finished. Every jot and tittle of the law, every word and deed, all that he had been given to do while on earth—finished. Then, still sovereignly in charge of the situation, he bowed his head and dismissed his spirit. Thus no man took his life from him. He laid it down of himself (10:17-18).

That triumphant word has been echoing down the centuries. The work that saves is finished. No one can add to a finished work. We can add nothing to the saving work of Christ.

IV. AN ACT OF GOD (19:31-42)

A. Divine Protection for the Lord's Bones (19:31-37)

The malice of the chief priests was still evident. Perhaps they would have dumped the Lord's body in a common criminal's grave or thrown it into the fire of the Gehenna garbage pit. They were given no opportunity even to touch it.

1. The Sabbath (19:31a)

"The Jews therefore, because it was the preparation, that the bodies should not remain upon the cross on the sabbath day, (for that sabbath day was an high day,) besought Pilate that their legs might be broken, and that they might be taken away."

This sabbath was not the ordinary weekly sabbath but "an high day" sabbath, the first day of the feast of Passover (15th Nisan; corresponding to our Wednesday sunset to Thursday sunset). It was unthinkable to the Jews that this high sabbath could be desecrated by having victims still hanging and dying on the nearby hill Golgotha (in violation of Deuteronomy 21:23).

2. The Sanhedrin (19:31b)

Such a request to Pilate was cruelty itself. True, breaking the legs of a crucified man was a common enough Roman practice. But that Israel's priests and religious leaders should formally request that this be done is a measure of their hate. They did not know that Jesus was already dead.

The breaking of the legs of a person hanging on a cross administered a terrible shock of pain to the victim. The whole weight of the body, no longer supported by the legs, dropped down, fixing the thoracic cage so that the lungs could no longer expel the air which was inhaled. Death was hastened by asphyxiation. Thus these men could preserve the sanctity of the sabbath.

3. The Soldiers (19:32)

"Then came the soldiers, and brake the legs of the first, and of the other which was crucified with him" (19:32). When faced with the request of the Sanhedrin, the Roman governor issued orders to the soldiers to proceed with their inhuman task. They carried out their orders, as far as the two malefactors were concerned, with prompt efficiency. Presumably the soldiers worked from either side, finishing off the two thieves before arriving at the center cross.

4. The Savior (19:33)

"But when they came to Jesus, and saw that he was dead already, they brake not his legs." The order was to hasten death. The method was terrible but the results were swift. When they arrived at the cross of Christ, death had already done its work. There was no need to break his legs. Sensibly enough, the soldiers (who, we can hope, did not relish this side of their business) stopped short. This man had made a deep impression on them all (Matthew 27:54). So they drew the line at smashing the legs of a dead man, especially this dead man. They must have been astonished to see that he was dead already. Death by crucifixion was never over in six hours.

5. The Spear (19:34)

"But one of the soldiers with a spear pierced his side, and forthwith came there out blood and water." In order to make quite sure that Jesus was really dead, one of the soldiers pierced his side with his spear. The flow of blood and water that followed satisfied the soldiers. There was no doubt he was dead.

Considerable discussion has been focused on the blood and water that flowed from the Savior's pierced side. It has been argued that the phenomenon indicates the immediate cause of Christ's death, a rupture of the heart followed by a large effusion of blood into the pericardium. The theory is that this blood separated quickly into its more solid and liquid parts, which then flowed out in a mingled stream when the pericardium was penetrated from below by the soldier's spear.

Many people however are skeptical about this explanation. Everything about Christ's death has overtones of the supernatural. The Lord dismissed his own spirit. He did not die from a rupture of the heart. We do not need a natural explanation of the outpoured blood and water that John clearly took to be a miraculous sign.

6. The Statement (19:35)

"And he that saw it bare record, and his record is true: and he knoweth that he saith true, that ye may believe." In the most solemn manner possible, John testifies to the fact that what he has just recorded is the accurate and reliable testimony of an eyewitness. John expounds on the water and the blood in his first epistle (1 John 5:6-8). There may also be here an echo from the Lord's own words to Nicodemus (John 3:5). In the

Old Testament, a similar truth was embodied in the tabernacle, where God put the brazen altar (blood) and the brazen laver (water) between the sinner and himself.

7. The Scriptures (19:36-37)

"For these things were done, that the scripture should be fulfilled, A bone of him shall not be broken." And again another scripture saith, They shall look on him whom they pierced." The references are to Exodus 12:46, Numbers 9:12, and Psalm 34:20, all of which were fulfilled. The Lord was the antitype indeed of the Passover lamb. When John then refers us to "another" Scripture he uses the word *heteros,* which means another of a different kind. This Scripture refers to Zechariah 12:10, which was only partially fulfilled at the cross. It was fulfilled inasmuch as those who were at Calvary were able to look on their handiwork and see his pierced hands and feet. But this Scripture awaits final and complete fulfillment in a future day, at the Lord's return, when a repentant Israel will indeed look on him whom they pierced.

B. Divine Provision for the Lord's Body (19:38-42)

But there was another act of God. The first one preserved the Lord's bones from being broken despite the power and malice of his foes. The second had to do with the Lord's body. From now on, only loving hands would touch it.

1. The Intercessor (19:38-39)

"And after this Joseph of Arimathaea, being a disciple of Jesus, but secretly for fear of the Jews, besought Pilate that he might take away the body of Jesus: and Pilate gave him leave. He came therefore, and took the body of Jesus" (19:38). All four gospels tell of Joseph of Arimathaea. He was a rich man (Matthew 27:57), an honorable counselor, that is, a member of the Sanhedrin (Mark 15:43), a good and just man (Luke 23:50). It was another fulfillment of prophecy that Jesus was to be buried by a rich man (Isaiah 53:9).

John might have had courage enough to seek an audience with Pilate and ask for the body of Jesus, but it is doubtful that he would have obtained even a hearing with the governor. Joseph of Arimathaea, an influential member of the Sanhedrin, would have both the ready access to Pilate and the commanding presence to give weight to his request. It was customary for the

Romans to allow relatives of executed criminals to have the body, except in cases of treason But Pilate most certainly knew that Jesus was no traitor.

Moreover, Joseph had another influential man with him to support his plea: Nicodemus, reputedly one of the three richest men in Jerusalem. "And there came also Nicodemus, which at the first came to Jesus by night, and brought a mixture of myrrh, and aloes, about an hundred pound weight" (19:39).

Up to now both these men had been secret disciples, but no longer. Calvary made the difference. Paul later wrote of the cross and the difference it had made in his life: "God forbid that I should glory, save in the cross of our Lord Jesus Christ, by whom the world is crucified unto me, and I unto the world" (Galatians 6:14). After what the world did to Jesus there could no longer be any compromise for these two believers.

Nicodemus lavished his wealth on the body of Jesus. He intended that Jesus should have a king's burial. He brought a hundred pounds of costly mixed spices and strips of linen cloth, another expensive item. The spices would be spread over the linen and the linen strips wound around the body.

2. The Interment (19:40-42)

"Then took they the body of Jesus, and wound it in linen clothes with the spices, as the manner of the Jews is to bury" (19:40). The body of Jesus was tenderly taken down and removed from the scene of the crucifixion for *the embalmment* (19:40). It was prepared for burial with all the care and protection that love could suggest or that wealth could provide. We can be sure that many a tear was shed over those terrible wounds that covered his beloved form. At last it was done. Rich swathings, not the old rags the rabbis say were used on criminals, hid the tortured body from mortal eyes. The aromatic fragrance of the spices filled the air. It was enough for now. More could be done later, once the sabbath was over.

Then there was *the entombment* (19:41-42): "Now in the place where he was crucified there was a garden; and in the garden a new sepulchre, wherein was never man yet laid. There laid they Jesus therefore because of the Jews' preparation day, for the sepulchre was nigh at hand." A garden, a new sepulcher, all that love could do to mitigate the indignity of death was done for Jesus. Haste? Yes, there was a measure of hurry because of the time and the day. But nothing was left undone that needed to be done.

Jesus died at three o'clock in the afternoon. Sundown would

bring an end to the work. It was a provision, foreseen by God, that Joseph's tomb should be so near the site of the crucifixion.

So in a clean new tomb, untainted by a previous occupant, dressed in linen and surrounded by perfume, in the cool dark interior, shut off from the din and noise of the world that had so shamefully used him, the Savior's body rested. The world went about its business.

We can imagine how things probably went. Pilate went home to supper and to make a report to his wife of the day's events. Annas and Caiaphas presided at their respective Passover feasts. Peter wept alone. The body of Judas lay forgotten. John sought to comfort his new mother. The other disciples hid themselves from public eye. Herod and his men of war mocked. Did Mary of Bethany have a sense of expectation in her heart? Did a Roman soldier try on his new robe, and another try to wash the blood of the Son of God off his spear?

The world spun 'round. Angels watched as some of their number went down to earth to prepare for the dawn of a new day.

Section 3. He Is Fully Conqueror (20:1-31)

Calvary was not the end of the story. The tomb was only a punctuation mark in a story that began before the foundation of the world. The resurrection of Christ was an important highlight of the story.

I. Revelations at the Empty Tomb (20:1-18)

The challenge of the resurrection, as recorded by John, proceeds along four lines. In chapter 20 the challenge is first to the intellect in the case of Peter and John, then to the emotions in the case of Mary Magdalene, then to the will in the case of Thomas. In chapter 21 the challenge is to the conscience in the case of Simon Peter.

The resurrection of Jesus satisfies the mind, stirs the heart, grips the will, and stabs the conscience. No wonder it was the predominant theme of apostolic preaching.

A. The Wondering Disciples (20:1-10)

1. Receipt of the News (20:1-2)

The resurrection story began with a woman whose love for Jesus was the most important thing in her life, in all the world.

It would not let her sleep. It drew her to the place where his remains lay buried. We note first *what Mary Magdalene discovered* (20:1): "The first day of the week cometh Mary Magdalene early, when it was yet dark, unto the sepulchre, and seeth the stone taken away from the sepulchre." A brave woman, she was not afraid of the dark, not afraid of the graveyard in the dark, not afraid of the guard. Perhaps the "perfect love" that "casteth out fear" so filled her heart that there was no room for any other thought (cf. 1 John 4:18).

What she saw must have first filled her with astonishment, then with apprehension. The tomb was no longer sealed. It was wide open. The soldiers were gone. The stone was rolled back.

Next we note *what Mary Magdalene decided* (20:2): "Then she runneth, and cometh to Simon Peter, and to the other disciple, whom Jesus loved, and saith unto them, They have taken away the Lord out of the sepulchre, and we know not where they have laid him." She knew where John was staying in the city. Evidently Peter had by now sought out John, or perhaps John had sought him out. They had been friends for many years. Peter had repented of his weakness and sin and was still a natural leader. By the time she arrived at the house, Mary had decided what had happened. The authorities, who had sealed the tomb at the time of the burial, must have ordered it opened and removed the body. Maybe they wanted to have it handy should rumors of a resurrection begin to circulate. Maybe they intended to dump it in a common grave after all. All she knew was that the grave was now open, and what other explanation could there be?

2. Reaction to the News (20:3-10)

The *first reaction* (20:3-7) to that news was one of action. Peter took the lead. The scene was still vivid in the mind of the aged John. Even as he wrote, as a very old man, he recalled the thrill and excitement of it all. "Peter therefore went forth, and that other disciple, and came to the sepulchre. So they ran both together: and the other disciple did outrun Peter, and come first to the sepulchre." We can picture the two of them racing toward the place. As they drew near, John, who was younger, put on an extra burst of speed and arrived at the tomb first.

"And he stooping down, and looking in, saw the linen clothes lying; yet went he not in" (20:5). Something was strange here. John's initial glance took in the evidence, but as yet the truth had not gripped him. Why would the authorities have bothered to unwrap the body? Why not take it, grave clothes and all? His

bewilderment and the strangeness of the situation made him
pause. Peter came up and, sure enough, Mary Magdalene was
right. The tomb was open. In he went, brushing right past John
who was still trying to make sense of the scene. "Then cometh
Simon Peter following him, and went into the sepulchre, and
seeth the linen clothes lie, And the napkin, that was about his
head, not lying with the linen clothes, but wrapped together in
a place by itself" (20:6-7). There was the evidence, all the clues
needed to solve the mystery. All that was required now was to
draw the right conclusions from the facts.

The body was gone; of that there was no doubt at all. There
was no evidence of haste or vandalism. Everything was orderly
and in place, the grave clothes, the napkin just a little apart
from the rest. It was as though the form of a dead man was
preserved, but the body itself was gone. Who could make sense
of that? Who would go to all that trouble?

Further reaction to the news (20:8-9) was more profound.
"Then went in also that other disciple, which came first to the
sepulchre, and he saw, and believed. For as yet they knew not
the scripture, that he must rise again from the dead." John
followed Peter into the obviously empty tomb. He too took in
all the items that cried out for the incredible but inescapable
conclusion. Jesus had risen from the dead. He had risen right
through the grave clothes. Of course! All the clues pointed to
that conclusion. Then and there he believed. It was incredibly,
gloriously true. Jesus was alive!

At this point, John pauses in his narrative to point out the
terrible dullness of the disciples in those days. "As yet they knew
not the scripture," he says. There was really no excuse for that.
Even if they were unable to grasp the truth of Psalm 16:10,
what about the Lord's repeated prophecies of his death, burial,
and resurrection? Mary of Bethany had believed. John himself
had seen three resurrections. They were "slow of heart to believe all that the prophets have spoken," as the Lord put it
shortly afterward to two of them on the Emmaus road (Luke
24:25). And surely we should be loathe to cast stones at them.
In the end they became magnificent believers who went out to
turn the world upside down.

Then came the *final reaction* (20:10): "Then the disciples went
away again unto their own home." By doing that, they missed a
blessing. We can imagine, however, what a stir they made at
home. They would go over the facts again and again. "I tell
you, he's alive!" John would say. "There's no other explanation
of the facts."

There is still no other explanation. Unbelievers have invented alternate theories—Christ did not really die, he only swooned on the cross and in the tomb recovered, escaped into the night, and later showed himself to be alive; the disciples stole the body and then made up a lie about Christ's resurrection based on the fact of an empty tomb; the women who came to the tomb were half expecting a resurrection and therefore had a hallucination.

One and all, those explanations are the desperate attempts of godless men to avoid the fact that Jesus is alive. God raised him from the dead. One and all, the clumsy attempts of an unbelieving world to deny the literal, bodily resurrection of Christ from the dead break down before the facts.

So then this resurrection story appeals first to the mind. It confronts us with facts. It presents us with the initial proofs, the evidence. Many more proofs followed, but these were enough to convince John.

B. The Weeping Disciple (20:11-18)

John turns next to the account of Mary Magdalene's unforgettable experience at the tomb.

1. Mary and the Lofty Messengers (20:11-14)

At this point it will be helpful to have a possible sequence of events before us *(op. cit.* Westcott, p. 288).

• About 5:00 a.m. Mary Magdalene, along with Mary the mother of James and Salome (and perhaps some others), set out for the sepulcher. It was still dark, but dawn was near. Mary Magdalene hurried on ahead of the others, found the tomb open, and ran to tell Peter and John.

• About 5:30 a.m. the other women arrived. By this time the sun was up (Mark 16:2f.). They saw an angel who sent a message to the disciples (Matthew 28:5f.; Mark 16:5f.).

• About 6:00 a.m. another group (among whom was Joanna) arrived at the tomb (Luke 24:1f.; Mark 16:1f.). They saw what they took to be "two young men" who gave them words of comfort and instruction (Luke 24:4f.).

• About 6:30 a.m. Peter and John come to the tomb. Mary Magdalene evidently followed them, but did not go home when they did. She saw two angels. About the same time the other women delivered their marvelous news to the other disciples (Luke 24:10f.).

• About 7:00 a.m. the Lord revealed himself to Mary Magdalene (John 20:14-18; Mark 16:9). Not long afterward he revealed himself, it would seem, to the company of women who by this time were returning to the tomb. They were charged by the Lord with a message to his disciples to meet him in Galilee (Matthew 28:9f.).

Later on, in the evening of this glorious day, there were other appearances of the Lord.

John tells us of *Mary's distress* (20:11): "But Mary stood without at the sepulchre weeping: and as she wept, she stooped down and looked into the sepulchre." The word for "weep" is *klaio*, the same word used of Mary of Bethany when she went out to meet Jesus at the tomb of Lazarus (11:31). It literally means "to wail." Mary Magdalene was heartbroken. Now she stood outside the sepulcher and did exactly what John had done (20:5); she "stooped down" to see inside. The word is the same, implying that she wanted to see more clearly what was inside.

Then comes *Mary's discovery* (20:12-13). "And seeth two angels in white sitting, the one at the head, and the other at the feet, where the body of Jesus had lain." At either end of the rock cut ledge on which the body of Jesus had lain sat two angels. The Lord's resurrection was an event of such significance in the annals of the universe that the presence of these mighty beings was required. The world should have been there with its homage—Caesar should have come from Rome, the wise men of Athens should have been there. Caiaphas and Annas and the Sanhedrin should have been there. People from the far flung Jewish Diaspora should have been there, along with Herod and his men of war. Pilate and his wife should have been there. The disciples should have been there, an eager, welcoming body. The roads to Jerusalem should have been crowded with pilgrims. All Jerusalem should have been arriving with triumphant palms.

Instead the world stayed away and shining ones from glory came instead. Whatever must those shining ones have thought? A few women come, and one of them leaves without much more than a startled glance. Two men come, one of them blunders about a bit, the other seems to have figured it out, but off they go. Now this woman is back, convulsed with sobs when she should have been shouting for joy. They allowed her to see them.

"And they say unto her, Woman, why weepest thou? She saith unto them, Because they have taken away my Lord, and I know not where they have laid him" (20:13). We are not told what they thought of her reply. It was evident that their beloved was her beloved, their Lord was her Lord. They made no attempt to dispel her confusion. She did not give them the opportunity, nor was there any need. They could see what she could not see: standing behind her was the one she sought.

We notice too *Mary's disinterest* (20:14): "And when she had thus said, she turned herself back, and saw Jesus standing, and knew not it was Jesus." When she turned away from them, she saw another figure standing there. She was so taken up with sad thoughts and her unutterable loss that she observed him but didn't see him. Not for a moment did she think it was he. She was no more interested in this anonymous visitor than she was in the angelic visitors. All she wanted was Jesus.

2. Mary and Her Living Master (20:15-17)

We note *her despair* (20:15): "Jesus saith unto her, Woman, why weepest thou? whom seekest thou? She, supposing him to be the gardener, saith unto him, Sir, if thou have borne him hence, tell me where thou hast laid him, and I will take him away."

He addressed her in the same way the angels did: "Woman, why weepest thou?" Those tears and sobs had touched his heart. With the angels was it perhaps a matter of academic interest, a mortal weeping? But Jesus had a human heart. He loved this forlorn woman. He knew the price and toll of her tears. In a moment he would greatly reward her for her constancy and for her love that was stronger than death. Further, he had a personal stake in this devotion. So he added, "Whom seekest thou?"

How wonderful these first words of Jesus are after his resurrection. He reminded her that it was not just something she was looking for, but someone. But she was still taken up with her grief. With the courage of despair she blurted it all out. She assumed, even if this was the gardener as she supposed, that he was a friend. One of the Lord's enemies would have roughly ordered her off the premises. If this friendly gardener had removed the body, maybe he would tell her where it was. Then she could run and get it and carry it away.

The Lord could contain himself no longer. Here was love indeed that many waters could not quench nor could the floods drown it. One word, and her despair was turned to *her delight* (20:16-17). "Jesus saith unto her, Mary. She turned herself, and saith unto him, Rabboni; which is to say, Master" (20:16). Such is the language of love. Each spoke just one word, and each spoke volumes. He said, "Mary." She said, "Master." For us to say more would be impertinence.

"Jesus saith unto her, Touch me not; for I am not yet ascended to my Father: but go to my brethren, and say unto them, I ascend unto my Father, and your Father; and to my God, and your God" (20:17). It would seem that the moment Mary Magdalene recognized Jesus she flung her arms around him as if to hold him and never let him go. The implication of the Lord's words is that she was clinging to him even as he spoke.

The Lord checked this demonstration of very human affection, telling her to let him go. All relationships were to be changed, and his ascension would bring a new situation. His followers would no longer be able to see and hear and touch him as before. A new and more permanent spiritual relationship was about to be forged. His Father was to be their Father; his God was to be their God. The ascension to which the Lord refers here might be different from the one that took place publicly five or six weeks later from Olivet. This seems to have been a private one.

It was the day after the sabbath. As required by Israel's annual religious calendar, on this day the high priest was required by law to take the sheaf of firstfruits and wave it before the Lord (Leviticus 23:10-11). The suggestion has been made that the Lord was about to ascend and, as the first fruits from the dead (1 Corinthians 15:23), to present himself before the Father. If that is so, then possibly the Old Testament saints, whose resurrection is recorded by Matthew (27:52-53), might have been taken up with him at this time.

3. Mary and Her Lord's Men (20:18)

"Mary Magdalene came and told the disciples that she had seen the Lord, and that he had spoken these things unto her." We are not told by John how the disciples received her testimony (cf. Mark 16:9-11). Thus Mary Magdalene, a woman, was the first to see the risen Christ, the first to hear his voice, the first to touch him, the first to be commissioned by him, and the first to tell the glad tidings to others.

II. REVELATIONS IN THE UPPER ROOM (20:19-31)

A. All Distress Banished (20:19-23)

The morning revelations now give way to the evening revelations. What a day it had been. What consternation reigned in the ranks of the Lord's enemies. In the Sanhedrin we can be sure that great displeasure was expressed at the defection of Nicodemus and Joseph of Arimathaea. A couple of days of calm had followed, with everyone busy in the rituals and traditions of the feast. But this morning, early, the guard had come terrified with tales of angels and a moving stone and an empty tomb.

In the praetorium, Pilate can scarcely have been less dis-

turbed. He had received the report of the centurion, his account of the strange happenings of Golgotha, not the least of
which was Jesus' extraordinary demise. Perhaps, under questioning, the centurion had voiced his personal conviction that
Jesus was the Son of God, not knowing how this piece of intelligence would awaken Pilate's fears afresh. Now, this morning,
had come news of his seal being broken and the tomb opened,
along with some highly suspicious story of the chief priests that
the disciples had stolen the body.

What expectations reigned in the ranks of the disciples? Some
were sure, some were skeptical, but most of them were together
in the evening. It is to be presumed that they were in the upper
room (Mark 14:15; Luke 22:12; Acts 1:13). Suddenly, he was
there! And he had come to bring peace.

1. His Peace—Triumphant in All Situations (20:19-20)

We note *the time* (20:19a): "Then the same day at evening,
being the first day of the week." The day was our Sunday. The
time was probably no sooner than eight o'clock since, according
to Luke, the two disciples the Lord had met on the road to
Emmaus had time to make the trip back to Jerusalem (Luke
24:13-36). We can imagine the hubbub of conversation, the
excited talk that evening. Some were still skeptical; Mark tells
us that they did not believe them either (Mark 16:12-13). Some
were convinced. The Lord had appeared to Mary Magdalene
and he had appeared to some of the other women—but the
testimony of the women was not taken seriously. But since then
he had appeared privately to Peter (Luke 24:34) and now it
seemed he had appeared to the Emmaus couple.

We note too *the terror* (20:19b): "When the doors were shut
where the disciples were assembled for fear of the Jews." The
disciples were naturally afraid that the Sanhedrin might at any
moment initiate proceedings against them. Maybe they had
heard that they were already being accused of stealing the body.
Men who had not hesitated to murder their master were not
likely to hesitate to attack them, if they decided that it was
expedient. So the door was firmly shut. It at least gave them
some sense of security.

Then came *the transformation* (20:19c-20): "Came Jesus and
stood in the midst, and saith unto them, Peace be unto you.
And when he had so said, he shewed unto them his hands and
his side. Then were the disciples glad, when they saw the Lord."
One moment he was not there; the next moment, there he was.
The reference to the shut door leads us to believe that he had

not come into the room the conventional way.

He greeted them with the everyday Jewish salutation, "Peace be unto you." They needed that familiar word, now vested with a new spiritual meaning. Not unnaturally, they thought they were seeing a ghost (Luke 24:37-39). The Lord quickly dismissed any such notion by showing them his hands and his side, tangible evidence of his resurrected body. It was really and truly their Lord. He had conquered death. He was alive. He was solid. Substantial. Real.

The transformation was swift: "Then were the disciples glad, when they saw the Lord." All of a sudden the whole situation was changed. What cause was there now to fear the Sadducees, the Sanhedrin, Pilate, the praetorium? Jesus was alive, come what may.

2. His Peace—Triumphant for All Service (20:21-23)

We note *their enlistment* (20:21): "Then said Jesus to them again, Peace be unto you: as my Father hath sent me, even so send I you." The disciples now became his "sent ones," commissioned by him as he had been commissioned by his Father. They were to carry on the work he had begun. There was a vast world still lying in the lap of the evil one waiting to be evangelized. Theirs was the mighty ordination of the nail pierced hands.

We note *their enablement* (20:22): "And when he had said this, he breathed on them and saith unto them, Receive ye the Holy Ghost." The word for "breathed" is *emphusao*, the same word used in the Septuagint in Genesis 2:7. The Lord as Jehovah Elohim breathed into Adam's nostrils the breath of life so that he became a living soul. The word means "to breathe with force." Now as the risen Lord he breathed on the apostles so that they might receive divine power in the person of the Holy Spirit. The task before them was a humanly impossible task: to evangelize a God hating, Christ rejecting world of unregenerate people, dead in trespasses and sins, and organized into a satanically energized system and society. How could they do it? By the Holy Spirit now indwelling their mortal bodies. The Son had received the Holy Spirit for his mission (John 1:32-34; 3:34) and now he gave them the Holy Spirit for their mission.

We note also *their ennoblement* (20:23): "Whose soever sins ye remit, they are remitted unto them; and whose soever sins ye retain, they are retained." It would seem an almost godlike power to forgive or not to forgive sins. Whatever else it means, we can be sure it does not mean that we can, in our own right or by virtue of some office, presume to cancel or confirm the sins of other human beings. The scribes were right, when Jesus said to the palsied man of Capernaum, "Son, thy sins be forgiven thee," to exclaim in their hearts, "Who can forgive sins but God only?" (Mark 2:5-7,10-11). The flaw in their reasoning lay in the fact that Jesus was God, a fact they did not grasp.

We recall the story of the dying woman who had been reared a Roman Catholic but who had for many years known Christ as personal Savior and who had long since left off going to confession, doing penance, and attending that church. Instead she studied her Bible and gathered with those of like faith. When she was on her deathbed some well-meaning relatives sent the parish priest around to see her. He offered to hear her confession and grant her absolution. The woman said to the priest, "Show me your hands." The priest extended his hands and the woman examined them. Then she turned to the priest and said, "You are an impostor, sir. The one who forgives my sins has nail prints in his hands."

That is what we have here in this context. The Lord had just shown his disciples the nail prints in his hands. Now he talked to them about forgiving and not forgiving sins. The prerogative is his and his alone. But so great is our ennoblement, having been brought by him into the royal family of heaven, that in a lesser and limited way we can convey the remitting or retaining in his name.

In this statement of the Lord the pronouns are not emphatic. There is nothing in text or context to indicate that this authority was exclusively the property of some special group such as the apostles or some ordained order of priests. It applies to the church as a whole and to all who serve the Lord in the power of his Spirit, no matter how high or how humble their places.

The church is the mystical body of Christ. He is the head, and every blood bought believer is a member. It is through us, the members of his body, that the Lord Jesus reaches out to the world today. It is the Holy Spirit who does the work. The function of the church in the world is to be the instrument through which the Holy Spirit deals with people about sin, righteousness, and judgment. It is through us, members of this mystical body, that he brings people to Christ, by whose blood alone sin is cleansed. As people respond to the gospel and put their faith in Christ, we can point them to the word of God and assure them that their sins are forgiven. When they refuse the gospel, we can tell them they retain their sins and unless they repent they will die in their sins. There are extreme cases when a child of God, indwelt by the Spirit of God in accordance with the word of God, can go further. Paul told Timothy about the wickedness of "Hymenaeus and Alexander; whom I have delivered unto Satan, that they may learn not to blaspheme" (1 Timothy 1:19-20). These men seem to have been apostates.

Within the church itself this authority seems to have unique force. The church is commanded to keep itself clean and to exercise discipline to this end. Several instances of disciplinary action are found in the New Testament. The case of Ananias and Sapphira had wholesome results not only in the church but in the world (Acts 5:1-14). In the case of Simon Magus, Peter warned but did not smite (Acts 8:18-24). It would seem that the principle of 1 Corinthians 5:12 has application to all this. It is a serious thing to be under church discipline, which is always aimed at the restoration of the excommunicated person (1 Corinthians 5:1-5; 2 Corinthians 2:6-8). The man in view in James 5:14-20 seems to have been under church discipline.

B. All Doubts Banished (20:24-31)

With John, the resurrection of Christ made a demand on the intellect; with Mary Magdalene, on the heart; now, with Thomas, it makes a demand on the will. The problem with Thomas was doubt, but doubt reinforced by stubbornness and will. In this segment all doubts are banished.

1. Then and There (20:24-29)

We look first at Thomas and his resolute unbelief.

We note *the doubts of Thomas declared* (20:24-25). John tells us *what Thomas missed* (20:24): "But Thomas, one of the twelve, called Didymus, was not with them when Jesus came." Thomas reminds us of all those believers who for one reason or another absent themselves from gatherings of God's people. The only other person who was absent from this meeting in the upper room was Judas. Indeed, the Holy Spirit draws oblique attention to this by use of the phrase "one of the twelve." The only other place it occurs in the gospel is in connection with Judas (6:71).

Why did Thomas stay away from this meeting? Why do people stay away from meetings of the assembly of God's people? Did he say, "I'm too busy," or "I'm tired tonight; I think I'll stay home," or "It's dangerous to go; I think it's courting trouble to gather in groups, given the political and religious climate right now," or "I can get more out of things by staying home and

reading my Bible and thinking it all through than by going to
that meeting," or "If Peter is going to be there, I'm not going—
not after what he did; and he'll be up front, bold as brass, if I
know him," or "There won't be any sense of the Lord's presence
in that meeting; it will be dead and dull, so why bother going?"
or "I think it's going to rain" (a popular excuse, the weather), or
"I want to stay here and get the news about what's happening at
the Sanhedrin"? Or—well, we all know the excuses.

But what Thomas missed! John is blunt about it: "But" (and
the "buts" of the Bible are all significant) "Thomas . . . was not
with them when Jesus came." He missed it. Whatever else he
was doing that night wasn't worth it. He missed a meeting with
Jesus. And that is always so. On the strength of Matthew 18:20,
we can positively affirm that people who absent themselves
from the meetings of the church always miss a meeting with the
Lord and a fresh revelation of himself.

John then tells us *what Thomas manifested* (20:25): "The other
disciples therefore said unto him, We have seen the Lord. But
he said unto them, Except I shall see in his hands the print of
the nails, and put my finger into the print of the nails, and
thrust my hand into his side, I will not believe." That was strong
language. Whether or not Thomas had actually seen the dead
body of Jesus we do not know, but he certainly had a vivid
picture in his mind of the terrible wounds inflicted on that
body.

What Thomas demanded was tangible proof. If the others
thought that their united testimony—"We have seen the
Lord"—was going to carry the day with Thomas, they were
mistaken. All he could think about were the wounds. The corporate testimony of the Lord's people to the reality of the Lord's
presence in a meeting leaves the absentee particularly cold. He
is not convinced by that at all.

When Thomas said he wanted to put his finger in the nail
prints and thrust his hand into the spear wound, he used the
same word both times. The word is *balo* and it is generally
translated "cast." It suggests a vigorous movement. The word
was used of the soldiers casting their lots (19:24).

The word for "print" is also an interesting one. It occurs in
Paul's word about the Thessalonians: "Ye were ensamples [a
pattern] to all that believe in Macedonia and Achaia" (1 Thessalonians 1:7). The word is *tupon*. What the print of the nail was
to Thomas, these Thessalonian Christians had been to the
world. They had on them the marks of Calvary. They were
branded, carrying with them the marks of the cross. The world
has every right to say to us, "Except we see the marks of the
cross on you, we will not believe." The world is not interested in

our doctrine, not interested in our views about life, not interested in our faith. Is there anything about us to remind them that Jesus died and rose again?

"I will not believe," Thomas said. It was there that the battle was joined—with the will. He was more honest than most skeptics. Most agnostics say, "I can't believe." Thomas said, "I won't believe." The corporate testimony of the disciples was this: "We have seen the Lord." Thomas discounted that. "I will not believe," he said, "until I myself have seen the proof."

Next we have *the doubts of Thomas discussed* (20:26-27). Look first at *the meeting* (20:26a): "And after eight days again his disciples were within, and Thomas with them." The eight days of course are inclusive. The festivities were now over and the disciples were preparing to head back to Galilee. This was probably a final gathering before leaving. We wonder what the disciples did all this week—where they went, what they did, whom they talked to, what they said. A week later, to the day, the second Sunday of the new resurrection era, the disciples were back in the upper room. And whatever Thomas said, he was there this time.

Now comes *the master* (20:26b): "Then came Jesus, the doors being shut, and stood in the midst, and said, Peace be unto you." The doors were shut as before, although this time there is no reference to any fear of the Jews. The reality of a living Christ had taken care of that. Perhaps Thomas insisted on the same physical arrangement as before.

And again, all of a sudden, the risen Christ was in the room, in the midst again, repeating his familiar "Peace be unto you."

The Lord turned at once to Thomas with *the message* (20:27): "Then saith he to Thomas, Reach hither thy finger, and behold my hands; and reach hither thy hand, and thrust it into my side: and be not faithless, but believing." The expression "be not" can be rendered "become not." Neither faith nor unbelief stands still; both either diminish or grow. Thomas was in peril of becoming a hardened unbeliever.

The Lord evidently knew the words Thomas had spoken in that room the week before. He had been a silent, unseen listener to that conversation. The Lord's omniscience made as deep an impression on Thomas as the clear-cut evidence of the Lord's miraculous appearance and the proffered proof of nail scarred hands and riven side. Every eye in the place must have been riveted to Thomas and the Lord to see what was going to happen next. But Thomas was already overwhelmed. The sight of his eyes, the evidence of his ears, was enough. He did not need to add the sense of touch. He was convinced.

So we see *the doubts of Thomas dispelled* (20:28-29). First comes *the great confession* (20:28): "And Thomas answered and said unto him, My Lord and my God." Here we have the first recorded postresurrection confession of the deity of Christ. "My Lord," he said; that put Jesus on the throne of his heart. "My God," he said; that put Jesus on the throne of the universe.

Then comes *the great contrast* (20:29): "Jesus saith unto him, Thomas, because thou hast seen me, thou hast believed: blessed are they that have not seen, and yet have believed." Thomas might have been more vocal and vehement in his expression of unbelief, but really none of them was in a position to criticize him. None of them believed until they saw. Even the beloved John, though he was ahead of the others because he was convinced by the visible evidence of the grave clothes and did not have to wait for the real life appearance of Jesus, "saw and believed" (20:8).

By the time John wrote this gospel the apostolic age was over. The visible appearances of the Lord had long since ceased. Faith had to replace sight. The "sign miracles" had ceased. It has been like that ever since. The Lord bestows a special beatitude on us: "Blessed are they that have not seen, and yet have believed."

Those today who crave miracles and signs are out of line with the Lord's method in this age of people's faith being based solely on God's word. As Paul put it, "Faith cometh by hearing, and hearing by the word of God" (Romans 10:17). Those who insist on signs, wonders, and miracles can have them—at a price. Satan is only too willing to oblige. After the church age when God once more takes up direct dealings with the nation of Israel, signs and miracles will resume. Pentecost was only a partial fulfillment of Joel 2:28-31. In the apocalypse we see God's "two witnesses" performing miracle after miracle (Revelation 11:3-6). They will be opposed by counterfeit, satanic miracles (2 Thessalonians 2:1-10). That will be an age of miracles. The church age however is one of faith, not sight. Hence the Lord's special beatitude for us.

2. Here and Now (20:30-31)

Doubts are also banished here and now. John adds his inspired comment to the Lord's beatitude: "And many other signs truly did Jesus in the presence of his disciples, which are not written in this book: But these are written, that ye might believe that Jesus is the Christ, the Son of God; and that believing ye might have life through his name."

John's mind went back. He was a very old man, and old men

dream. He began to recall miracle after miracle he had seen Jesus perform—more than he could count. Only thirty-six are recorded in the gospels (so few in relation to the total sum in order to de-emphasize miracles as a basis for faith), but John knew of many more than that. Out of that treasury he himself had selected only eight—special signs to help him achieve his objective.

In John's day a twofold attack had been mounted against the person of Christ. There were those who were emphasizing his deity at the expense of his humanity. There were those who were emphasizing his humanity at the expense of his deity. To combat those heresies John wrote two books: his gospel and his first epistle. In his gospel John shows that the Jesus of history was more than a mere man, he was the Son of God (as opposed to mere "flesh"). In his first epistle he shows that the Son of God was a true man (as opposed to mere "spirit").

Thomas had just confessed Jesus as God—absolutely, unconditionally, incontrovertibly God. John says, "True." And there are signs without number that Jesus of Nazareth was the Christ, the anointed of God, the promised messiah of Israel, and God over all, blessed for evermore. To believe *that* is the basis of having "life through his name." His name here, "Christ, the Son of God," reveals his twofold nature.

PART FIVE

The Epilogue
John 21:1-25

The epilogue of John's gospel marches in step with the prologue. We cover the same ground, we salute the same ensigns: life, love, and light.

I. THE SAME DYNAMIC LIFE (21:1-14)

It begins with the same dynamic life. Here, however, all is centered around Peter, and Peter's terrible failure. This is the fourth feature of the resurrection of Christ. It speaks not only to the mind, the heart, and the will; it speaks to the conscience.

A. A Presumptuous Move (21:1-3)

1. The Place (21:1)

"After these things Jesus shewed himself again to the disciples at the sea of Tiberias; and on this wise shewed he himself." After the appearance to Thomas, the disciples seem to have packed their bags and headed back home to Galilee. The feast of unleavened bread was over. There was no point in staying in Jerusalem where their presence invited further action of the authorities, although the authorities seem to have been subdued for the time being by the intimidating fact of an empty tomb and by rumors of a resurrection.

In any case, the Lord had already told them he would meet them in Galilee. They would all be back in Jerusalem a few weeks later for the feast of Pentecost. Thus it is we find them in their old familiar haunts by the shore of Lake Galilee.

Time passed and nothing happened. Peter made a decision. He was tired of inaction. He was going to do something and the thing he knew best to do was fish.

2. The Partners (21:2)

"There were together Simon Peter, and Thomas called Didymus, and Nathanael of Cana in Galilee, and the sons of Zebedee, and two other of his disciples." They all seem to have been from the same neighborhood.

We wonder, of course, who the other two were. Nathanael was one of them, so it is likely that his good friend Philip was one of them (1:43-51). Peter was there, so his brother Andrew might have been the other (1:41). But still the fact remains that two are left anonymous by the Holy Spirit—perhaps so that you and I can take our seats in the boat!

3. The Proposal (21:3)

"Simon Peter saith unto them, I go a fishing. They say unto him, we also go with thee. They went forth, and entered into a ship immediately; and that night they caught nothing." Years ago, Peter "forsook all" to follow Jesus (Luke 5:11). No matter. He was going to try his hand at fishing again. The boat in question here might have belonged to the Zebedee family (Matthew 4:21). Perhaps Peter was already thinking of going back into business again. If so, the results of that night's efforts were not encouraging. The fish stayed far away from Peter's net, nor could Peter for all his skill coax them anywhere near. There is nothing more discouraging, as anyone who has tried it knows, than to fish for hours and to catch nothing. The Lord simply was not leading Peter back into the fishing business.

After I had been in fulltime Christian service for some fifteen years, circumstances arose that led to my resigning from further involvement in a particular Christian enterprise. The situation was not a happy one, so, discouraged and in a measure disillusioned, I went back into secular employment. I worked for a large corporation owned by a very good friend of mine. The work was interesting, my friend was supportive, I had some good friends in the corporation, my immediate boss was a very close friend, the salary was attractive, the possibilities were inviting. I stayed there trying to convince myself that I was through forever with fulltime Christian work. And I was thoroughly miserable. Like Peter I "toiled all night" so to speak "and caught nothing."

One of my colleagues came one night when I was preaching in a local church near where he lived. He said, "If I could preach like that, I'd sure not waste my time working for a trucking company even if the big boss was my friend." The Lord allowed me to toil on at that job for a year, allowing me to become more and more dissatisfied with my decision. Then one day a Christian friend of mine took me out for lunch. He was a retired and successful businessman, a wise man, the elder in one of the churches where I ministered on weekends. He was blunt about it. "John," he said to me, "you are wasting your time." I knew he was right. Within a month I was back in fulltime Christian work. The Lord was no more in my decision to go back into secular work than he was in Peter's decision to start fishing again.

B. A Patient Master (21:4-14)

1. The Master's Presence (21:4-7)

Jesus knew where they were and what they were up to. He knew that Peter was toying with the idea of giving up and going back into business and that the others would follow his lead. He allowed them to have a thoroughly disappointing night of it. Then in the morning he showed up on shore and he was *ready for them* (21:4-6). "But when the morning was now come, Jesus stood on the shore: but the disciples knew not it was Jesus. Then Jesus saith unto them, Children, have ye any meat? They answered him, No."

The discouraged disciples were pulling for shore when a voice reached them across the still waters of the lake. The day was breaking. There on the shore was a man. He called them "children." The word is *paidon*, the diminutive of *pais*, a word used of a child. It was used in law, of a son or a daughter; it was used in terms of age, of a boy or a girl; it was used in terms of condition, of a servant. Thus it was like the French word *garçon*. The diminutive was also used as a term of endearment. F. F. Bruce translates it "boys."

The disciples, John recalls, did not recognize the man standing on the shore as their loved Lord (cf. 20:14; Luke 24:31). They answered the stranger's question with a monosyllabic no.

"And he said unto them, Cast the net on the right side of the ship, and ye shall find. They cast therefore, and now they were not able to draw it for the multitude of fishes" (21:6). The Lord knew where the fish were. They had confessed their failure, and therefore it was safe to let them have an overabundance of fish. In a few minutes they were to be put forever beyond any likelihood of ever going back to the old way of life again.

Now he was *recognized by them* (21:7). With their net full to bursting point, they began to pull in their catch. Then it dawned on John who the stranger on shore was. Perhaps he remembered a similar occasion on this lake some years ago (Luke 5:1-11). That was the occasion when "they forsook all, and followed him."

No sooner had John spoken than Peter recognized the truth of what he said. "Therefore that disciple whom Jesus loved saith unto Peter, It is the Lord. Now when Simon Peter heard that it was the Lord, he girt his fisher's coat unto him, (for he was naked), and did cast himself into the sea" (21:7). Impulsive as ever, Peter nevertheless remembered that he was in no condition to appear before his Lord. Hastily he seized his coat, threw it about himself, and jumped into the lake. The progress of the boat was far too slow for him.

2. The Master's Provision (21:8-14)

We note first *how the Lord involved them* (21:8-11) all. The other disciples were more orderly than Peter: "And the other disciples came in a little ship; (for they were not far from land, but as it were two hundred cubits,) dragging the net with fishes." They were only about a hundred yards off shore. We can picture the scene as the small boat came into the shallows and the other half dozen disciples poured over the side and waded ashore pulling the heavy dragnet with them, bursting with struggling fish. It was all so natural, yet supercharged with the supernatural.

On shore the Lord had prepared a fire: "As soon then as they were come to land, they saw a fire of coals there, and fish laid thereon, and bread." These were the first things designed to probe Peter's conscience. This was a fire of charcoal, like the one at which Peter had warmed his hands the night he denied the Lord. The word is the same, *anthrakia*, and occurs in only these places in the New Testament (cf. 18:18). The fish and the bread perhaps reminded Peter of the meal the Lord had provided to feed the multitudes. He was the same Lord, able to spread a table for his own. The word used for the fish broiling on the charcoal fire *(opsarion)* is found only in John's gospel. John used it to describe the two fish used in feeding the five thousand (6:9,11).

Before anything else could be done, the Lord commanded them to bring some of the fish they had caught: "Jesus saith unto them, bring of the fish which ye have now caught. Simon Peter went up, and drew the net to land full of great fishes, an hundred and fifty and three: and for all there were so many, yet was not the net broken" (21:10-11). Peter, glad to be up and doing, hurried down to where the others had evidently left the net, still in the water, and single-handedly hauled it in, a tacit tribute to his physical strength. Peter was no weakling. The unbroken net had a message for him also, of an earlier failure (Luke 5:4-6). All kinds of suggestions have been made to explain the significance of the 153 fishes. It possibly symbolizes the completeness, down to the very last one, of those caught in the gospel net and brought safely to shore. One ingenious view (attributed to Cyril of Alexandria) breaks the number into its three simple elements (100 + 50 + 3). The number 100 is said to represent the fullness of the gentiles (10 x 10), a number used to describe the Lord's flock (Matthew 18:12); the number 50 is supposed to indicate the remnant of Israel according to election; the number 3 is said to represent the trinity to whose glory all are gathered. Probably, however, the number is simply an indication of the meticulous care with which the disciples counted their catch. It probably had considerable market value. Having an exact count of the fish, they were then able to divide it equally among themselves.

Then we see *how the Lord invited them* (21:12a): "Jesus saith unto them, Come and dine." As far as John was concerned, it had all begun in very much the same way right here near this lake. He and Andrew had been listening to John the baptist, who had pointed out Jesus to them. They had left John to follow Jesus. They had asked him about himself, where he lived. He had said, "Come and see" (1:35-39). Now he said, "Come and dine." Countless books could be written about all that had happened in between.

"Come!" It is the grandest word in the gospel. God first used the word in Genesis, inviting Noah to join him in the ark (Genesis 7:11). He keeps on using the word and closes the Bible by using it twice (Revelation 22:17). It dissolves distance. It brings saint and sinner alike to him who takes away sin and sadness and replaces them with joy and gladness.

He had anticipated their needs and made provision for them. Literally he said, "Come and have breakfast." The word for "dine" is *aristao*, which indicates a morning meal. The only other place it occurs in the New Testament is in Luke 11:37.

We note however *how the Lord intimidated them* (21:12b-14). "And none of the disciples durst ask him, Who art thou? knowing that it was the Lord" (21:12b). The Lord, it would seem, was standing at some distance from them. Although they knew it was he, they hung back. They were awed by him. They knew him but they didn't know him, so to speak. They felt they ought to ask him who he was, but they already knew who he was. He was the same—but he was different. They loved him, but could no longer be familiar with him—not like in the old days. Before, they had always been more aware of his humanity than of his deity. Now they were more conscious of his deity than of his humanity.

But this would never do. The Lord took the initiative: "Jesus then cometh, and taketh bread, and giveth them, and fish like-wise" (21:13). In that culture to eat someone's food created a bond of friendship. John notes: "This is now the third time that Jesus shewed himself to his disciples, after that he was risen from the dead" (21:14). John seems to have in mind the appear-ances of the Lord to the disciples as a group.

All that had happened so far in this remarkable incident was to set the stage. The Lord now had to minister directly to Peter's conscience. He had already awakened that conscience by having a charcoal fire. It was such a simple thing, an ordi-nary, everyday thing, but it must have evoked painful memories.

We know what that is like. There was a place, once, where something happened, something of which we are now ashamed, something we regret with all our hearts, something we would give anything to undo. We wish we could go back and live the incident over again, only doing it differently this time. We avoid that spot. The sight of it awakes pangs of conscience. Neverthe-less, it haunts us. We cannot erase the memory. And if we happen by the spot, our remorse is stirred up again. Or maybe what quickens conscience is not a place but a thing, or the sound of a voice, or a photograph, a forgotten letter, a chance meeting.

Peter was tormented by his conscience. I have been torment-ed by mine, you by yours. Here the Lord deals with conscience and its agonizing sting. It is no use for us to call out across the distance that now separates us from that scene of our sin and across the many years since it took place: "I'm sorry! Forgive me! Lay not this sin to my charge!" The injured party cannot hear. The one so grievously wronged may be dead, or certainly is dead to us. Would God it were otherwise. Here the great physi-cian shows us how he deals with consciences, how he lays even the persistent ghosts of our past to rest.

II. THE SAME DETERMINED LOVE (21:15-17)

A. Recalling Peter's Failure (21:15)

"So when they had dined, Jesus saith to Simon Peter, Simon, son of Jonas, lovest thou me more than these? He saith unto him, Yea Lord; thou knowest that I love thee."

1. The Old Name (21:15a)

The Lord used the name Peter had in his unregenerate days, before he met the Savior: Simon, son of Jonas. On the night of the betrayal, Peter had used the lies and even the coarse language of his old nature. So Jesus called him by his old name.

That stabbed Peter's conscience. When Peter first met the Lord, Jesus had said to him: "Thou art Simon the son of Jona: thou shalt be called Cephas, which is by interpretation, A stone" (1:42). When Peter had made his great confession, the Lord had reconfirmed that: "Blessed art thou, Simon Bar-Jona . . . And I say also unto thee, That thou art Peter" (Matthew 16:17-18). But now the Lord went back to the old name and left it at that. It is no part of healing a guilty conscience to minimize the seriousness of the offense, nor to conceal the source in the old evil nature from whence it came.

"Lovest thou me more than these?" The Lord's word was *agapao*, the word for the highest kind of love, the word used for God's love, love that is lofty, spiritual, pure. It is not certain what Jesus meant by "more than these." Did Peter love Jesus more than the fish? After all, he had taken the initiative, he had influenced the others into going back into the fishing business. If he wanted to settle for fish, well, there were plenty of them. Peter could go and sell them and get a good start back in business.

More probably, "more than these" refers to the disciples. Peter had boasted, "Though all men shall be offended because of thee, yet will I never be offended . . . Though I should die with thee, yet will I not deny thee" (Matthew 26:33,35). He said this in the face of the Lord's prophecy that he would deny him three times (Matthew 26:34). "Do you love me more than these other disciples, Peter?" Was that what the Lord meant? In either case, the Lord was probing Peter's conscience.

2. The Old Claim (21:15b)

Peter's answer was prompt, but marked by caution: "Yea, Lord; thou knowest that I love thee." Peter used the word *phileo*, meaning brotherly love. "You know, Lord," Peter said, "I have deep affection for you."

"He saith unto him, Feed my lambs." The word for "lambs" is *arnion*, a diminutive. It occurs only here and in the book of Revelation, where it is used of Christ twenty-eight times. The other word for "lamb" is used solely of Christ (1:29,36; Acts 8:32; 1 Peter 1:19). The Lord accepted Peter's genuine profession of love and directed him once and for all away from the secular to the spiritual, from the fishing business to the work of a shepherd of God's lambs.

B. Rekindling Peter's Fervor (21:16-17)

The Lord repeated his question. Peter had used a lesser word for love. The Lord asked Peter the same question. He wanted to lift him to higher ground.

1. Do You Have a Burning Love for Me? (12:16)

We read: "He saith to him the second time, Simon, son of Jonas, lovest thou me? He saith unto him Yea, Lord; thou knowest that I love thee. He saith unto him, Feed my sheep." This time Jesus did not ask Peter to state his love comparatively ("more than these"), whether in terms of his business or his brethren. He asked him to state his love absolutely. "Lovest thou me?" Peter answered the same way as before. "Lord, you know I have deep affection for you."

"Feed my sheep," the Lord replied. This time he used a different word for "feed" and a different word for the flock. The first time the word was *bosko,* which expresses the idea of providing the flock with food (21:15). This time the word is *poimaino,* which means "to tend" or "to shepherd" the flock. The word for "sheep" is *probatia.* He added to Peter's commission. Lambs need to be fed: sheep need to be led.

2. Do You Have a Brotherly Love for Me? (21:17)

Since Peter had twice used the word for brotherly love, the Lord changed the question. He asked him, "Do you have a brotherly love for me?" We read: "He saith unto him the third time, Simon, son of Jonas, lovest thou me? Peter was grieved because he said unto him the third time, Lovest thou me? And he said unto him, Lord, thou knowest all things; thou knowest that I love thee" (21:17). This time Jesus had used Peter's own word. He said, "Do you have personal affection for me?" That broke Peter completely.

The threefold question matched the threefold denial. Peter had been vehement when he denied the Lord the third time; he is passionate enough now. "You know I have personal affection for you. You know me through and through. You know everything. You know what I said and what I did and what I am. You know me better than I know myself. Lord, out of all your knowledge of me you know I have brotherly love for you. You know I love you *(phileo)* and I know I can never love you the way you love me *(agape)."* It was the confession of a man who had been put to the wall by his conscience and who stood now before the Lord, broken, aware of his weakness, sensitive to his limitations, and afraid ever to boast again.

"Feed my sheep," Jesus said. This time the word for "feed" is *bosko*, the same word used for the lambs (21:15). The sheep need not only to be led, they need to be fed. So Peter was installed into office as an under-shepherd, aware now of his calling to tend God's flock. The flock of God needs two things: good pastorage and gracious pastoring. Peter henceforth was to provide both. How he discharged his duty we learn from the book of Acts and from his two epistles.

III. THE SAME DISCERNING LIGHT (21:18-25)

A. A Word of Revelation (2:18-19)

Now come the final words of the epilogue: "Verily, verily, I say unto thee, When thou wast young, thou girdest thyself, and walkedst whither thou wouldest: but when thou shalt be old, thou shalt stretch forth thy hands, and another shall gird thee, and carry thee whither thou wouldest not. This spake he, signifying by what death he should glorify God."

The word translated "young" is *neoteros*, literally "younger." This verse, coupled with John 20:4, gives the idea that Peter was a middle-aged man. By the time John wrote these words, Peter was dead, a victim of Nero and a martyr of the faith. He had no blessed hope of being taken home in the rapture. Paul knew toward the very end that he was almost certain to be martyred (2 Timothy 4:6), but Peter lived all the rest of his life under the shadow of a cross. The Lord promised Peter that, his past faults and failings notwithstanding, he would glorify God in his death.

The Lord added a challenge, "Follow me." He had gone before them. He had endured the cross, despising the shame, for the joy that was set before him. "Just follow me, Peter," he said.

B. A Word of Rebuke (21:20-23)

"Then Peter, turning about, seeth the disciple whom Jesus loved following, which also leaned on his breast at supper, and said, Lord, which is he that betrayeth thee? Peter seeing him saith to Jesus, Lord, and what shall this man do? Jesus saith unto him, If I will that he tarry till I come, what is that to thee? follow thou me" (21:20-22). It might well have been that the Lord and Peter had taken a walk along the lake so that the above talk with Peter was private. If so, at this point they must have turned back to rejoin the group. John, it would seem, had detached himself from the group and was following Peter and the Lord. Thus, as they turned to go back, Peter saw John.

John describes himself in the usual way and adds the note that he was the one who "leaned on his breast at supper," a reference to the time in the upper room when Peter had beckoned to John to ask Jesus about the traitor. One wonders why John introduces this incident here. Could it be that Peter, perhaps slightly, even subconsciously, was jealous of John's special closeness to Jesus? Is that why Peter asked this question about John's future?

The Lord told him to mind his own business. If Peter was to have no "blessed hope" of being alive at the rapture, that was the Lord's will for him. If John was to be still alive when the rapture took place, that was no concern of Peter's. Peter would have all he could manage just following the Lord without prying into someone else's future.

This incident started a rumor: "Then went this saying abroad among the brethren, that that disciple should not die: yet Jesus said not unto him, He shall not die; but, If I will that he tarry till I come, what is that to thee?" It is extraordinary how rumors get started, how they change color, and how tenaciously they take root. Word was soon circulating that John was not going to die, even though that was not what Jesus said.

When John wrote this gospel, well over half a century had passed and that rumor was still being repeated. John's great age undoubtly gave it greater credence. Even after his death and burial at Ephesus the story persisted (it was claimed that John was still alive in his tomb).

C. A Word of Reassurance (21:24-25)

The gospel concludes with two words of testimony.

1. The Inerrancy of the Statements of John (21:24)

"This is the disciple which testifieth of these things, and wrote these things: and we know that his testimony is true" (21:24). John was a credible witness. He had been with Jesus from the beginning of his public ministry. He had been close to him. As his first cousin, he had known him for years. He had been a loyal disciple from beginning to end, an eyewitness of the magnificent drama of God's manifestation in human flesh. He had stored up in his tenacious memory the deep sayings of

Jesus. He had been in on the beginning of the church, followed its progress, suffered for its cause, undergirded its doctrines. He had known nearly all its principal actors. He had given much thought over more than half a lifetime to the story. Now as a mature believer his memory quickened and his pen guided by the Spirit, he had undertaken to write a gospel. It was *true*. What he wrote was inerrant, part of that "God-breathed" Scripture of which the Holy Spirit was the ultimate author (2 Timothy 3:16).

2. The Inexhaustibility of the Story of Jesus (21:25)

"And there are also many other things which Jesus did, the which, if they should be written every one, I suppose that even the world itself could not contain the books that should be written." An old man's memory is long. Doubtless John had read Matthew's account of the royal messiah, Mark's account of God's perfect servant, and Luke's well researched gospel of the glorious humanity of Jesus. The sum total of all that had been written was but the fringe on the hem of the garment of that glorious life.

When the queen of Sheba came to visit Solomon she was overwhelmed by his wisdom and wealth. "The half was never told me," she said. John, pen in hand, exclaimed, the world itself could not contain all the books that could be written about that life. A complete account of the human life of Jesus, even supposing anyone were competent to write it, would be infinite.

We have much to look forward to with joy. When we get to heaven and receive our resurrection bodies, when we see him as he is, sit at his feet and listen to his voice, when face to face we shall know even as we are known (1 Corinthians 13:12), then we shall say to him, "Lord, the half was never told us."

Perhaps, then, he will tell us the rest of the story.

COMPLETE OUTLINE

PART ONE. The Prologue (John 1:1-18)

I. THE DIVINE LIFE IN ESSENCE (1:1-5)
  A. The Lord's Ineffable Person (1:1-2)
   1. Jesus Is Eternally God (1:1a)
   2. Jesus Is Equally God (1:1b)
   3. Jesus Is Essentially God (1:1c-2)
  B. The Lord's Infinite Power (1:3-5)
   Jesus is unique in:
   1. His Power of Creation (1:3)
   2. His Power of Communication (1:4-5)
    a. Communicating Life (1:4)
    b. Communicating Light (1:5)
II. THE DIVINE LIGHT IN EVIDENCE (1:6-13)
  A. The Witness and the Light (1:6-8)
   1. The Messenger (1:6)
   2. The Motive (1:7)
   3. The Method (1:8)
  B. The World and the Light (1:9-13)
   1. The Light Revealed (1:9)
   2. The Light Resisted (1:10-11)
    a. By His Own Creatures (1:10)
    b. By His Own Countrymen (1:11)
   3. The Light Received (1:12-13)
    a. The Spiritual Birth of the Child of God (1:12)
    b. The Supernatural Birth of the Christ of God (1:13)
     (1) Not of Human Descent (1:13a)
     (2) Not of Human Desire (1:13b)
     (3) Not of Human Design (1:13c)
III. THE DIVINE LOVE IN EXPERIENCE (1:14-18)
  A. Incarnation (1:14)
  B. Identification (1:15)
   1. His Person (1:15a)
   2. His Pre-eminence (1:15b)
   3. His Pre-existence (1:15c)
  C. Imputation (1:16)
  D. Implementation (1:17)
  E. Illumination (1:18)

PART TWO. The Signs of the Son of God (John 1:19–12:50)

Section 1. His Deity Is Declared (1:19–4:54)
I. THE TESTIMONY OF JOHN (1:19-51)
  A. The Faithfulness of His Testimony (1:19-34)
    1. Questions Asked (1:19-28)
      a. About John's Identity (1:19-23)
        (1) The Delegation (1:19)
        (2) The Denials (1:20-21)
        (3) The Demand (1:22-23)
      b. About John's Ideology (1:24-28)
        (1) The Pharisees' Attack on His Baptism (1:24-25)
        (2) John's Attack on Their Blindness (1:26-28)
    2. Questions Answered (1:29-34)
      a. The Arrival of Jesus (1:29a)
      b. The Announcement of John (1:29b-34)
        (1) A Proclamation (1:29b-30)
        (2) A Problem (1:31-34)
          (a) The Problem Stated (1:31)
          (b) The Problem Solved (1:32-34)
  B. The Fruitfulness of His Testimony (1:35-51)
    1. Disciples of John in View (1:35-39)
      a. How They Found the Lord (1:35-37)
      b. How They Followed the Lord (1:38-39)
    2. Disciples of Jesus in View (1:40-51)
      a. How Peter Was Drawn to Jesus (1:40-42)
      b. How Philip Was Discovered by Jesus (1:43-51)
        (1) Philip's Call (1:43-44)
        (2) Philip's Concern (1:45-51)
          (a) Nathanael Was Introduced to Jesus (1:45-46)
          (b) Nathanael Was Interested in Jesus (1:47-48)
          (c) Nathanael Was Inspired by Jesus (1:49-51)
            i. His Confession of Christ (1:49)
            ii. His Comprehension of Christ (1:50-51)
II. THE TRIUMPHS OF JESUS (2:1–4:54)
  A. The Wine at the Wedding (2:1-12)
    Triumph over Life's Sudden Disappointments
    1. Jesus and the Marriage (2:1-2)
    2. Jesus and His Mother (2:3-5)
      a. Mankind's Problem (2:3a)
      b. Mary's Proposal (2:3b)
      c. Messiah's Prerogative (2:4-5)
    3. Jesus and the Miracle (2:6-11)
      a. Its Preliminary Purpose (2:6-10)
      b. Its Primary Purpose (2:11)
    4. Jesus and His Move (2:12)
  B. The Traffic in the Temple (2:13-25)
    Triumph over Life's Secular Debasements
    1. Jesus and the Building (2:13-17)

2. Jesus and His Body (2:18-22)
3. Jesus and the Believers (2:23-25)
    a. The Foundation of The Faith (2:23)
    b. The Flaw in The Faith (2:24-25)
C. The Night with Nicodemus (3:1-21)
   Triumph over Life's Spiritual Deceptions
   1. The World's Greatest Tragedy (3:1-10)
    a. Nicodemus and His Belief (3:1-2)
    b. Nicodemus and His Blindness (3:3-8)
      (1) The Need for a New Birth Was Expressed to Him (3:3-5)
      (2) The Need for a New Birth Was Explained to Him (3:6-8)
        (a) Different Worlds (3:6-7)
        (b) Different Winds (3:8)
    c. Nicodemus and His Bewilderment (3:9-10)
   2. The World's Greatest Truths (3:11-15)
    a. The Secret of Salvation (3:11-12)
      (1) Great Facts Are Revealed (3:11)
      (2) Great Faith Is Required (3:12)
    b. The Source of Salvation (3:13)
    c. The Simplicity of Salvation (3:14-15)
   3. The World's Greatest Text (3:16)
   4. The World's Greatest Test (3:17-21)
    a. Why Jesus Came (3:17)
    b. Whom Jesus Condemns (3:18-19)
    c. What Jesus Contrasts (3:20-21)
      (1) Those Who Loathe the Light (3:20)
      (2) Those Who Love the Light (3:21)
D. The Jews and John (3:22-36)
   Triumph over Life's Saddening Discouragements
   1. John the Baptist's Witness (3:22-30)
    a. John and His Baptism (3:22-27)
      (1) The Baptism of Jesus (3:22)
      (2) The Baptism of John (3:23-24)
    b. John and the Bridegroom (3:28-30)
      (1) Positive Denial (3:28)
      (2) Personal Delight (3:29)
      (3) Precious Desire (3:30)
   2. John the Beloved's Witness (3:31-36)
    a. The Testimony of God (3:31-33)
      (1) Adequately Declared (3:31)
      (2) Actually Disbelieved (3:32)
      (3) Absolutely Dependable (3:33)
    b. The Truth of God (3:34-36)
      (1) The Spirit of God (3:34)
      (2) The Son of God (3:35)
      (3) The Salvation of God (3:36)
E. The Woman at the Well (4:1-42)

Triumph over Life's Sordid Defilements
1. The Detour (4:1-8)
    a. A Necessary Way (4:1-6)
6 b. A Needy Woman (4:7-8)
2. The Discussion (4:9-30)
    a. A Word of Indignation (4:9-10)
    b. A Word of Indecision (4:11-14)
        (1) The Woman's Innate Thoughtfulness (4:11-12)
        (2) The Woman's Inner Thirstiness (4:13-14)
    c. A Word of Intimation (4:15)
    d. A Word of Insulation (4:16-18)
        (1) A Disturbing Reservation (4:16)
        (2) A Defensive Reaction (4:17a)
        (3) A Damaging Revelation (4:17b-18)
    e. A Word of Inspiration (4:19-24)
        (1) A Notable Tribute (4:19-20)
        (2) A Notable Truth (4:21-24)
            (a) A Word about the Future (4:21)
            (b) A Word about the Faith (4:22)
            (c) A Word about the Father (4:23-24)
                i. His Passion (4:23)
                ii. His Person (4:24)
    f. A Word of Indoctrination (4:25-27)
    g. A Word of Invitation (4:28-30)
3. The Disciples (4:31-42)
    a. Their Meat (4:31-34)
    b. Their Mission (4:35-42)
        (1) The Time of the Harvest (4:35-38)
            (a) The Need for Reapers (4:35)
            (b) The Nature of Rewards (4:36-38)
        (2) The Token of the Harvest (4:39-42)
F. The Faith of a Father (4:43-54)
    Triumph over Life's Sorrowful Disasters
    1. The Return to Cana (4:43-46a)
    2. The Request from Capernaum (4:46b-54)
            (a) His Plight (4:46b)
            (b) His Plea (4:47-49)
            (c) His Path (4:50)
            (d) His Proof (4:51-54)
Section 2. His Deity Is Disputed (5:1–10:42)
I. THE IMPACT OF HIS LIFE (5:1–6:71)
    A. In Urban Jerusalem (5:1-47)
        1. The Impotent Man Challenged (5:1-15)
            a. The Multitude (5:1-4)
            b. The Man (5:5)
            c. The Master (5:6-15)
                (1) The Situation (5:6-9a)
                (2) The Sabbath (5:9b-15)
                    (a) The Man's Intelligence (5:9b-11)

1. Convicting Them (8:2-11)
   a. The Time (8:2a)
   b. The Temple (8:2b)
   c. The Teacher (8:2c)
   d. The Trap (8:3-6)
      (1) The Scribes (8:3a)
      (2) The Sinner (8:3b)
      (3) The Story (8:4)
      (4) The Scripture (8:5-6a)
      (5) The Savior (8:6b)
   e. The Truth (8:7-9)
   f. The Terms (8:10-11)
      (1) He Faced Her (8:10)
      (2) He Forgave Her (8:11)
         (a) A New Lord (8:11a)
         (b) A New Life (8:11b,c)
2. Contradicting Them (8:12-59)
   a. His Witness (8:12-19)
      (1) The Light of the World (8:12)
      (2) The Lies of the World (8:13-19)
         (a) The Lord's Testimony (8:14-16)
         (b) The Law's Testimony (8:17-18)
   b. His World (8:20-24)
      (1) The Portals of His World (8:20a,b)
      (2) The Protection of His World (8:20c)
      (3) The Pathway to His World (8:21-22)
         (a) Its Godly Direction (8:21a)
         (b) Its Great Divide (8:21b-22)
      (4) The Passport for His World (8:23-24)
         (a) The Need (8:23)
         (b) The Nature (8:24)
   c. His Word (8:25-45)
      (1) Identification with His Father Above (8:25-32)
         (a) Those Who Tested Him (8:25-29)
            i. A Word about His Father (8:25-27)
               a. His Previous Testimony (8:25b)
               b. His Present Testimony (8:26-27)
                  1. Things He Could Not Unveil (8:26)
                  2. Things They Could Not Understand (8:27)
            ii. A Word about His Future (8:28-29)
               a. What the Cross Reveals (8:28a)
               b. What the Christ Reveals (8:28b-29)
                  1. The Son's Absolute Dependence on His Father (8:28b)
                  2. The Father's Abundant Delight in the Son (8:29)
         (b) Those Who Trusted Him (8:30-32)
            i. An Easy Profession of Faith (8:30)

         (1) The Jewish Priest (11:47-54)
             (a) His Companions (11:47-48)
             (b) His Counsel (11:49-52)
                 i. His Person (11:49a)
                 ii. His Pride (11:49b)
                 iii. His Policy (11:50)
                 iv. His Prophecy (11:51-52)
             (c) His Crime (11:53-54)
                 i. The Motion Was Passed (11:53)
                 ii. The Murder Was Postponed (11:54)
         (2) The Jewish Passover (11:55-57)
             (a) The Pilgrimage (11:55)
             (b) The People (11:56)
             (c) The Priests (11:57)
     b. An Interlude of Peace (12:1-11)
         (1) The Date of the Lord's Visit to Bethany (12:1)
         (2) The Details of the Lord's Visit to Bethany (12:2-11)
             (a) A Worker (12:2)
             (b) A Worshiper (12:3-8)
                 i. Her Worship Was Expressed (12:3)
                 ii. Her Worship Was Examined (12:4-6)
             (c) A Witness (12:9-11)
                 i. The Tremendous Reality (12:9)
                 ii. The Terrible Reaction (12:10-11)
B. Rejected in spite of His Fulfillment of Prophecy (12:12-19)
   1. The Pilgrims (12:12-13a)
      a. The Importance of the Day (12:12)
      b. The Implications of the Deed (12:13a)
   2. The Praise (12:13b)
   3. The Procession (12:14a)
   4. The Prophecy (12:14b-16)
   5. The People (12:17-18)
   6. The Perception (12:19)
C. Rejected in spite of His Fervor in Prayer (12:20-36)
   1. The Visit of the Greeks (12:20-26)
      a. A Plea (12:20-24)
         (1) A Spontaneous Request (12:20-22)
         (2) A Specific Reply (12:23-24)
             (a) The Lord Glorified (12:23)
             (b) The Lord Crucified (12:24a)
             (c) The Lord Multiplied (12:24b)
      b. A Paradox (12:25)
      c. A Principle (12:26)
         (1) The Lord's Followers (12:26a,b)
         (2) The Lord's Father (12:26c)
   2. The Voice of God (12:27-36)
      a. The Lord's Distress (12:27)
      b. The Lord's Desire (12:28-30)

            (1) What Was Expedient for Them (16:7)
            (2) What Was Expounded to Them (16:8-11)
                (a) The Spirit's Reproving Ministry Declared
                    (16:8)
                        i. The Nature of Sin (16:8a)
                        ii. The Need for Righteousness (16:8b)
                        iii. The Nearness of Judgment (16:8c)
                (b) The Spirit's Reproving Ministry Detailed
                    (16:9-11)
                        i. The Jurisdiction of Sin (16:9)
                        ii. The Justification of Saints (16:10)
                        iii. The Judgment of Sinners (16:11)
    3. His Revealing Ministry (16:12-15)
        a. The Ecclesiastical Truth (16:12-13b)
            (1) The Dispositional Barrier (16:12)
            (2) The Dispensational Barrier (16:13a,b)
                (a) A Revealing Process (16:13a)
                (b) A Revealing Principle (16:13b)
        b. The Eschatological Truth (16:13c-15)
            (1) The Things to Come (16:13c)
            (2) The Things of Christ (16:14-15)
                (a) The Person of Christ (16:14a)
                (b) The Pre-eminence of Christ (16:14b-15)
C. Revelations about God the Father (16:16-33)
    1. Wonderful Words of Life (16:16-28)
        a. A Little While (16:16-19)
            (1) What Jesus Declared (16:16-18)
                (a) Uttered to the Disciples (16:16)
                (b) Undeciphered by the Disciples (16:17-18)
            (2) What Jesus Discerned (16:19)
        b. A Little Weeping (16:20-22)
            (1) A Word of Information (16:20)
            (2) A Word of Illustration (16:21-22)
        c. A Little Word (16:23-24)
            (1) Whom We Are to Ask (16:23)
            (2) Why We Are to Ask (16:24)
        d. A Little Wait (16:25-28)
            (1) Speaking Distinctly about the Father (16:25)
            (2) Speaking Directly to the Father (16:26-28)
                (a) The Son's Father Loves the Son's Followers
                    (16:26-27a)
                (b) The Son's Followers Love the Son's Father
                    (16:27b-28)
    2. Warning Words of Love (16:29-33)
        a. Their Overconfidence Was Revealed (16:29-30)
            (1) His Proverbs (16:29)
            (2) His Person (16:30)
        b. Their Overconfidence Was Rebuked (16:31-33)
            (1) To Be Tested (16:31-32)

C. The World and Who He Was (17:24-26)
    1. His Pre-existence in That World (17:24)
        a. His Desire (17:24a)
        b. His Deity (17:24b)
    2. His Presence in This World (17:25-26)
        a. Blind Majority (17:25a)
        b. Believing Minority (17:25b-26)
            (1) His Light Is Their Light (17:25b-26a)
            (2) His Love Is Their Love (17:26b)

PART FOUR. The Sorrows of the Son of God (John 18:1–20:31)

Section 1. He Is Falsely Condemned (18:1–19:15)
I. JESUS WAS ARRESTED (18:1-12)
    A. His Departure (18:1)
    B. His Deity (18:2-9)
        1. The Coming of Judas (18:2-3)
        2. The Comprehension of Jesus (18:4-9)
            a. Supernatural (18:4-6)
                (1) His Omniscience (18:4)
                (2) His Omnipotence (18:5-6)
                    (a) How Jesus Confronted His Foes (18:5)
                    (b) How Jesus Confounded His Foes (18:6)
            b. Scriptural (18:7-9)
    C. His Defender (18:10-12)
        1. Peter's Fervor (18:10)
        2. Peter's Failure (18:11-12)
II. JESUS WAS ARRAIGNED (18:13–19:15)
    A. Before the Priests (18:13-27)
        1. The Tribunal (18:13-14)
        2. The Trial (18:15-27)
            a. The Disciples (18:15-18)
                (1) Peter's False Profession (18:17)
                (2) Peter's False Position (18:18)
            b. The Defense (18:19-24)
                (1) Asked (18:19)
                (2) Answered (18:20-24)
                    (a) The Rebuttal (18:20-21)
                    (b) The Reaction (18:22)
                    (c) The Response (18:23-24)
            c. The Denial (18:25-27)
                (1) Where Peter Stood (18:25a)
                (2) What Peter Said (18:25b)
                (3) Whom Peter Saw (18:26)
                (4) When Peter Sinned (18:27)
    B. Before the Procurator (18:28–19:15)
        1. The Accusation (18:28-32)
            a. The Scruples of the Priests (18:28)